THE MAKING OF FRIEDRICH NIETZSCHE

How did Nietzsche the philosopher come into being? The Nietzsche known today did not develop "naturally," through the gradual maturation of some inborn character. Instead, from an early age he engaged in a self-conscious campaign to follow his own guidance, thereby cultivating the critical capacities and personal vision which figure in his books. As a result, his published works are steeped in values that he discovered long before he mobilized their results. Indeed, one could argue that the first work which he authored was not a book at all, but his own persona. Based on scholarship previously available only in German, this book examines Nietzsche's unstable childhood, his determination to advance through self-formation, and the ways in which his environment, notably the Prussian education system, alternately influenced and impeded his efforts to find his own way. It will be essential reading for all who are interested in Nietzsche.

DANIEL BLUE is an independent scholar. He is the author of many articles on Nietzsche in journals, including *Journal of Nietzsche Studies* and *Dialogue*.

THE MAKING OF FRIEDRICH NIETZSCHE

The Quest for Identity, 1844–1869

DANIEL BLUE

CAMBRIDGE UNIVERSITY PRESS

CAMBRIDGE
UNIVERSITY PRESS

University Printing House, Cambridge CB2 8BS, United Kingdom

Cambridge University Press is part of the University of Cambridge.

It furthers the University's mission by disseminating knowledge in the pursuit of education, learning and research at the highest international levels of excellence.

www.cambridge.org
Information on this title: www.cambridge.org/9781107134867

© Daniel Blue 2016

This publication is in copyright. Subject to statutory exception and to the provisions of relevant collective licensing agreements, no reproduction of any part may take place without the written permission of Cambridge University Press.

First published 2016

Printed in the United Kingdom by Clays, St Ives plc

A catalogue record for this publication is available from the British Library

Library of Congress Cataloguing in Publication data
Blue, Daniel, 1946– author.
The making of Friedrich Nietzsche : the quest for identity, 1844–1869 / Daniel Blue.
New York : Cambridge University Press, 2016. | Includes bibliographical references and index.
LCCN 2016005742 | ISBN 9781107134867
LCSH: Nietzsche, Friedrich Wilhelm, 1844–1900.
LCC B3316 .B58 2016 | DDC 193–dc23
LC record available at http://lccn.loc.gov/2016005742

ISBN 978-1-107-13486-7 Hardback

Cambridge University Press has no responsibility for the persistence or accuracy of URLs for external or third-party internet websites referred to in this publication, and does not guarantee that any content on such websites is, or will remain, accurate or appropriate.

*For Adrienne Fried Block
who told me to write it again*

Contents

Texts and citations		*page* viii
	Introduction	1
1	The legacy	13
2	Half an orphan	34
3	The discovery of writing	57
4	The discovery of self	73
5	Soul-building: the theory	93
6	The turn to naturalism	115
7	The underworld of Pforta	139
8	The lottery	161
9	Soul-building: the practice	178
10	The fourth cycle	208
11	"The end of the first act"	231
12	An education in mistrust	248
13	"Become what you are"	271
14	The gift horse	293
	Afterword: the autobiographer	314
Bibliography		321
Index		336

Texts and Citations

Because this work confines itself to Nietzsche's early years, citations in the text refer almost exclusively to collected editions of his work. Editions of individual books by Nietzsche are given only for those mentioned in the text and are provided mostly to source translations. Any unattributed translations are the author's own.

Abbreviations of collected works of Nietzsche

BAW
Historisch-kritische Gesamtausgabe: Werke. 5 vols. Hans Joachim Mette, Karl Schlechta, and Carl Koch eds. Munich: C.H. Beck'sche Verlagsbuchhandlung. 1933–1940. Reprinted 1994.

KGW
Kritische Gesamtausgabe: Werke. Begründet von Giorgio Colli und Mazzino Montinari. Weitergeführt von Volker Gerhardt, Norbert Müller, Wolfgang Müller-Lauter und Karl Petalozzi. Erste Abteilung. Johann Figl, Hans Gerald Hödl, Ingo W. Rath *et al.* eds. Berlin: Walter de Gruyter. 1967–.

KGB
Kritische Gesamtausgabe: Briefwechsel. Giorgio Colli and Mazzino Montinari eds. Berlin: Walter de Gruyter. 1975–.

KSA
Sämtliche Werke: Kritische Studienausgabe. 15 vols. Giorgio Colli and Mazzino Montinari eds. Berlin: Walter de Gruyter. 1988.

KSAB
Sämtliche Briefe. Kritische Studienausgabe. 8 vols. Giorgio Colli and Mazzino Montinari eds. Berlin: Walter de Gruyter. 1986.

Abbreviations of individual works by Nietzsche cited in text

UO
Unfashionable observations. Richard T. Gray tr. Stanford University Press. 1995.

HAH I
Human, all too human I. Gary Handwerk tr. and Afterword. Stanford University Press. 1995.

HAH II
Human, all too human II and unpublished fragments from the period of Human, all too human II (Spring 1878—Fall 1879). Gary Handwerk tr. and Afterword. Stanford University Press. 2013.

D
Dawn: thoughts on the presumptions of morality. Brittain Smith tr. Afterword by Keith Ansell-Pearson. Stanford University Press. 2013.

GS
The gay science with a prelude in rhymes and an appendix of songs. Walter Kaufmann tr. and commentary. New York: Random House. 1974.

Z
Thus spoke Zarathustra, a book for all and none. Adrian Del Caro tr. Adrian Del Caro and Robert B. Pippin eds. Cambridge University Press. 2006.

BGE
Beyond good and evil: prelude to a philosophy of the future. Walter Kaufmann tr. New York: Random House. 1966.

GM
On the genealogy of morality: a polemic. Maudemarie Clark and Alan J. Swensen tr. with notes. Indianapolis, IN: Hackett Publishing Company. 1998.

TI
Friedrich Nietzsche. *Twilight of the idols* in *The Anti-Christ, Ecce homo, Twilight of the idols, and other writings.* Judith Norman tr. Aaron Ridley and Judith Norman eds. Cambridge University Press. 2005.

EH
    Friedrich Nietzsche. *Ecce homo* in *The Anti-Christ, Ecce homo, Twilight of the idols, and other writings*. Judith Norman tr. Aaron Ridley and Judith Norman eds. Cambridge University Press. 2005.

CW
    Friedrich Nietzsche. *The Case of Wagner* in *The Anti-Christ, Ecce homo, Twilight of the idols, and other writings*. Judith Norman tr. Aaron Ridley and Judith Norman eds. Cambridge University Press. 2005.

Introduction

The product of the philosopher is his life (first, before his works). That is his work of art.[1]

I

This biography of Friedrich Nietzsche is traditional in the sense that it provides a narrative account of his early years, beginning before he was born and chronicling his development up to the age of twenty-four. It also embeds that life within larger intellectual, social, and political contexts, showing how these shaped and sometimes obstructed his progress in ways of which he was not always aware. While the treatment here is significantly larger in scale than previous attempts, the intent itself is also traditional. Many biographers have recognized the importance of Nietzsche's environment and sought to do it justice.

What makes this book new is that it takes a distinctive and practically unnoticed ambition of the early Nietzsche and seeks to give it a prominence commensurate with the value he assigned it himself. From at least the age of thirteen he sought to direct his own development, and he did so with a steadiness of purpose and flexibility of intellectual insight which might be difficult to believe if it were not documented by texts. Fortunately, Nietzsche was an inveterate archivist in the sense that he wrote so much down. The private progress of his intellect and psyche is recorded in five volumes of juvenilia and three volumes of early letters – four, if one counts the commentaries – which chronicle his life up to the age of twenty-four. This was a particularly fraught and fecund era in his development, and when one examines the record, a remarkably complete and coherent process of self-education comes into view. As these writings attest, he did not become the Nietzsche known today "naturally,"

---

[1] KSA VII: 712.

through the graceful maturation of some inborn character. He engaged rather in a self-conducted and self-conscious campaign to follow his own guidance, in the process cultivating the critical capacities and personal vision which figure so strikingly in his books. As a result, Nietzsche's published works are steeped in values that he discovered and internalized long before he mobilized their results. Indeed, one could argue that the first work which he authored was not a book at all but the persona who wrote them. In his notebooks and letters one can watch this somewhat artificial figure being constructed, action by action, as the developing boy and youth defined positions *vis-à-vis* family, friends, authorities, and on occasion himself.

2

Although Nietzsche practiced many literary genres, this book will often focus on the one which poses the most direct challenge to the biographer, the autobiographies which he wrote up through the age of twenty-four. These were not just journalistic narrations of facts, although they provide a great deal of data which can be used to fill in biographical gaps. Rather they functioned as strategic instruments through which he tried to understand a certain concept of the self – to present through self-portraiture his psychology and values, and sometimes to decide what he should do next.

To be more specific, between the ages of thirteen and twenty-four Nietzsche produced at least six autobiographies, depending on how one counts them:[2]

(1) "From my life," composed in August 1858 (KGW I-1: 281–311);
(2) "The course of my life," three attempts to address the influence of environment, composed in the spring of 1861 (KGW I-2: 255–263);
(3) "My life," written in September 1863 (KGW I-3: 189–192);
(4) "Farewell" (also called "My life"), Nietzsche's goodbye to Schulpforte, which dates to October 1864 (KGW I-3: 417–419);

---

[2] Nietzsche actually wrote more than six autobiographies between 1858 and 1869. (Sommer 2013: 325, counts ten.) Some go unconsidered here because they offer no new information and seem largely parasitic on earlier attempts (KGW I-2: 3–4, for example). In other cases when several sketches were composed at the same time and run parallel to one another, they are construed as one. Thus, the three accounts written in 1861 (all called "The course of my life") are considered a unit, as are the several sketches made in 1869. It should be noted that Nietzsche probably wrote a seventh autobiography, covering his stay at Bonn. If so, it has been lost. See Chapter 10, Section 1.

(5) "Retrospect of my two years at Leipzig," written in late summer / early autumn, 1867 (KGW I-4: 506–530); and
(6) the preliminary versions of Nietzsche's curriculum vitae, January 1869 (KGW I-5: 40–42, 44–50, 52–54).[3]

Each such autobiography was distinctive, not only in content but in the problems addressed; and sometimes they differed in form. He issued these with remarkable regularity, composing them at the ages of thirteen, sixteen, eighteen, nineteen, twenty-two, and twenty-four, that is, at two- to three-year intervals throughout his adolescence and youth. Their approach was not just narrative but conceptual. In addition to describing his life they proposed psychological and even philosophical positions vital to the enactment of his youthful ambitions. Unlike his memoranda – the sundry lists and brief accounts which populate his notebooks – these attempted an overview, a bid to plot the course of his existence, not just as a series of incidents, but as the sequent development of an autonomous self.[4]

Nietzsche took these narratives seriously. While some were created on demand and to meet external requirements (at least two were written for school and one provided the basis for a curriculum vitae) the two longest and most comprehensive were composed for himself alone, and he put several to explicit use. Sometimes he seems to have treated autobiography as a kind of report card, to assess his progress. On other occasions he employed them to draw up a balance sheet of his proclivities when confronting a major decision. At least one led him into the abysses of a philosophic problem that it took nearly a year to resolve. All allowed him to sketch a somewhat objective representation of himself, an externalized portrait, and thereby to see himself as a figure deployed against (and to an extent intrinsically different from) the world in which he lived.

As the very fact that they had uses indicates, Nietzsche's autobiographies were not theoretical treatises, to be considered apart from the life they described. They were maps in progress, sketches of psychical terrain that allowed him to advance a bit further, then to reconstruct his views in the light of further experience. This book accordingly will locate Nietzsche's autobiographies within the contexts in which they first appeared, as

---

[3] The final version (KGW I-5: 55–57, also given in KSAB II: 366–368) is so discreet as to be of inferior interest.
[4] While this approach to Nietzsche's life was begun and largely developed independently, it was later influenced by Schmidt's and Kjaer's insistence that Nietzsche's early work performs an emancipatory function in his struggle with the forces of socialization. Hödl calls this Nietzsche's "*Bildungsprogramm*" and contrasts it with the "exterior" *Bildung* (education) he received in school and elsewhere. See Schmidt 1991–1994, Kjaer 1990, and Hödl 2009: 132–133.

engagements within his battle with his environment. It will also show how his fascination with the self and the course of its development forced him to confront psychological and philosophical issues that might otherwise have gone unobserved. The autobiographies proper are sometimes surrounded by satellite entries which examine these insights through the non-narrative means of philosophical analysis. As will be shown, Nietzsche's first extant philosophical essays, "Fate and history" and "Freedom of the will and fate," as well as "On moods" and "Self-observation" can usefully be interpreted as extensions of his autobiographical enterprise.

Despite their inherent interest, it is not the autobiographies themselves but rather the ongoing project they embody which underwrites this book. Some will be only fleetingly mentioned, for their importance here lies less in what they say than in what they represent, yet another attempt by the philosopher to examine the terms by which he lived. Further, as will be explained in the text, Nietzsche considered autobiography important, not for its overt content and certainly not for individual instances that he composed, but for what he believed that these revealed: that he had a latent self, construed along Humboldtian lines as a complex of drives and talents, and beyond this a native character not to be accounted for by his environment and in some ways beyond his personal control.[5] From his earliest attempt he saw autobiography as a mirror (his term) through which that unseen personage emerged into view.[6] He did recount his deeds, but only because these actions were manifestations – sometimes inscrutable – of a hidden self; and autobiography served as a record of its mysterious development. Autobiography might meet other needs as well, as mentioned earlier, but this sense of involuntary revelation was always present and sometimes primary. Autobiography was a book which he wrote in order to see who he was.

Although Nietzsche made his first such attempt at this genre somewhat spontaneously, his later attempts were composed under the influence of various ideologies and theories. As will be seen, the Humboldtian notion of *Bildung*, a spiritual underpinning of the Prussian educational system, would foster this vision and provide the boy with a metaphysic of discovery

---

[5] The qualifier "believed" is introduced because "self" is philosophically a problematic term. This book does not seek either to endorse or to critique Nietzsche's vocabulary and the metaphysical and psychological worlds he envisioned. He was capable of criticizing these on his own, as will appear as the book proceeds. See particularly Afterword, Section 2.

[6] For Nietzsche's mirror analogy, see Chapter 4, Section 5. As late as his final lucid year he could conceive a work entitled, "The Mirror / Attempt / at a self-valuation." KSA XIII: 633, cited in Hödl 2009: 166.

that would allow him to deepen his appreciation of his new powers and inspire him to direct them in new directions, notably toward scholarship.[7]

During adolescence Nietzsche made two new discoveries concerning the self and its manifestations. The first occurred at the age of seventeen and was composed in the wake of two anthropological essays that stressed the importance of environment for the emergence of various peoples. He applied this same approach to himself and was alarmed by the implication that the influence of one's habitat could inhibit and even warp the expression of a supposedly autonomous self. For the first time he considered the possibility that he might be a mere puppet of the world in which he lived. This scenario troubled him and initiated one of his first visceral encounters with philosophic issues, an effort considerably eased by his reading of Ralph Waldo Emerson.

If Emerson provided a balm for Nietzsche's anxieties, he deepened the latter's appreciation for an aspect of self-revelation of which he was already aware. The self tended to operate beyond the reach of consciousness. It did not lay itself open to introspection or make itself available to deliberate examination. It could only be tracked through its expressions, that is, *post facto*, through its actions. All the young Nietzsche could consciously do was to run after his deeds like an eager reporter, noting what had happened and occasionally surmising what it meant. As the Afterword will suggest, he eventually entertained doubts concerning even this oblique approach and in the process grew skeptical of self-knowledge altogether. Possibly as a result, he ceased writing self-portraits of this kind after 1869. He would continue to evoke his past and even write narratives which could be construed as autobiographies. These later efforts, however, were different – less factually oriented, less suitable for use in self-formation, and directed to other uses than the accounts produced in his youth.

Having said all this, one must issue a qualification. Nietzsche's autobiographical project plays a large role in this book. However, it is not itself the book's center. That would be to intellectualize an inherently factual exercise and to make the biography tendentious. Neither lives nor history lend themselves to intellectual simplification. To propose Nietzsche's use of autobiography as a universal, pan-explanatory theory would falsify the way he in fact negotiated the world.

It would also misrepresent the scope of his ambition. Ultimately, as will be seen, Nietzsche was interested in the self, not just because it was his, but because of what he could do with it. Once he had identified his distinctive

---

[7] The Humboldtian notion of *Bildung* will figure in Chapters 5, 12, and 13.

abilities and interests, he wanted to develop these and display them in the world. Autobiography might show the nature of such capabilities; it could not of itself animate or apply them. Accordingly, after every revelation, a period of gestation and response followed, as he drew out the implications of his findings and put them to work. Such generative ruminations were at least as important as the initial process of self-discovery, but they are far more difficult to categorize and describe because they were implemented ad hoc – within the strictures of specific circumstances and under the impress of immediate needs.

For these reasons, the topics of self-discovery and autobiography will surface only intermittently in this book and even then amid a welter of other material. Nonetheless, such themes are pivotal, for they provide the interpretive principles Nietzsche himself used to understand his actions and to direct his life. They permit this book to depict his development as he himself saw it, or at least according to principles which he would recognize and approve. To that extent this book aspires to be the biography Nietzsche himself might have composed if he had possessed the inclination and the time.

3

If Nietzsche's own account of his life, as recovered here, may be described as his lost biography, there exists a second *Urbiographie* of Nietzsche which this book aspires to dislodge, that of his sister Elisabeth Förster-Nietzsche. This is not the place to describe in detail the weaknesses of her two presentations of his life, although her unreliability is well known.[8] It need only be noted that she was not herself a scholar and that she actively ignored scholarship when it threatened her preconceptions.[9] She further deployed the narration and the character descriptions given in the biographies for personal ends: first, to glamorize her brother and increase his public, and second, to downplay the contributions and malign the characters of people she disliked, which included virtually everybody who might rival her claim to be her brother's closest confidante. As Renate Müller-Buck has argued, she sought in particular to discredit those who might reveal the deterioration of her relations with her brother during his

---

[8] See Podach 1932: 7–8; Blunck 1953: 32; Schlechta 1956 III: 1408 ff; Janz 1972: 60; 17–20; 63–101, 151; Pernet 1989: 27, 51. For more global arraignments see Müller-Buck 1998 and Niemeyer 2014. (Paul Loeb brought the final article to my attention.)

[9] See her response to Hans von Müller's evidence that Nietzsche had no Polish ancestors. Müller 2001: 260–264, 266–268.

final productive years, that is, her mother, Franz Overbeck, and Lou Andreas-Salomé.[10] Her books are further replete with questionable anecdotes, which would have to be examined individually to show their implausibility and common imaginary features. The interested reader is directed to read the accusations made by Karl Schlechta and Curt Paul Janz or the summary of charges contained in Renate Müller-Buck's article from 1998.[11] Or, they can simply turn to a remark by Carol Diethe, Förster-Nietzsche's principal biographer in English: "one can never take a quotation from the pen of Elisabeth Förster-Nietzsche at face value."[12]

Most readers will think this disclaimer unnecessary, for they have never read Förster-Nietzsche's biographies and have no intention of doing so. Yet virtually all non-specialized biographies of Nietzsche are indebted to her work in two ways. First, they cite many of her statements and stories as uncontroversial facts. Sometimes they will not even bother to attribute them to her, so that the reader does not know the problematic source of their assertions.[13] In other cases they cite Förster-Nietzsche's books in the footnotes as though her claims carried the same weight as those of conscientious scholars, an equivalence which cannot be sustained. Yet if biographers err in accepting Förster-Nietzsche as a factual resource, they compound the damage by taking her account in general as their template and model. If one has read any biography of Nietzsche, one is probably reading one that implicitly follows her vision.[14] Biographers do not do this deliberately, of course. Each brings individual interpretations to bear and consults a variety of sources. However, it takes a good deal of deliberate work to escape the seductions of a powerful and established paradigm, and few biographers have mustered the resources or even seen the necessity of eluding this wily precursor.[15] As a result and regardless of personal intent, virtually all stress the figures that Förster-Nietzsche stressed (Nietzsche's

---

[10] Müller-Buck 1998: 322.
[11] See n. 8. See also Däuble 1976: 325–326, 328. Most of these criticisms are directed against her editions of the letters and her misuse of documentation. However, they apply the more forcefully against the biographies which with rare exceptions are backed by no documentary evidence whatsoever.
[12] Diethe 2003: 24.
[13] The entirety of Hayman's paragraph beginning, "Fritz was sent," is drawn from Förster-Nietzsche. Hayman 1980: 20. Cate gives Förster-Nietzsche's account of Nietzsche's education without citation. Cate 2002: 11. Young's paragraph at the base of p. 13 is largely derived from Förster-Nietzsche. Young 2010: 13.
[14] Two biographers who largely sidestepped Förster-Nietzsche are Blunck 1953 (subsequently incorporated with minor changes into Janz 1978) and Ross 1980. Specialized biographies such as Bergmann 1987 and Parkes 1994 use her more sparingly.
[15] Compare Janz 1972: 151. "Elisabeth could carry out her office only through the most massive fabrications, and what she did in this arrogated office had the most fatal consequences."

"saintly" father, paternal grandmother, maternal grandfather); recirculate the characterizations she made (the helpful grandmother, the happy household in Naumburg, the cultural homogeneity of Naumburg and Schulpforte); and they downplay the persons she either sidelined or overlooked (Nietzsche's mother, Friedrich Ritschl, the Mushacke family). The same anecdotes are repeated, the same explanations accepted, and the same events that she stresses are stressed by them as well. They can and do supplement her account, but they do not alter it fundamentally. This book aspires to end all that. It does not intend merely to correct previous versions of Nietzsche's biography but to reconsider it on a fresh basis. If its first goal is to reframe his biography in Nietzsche's own image, its second is to seize control of its narrative from Förster-Nietzsche's hands and to restore it to the custody of her brother, using his autobiographies for guidance.

After that proud claim, a concession must be made. Förster-Nietzsche has often been cited in Nietzsche biographies for the very good reason that she is the sole family member to record impressions of Nietzsche's early life.[16] This is not an accident. She broke relations with family members who criticized her own account,[17] and her appetite for lawsuits (in which she enjoyed extraordinary success) soon stilled those who might offer doubts or protests.[18] This book accordingly has little recourse but occasionally to resort to her stories. In no case, however, has she simply been listed in the footnotes as though she merited the same deference as scholars. Rather, the main text always explicitly acknowledges that a statement comes from her so that the reader knows to exercise caution. One can only hope that in the future some ingenious researcher will be able to circumvent her entirely. In the meantime, Nietzsche's life has been fundamentally reconsidered and ordered according to principles which certainly do not derive from Förster-Nietzsche. These would include reliance on Nietzsche's own notions of self-development and autobiography; an effort to restore credit to persons previously neglected, especially Franziska Nietzsche; and a stress on contingencies that Förster-Nietzsche never considered, such as the financial situation of the Nietzsche household,

---

[16] Her mother wrote an account of her own girlhood but never published it and brought it to a close with her wedding. Goch 1994: 32–64.
[17] For Förster-Nietzsche's rejection of the Schenkel family, see Franziska Nietzsche 1984: 51, 85; for her quarrel with Oscar Oehler and the Lachauers, Franziska Nietzsche 1984: 81, 85.
[18] Müller-Buck 1998: 321, 322. "It would be valuable to study the lawsuit documents in order to understand how it was possible that Elisabeth Förster-Nietzsche could win practically all suits, especially those in which everything spoke against her."

educational assumptions of the time, and the ways Nietzsche's study of philology affected his attitudes and modes of thought.

4

Despite his many notes on his surroundings, Friedrich Nietzsche's own words are insufficient to ground an account of his life. At a minimum some control is needed to assess the accuracy of his own claims, not to mention the truth of statements made by his sister and other memoirists. This book is therefore at pains to specify the historical world which Nietzsche inhabited and the customs, attitudes, and constraints operative when he lived. He did not grow up in a vacuum; and if he sought to disengage himself from local attitudes, it is important to know what these were and why they might oppress him. Before he could transcend his time, he had first to address it and, further, to communicate his findings in terms that his contemporaries could understand. This book accordingly calls upon the resources of history and social sciences to fill in some of the blanks and to discern what Nietzsche never thought to record and sometimes may not have recognized, namely, the dynamics and limits of the world he inhabited. Regardless whether he saw these factors as hostile or helpful, they were part of his ecology and inevitably inflected his personality and his views.

If this book includes more historical background than is customary in biographies of Nietzsche, it also lays greater stress on his actual writing. Readers sometimes complain that biographies of artists and thinkers depict the human being in their everyday activities but not that second self, the paradoxically mute creature whose hand moves silently over the page. This biography aspires to display both and, further, to show how the two beings intertwined and affected one another. It presents the shy and obedient son who pursued his studies and frequented small, choice collections of friends. It also depicts the brooding poet and thinker, hunched over his manuscripts. While we cannot call these creatures different, they are not quite the same either; and this book attempts not only to do justice to both but to show how each required the other, how the boy and youth encountered puzzles in his life that he took to creative means to resolve; and how the writer and composer produced works with implications which were then carried back to his life away from the desk. One might call this "the double aspect of Friedrich Nietzsche," and it lies at the heart of this book.

Nietzsche's life is so rich and the current knowledge of it so extensive, that any account must discipline itself through limiting parameters and principles. This book accordingly confines its time frame to the years before 1869, and it centers on the interplay between Nietzsche's ambitions and the world within which he developed, between the cultural legacy that he received and the ways he turned this to his own uses. The book could have concentrated on his music, but others have done this;[19] and it could have paid greater attention to his writing in general, but Hermann Josef Schmidt has devoted four large volumes to this project, even if he stops just before Nietzsche reaches the age of twenty.[20] This biography could have covered his philosophic development in much more detail, an invaluable approach which was envisioned by an earlier version. However, that would require a book in itself, and it seemed better here to adhere to the focus most germane to biography. The ordering topic of this volume is accordingly Nietzsche's attempt to direct his own life and thereby to develop and display his own character. Once he explicitly begins this process (in his thirteenth year), other themes will be considered largely as they bear upon this quest.

This book ends with Nietzsche's twenty-fourth year for three reasons. First, at that age the philosopher was involuntarily plucked from postgraduate studies, awarded a doctorate, and installed in an academic position in another country far from home. His life thenceforward was radically different. Second, upon turning twenty-four he was emancipated from the supervision of his guardian, allowed to administer his own finances, and to that extent accorded the dignity of adulthood. Finally, and most importantly given the focus of this book, Nietzsche considered the age of twenty-four climactic since by then one's character had received its fundamental impressions. It might develop further and produce the works distinctive of itself. However, by twenty-four it had defined the kind of self it was and would not radically change.[21] In his view, "Friedrich Nietzsche" was decisively in place.

Some readers will be disconcerted by the occasional use of German words when it would seem English would do. I insist on using "*Bildung*" and "*Wissenschaft*," among others, because these words are so enmeshed in the assumptions of the culture that produced them that they cannot be translated, and it is misleading to replace them with an English simulacrum. Worse, any pseudo-translation will not communicate the *changes* in meaning that these terms underwent over the course of the nineteenth century, transformations which influenced Nietzsche's own shifts in attitude.

---

[19] See Love 1963; Janz 1972: 113–142; Janz 1976. See also Liébert 2004.   [20] Schmidt 1991–1994.
[21] KGW I-5: 45. See Chapter 14, Section 1.

Introduction

This book relies heavily, and indeed almost exclusively, on the archival work of Continental scholars, most of it written in German. Indeed, if this book offers any groundbreaking novelty, beyond the use of Nietzsche's self-analyses, it is in its reliance on a fund of scholarship untouched by any biographies written in English. Martin Pernet's groundbreaking account of Nietzsche's religious upbringing is replete with invaluable information on mid-nineteenth-century Röcken, Naumburg, Pforta, and Bonn.[22] To it must be added Johann Figl's own investigations of Nietzsche's religious development and the many articles he has written on individual aspects of the philosopher's early life.[23] I have used Figl less than I might have wished, but my debt to him as a model of biographical scholarship is fundamental. Klaus Goch has produced a solid history of Nietzsche's mother and an outstanding account of his father.[24] Giuliano Campioni and his co-workers finally achieved what neither Rudolf Steiner nor Max Oehler could produce: a full and scholarly examination of the books in Nietzsche's personal library.[25] Hermann Josef Schmidt has examined Nietzsche's writings and religious views in the four volumes of *Nietzsche absconditus*.[26] While some of his interpretations seem questionable, he has rightly stressed the importance of Nietzsche's juvenilia and explored them with such pertinacity and respect that they became fascinating to this reader as well.[27] Finally, Thomas Brobjer, the lone writer in English here, has examined the books Nietzsche read and consulted his school records.[28] Brobjer's work awakened me to the possibility of constructing a biography based on facts rather than memoirs. My debt to him is incalculable.

While this book is primarily indebted to the above specialized accounts, the author is of course familiar with the more general biographies of Ronald Hayman, R.J. Hollingdale (both studies), Curtis Cate, Julian Young, Peter Bergmann, Graham Parkes, and Carl Pletsch (among others), and in German Erich Podach, Richard Blunck, Curt Paul Janz, Werner Ross, Jørgen Kjaer, Ulf Heise, Anacleto Verrecchia, and Christian Niemeyer.[29] While all these have no doubt exercised subliminal influence on the current account – and they certainly constituted the starting point for its researches – the only one in English which is directly comparable

---

[22] Pernet 1989.   [23] Figl 1984.   [24] Goch 1994 and 2000.   [25] Campioni *et al.* 2003.
[26] Schmidt 1991–1994.   [27] For a summary of Schmidt's positions, see Hödl 2009: 73–74.
[28] Brobjer has been prolific, but the two pieces which most influenced this book were Brobjer 1999 and 2001b.
[29] Hayman 1980; Hollingdale 1973 and 1999; Cate 2002; Young 2010; Bergmann 1987; Parkes 1994; Pletsch 1991; Podach 1930 and 1932; Blunck 1953; Janz 1978; Ross 1980; Kjaer 1990; Heise 2000; Verrecchia 1986; and Niemeyer 1998.

and to which I knowingly owe a significant debt is Carl Pletsch's *Young Nietzsche: becoming a genius*.[30] Pletsch stresses Nietzsche's attempts to pursue agency in his life and in particular his efforts to "become a genius." While I cannot follow his stress on "genius," I do assume that Pletsch was correct insofar as he claimed that Nietzsche aspired actively to direct his life and toward specific ends. We disagree only as to the object of that ambition, although the implications of that one shift are enormous. Pletsch's book proved stimulating when I first read it, and I have tried to remain true to the significant elements of his vision.

It is a pleasure to close with a list of personal debts. First, I must thank Paul Loeb, who has always encouraged me in this project, provided venues for me to appear before the public, and frequently offered invaluable advice. I also owe an incalculable debt to Christa Davis Acampora, who recommended my work to others and offered opportunities to put my views in print. I have met and often corresponded with Laurence Lampert, whose kindness, enthusiasm, and stimulating books have steadily encouraged and inspired me. Mark Anderson came to my assistance concerning a point in Greek, and David Tinsley greatly improved a translation. Rainer J. Hanshe asked me to write book reviews and to conduct interviews on The Nietzsche Circle website when this project was just beginning. Two anonymous reviewers read the whole and offered valuable recommendations. I have often profitably discussed Nietzsche with Dan Fincke. Major Woolard, David Blue, Karen Ball, Ana Eliasen, and Sophie Appell read drafts or provided practical help. Lee Quinby surfaced when the book was nearly complete, later read it in its entirety, and offered such excellent advice that I wonder how I could have finished without her. Hilary Gaizler, Rosemary Crawley, Christofere Nzalankazi, Bronte Rawlings, Elizabeth Davison and Barbara Docherty of Cambridge University Press were unfailingly courteous and helpful. Finally, I must thank the dedicatee of this book, Adrienne Fried Block, former co-chair of the "Music in Gotham" project and herself the author of a much-esteemed biography of the composer, Amy Beach. Adrienne Block was my first audience and most generous critic. Although she did not live to see the completion of this project, I hope that she would be pleased with the result and think of it as in some sense hers.

---

[30] I am indebted to Paul Loeb for pointing out similarities between my own views and Pletsch's.

CHAPTER I

The legacy

Since, like it or not, we are the result of earlier generations, we are also the result of their aberrations, passions, and mistakes, indeed crimes; it is not possible to free ourselves entirely from this chain.[1]

Friedrich Nietzsche was raised to revere his father. The man died young but was constantly invoked as a model for his son – partly because the family genuinely loved the departed, but also because Nietzsche was the sole surviving boy in his family and, in those days of male dominance, the vehicle of its profoundest hopes and ambitions. It was understood by relatives that he would take up where the older man had faltered and retrieve the fallen man's torch.

Such an inheritance would have been burdensome under any circumstances. It was acutely so in Nietzsche's case because he was raised to view his father as a sainted ancestor, "the perfect image of a country parson."[2] His sister Elisabeth Förster-Nietzsche was assiduous in communicating this image to posterity, and many biographers have taken her at her word. Because the son is so famous, however, the father's life has been exhumed, and today, thanks notably to the efforts of Klaus Goch, readers know far more about Carl Ludwig Nietzsche than the son was likely to discover.[3] In the process they have learned, unsurprisingly, that the actual man was more frail and vulnerable than the myth allows. This is not to deny that he was in many ways heroic and amply deserving of his family's respect. He simply was not, as no human could be, the ideal figure presented as a model to his son.

This biography begins with an account of Nietzsche's father's career because the events of the philosopher's toddler years (and those regarding his father, in particular) were rightly regarded by him as among the most pivotal in his life.[4] Further the phrase "as the twig is bent" applies to

---

[1] UO II: 3; KSA I: 270. [2] KGW I-1: 282. [3] Goch 2000. [4] KGW I-3: 417.

families as well as individuals. Carl Ludwig Nietzsche played a decisive role in establishing the tone and behavioral dynamics of his household. Those customs had a life of their own and would not disappear merely because their progenitor had died. The decorum and emotional tone that the deceased man had instilled in those closest to him – and the social tensions that beset his wife – would continue to inform their actions and shape the children that he left behind.

I

If the early formation of Friedrich Nietzsche was rooted in family history, that of his father began in historical circumstances considerably more grand. Nietzsche himself drew attention to this when he noted in one version of his final autobiography that his father had been born in Eilenburg, Saxony, on October 10, 1813, just a few hours after Napoleon with his staff had entered that town.[5] In his own time Nietzsche could depend on readers to recognize the significance of this event. His reference, however, will probably be lost on today's public, who will be unaware that on that date the emperor was already pondering the decision to meet the enemy in the Battle of Leipzig. This was the engagement in which Prussian, Russian, Swedish, and Austrian troops dealt the French general a defeat from which he never recovered. By associating his father's birth with the event that triggered Napoleon's downfall, Nietzsche was not just linking him with an imposing figure and historic battle. He was placing that incident within the context of a turning point for Europe, the end of the revolutionary age and the start of an era one might recognize as modern.

These were not easy times, either for the citizens of Eilenburg or for the infant's parents. Their town lay 25 kilometers to the northeast of Leipzig, in a region prey to bivouacked armies. These were putatively friendly forces, but they lived off the land, and civilians found their livestock slaughtered, their homes plundered, and their shelters dismantled for use as firewood.[6] In the midst of so much tumult the child's parents had little chance to celebrate the arrival of their son or even to baptize him. The father Friedrich August Ludwig Nietzsche served as a superintendent in the Lutheran Church and had not only to advise his ministers but to answer

---

[5] KSA 14: 472. Napoleon actually arrived late on October 9. However, since Carl Ludwig Nietzsche was born in the early hours of October 10, his son is correct in his description.
[6] Goch 2000: 4. See also Colson 2013: 35.

to authorities and to guide the desperate members of his congregation.[7] He was fifty-seven years old – an advanced age for such pressures – and in the midst of official duties he had to protect and tend to his much younger and comparatively new wife Erdmuthe, née Krause. (Both spouses were on second marriages after the death of previous partners.) Aged thirty-four and prostrate after delivery, she could be of little help except to care for the newborn child and to watch in her weakened state as the armies in her vicinity began to march south. Between October 16 and 19, 1813, half a million troops assembled for what one historian has recently called "the greatest single military engagement to that date in the history of continental Europe, and probably of human warfare."[8] The pounding of cannons in Leipzig was severe enough to shake the ground and rattle the windows, even in Eilenburg,[9] and Erdmuthe may never have fully recovered psychologically. According to her granddaughter, she experienced terrors that afflicted her for the rest of her life.[10]

Friedrich August Ludwig Nietzsche appears to have been a man of considerable enterprise, and, after the war, political flexibility. Although he had once sworn an oath of loyalty to the king of Saxony, he accepted the new treaties which awarded the town to Prussia and threw in his lot with the victors. It would of course take decades for a people to heal from such disruption, and it is probable that most of the generation immediately affected never quite forgot the devastations they had experienced.[11] Nonetheless, circumstances changed rapidly over the next two years. Napoleon abdicated, a treaty of peace was negotiated, many of the former rulers resumed their powers, and the city of Eilenburg, hitherto part of the Kingdom of Saxony, was awarded to its hated rival. It fell to Friedrich August Ludwig Nietzsche, as a civic authority, to persuade his congregants to accept the new government and to enjoy the economic benefits that Prussia could provide.[12]

Superintendent Nietzsche's efforts were no doubt eased by a general sense of exhaustion and relief.[13] After a quarter of a century of violence, much of Continental Europe embraced a return to pious conservatism. Behind this facade of a return to the status quo, however, both royalty and

---

[7] Goch 2000: 46–47.   [8] Clark 2006: 367. Compare Esdaile 1995: 251.   [9] Goch 2000: 4.
[10] Förster-Nietzsche 1912: 2.
[11] For more on the sense of dislocation induced by the treaty, see Blue 2007.
[12] Goch 2000: 5–11.
[13] This paragraph is based on numerous historical accounts, of which the following have proved particularly helpful, both here and later in this book: Brose 2013; Carr 1991; Clark 2006; Nipperdey 1996; Schulze 1998; Sheehan 1989; and Simms 1998. Obviously this account is simplistic but it is designed merely to offer a context for the Nietzsche family and their new historical situation.

their subjects knew that little could be the same. The people had seen their kings flee ignominiously before the invading armies. The populace had itself participated militarily in the eventual victory and learned that they were potential wielders of power themselves.[14] They had further been exposed to a secular and politically inflammatory ideology (symbolized by the slogan, "Liberty, equality, fraternity"), which they might reject but could not quite forget. A comparatively new and far more dangerous ideology, that of nationalism, was beginning to spread to the populace at large.[15]

It was in this resolutely peaceful world with a lid clamped on the unspoken that Carl Ludwig Nietzsche (or Ludwig, as he was generally known) grew up, himself a member of the first post-war generation and fervently committed to its conservative values. Unlike certain restive political malcontents, who were already beginning to appear, Ludwig accepted the world acclaimed by the authorities and grew to be a genuinely pious boy, industrious in his lessons and aware that his God was a fearsome judge who must be obeyed in all particulars.[16] Friedrich August Ludwig Nietzsche, a lifelong proponent of education, supervised his son's schooling with particular care. The boy proved poor in mathematics, excellent in literary studies, and showed an aptitude for music. His father probably took note of his verbal skills, for the whole family assumed (and Ludwig no doubt was nudged to believe) that he would become a minister himself.

This early push towards a career was pressing for economic reasons. As Friedrich August Ludwig Nietzsche entered his late sixties and began to feel signs of mortality, he recognized that the financial fate of his prospective widow and probably of his two youngest daughters would rest on the shoulders of his son. The seven surviving children from his first marriage were now comparatively stable adults.[17] This could hardly be said of his current offspring who, in 1826, were fifteen, twelve, and ten years old. His daughters were particularly vulnerable, for they would enjoy financial security only if linked to a financially secure male. Unless they married, their only source of future funds would have to come from Ludwig himself.

---

[14] The people's view of their military participation appears to be largely a myth, but it was a myth widely believed and a source of considerable pride. See, for example, Clark 2006: 379–385.

[15] For a discussion of the ideologically fraught "restoration" of monarchy in Prussia and elsewhere, see Barclay 1995: 4–16. For a geographically nuanced discussion of the effect in Saxony and other states, see Green 2001: 62–96, especially 62–67.

[16] One drawing he made as a child depicts a fierce man brandishing a rod while standing over a Bible on which is written, "One must reverence the word of God." Goch 2000: 89.

[17] Comparatively speaking, of course. His youngest daughter Lina, for example, never married and lived with siblings.

The legacy

The obedient son seems to have understood this obligation and acceded. At the age of twelve he composed his first sermon.[18]

On March 16, 1826, aged seventy years old, Friedrich August Ludwig Nietzsche passed away, leaving his family economically vulnerable.[19] Erdmuthe Nietzsche, his much younger wife (she would now be forty-seven) found that her pension came to 100 talers per year,[20] an absurdly low amount in an era when a cultured bourgeois family required at least six times that much for expenses.[21] Her dying husband had no doubt counseled her on how best to navigate the future, and she seems to have been equal to the occasion. Indeed, Erdmuthe was a veteran of disasters, some much worse than the aforementioned battle. She had married for the first time at the age of twenty-three and given birth to a son, who died just after his first birthday.[22] Shortly thereafter, she had been living in Weimar when French marauders looted that town, committing rape, arson, and murder.[23] Her husband, long ill from consumption, died a month later, the brutality of the French probably hastening his demise.[24] Thus, at the age of twenty-eight, Erdmuthe had found her entire first family – and probably her youthful hopes – extinguished.[25] She had repaired to the nearby town of Naumburg, where her brother was preacher at the cathedral and there she made powerful friends. It was in this town that she met and married the much older Friedrich August Ludwig Nietzsche and had begun the era of seventeen years of stability that had just ended. Having now outlived all these males (both husbands, a first son, and the protective brother), she of necessity turned her eye to the family's remaining boy and considered the possibilities.

---

[18] Goch 2000: 69–70.
[19] For short biographies of Friedrich August Ludwig Nietzsche, see Pernet 1989: 37–42 and Goch 2000: 41–55.
[20] Goch 2000: 60–61, n. 126. For purchasing power, McClelland 1980: 210–211. See also Turner 1980a: 132–133.
[21] For Erdmuthe's finances see Bohley 1989: 385, n. 48. Förster-Nietzsche indicates that the Nietzsche family inherited money from a half-brother who died childless. (Förster-Nietzsche 1912: 4.) A half-brother matching her description did exist and may have left funds. Erdmuthe also probably received a bequest from her first husband Christoph Krüger.
[22] All information on Erdmuthe Nietzsche's first family is taken from Rosmiarek et al. 2003: 351 and Bohley 1989: 380. Incidentally, Erdmuthe's first husband Carl Christoph Heinrich Krüger was cousin to August von Kotzebue, the well-known playwright. For more on the implications of this relationship, see Chapter 9, Section 2. Nietzsche's stories about his grandmother's supposed acquaintanceship with Goethe are fictional. Goch 2000: 61, n. 128; 65–66, n. 135.
[23] Fürster-Nietzsche tells some melodramatic tales (Förster-Nietzsche 1895: I 63–64), and Erdmuthe possibly did see violence. See Safranski 1989: 76–78.
[24] The Battle of Jena occurred October 14, 1806. Erdmuthe's first husband died on November 16, "from consumption." Rosmiarek et al. 2003: 351.
[25] Goch 2000: 130.

2

At the age of twelve, Ludwig Nietzsche was well meaning but unfledged. A sickly and apparently excitable child, he seemed to show little ambition beyond a wish to follow his father's footsteps into the ministry and an evident desire to remain at his beloved mother's side. These desires were incompatible, as Erdmuthe recognized. If he was to become a minister, he would have to learn French and master Latin (requirements for admission to the preparatory school for the seminary) and work his way with little financial backing through ten years of rigorous schooling, all of it away from home. This called for heroic measures, and Ludwig would require stern handling if he was to live up to them.[26]

By all accounts Ludwig was unusually attached to his mother, and Erdmuthe put this devotion to use.[27] Her first move was to send the boy away and to keep him away, so that he would see her at most on the holidays, such reunions being treated as rewards for good behavior. She dispatched him first to relatives in Halle to study French, then arranged for him to attend a preparatory school at the even further distant Rossleben. Ludwig was homesick while with the relatives and desperately unhappy at Rossleben, yet Erdmuthe instructed him to endure these tribulations both for his own sake and hers. She had found life difficult, and she made clear to her son that no success would come without hardship. Trust God and stick to your last, she commanded, hinting that he could best win her love through stern application to his studies. Above all, she promised to advise and help him throughout, as she did through her letters. Indeed, the correspondence between mother and son indicates that the boy's education was in some ways a joint enterprise, Ludwig reporting, Erdmuthe advising and exhorting. Although this partnership had its manipulative and even psychologically disquieting aspects, much noted by Ludwig's biographer, it would be unfair to either party to overlook the larger religious context. On the one hand Erdmuthe would sweeten her requests by promising to give Ludwig a kiss for good grades. On the other she appealed to an Enlightenment-inflected version of Christianity which stressed the sacrifice of transient pleasures for the satisfactions of transcendent purpose. In the eyes of mother and son, they were embarked on a joint spiritual

---

[26] Unless otherwise stated, this account of Carl Ludwig Nietzsche's life is based on Goch 2000. See also Bohley 1987.
[27] Goch 2000: 59–60, 130, and *passim*; Pernet 1989: 44; Schmidt 1991–1994 II: 863.

journey – one that invoked duty, led to practical success, and fostered compliance with God's will.[28]

For ten years Ludwig endured almost Dickensian misery (freezing winters, petty bullying, mice in his mattress), to most of which Erdmuthe was strategically unsympathetic. He was a lonely boy with few social skills, and he was disliked by schoolmates because of his pious demeanor.[29] On the few occasions when he tried to make friends, his mother wrote in disapproval, afraid that socializing would lead him into trouble or distract him from his studies.[30] When he wanted to come home for the holidays, she worried over the expense,[31] and one year she flatly forbade him to return for Christmas, a devastating decision for the boy.[32] When he suffered painful headaches, stomach upsets, and had trouble breathing, she said he had probably brought these on himself, not wearing proper clothing in the cold.[33] As a kind of nadir of discomfort and humiliation Ludwig found at the age of eighteen that his spine was curving, a condition so severe that it threw him off balance, causing him to fall.[34] For at least two years he wore a corrective leather corset that hoisted his chest and ensured good posture. Although he was eventually able to forgo the harness, difficulties with his back and hips persisted well into his twenties and possibly beyond.[35]

Throughout these difficult times, Ludwig was sustained by a double faith: that he was serving God and making his mother happy. Indeed, the experience seems to have brought out a dogged, patient, and industrious side to him that might never have been suspected when he was living with his mother at Eilenburg. "*Constantia et labore*" ("Perseverance and work") was his motto,[36] and he succeeded in each of his tasks. He mastered French with the relatives, he graduated with honors at Rossleben, and he impressed his exacting and contentious teachers at the prestigious seminary at Halle. Klaus Goch, Ludwig's principal biographer, has suggested that these achievements came at a cost.[37] In his view Ludwig succeeded by more or less eviscerating himself of his personal values and indefinitely postponing any life beyond one spent following rules and earning good grades. He had committed himself to Christ

---

[28] Goch 2000: 128–132, 65, 77, 116. For Erdmuthe's "philosophy of life" see Goch 2000: 66–70, 162–163.
[29] Goch 2000: 114–115, 139–140, 170–172.
[30] Goch 2000: 218–219. See also 99 (nn. 23, 24), 134–136, 139–140. Erdmuthe also disapproved of the arts because she feared they would distract her son. Goch 2000: 168.
[31] Goch 2000: 131.   [32] Goch 2000: 130–132.   [33] Goch 2000: 81, 82, 133.
[34] Although Ludwig was first treated for his condition in 1831 (when he would have been seventeen years old), it had first been noted as early as February 1828, when he was fourteen. Goch 2000: 82, 153–154.
[35] During his university years (in 1833 and 1836) the military twice exempted him from service on grounds of physical unsuitability. One citation mentioned "twisted hips." Goch 2000: 259.
[36] Goch 2000: 230.   [37] See, for example, Goch 2000: 35–36, 59–60, 93–94.

(who was in heaven) and his mother (in distant Eilenburg) and in pursuit of a goal which (until now) had been some years distant. He was thus unprepared for the inevitable day when he would graduate from school and be expected to navigate the world under his own direction.

If so, there were signs that Ludwig recognized these dangers and that he quietly maneuvered to exert a will of his own. Once, when his mother demanded that he wear heavy coats in September, he wrote in gentle remonstrance that if he bundled up in September, what would he wear in December?[38] During his university days at Halle he not only enrolled in a dance course but sang in a mixed choir that included forty to fifty women. He found himself attracted to one of them and appears to have nursed romantic hopes, although these were swiftly crushed. "Such women are not meant for lopsided people,"[39] he told his mother, his adjective apparently referring to his spinal condition. These diversions, while tame by comparison with those pursued by rowdier male students, suggest that Ludwig was beginning to wean himself from his mother's dominance. He also seems to have moved from her rationalistic version of Pietism to a more fervent persuasion known in German as the *Erweckungsbewegung*, the "Awakening Movement."[40] This was a far more radical assertion of his values, for it involved nothing less than the religion which governed both his own and his mother's lives. Erdmuthe disapproved of this new approach to Pietism, and Ludwig never professed this faith in public, possibly out of deference to her views.[41] Nonetheless, the religious leaders who most influenced him, both in his final years at Halle and in the aftermath, were those of the "Awakened" persuasion.[42]

More puzzling in view of his previous persistence was Ludwig's apparent reluctance to graduate. He had to take two final examinations, and he waited a year to take the first,[43] possibly discouraged because he finished his studies at a time when job prospects for clerics were poor.[44] If so, he failed to reckon with his mother, who intervened yet again. This time Erdmuthe wrote to a relative, a captain in the ducal city of Altenburg, to arrange for her son to teach the man's eight sons and daughters. This was a formidable task, particularly since Ludwig knew nothing of children, yet he applied

---

[38] Goch 2000: 157.   [39] Goch 2000: 220.
[40] This movement will be discussed in detail in Chapter 2, Section 3.
[41] Three of Ludwig Nietzsche's biographers share unanimity on this point: Pernet 1989: 11, 17 ff., 22, 26, 44; Bohley 1987: 172; Goch 2000: 271–278, 300–303.
[42] Goch 2000: 241–245, 271–278, 300–303.
[43] Goch 2000: 256, n. 171. The delay may also have been due to health issues. Goch 2000: 256–260. For details, see Bohley 1987: 176–177, especially n. 75.
[44] Goch 2000: 267, n. 5.

himself with his practiced dedication, patience, and stoicism; and apparently he succeeded. The captain was delighted. Through his preaching skills and the adroit politicking of a friend, Ludwig was able to parley this job into a position with Joseph, the Duke of Saxe-Altenburg, who was looking for someone to instruct his three younger daughters, particularly his fifteen-year-old, who was beginning Confirmation instruction.[45] By November 1838 Ludwig found himself a prized employee at the palace, a position he would hold for three years.

Everyone in the royal household, even the difficult duchess, were apparently impressed with the new employee, who was both eager to please and industrious. Ludwig seems besides to have been gifted with a warm and affectionate nature, a quality which apparently impressed at least two of the princesses, who would keep in touch with his family for decades.[46] He turned out to be so popular with the royal household that he dreamed of remaining at Altenburg longer and asked the consistory to postpone his second examination. To Ludwig's chagrin, however, his supervisor Court Preacher Friedrich Heinrich Sachse grew jealous of this popular young assistant and thwarted his retention. After the duke's daughter was confirmed in August, 1840, Sachse informed Ludwig that his services were no longer needed.[47]

The young man was devastated, and the duke too seems to have regretted this turn of events. Seeing that he could no longer keep his employee, he took the exceptional step of sending him to Berlin with letters of recommendation to the newly crowned king of Prussia, Friedrich Wilhelm IV, as well as to other members of the court. That monarch interviewed the young man and apparently found him suitable to be a Prussian cleric. Ludwig had already reapplied to take his clerical examination and had passed it with dispatch.[48] In the autumn of 1841 he received a pastoral assignment to four country villages (principally Röcken but also Michlitz, Bothfeld, and Schwessnitz), all about 30 kilometers southwest of Leipzig.[49]

3

On January 9, 1842, as he ascended the pulpit to deliver his introductory sermon at Röcken, Ludwig expressed gratitude to God and king, a sense of

---

[45] The duke had a fourth daughter, Maria Alexandrine Wilhelmine Katherine von Sachsen-Altenburg, who had already completed her education. She would eventually marry George V of Hannover. Goch 2000: 287, n. 41.
[46] Goch 2000: 293, n. 51.   [47] Goch 2000: 304.
[48] He took the second exam on July 15, 1841, four years after the first. Pernet 1989: 21.
[49] Pernet 1989: 112, n. 65.

thankfulness which was doubtless sincere. At last he was a functioning pastor and had arrived at the future he had envisioned for himself as a child of twelve. Yet as he took up residence in the village, it is unlikely that he didn't suffer some disappointment at the reality of the situation. He had grown up in the city, served a duke, taught princesses, and met one of the most prominent monarchs in Europe. Now he lived in a frequently waterlogged, rural community of approximately twenty-eight homes and 202 inhabitants,[50] where the previous pastor (who had neglected his congregation and left the rectory in disorder) refused to retire until paid a large sum out of Ludwig's own pocket.[51] His parishioners were largely farming folk who would be expected to contribute to his upkeep in the form of agricultural products for food, the notoriously parsimonious Prussian government offering little in the way of salary.[52] Further, Ludwig found himself saddled with the local schoolmaster Gustav Dathe, who happened also to be church organist and Ludwig's representative when he was away on trips. Dathe was apparently brutal to his students, a bully to his wife and eleven children, and an impertinent assistant to the gentle Ludwig.[53] On one occasion he so upset the minister that the latter gave way to tears and tremors during a church service and had to leave and recover, only later returning to complete the ceremony.[54] The high-strung minister's partnership with this insensitive assistant must have often led to pain.

None of these factors should have daunted a man so inured to misery as Ludwig Nietzsche. Yet now that he held the job he had long sought, he experienced a curious diffidence. On the surface, Ludwig performed his duties well. He knew how to be practical, work hard, and both to envision and inculcate ideals. He was by all accounts a far more capable parson than the man he succeeded, and both his parishioners and supervisor declared themselves satisfied and even pleased with his labors.[55] Privately, he admitted that he was terrified. Even before his arrival he had written a friend, "In my ear and heart sounds [the saying,] 'Of those who has been given much, much will be demanded.' Trembling and faint of heart, I wonder over my competence, and such terror often seizes me that I would rather not take my office."[56] Ludwig's guttering confidence may have been

---

[50] Pernet 1989 123, n. 9.
[51] An incoming pastor was supposed to pay his predecessor a sum to eke out the latter's finances. However, the departing pastor in this case demanded an exorbitant amount, which Ludwig was able to bargain down somewhat. Goch 2000: 330.
[52] Oehler 1940: 47.   [53] Reich 2004: 51–52; Goch 2000: 332–333.
[54] Goch 2000: 377–378. This story was originally told in Bohley 1987: 177.
[55] Pernet 1989: 25–26; Goch 1994: 368, n. 148; Goch 2000: 331–336.
[56] Goch 2000: 329. The quotation is from John 12:48.

due to his health. He suffered migraine headaches, along with tiredness and exhaustion, and a letter from a sister indicates that rumors of his death had begun to circulate.[57]

His daughter reports rumors among Ludwig's parishioners[58] that he would eventually be promoted from this first assignment and even be called to the post of court chaplain at Berlin.[59] Such prospects seem unlikely in view of the realities of the situation, and the pastor had no such illusions. In another letter he stated flatly that his professional career had begun and would end in that country village: "I have long ago taken leave of high hopes to move to a large city."[60] Ludwig did not give reasons for this despair, but it must have been due partly to the scarcity of open positions, partly to the damage done his career by the postponement of his second examination, and perhaps he recognized that between illness and his own lack of forcefulness, he would not be able to rise above his current inglorious situation. Threatened by depression and poor health, he turned to the woman he had relied upon from the beginning. He wrote to his mother and asked her to join him.

Erdmuthe had been settled for thirty years at Eilenburg and might have been reluctant to leave the comfort and prestige she enjoyed there for the indignities of a country village. She did eventually accede but warned her son that if she moved, he would have to accept his two sisters as well, for neither had married and both were dependent on their mother. Ludwig had no trouble welcoming Auguste, the youngest child, although she was chronically ill and her doctors' bills had probably drawn heavily on Erdmuthe's resources.[61] Auguste, at least, had an undemanding personality, and she made a sterling housekeeper. Ludwig was less hospitable to Rosalie, his older sister, for she was high-strung, quarrelsome, and certain to be a source of unrest. Somehow an arrangement was made to relocate Erdmuthe and Auguste to Röcken, while the more pugnacious thirty-three-year-old was persuaded to live with relatives in Plauen, Saxony. Rosalie, however, was not inclined to be submissive. Through a campaign of wheedling letters and repeated visits (each of which seemed to last longer), she managed in 1844 to descend on the rectory and never to leave. The family in Plauen was told to forward her belongings permanently to Röcken.[62]

---

[57] For the headaches and exhaustion, see Goch 2000: 332; for the rumors of death see 331.
[58] Goch 1994: 96–97; Goch 2000: 335.
[59] Förster-Nietzsche 1912: 7. In his biography of Franziska Nietzsche, Adalbert Oehler suggests similar possibilities, although he does not mention Berlin. Oehler 1940: 41.
[60] Goch 2000: 335–336.   [61] A doctor treated Auguste weekly. Franziska Nietzsche 1994: 173.
[62] Goch 2000: 337–339; Bohley 1989: 388.

4

With the arrival of mother and sisters, the old household reconstituted itself, reverting to the structure of seventeen years earlier, before Ludwig had been sent away to school. Inevitably, there were tensions. Rosalie proved predictably high-strung and prone to quarrels. Auguste's health required weekly visits by the doctor.[63] Nonetheless, both sisters seem to have idolized their brother, and the family reunited with warmth and glee. As Ludwig well knew, the Nietzsche women were splendid administrators, and the Röcken parsonage was probably never run so well.[64]

Now that he had a situation and income, Ludwig would be expected to marry, and he began to canvass the countryside for a bride. Among the families he visited was that of David Ernst Oehler, a parson at Pobles, a village even smaller than Röcken. (It consisted of eighteen buildings and 130 inhabitants.)[65] Oehler was of a looser disposition than Ludwig and indeed than any of the other local ministers, somewhat to the chagrin of his superintendent who tended to be critical of him.[66] The man ran a farm, served beer, was a Freemason, and he had once harangued the local landowner (his social superior and paymaster) concerning the division of harvest monies. (The landowner paid but never came to Oehler's church again.)[67] In addition to his farming and bee-keeping the industrious parson pursued music (as a boy he had sung well enough to be paid for it), literature (each of his children was required to recite a poem by heart every week), and he was often immersed in his library, which was by no means exclusively theological.[68] The Oehler household with its several dogs, eleven children, and many guests (the Oehlers were highly hospitable), was loud and, as even Förster-Nietzsche admits,[69] somewhat quarrelsome – not the sort of ambience likely to appeal to Ludwig Nietzsche. Perhaps he was drawn by its very difference, and besides, he here encountered five daughters, including a sixteen-year-old named Franziska, generally known as Fränzchen. Soon he arranged for the girl to meet his mother, and after nearly a year of consideration, he proposed marriage.

Even during this era, it struck many as odd that a twenty-nine-year-old man would select a girl nearly half his age for his bride, particularly as she had three marriageable sisters, aged twenty-five, twenty-four, and

---

[63] Franziska Nietzsche, quoted in Goch 1994: 173.   [64] Goch 2000: 339–340.
[65] Goch 1994: 66. Oehler was also pastor of Sössen, Gostau, and Stösswitz. Pernet 1989: 46.
[66] See the transcripts given in Goch 1994: 72 and Pernet 1989: 48.
[67] Goch 1994: 69, 78–79, 81–82, 358–359, n. 80. See also Oehler 2002: 276–277.
[68] Goch 1994: 75; Oehler 1940: 10.   [69] Förster-Nietzsche 1912: 9–10.

twenty-three. Franziska was also a questionable fit temperamentally. Raised with ten rather wild siblings, and herself coming in the midst of a brood of five brothers, the girl tended to be forthright and physical. (She excelled at the toboggan.)[70] Poorly educated, like most country girls of the time,[71] she was beautiful, but inexperienced – she had only just stopped playing with dolls[72] – and she certainly knew little of the social decorum the Nietzsche family prized. Her outgoing and even obstreperous demeanor may have charmed the repressed Ludwig but would have raised eyebrows among both family and friends. (At least one of Ludwig's colleagues regarded a marriage into the Oehler family as a baffling misalliance.)[73] It was clear that his choice could not help him politically, and if Ludwig decided to marry out of policy, he selected his spouse out of sentiment. He seems never to have had a romantic relationship before – certainly none he acknowledged – and his affection for Franziska proved to be genuine and enduring. "My Franziska may not have a rich and educated intellect . . . but she has . . . a heart which is open to all things," he wrote a friend.[74] As for Franziska, she certainly did not choose Ludwig and seems never to have thought of marriage before the proposal. However, she was not averse to the unexpected honor, and whatever happened, she would never express regret in the future.[75]

The wedding followed village customs and lasted three days, the exchange of vows occurring on the groom's thirtieth birthday, October 10, 1843. The couple spent their honeymoon in Plauen in Saxony, near where Ludwig's beloved mother had grown up and where members of his father's first family resided. They then returned to Röcken to settle in. This was a decisive moment for the guileless Franziska. Erdmuthe probably did not envision relaxing her grip on her son, nor did her daughters expect interference in the household arrangements. Franziska might henceforward enjoy the title "wife," but at seventeen (the age she actually wed) she could be no match for the united front of the three Nietzsche women.[76] Franziska herself was slightly in awe of the household and quite aware of her own ignorance. She had already confessed to her mother that she felt too young for marriage, to which the latter responded, "That, my child, is a flaw that mends itself each day."[77] Anxious to prove herself worthy of her distinguished husband, she tried to be as docile as her temperament allowed. Nonetheless, her assimilation cannot have been easy for any of

---

[70] Goch 1994: 32–64; Oehler 1940: 15.   [71] Goch 1994: 94–95; Oehler 1940: 8–10.
[72] Oehler 1940: 17–18.   [73] Goch 2000: 345.   [74] Pernet 1989: 29.
[75] Goch 1994: 55–60, 99–100.   [76] Apparently, even the maid offered advice. Oehler 1940: 41.
[77] Goch 1994: 59.

the parties. By all accounts, Rosalie was particularly irritable and overbearing. (Franziska would call her "dreadfully nervous.")[78] Apparently a woman of imposing intellectual habits, although we only have Förster-Nietzsche's word for this,[79] Rosalie took the lead among the women in spiritual matters and probably dispensed advice to Franziska as well. Auguste, by contrast, was a quietly industrious housekeeper, who shared the cooking duties with Franziska but, according to her niece, insisted on cleaning the rectory alone.[80]

If the Nietzsches joined forces against the interloper, Franziska in turn marveled at the peculiarities of her new family. When the brittle Rosalie complained of her nerves, the country girl was baffled because she had never heard the term used in this sense before. "I hadn't the least idea what it meant," she confessed, and she had to ask her mother for information. ("I think it's a kind of general weakness," Wilhelmine Oehler darkly replied.)[81] "Nerves" with its demands carried many implications. According to Goch it meant that all quarrels must be suppressed and that the home must be kept orderly and quiet. Franziska herself had grown up amid the hubbub of eleven children, two loud-tempered parents, and the country manners of farm hands. (One of her brothers remembered their upbringing as "organized chaos.")[82] Indeed, when her mother Wilhelmine assigned her eleven children household chores, she directed them to sing vigorously so that she could keep track of their whereabouts by ear.[83] Such raucousness was probably unknown in the decorous rectory in Röcken, where it is doubtful that anyone (except Franziska) ever spoke other than in low tones.[84]

Franziska accepted the matriarchal Erdmuthe as a substitute parent and sought to conform to her strictures. Ludwig wrote a friend that his new wife "submits with charming humility and devotion... not just to me but with enchanting childlikeness to my good mother."[85] However sweetly she might defer to Erdmuthe, the newcomer found it difficult to bend before the less tactful Rosalie. Förster-Nietzsche relates that on such occasions Ludwig could hardly stand up for himself, much less defend his wife. Rather than adjudicate or take Franziska's side, he would lock himself in his study and refuse food and drink until the women made peace.[86]

---

[78] Goch 1994: 172.   [79] Förster-Nietzsche 1895: I 26; 1912: 29.
[80] Förster-Nietzsche 1895: I 26; 1912: 29. Franziska shared the cooking (Goch 1994: 64) and she tended the garden. Oehler 1940: 43.
[81] Goch 1994: 54.   [82] Quoted in Goch 1994: 90.   [83] Oehler 1940: 13.
[84] Goch 1994: 120; Oehler 1940: 43–44.   [85] Quoted in Pernet 1989: 28.
[86] The only source for this account of Ludwig's purported behavior is Förster-Nietzsche, who interprets it positively as a sign of her father's sensitivity. Förster-Nietzsche 1912: 15. Compare Goch 1994: 125–126.

The legacy

Abandoned by her only source of support, Franziska seized opportunities to decamp to her own parents' home, which was within only a few kilometers of the Röcken parsonage. This can neither have helped the marriage nor eased relations between the two families, and Ludwig came to detest the Oehlers. "The longer I know them, the less I can respect them," he wrote a friend. "It oppresses and pains me terribly that I must be ashamed of my in-laws ... and unfortunately, this difference with [them] has already led to many hours of misunderstanding with my dear Franziska. It hurts her so that I cannot stand her parents."[87]

One niche remained for this abruptly thwarted and marginalized woman – to produce children and see to their needs. Accordingly, it was almost certainly with relief that she discovered she was pregnant, and on October 15, 1844, she gave birth to a son. This happened to be the birthday of the king of Prussia, and the date was usually celebrated with cannon salutes, religious services, public speeches, and (in large cities) balls.[88] After considerable deliberation Ludwig chose to name the boy after his royal benefactor – Friedrich Wilhelm – although he rejoiced that the name "Fritz," a diminutive of Friedrich, would please his mother, whose long-deceased first son had borne that name.[89]

After the birth Franziska stayed in bed for a time because of a breast inflammation and missed her own son's baptism.[90] Perhaps because of this invalidism, and perhaps because she was untrained and inexperienced, she found that many of the early child-rearing decisions were taken from her and assigned to Erdmuthe. Nonetheless, Franziska was expected to perform the more menial tasks, and she seems to have embraced motherhood with the vigor and enthusiasm of an active young woman who has at last been given something to do. According to her daughter, she so single-mindedly practiced her maternal role that the boy didn't learn to speak until he was two-and-a-half. (Franziska supposedly leapt too quickly to see to his needs and did not allow him to ask for help.) This story is mentioned here only because it is so often repeated, but it is almost certainly false. Aside from its inherent implausibility – this is not how children learn to talk – Franziska herself denied it. "Nonsense," she said when she read her daughter's account. Further, a

---

[87] Pernet 1989: 29. This letter was written February 22, 1844, only four-and-a-half months into the marriage. For the causes of this estrangement, see Pernet 1989: 48; Goch 2000: 349; Goch 1994: 127–129; Bohley 1980: 389–390, n. 37.
[88] Barclay 1995: 112–113.   [89] Bohley 1980: 386; Goch 2000: 61, n. 127.
[90] Ludwig hastened the ceremony so that his son could be christened on Ludwig's own baptismal date (October 24). Hödl 2009: 31.

letter from Ludwig written shortly after his son's second birthday takes for granted that the boy is already talking.[91]

It does appear, however, that Franziska left most disciplinary matters to her husband and with good reason. Friedrich didn't like to be balked and was described as a "boisterous child" who, when angry, would throw himself on the floor in what was apparently a tantrum.[92] According to Förster-Nietzsche (seconded by Adalbert Oehler, Franziska's confidant for a time), his parents soon discovered a swift means of relief. Ludwig had always loved music – it had been the one amusement he allowed himself outside of study – and he was an exceptional improviser. Now he found that he had only to touch the piano, and the boy would grow "still as a mouse."[93] Soon Franziska was begging her husband to play whenever the son was grumpy.[94] Of course, Ludwig also practiced more conventional modes of discipline – physical punishment, warnings about the wrath of God, and modeling a good example for the boy to imitate.[95] He had twice held tutoring posts in Altenburg, and he was probably quite skillful in dealing with children. Friedrich seems to have responded to his guidance with a willingness which the family probably found winning and reassuring. He was, by all accounts, an exceptionally "good," dignified, and above all self-controlled child, his only flaws being the above-mentioned tantrums and occasional stubbornness.

Two siblings soon shared the attentions of the rapt Franziska, and they too were named after royalty. A daughter (born July 10, 1846) was baptized Therese Elisabeth Alexandra after the three princesses; and a second son (born February 27, 1848) was called Ludwig Joseph, the second name after the duke.[96] In view of these later arrivals, one might expect sibling rivalry, but if this occurred, no record survives. Friedrich later wrote that he liked to wander along the ponds just outside the house and play in the graveyard, which adjoined the parsonage.[97] He also made friends with the local children and later remembered them with wistful fondness. He took long walks with his father (often past the nearby doubly historic battlefield of Lützen)[98] and developed a love of nature that would nourish and inspire him for the rest of his life.

---

[91] Franziska Nietzsche 1994: 34–35. For Ludwig's letter, dated December 15, 1846, see Bohley 1987: 171. This discrepancy is noted by Schmidt 1991–1994 II: 840.
[92] Franziska Nietzsche 1994: 38.   [93] See Förster-Nietzsche 1912: 16; Oehler 1940: 44.
[94] Goch 1994: 135–136.   [95] Goch 2000: 358–9.
[96] According to Bohley 1987: 167 and Rosmiarek et al. 2001: 373, the name "Therese" precedes "Elisabeth." Cf. Goch 2000: 359.
[97] KGW I-1: 283.
[98] Lützen was the site of the 1632 engagement between the Swedes and Austrian Empire in which Gustavus Adolphus was slain and the 1813 victory of Napoleon over the Prusso-Russian army.

The legacy

5

Meanwhile, far from this bucolic retreat, political unrest was sweeping Europe. The pretense that the kings of Europe could resume their autocratic prerogatives after Napoleon's defeat had become ever less tenable, and restive subjects began to sense their own power. A riot disturbed Berlin in 1847, and in 1848 revolutions toppled the monarchy in France and drove the conservative chancellor Klemens von Metternich from Vienna. In Altenburg where Ludwig had been so happy, his beloved employer Duke Joseph was forced to abdicate, and the imperious duchess died.[99] Ludwig's other sponsor, the Prussian king Friedrich Wilhelm IV, was taken hostage by his own subjects and, to his army's horror, was persuaded to wear a revolutionary cockade through the streets of his capital. This last event seems to have outraged the hitherto loyal Ludwig. "I lament that our *king* is dead," he wrote a friend, "for the Friedrich Wilhelm who rides around the streets of Berlin [bearing revolutionary insignia] is no longer the king whom I once regarded with deepest reverence." (Emphasis Ludwig's.)[100]

Since Röcken was a backwater, the revolution seems to have passed there largely without incident, although Friedrich would claim to remember isolated incidents.[101] Nonetheless, Ludwig had been weaned on monarchism and had spent some of the happiest years of his life at the court of a duke. In the summer of 1848 as the traditional social order collapsed, he became profoundly depressed.[102] Already the headaches which had been chronic since he was a boy grew worse, and strange fits of behavior began to puzzle his family, parishioners, and Ludwig himself. During the previous two years he had become increasingly restless and spent much time outdoors because he couldn't bear to sit in his room and study.[103] Every Sunday he was sick, and his sermons, which had been a source of pride,[104] now inspired fear. "I have to do something for my nerves," he wrote a friend.[105] The Nietzsches were homeopaths but seem also to have

---

[99] Goch 2000: 286, n. 39, 376. See also Pernet 1989: 110, n. 52.
[100] Goch 1994: 139; Goch 2000: 376. The versions in these books are slightly different.
[101] In KGW I-1: 284, he recalls groups in wagons waving banners and singing. In KGW I-2: 258, he remembers hussars being quartered on the village.
[102] On Ludwig's despair, see Goch 2000: 375. On the reasons for his depression, Goch 1994: 109–110.
[103] Goch 2000: 378.
[104] For Ludwig's expertise in sermons, see Pernet 1989: 19. This skill is repeatedly stressed in Goch 2000. See, for example, 246.
[105] Goch 2000: 378.

tried other remedies, to no avail.[106] His family had already noticed absent-minded spells, when he ceased conversation and stared into space.[107] Such episodes grew more severe, and he began to suffer from insomnia and dizziness. Eventually, speech became difficult, and on September 17, 1848, he gave what was to be his final sermon. Fits of vomiting ensued, along with fiercely painful headaches, and eventually, Ludwig went blind.

The source of his illness remains unknown. The doctors termed it "softening of the brain," a diagnosis which seems to have satisfied the medical community of the time.[108] Conditions as varied as stroke, tumor, concussion, encephalitis, tuberculosis of the brain, and even syphilis have been suggested.[109] Whatever the cause, the effect on the preschool Friedrich must have been disturbing. During the time that Ludwig's brain was "softening" (and an autopsy is said to have revealed that a quarter of that organ had been affected),[110] he experienced severe pain as well as the motor deterioration wrought by nerve damage. Friedrich was still three years old when these sufferings began, and he turned four shortly after his father preached his final sermon. The sight and sounds of the man's abrupt deterioration could scarcely be hidden in the small, crowded house,[111] and thirteen years later the boy would recall, "The increasing suffering of my father, his blindness, his haggard face and figure, my mother's tears, the doctor's portentous mien, and also the incautious remarks of some villagers must have given me a sense of impending doom."[112]

---

[106] See treatment of Auguste in Bohley 1989: 387, n. 53. Ludwig's own early consultations were with homeopathic doctors (Goch 2000: 378, 381), although he indicates in a letter that he also tried other remedies. Bohley 1987: 177. See also Franziska's letter, Oehler 1940: 42.

[107] Goch 2000: 377.

[108] It did not, however, satisfy Dr. Otto Binswanger, head of the psychiatric clinic at the University of Jena, who handled Nietzsche. Volz 1990: 35.

[109] Pletsch proposes concussion, stroke, and tumor. Pletsch 1991: 25–26. Blunck suggests no diagnosis (Blunck 1953: 31–33) but in his rewrite Janz introduces the possibility of tuberculosis of the brain. Janz 1978 I: 46–47. Goch proposes encephalitis (Goch 2000: 384, n. 119; see also Goch 1994: 369–370, n. 183). Heinrich Köselitz proposed a brain tumor. See Goch 2000: 384–385, n. 119. Hayman surmises that Carl Ludwig had syphilis, infected Franziska, and passed the disease to Friedrich. Hayman 1980: 24.

[110] Blunck 1953: 32. This dramatic and often-cited piece of information comes from a letter written by the medically uneducated Friederike Daechsel and is to that extent questionable. The autopsy report itself, supposedly composed by Dr. Oppolzer and an army doctor, has vanished. Volz 1990: 33.

[111] In her memoir Franziska says that the areas of the rectory available for private family life consisted only of a living room and two bedrooms. Oehler 1940: 36. She tells a friend that she sends the children out of the house as much as possible. Bohley 1987: 179.

[112] KGW I-2: 259. Although a swift reading might interpret this as an eyewitness report, one should not overlook the qualifying words, "must have." Nietzsche doesn't depict himself as actually remembering; he is rather recording a probability.

While Ludwig alternated between painful waking hours and the oblivion of sleep, the family coped as best it could, wavering between hope that the illness would pass and resignation that their respective son, brother, husband, and father would shortly be relieved of his sufferings in the most final way possible. They consulted doctors in Lützen, Naumburg, and Leipzig. They tried to maintain a normal life, celebrating the distribution of Christmas gifts to the apparently delighted children while leaving Ludwig secluded upstairs.[113] Meanwhile, local pastors assumed the man's lapsed duties, and his supervisor persuaded church authorities to wait before replacing the now useless minister, so as to spare the family further sorrow and devastation.[114]

The increasingly grim process drew on for another half-year until July 30, 1849, when the end came.[115] There are several accounts of Ludwig's final hours, but perhaps the most telling was given by a half-sister, Friederike Daechsel, who related that when Auguste had stood beside his bed weeping, Ludwig had responded, "Don't cry," only to break into tears himself. Afterwards he was calm, and the dreadful final symptoms began to take their course. Auguste herself recalled him as saying, "Listen," then "My mother – oh my God." A painful trembling followed, then sleep, then "heart-rending" death rattles and the final moments.[116] "When I woke up in the morning," young Friedrich recalled, "I heard all around me loud weeping and sobbing. My dear mother came to me with tears in her eyes and cried out: 'O God! My good Ludwig is dead!' Although I was very young and inexperienced, I still had some idea of death; the thought that I would be separated forever from my dear father seized me, and I wept bitterly."[117]

The funeral was particularly bleak, for the family had not only lost a beloved member but its social and economic keystone. Franziska seems to have been particularly distraught, and one of Ludwig's half-sisters noted dourly, "It was hardest for her since she had the longest life ahead of her with all its sorrows and privations."[118] As for Friedrich's reaction, no record remains, but he was just old enough to register the decline of his father from warm benefactor and stern authority to the status of a blind and

---

[113] For Franziska's account, see Goch 2000: 382.   [114] Goch 2000: 386–387.
[115] See Goch 2000: 388, which quotes Auguste and Rosalie; and 390, n. 131, which cites the Leipzig obituary. Nietzsche incorrectly gives the date as July 27 in his memoir, "From my life." KGW I-1: 285.
[116] For Friederike Daechsel's account see Goch 2000: 389, n. 128. For Auguste Nietzsche's, see Goch 2000: 388.
[117] KGW I-1: 285.   [118] Goch 2000: 389.

pitiable invalid. Much would depend on his family response to the event, but the effect may have been lasting and deep.[119]

The next months represented a time of reconsolidation. Franziska had made some effort to teach her son to read and write,[120] but the family was dissatisfied with this, and it was decided to send the boy to the village school supervised by the redoubtable Dathe. In October Friedrich returned home from his first classes, to receive from his grandmother the paper horn filled with candies traditionally given to German children on the first day of school. He had never experienced such joy, he announced.[121] Christmas was a grim affair for the stunned adults, although the children enjoyed it, and Friedrich received his first musical instrument, a harmonica.[122] Then, in early January 1850, five months after Ludwig's death, Friedrich's little brother, not yet two, abruptly went into convulsions and died of causes unknown.[123] Franziska was bereft[124] and it was surely a heavy blow for the entire family. Friedrich rarely mentioned it,[125] which suggests that he was less affected by the event, but it had consequences which a five-year-old could not appreciate. Joseph's death left him as the family's last surviving male.

By this time, the family had to vacate the parsonage for the incoming pastor. Erdmuthe resolved to move to Naumburg, where she had recovered from earlier deaths, married both her husbands, and still had friends.[126] Auguste and Rosalie would accompany her, and an offer was made to include Franziska and the children. Franziska agreed, thus ensuring further subservience to the Nietzsches. This might seem surprising, given her previous difficulties, but the young mother probably believed that she had little alternative. Already psychologically undermined by years spent under her in-laws' dominance, she found herself reduced overnight from the wife of a distinguished figure to a charity case. With two small children

---

[119] Several commentators regard the decline and death of his father as a shock to the young Nietzsche's psyche from which he never fully recovered. See, for example, Volz 1990: 28; Schmidt 1991–1994: *passim*.
[120] Franziska Nietzsche 1994: 35. See also Figl 1999: 25–29. For details, see Chapter 2, Section 2.
[121] From a letter written by Franziska. Goch 1994: 144.
[122] Bohley 1987: 184. The German word may also mean "accordion."
[123] Janz gives the death date as January 9 (Janz 1978 I: 47). Since the date is not specified in Blunck's account (Blunck 1953: 33), Janz must have added the specification himself. See also Bohley 1987:183; Goch 1994: 145.
[124] See her account of how these events "broke" her bodily strength. KGB VI-1: 516–517.
[125] In "From my life," written when he was thirteen, Nietzsche recounts a morbid dream concerning his brother and father. This remembrance was written long after the event, however, and Nietzsche otherwise leaves his brother unmentioned. KGW I-1: 286.
[126] Her first husband was buried there. Bohley 1989: 381.

The legacy

she could scarcely live on her husband's pension,[127] and she would not wish to be a burden to her parents. As will be seen, she may also have recognized that her children had better social prospects with her husband's family. Whatever her reasons, she bade farewell to her nearby family and joined the Nietzsches for good.

Such was the situation when in April 1850, a wagon drew up and members of the Nietzsche family packed their belongings and prepared to leave.[128] The departure from his birthplace, the only world he had known, seemed particularly difficult for the now five-year-old boy. He had lost his father. Now he lost his home, a deprivation which in retrospect would seem almost as painful. Unable to sleep, he crept downstairs and spent much of the night in vigil, contemplating the waiting wagon. The next day, the household loaded its bags and departed.[129]

Left behind was the grave of Carl Ludwig Nietzsche, who had worked so hard and come to such an unfortunate end. Yet one might argue that his memory and tomb would consecrate Röcken for the entire generation of younger Nietzsches. They had lived there for seven years, at most, yet seemed to regard it as the true family home. In that sense his sustained longing for family affection had taken decisive root. Not only was Ludwig himself buried in the parsonage graveyard, but later when Franziska, Friedrich, and Elisabeth died, each was interred in the village from which they had departed forty-eight, fifty, and eighty-five years before. It was Elisabeth who ultimately selected this final dwelling place, and she may have had myth-making purposes in mind.[130] If so, the myth reflected a reality. The father's grave would be a constant theme in Friedrich's early poems, and he honored it again as late as 1886.[131] For his mother it was practically a holy site, and his sister viewed it with respect. All their lives it would function as a symbol of a lost paradise, a place where a certain kind of happiness once seemed possible. In that sense they never left Röcken, and to Röcken they returned.

---

[127] For Franziska's income see Oehler 1940: 47 and Goch 1994: 378–379, n. 272. For more on her sources of income as she aged, see Chapter 4, n. 9.
[128] According to Friedrich's first memoir, Erdmuthe, Rosalie, and the maid Mine were already in Naumburg. That would have left him, Elisabeth, Franziska, and Auguste still in Röcken. KGW I-1: 287.
[129] KGW I-1: 287.
[130] In fact, Friedrich Nietzsche had told his mother that he wanted to be buried "in the south, on a headland." Franziska Nietzsche 1994: 70.
[131] KSAB VII: 138.

CHAPTER 2

Half an orphan

> *It is not only interesting but even necessary to place the past, particularly the childhood years, as faithfully as possible before one's eyes, for we will never be able to come to a clear judgment of ourselves unless we closely inspect the circumstances in which we were raised and take the measure of their influence.*[1]

I

When examining Friedrich's first years in Naumburg, it is useful to recall that he came there from somewhere else. He was only five years old when he arrived, and his memories of earlier times might be weak. His family's mourning and repeated stories, however, would remind him of what he might otherwise forget, that life had been better elsewhere. Perhaps he would have found the town unappealing under any circumstances, but the terms under which he arrived virtually ensured that he would respond to its customs negatively, as an inferior replacement for life as it should have been.

Certainly he seems to have disliked Naumburg from the day he arrived. "It was terrible for us, after we had lived so long in the country, to live in the city," he wrote, and he objected particularly to its size.[2] Whereas Röcken was a village with a population of 202, Naumburg with its 13,500 inhabitants[3] qualified as a town, complete with separate neighborhoods and a tangle of bewildering streets. The community had two centers: the marketplace adjacent to a major church (Saint Wenceslas) and the renowned cathedral, elevated on a hill. The perimeter was defined by the remains of a medieval wall that had begun to be dismantled only three decades earlier.[4] While Naumburg probably seemed provincial to anyone familiar with Leipzig or nearby Weimar, Friedrich found it a comparative metropolis. "Nothing but Christmas trees!" he exclaimed

---

[1] KGW I-3: 24. [2] KGW I-1: 287. [3] Bergmann 1987: 13; Pernet 1989: 51.
[4] Biller and Häffner 2001: 251–252; Schubert 1989: 31, 49. Despite Förster-Nietzsche's claim that the walls were intact, all the gates except the Marientor had been dismantled by 1830, two decades before the Nietzsche's arrival.

Half an orphan

the first time he saw the public gardens, and he was not only overwhelmed by the town's large population but amazed that its inhabitants seemed not to know one another.[5]

That he noticed crowds and the artificiality of the trees tells us much about his needs. At Röcken Friedrich had liked to wander outdoors and watch the sunlight play on the ponds. In Naumburg, he would leave his shared rooms only to find himself hemmed in by buildings and jostled by busy townspeople. The anonymity and absence of privacy suggest a lack of breathing space, and he would write, "We avoided the dusty streets and sought the open air like a bird escaping its cage."[6] The rooms he occupied were particularly dark. Erdmuthe had rented the flat, and as matriarch and the family's social representative, she claimed the apartment's front room with its open windows beside the parlor.[7] Her daughters received the adjacent chamber, and Franziska and the children were relegated to two rooms in the rear, lit largely by oil lamps and candles.[8] This division of space was hierarchical by age and probably meant to keep the noisy children away from the quieter front. Nonetheless, the effect was to confirm the younger family's diminished status. "We were boarders [*Kostgänger*]," Franziska would recall,[9] that is, poor relations to whom family charity was extended. The children were permitted into the front rooms only twice a day, for lunch and dinner. Since "absolute peace must reign," they were subject to expulsion if they misbehaved.[10]

The rigidity of household arrangements might reflect the demoralized state of the Nietzsches. Even Förster-Nietzsche, who in her reminiscences tends to put a cheerful gloss on hardship, conceded, "It seems to me that we cried quite a lot."[11] Years earlier each of the adults (Rosalie excepted) had left a long-established home to join forces with Ludwig and to create a fresh household. At the time the daring of the sacrifice and the joy of creating a new family must have given them a sense of giddy hope; and the beloved man had served as a family axis, the center around whom they revolved. With his death, that system collapsed, and it is not clear that it recovered. The women continued to live together, but each adult seems to have kept largely to herself. Erdmuthe ruled the front areas like a remote but kindly monarch. Rosalie joined religious organizations; Auguste (with the assistance of the maid Mine) cleaned house; and Franziska immersed herself in the children.

---

[5] KGW I-1: 287–288. [6] KGW I-1: 287. [7] Oehler 1940: 48. [8] Oehler 1940: 48.
[9] Quoted in Goch 1994: 172. [10] Oehler 1940: 48. The quoted phrase is from Oehler himself.
[11] Förster-Nietzsche 1895: I, 25.

In some ways this arrangement worked to Franziska's advantage. In the public rooms of Röcken others had questioned her child-rearing habits, and important functions had been reassigned to her mother-in-law. In Naumburg, confined as she was to the back quarters, she was no longer burdened with immediate supervision, and she became the dominant human in the children's tiny world. It is unclear to what extent Erdmuthe made ultimate decisions concerning her grandson – Förster-Nietzsche indicates that she did; Franziska protests that she did not[12] – but the older woman surely had veto power, if only because she held the purse strings.[13] Nonetheless, Franziska was responsible for the day-to-day discipline and nurturance of the children, and possibly a good deal more, regardless whether she was qualified.

One can therefore appreciate the poignancy and the implications of a remark Friedrich made in an autobiography written when he was thirteen. Lamenting his father's death, he remarked, "I was now a fatherless *Waisenkind*," that is, in this context, a half-orphan.[14] Had his father survived, Friedrich would have been subject to the direction and leadership of a male who, in that patriarchal society, could more knowledgeably steer the children through their social and professional environments. With Ludwig dead, this task fell to Franziska, who because of her lack of education could not direct her son with comparable knowledge and authority, particularly in a large town like Naumburg, which must have appeared almost as alien to her as to her son. Aware of her limitations, she consulted relatives and friends of varying insight and sensitivity.[15] One might say then that Friedrich was raised, not by either parent but by a kind of committee of which his mother was the somewhat erratic director. Sometimes Erdmuthe Nietzsche offered counsel, sometimes David Oehler, and sometimes a neighbor down the street. Through it all Franziska sifted suggestions and fostered her son's advances as best she could. Nonetheless, the haphazard nature of that guidance was later to be a source of chagrin to Friedrich who (to some extent rightly) recognized that much would have been different had his upbringing been overseen by his father.[16]

---

[12] Quoted in Goch 1994: 173–174. Franziska wrote this when trying to counter what she construed as Förster-Nietzsche's attempt to write her out of her own son's biography.
[13] For discussion of the child-rearing dynamics in the Nietzsche family, see Goch 1994: 169–172.
[14] KGW I-1: 285.
[15] For examples of consultations Franziska made with friends and authorities on child-rearing, see Goch 1994: 179–180.
[16] That he had been inadequately raised would become an article of faith with Nietzsche: see Chapter 5, Section 3; Chapter 8, Section 5; and Chapter 14, Section 5.

2

This committee process is amply evident in the way Friedrich was first sent to school. He was now five, and it was time seriously to consider formal instruction. Of course, he had already attended school for a time in Röcken,[17] but he had gone only an hour a day and, according to Franziska, he was enrolled less in the expectation of academic instruction than in an attempt to accustom him to the mechanics of a regular schedule before he moved to Naumburg.[18] His first lessons in reading and writing had actually come from Franziska herself, who taught both Friedrich and Elisabeth the relationship between sounds and letters phonetically by encouraging them to make up rhymes, then showing them the corresponding signs on paper.[19] This pedagogy, which might seem sensible today, was anomalous at the time and greeted with dismay by family and friends, who were concerned that the boy was not being properly educated.[20]

After these ad hoc introductions to learning, the time had come to enroll the boy in a formal school. That he would eventually attend a Gymnasium, a nine-year middle and high school, was a given.[21] Only if he graduated from such an institution could he secure the *Abitur*, a degree necessary to attend a Prussian university.[22] The issue lay rather in what kind of school Friedrich would attend *before* the Gymnasium. Boys in the upper classes were generally privately tutored or sent to a preparatory school,[23] but the Nietzsches' finances were limited, and probably for this reason they elected not to take this approach.

They did eventually enroll the boy in a preparatory school, but he would first spend two-and-a-half to three years in the burgher school,[24] a public institution which catered to the sons of handworkers and merchants, but

---

[17] Nietzsche had begun attendance on his fifth birthday (October 15, 1849). See letter from Franziska in Goch 1994: 144.
[18] Goch 1994: 144; Bohley 1987: 183. A letter from Erdmuthe suggests that he also received instruction under David Oehler during the late spring and early summer of 1850. KGB I-1, 302. Significantly, Friedrich's first (very short) letter is dated June 1, 1850, that is, at most two months after leaving Röcken and probably represents an educational coup on the part of his grandfather. KSAB I: 1.
[19] Franziska Nietzsche 1994: 173; Figl 1999: 24–29.   [20] Oehler 1940: 59–60.
[21] Daum 2004: 145.   [22] The *Abitur* was made a requirement in 1834.
[23] Friedrich's later friends, Wilhelm Pinder and Gustav Krug, received this sort of introductory education. Girls were sidelined to other institutions, as will be seen with Elisabeth.
[24] As Reiner Bohley was the first to discover, Nietzsche left the burgher school at Easter 1853, and not as Nietzsche's sister had claimed, sometime in 1851. Bohley 1987: 167. However, when precisely Friedrich *entered* the burgher school remains a vexed topic. See Pernet 1989: 59; KGB I-4: 33–34; Bohley 1987: 167; Hödl 2009: 133. A letter from Erdmuthe (August 2, 1850) specifically states that Friedrich is now a "*Bürgerschüler*," as he had not been before, and this would seem definitive.

not the poor.[25] The boys from these backgrounds would have little use for Latin and Greek, and they generally attended only to the age of fourteen, when, unless they had shown higher aspirations, they were set to work.[26] Such burgher schools tended to concentrate on religious instruction but would also cover German, "practical arithmetic," geography, history (particularly Prussian), and a smattering of other subjects.[27] Such a curriculum seems limiting for a potential university student, and it is clear that sending Friedrich to such a school was a bit *déclassé*.

Indeed, forty-five years afterward, his sister still found its selection difficult to explain.[28] As stated, the family probably believed that hiring a good tutor or sending the boy immediately to a preparatory school was beyond their means. Förster-Nietzsche, however, could not say this, for she never mentioned money and probably would have taken it as a slur on her family to have done so. While her omission may be honorable, the lengths she went to disguise it were not. In her two biographies she made two claims concerning this first school: that its selection had been Erdmuthe's idea and that Friedrich had found it so unpleasant that he was withdrawn in less than a year.[29] In the first biography Förster-Nietzsche also stated that Friedrich's eventual friends, Wilhelm Pinder and Gustav Krug, attended the burgher school with him.[30] These three claims have been much repeated, yet two are unquestionably false and the remaining third is problematic.

The assertion regarding Friedrich's friends seems *prima facie* improbable and has been shown to be incorrect.[31] Neither Wilhelm Pinder nor Gustav Krug attended the burgher school, nor should the reader expect these patrician boys to patronize an institution intended for people in trade. Förster-Nietzsche's second claim is also mistaken. School records indicate that Friedrich remained there, not, as she said, for "less than one," but for

---

[25] See translator's footnote, Cousin 1833: 51. Not all inhabitants of the town were citizens (burghers), but only those who paid taxes. Cousin 1833: xxx. Thus the lower classes would be excluded from the burgher schools. Enrollment in these schools nonetheless required fees, which the Nietzsches would have had to pay. See Müller and Zymek 1987: 40.

[26] For the age of fourteen, see Cousin 1833: 517. For the use of burgher schools as preliminary tracking, see 51.

[27] Pernet suggests that primary subjects of study would be the catechism and hymnbook. Pernet 1989: 59–60. According to Victor Cousin, however, every burgher school was required to teach ten fields, most of them secular. Cousin 1833: 523.

[28] Förster-Nietzsche 1912: 24. [29] Förster-Nietzsche 1895: I, 29; Förster-Nietzsche 1912: 24.

[30] For Erdmuthe's supposed decision see Förster-Nietzsche 1912: 24; for length of enrollment, 25; for the enrollment of Wilhelm and Gustav in the burgher school see Förster-Nietzsche 1895: I, 31.

[31] Rosmiarek *et al.* 2003: 357, 349. Förster-Nietzsche silently withdrew the claim in her second biography.

at least two-and-a-half years and possibly three.[32] As for her statement that the decision was Erdmuthe's (with the supposed explanation that she wanted her grandson to be exposed to lower classes), this assertion was vehemently disputed by Franziska herself. The latter was quite upset when Förster-Nietzsche's first biography appeared, and she complained that the book was "nonsense." Her daughter had not only made up fictions but had done so with the purpose of minimizing the mother's role in her son's life.[33] In a letter to a nephew Franziska specifically deplored "the stuff Lieschen concocts concerning her grandmamma when Fritz was sent to the burgher school, Lieschen who wasn't even four years old at the time."[34] Franziska proceeded to give her own version of how the decision was made, as will be presented in the following paragraph. Meanwhile, she saw in her daughter's tales an attempt to marginalize her in the annals of history and thereby to subject her again and permanently to the degradation that she had suffered forty-five years earlier when she moved in with the Nietzsches. The worst of the Förster-Nietzsche's biography, she wrote, was that "there appears not the least intellectual influence on the Oehler side, but everything derives from the Nietzsches alone."[35] In another letter she complains that the biography stripped her of everything she had done besides giving her children birth.[36]

Over a hundred years later it is difficult to adjudicate claims, although it is known that Förster-Nietzsche deliberately published falsehoods, whereas no such imputation attaches to Franziska.[37] It is also telling that when Erdmuthe and Franziska later disagreed over a school for the boy, the decision was unquestionably left to Franziska, and she alone prevailed against a united front, a front that included Erdmuthe Nietzsche.[38] Finally, even if, as seems doubtful, Erdmuthe made the ultimate decisions

---

[32] See n. 24. Adalbert Oehler suggests that the boy was to be kept at the burgher school indefinitely and until he entered the Gymnasium, that is, for the entirety of his pre-Gymnasium education. If so, then an explicit decision must have been made to remove him, one presumably based on the boy's unhappiness in that school. Oehler 1940: 63.
[33] In the first chapter of Förster-Nietzsche's book, nine-and-a-half pages are devoted to the Nietzsches, and one to the Oehlers. Franziska receives thirty-six words. Förster-Nietzsche 1895: I, 12. Förster-Nietzsche's second biography is far more appreciative of the Oehlers in general and of Franziska in particular, although arguably in a patronizing way.
[34] Franziska Nietzsche 1994: 35.
[35] Franziska Nietzsche 1994: 54. In an earlier letter, written before the biography appeared, Franziska records a terrible quarrel in which she says of her daughter, "the only thing she cannot dispute is that I bore [Fritz]." Franziska Nietzsche 1994: 32.
[36] Franziska Nietzsche 1994: 60. Franziska is at pains to claim that the decision involving the burgher school was hers.
[37] For Förster-Nietzsche's questionable veracity, see Introduction, Section 2.
[38] See Chapter 4, Section 2.

with regard to school, Franziska certainly made inquiries on her own. Throughout her son's childhood she would quiz relatives and acquaintances on this subject and copy extracts on educational issues from newspapers and church bulletins.[39] On this occasion she was struck by advice given by Bernhard Daechsel, the stepson of one of Ludwig's half-sisters. When queried, he observed that he himself had attended the burgher school and found the experience satisfactory.[40] Daechsel spoke with authority, for he was not only related by marriage but had been appointed Friedrich's guardian and would remain in that capacity until the boy turned twenty-four. His word, therefore, would be taken very seriously, and Franziska records that his endorsement was decisive. It was on his authority that she chose to enroll her son in the burgher school.[41]

The boy remained in that institution for at least two-and-a-half and possibly three years. He was probably unhappy during this time, but little documentary evidence exists to support this, aside, of course, from anecdotes provided by Förster-Nietzsche.[42] Only once in his early years does the boy himself mention the school, and there he indicates that he was indeed morose but this was due more to his temperament and early experiences than to the immediate effect of environment. In other words, he *was* unhappy, but he did not blame this directly on the school.[43]

In Franziska's eyes, all was not well with her son. She worried that he was shy and fearful, and she sought to "toughen him up" (her words) by making him do things for himself and by dousing him with cold water in summer.[44] She also worried that Friedrich was becoming "pedantic," by which she apparently meant that he was inordinately devoted to rules.[45] Förster-Nietzsche tells several stories about her brother which, even if exaggerated, illustrate what his mother had in mind. In what is probably the best known of her anecdotes, she records an occasion when heavy rain erupted, just as school was dismissed. A swarm of boys raced through the downpour, while Friedrich walked through the torrents at a stately pace,

---

[39] Goch (1994): 211. Franziska wrote her nephew that at that time she read books on education by Pestalozzi and von Stein. She also received advice from her oldest brother Ernst and from an aged professor and his ward. Franziska Nietzsche 1994: 36.
[40] Franziska Nietzsche 1994: 35. Daechsel later studied at Schulpforte and eventually took university degrees. Franziska would be aware that attendance at the burgher school did not preclude these prospects.
[41] For a biography of Daechsel, see Rosmiarek *et al.* 2003: 346–347.
[42] Förster-Nietzsche 1912: 24–25.   [43] KGW I-1: 288.   [44] Goch 1994: 179–180.
[45] Quoted in Goch 1994: 180.

Half an orphan

his cap and handkerchief pressed protectively over his slate and books. Asked what he was thinking, he explained that the school rules called for the boys never to jump or run in the street but always to walk decorously to their homes.[46]

If this tale is true, then Friedrich's behavior might be viewed as admirable, neurotic, or as just a typical childhood phase. It certainly displays a certain independence of mind *vis-à-vis* his fellow students and possibly his mother, who in this case sided with the boys. By submitting to the impersonal authority of rules, Friedrich could separate himself from all these persons and show allegiance instead to principles that were abstract. Nor was this adherence to rules – what his mother called "pedantry" – limited to school. Förster-Nietzsche records that he refused to accept treats offered by his grandmother on the grounds that these had been forbidden by Franziska. Further, when told he had done something wrong, Friedrich would withdraw to the only private place available (the privy, as Franziska informs us), consider his transgression, and only then emerge to apologize, a maneuver which took authority out of the adults' hands.[47] Outwardly he would obey his mother. Inwardly, he would obey the rules and, implicitly, himself. It is also possible that he was showing obeisance to a third, unseen party. In notes written long afterward he recorded, "Then in the Neugasse, where I always heard the cautionary voice of my father," and later, "Daemon – warning voice of [my] father."[48]

If such distancing tactics allowed Friedrich to affirm his autonomy, they also undermined it fatally. One of the rules called for him always to heed his mother – it was, after all, the Fourth Commandment[49] – and Friedrich did as Franziska wished. This precluded any active assertion of his own needs and tastes, and from an external point of view it could be said that he had no self at all. He could not reply to the boys who teased him. He could not protest when sent to an inappropriate school. It would appear then that Friedrich Nietzsche spent his formative years, from ages five to eight and to an extent through thirteen, in a state of suspended animation: uncannily perfect on the surface, impotently resistant beneath. As will be seen, that is not quite true, but impeccable deportment did figure as one of the more prominent aspects of his persona.[50]

---

[46] Förster-Nietzsche 1912: 25.
[47] See Förster-Nietzsche 1912: 12–13, 28. The third story is the most reliable, since it is confirmed by Franziska. Franziska Nietzsche 1994: 38.
[48] KSA VIII: 194, 505.   [49] Goch 2000: 24.
[50] Chapter 3 will be concerned almost exclusively with the ways Friedrich resisted and eventually transcended his environment.

3

Friedrich's fundamental passivity during those early years meant that his surroundings – the town of Naumburg, in particular – would loom larger than any forces that he could array against them. He lived in that community from the ages of five through thirteen, nine impressionable years, and inevitably he absorbed its attitudes in ways that he would find difficult to recognize, much less to elude. Naumburg provided his first sustained instruction in manners and mores and, except for the crude country villages where he and his mother had been born, it was his only source of social instruction until he was well on his way toward adulthood. A friend would recall that when they were both nineteen years old, Friedrich assured him that the elevated manners of Naumburg's upper crust were the epitome of "elegant tone and elegant society."[51] While such views might eventually be outgrown, they served as his point of departure.

The first impression made on a visitor to Naumburg today is that it is an old town and one so unmistakably saturated in history that to live there must force on its inhabitants a sense of the abiding past. The first mention of the location dates from the early eleventh century,[52] and to this day buildings dating from the twelfth to the seventeenth centuries crowd the central historical district, making it in effect an inhabited museum. A similar impression was made on visiting Germans during a time when Nietzsche was yet alive. Touting its architectural heritage and its exemption from the blights of the Industrial Revolution, a mayor pitched it to potential tourists as a town that time had passed by.[53]

Nonetheless, one change occurred which was decisive not just for Naumburg but for the education of Friedrich Nietzsche. In 1815, after Napoleon's defeat and after nearly a millennium of fealty to Saxon rulers (either directly or through the medium of church authorities), Naumburg was handed to the Prussian state.[54] Quite apart from the civic shock of being reassigned to another country, Naumburg now found that many of its former trading partners lay on the wrong side of the border. In a move to compensate the commercial losses (and probably to shore up the loyalty of the populace by importing people loyal to the state), Prussia installed a

---

[51] Deussen 1901: 16. For an English translation, see Gilman 1987: 18.   [52] Hege 1958: 8.
[53] Wagner 2001.
[54] Prussia had demanded the whole of Saxony but was offered large properties in the Rhineland instead.

provincial court of justice in the town. The arrival of judges, lawyers, clerks, and itinerant plaintiffs somewhat revived Naumburg's economy by supplementing its focus on trade with one on law.[55] This change also altered the social structure of the town, for it brought into prominence a social status which has no equivalent in the English-speaking world but into which Friedrich Nietzsche was inducted, possibly from birth, but certainly from around the age of nine.

To understand the hierarchical position which Nietzsche would inhabit for most of his life, one must consider the so-called "cultivated classes," (*gebildeten Stände*), or, as they were called in the mid- and later twentieth century, the "cultivated (or educated) middle class" (*Bildungsbürgertum*).[56] This group is difficult to define, for it was delimited neither by its members' professions nor by their level of education but through an amalgam of the two, with education perhaps the more prominent characteristic. Even this does not suffice to explain its prestige, for "*Bildung*" in German has three meanings of relevance here: education, cultivation, and most importantly, self-cultivation, the melding of one's character, talents, sensibility and judgment into an amalgam of wisdom and insight. Discussion of this third aspect is best delayed until Chapter 5, but the two more sociologically relevant factors bear inspection here.

The cultivated (or educated) middle class had emerged during the Enlightenment, thanks to certain economic and social developments, but also through a double liberation. As against the church with its emphasis on salvation in the afterlife, this group had come to esteem the beauties and happiness to be found in this world, particularly through cultivation of the arts and, theoretically, through immersion in the accomplishments of the Romans and Greeks. Paradoxically, this grouping emerged just as knowledge had come to be liberated from its association with the crabbed Latin of the Middle Ages and to be promulgated gracefully and elegantly in a language which could be spoken in the drawing room. As good students of such Enlightenment masters as Lessing and Nicolai, not to mention the later Goethe and Schiller, its members began to discover and to canonize their own literature and to esteem it as a vehicle for self-cultivation and

---

[55] Pernet 1989: 51.
[56] The terms "*gebildeten Stände*" and "*Bildungsbürgertum*" are notoriously difficult to translate, and this is sometimes seen as a reflection of their peculiarly German provenance. Kocka 1989: 15–16. Kocka also argues that the term "*Bildungsbürger*" has become problematic. Kocka 1989: 9–20. It was not coined until 1920 and was originally used as an informal pejorative term along the lines of Nietzsche's own "*Bildungsphilister.*" See Engelhardt 1986: 189–192.

self-development.[57] Professionally, the group was particularly associated with civil servants, a wide-ranging collection under the highly regulative Prussian state. However, its membership could extend far beyond those professions, and, depending on their degree of self-cultivation, it could include, later at least, lawyers, judges, doctors, pastors, teachers, professors, persons of leisure, and even artists.[58] Over time members became enormously powerful culturally, evolving into a parallel aristocracy, without, however, forfeiting their claims to belong to the middle class. Since the stock-in-trade of this "spiritual nobility" was knowledge, but not necessarily applied knowledge, such professionals took pride in the thoroughness and range of their learning. This self-confidence was further enhanced by their implicit term of opposition, for (to put it crudely and for heuristic purposes only) these quasi-aristocrats tended to think of themselves as superior to engineers, merchants, and manufacturers, who, whatever their accomplishments, were devoted to making money and ignorant of what some might call "the finer things." The cultivated middle classes, by contrast, prided themselves on being enlightened professionals, and it was these educated mandarins (in the shape of judges and lawyers) who took up residence and authority at Naumburg, making it, in Goch's words, "a town of civil servants."[59]

This point is being made for two reasons. First, as has been mentioned, Friedrich Nietzsche would be raised to be a member of this cultivated caste and would enjoy membership, implicitly at least, even after he left Germany. Second, he was entering this class just as its power was beginning to be challenged. The Industrial Revolution was already beginning to transform the German states, and while this would not reach critical mass until the 1870s, suddenly the *Wirtschaftsbürger*,[60] that is, those whose status was due to possessions, factories, and money, were no longer minor players to be treated with polite disdain. Proportionately as economics, material production, and the technical advances of the physical sciences came to the fore, the cultural and intangible accomplishments of the learned bureaucrats came to be less esteemed or, at least, less shared.[61]

---

[57] There have been many efforts, not all consistent, to describe the origins, development, characteristics, and decline of this class. The foregoing is largely based on Lepsius 1992: 8–18. See also Bödeker 1989: 21–52. For a good account in English, although it focuses on the Enlightenment, see Zammito 2002: 15–41.

[58] Lepsius 1992: 8. Although *Bildung* is most associated with the middle classes, it was cultivated by the aristocracy as well. Rosenberg 1958: 186.

[59] Goch 1994: 195.

[60] Often called "*Besitzbürger*," a term that has the same problems as "*Bildungsbürger*." See n. 56.

[61] Ringer 1969 describes this process in book-length detail. For a swift synopsis, see Wehler 1989: 218–219.

This would not be so evident in Naumburg where, thanks to its judicial status, the citizenry was insulated from the social and economic convulsions shaking the rest of the country. Nonetheless, Friedrich Nietzsche was being inducted into the ways of a class that would find itself increasingly under threat – and that would respond to the materialistic interlopers largely by withdrawal into a brittle cult of social insignia and pretension.

The primacy of the cultivated classes in Naumburg meant that, for all its provinciality, the town was by no means devoid of artistic or intellectual vitality. The term "*gebildet*" can be rendered either as 'educated' or as 'cultivated' in English, and it was the duty of those so described to demonstrate both aspects of their heritage. If they so often learned to write poems, sing, draw, or play the piano, this was not just a manifestation of talent or enjoyment of the arts. It implied rather that they were exploring and expressing their sensibility through engagement with aesthetic forms.[62] Significantly, it was during this period that the term "dilettante" first became prominent, reflecting the understandable desire of the *Gebildeten* to participate in the now-prestigious arts themselves.[63] It is thus unlikely to be an accident that several intellectual figures, quite apart from Nietzsche himself, emerged from Naumburg during this period. The best known of German Egyptologists, Karl Richard Lepsius, was grandson to a deceased mayor, and the philologist, Curt Wachsmuth (with whom Nietzsche was later a colleague), also came from this town. (Richard Lepsius's mother and stepmother had been among Erdmuthe's closest companions, and the young Nietzsche knew both men's families.)[64] The *gebildeten Stände* had intellectual and cultural pretensions to live up to, and they did their best to meet these. Concerts were given, plays produced, and a club known as the Literaria was established in 1821 and maintained by the highest levels of local (male) society.[65] Not only did the city fathers themselves contribute lectures on such topics as Goethe and Hegel, but professors from the nearby and highly prestigious school, Schulpforte, attended and lectured too. Such presentations were probably a bit fustian and reflected more pose than insight, but that they occurred at all says a great deal about the pretensions of the city's leaders.

Meanwhile, if Naumburg was insulated from the economic upheavals of its time, it enjoyed no such exemption from contemporary religious

---

[62] Koselleck 1990: 36–37. [63] Bödeker 1989: 37–38.
[64] For more on the Lepsius family, see Dorgeloh 2003: 16–18.
[65] Pernet 1989: 56. Among prominent members from nearby Schulpforte one might name David Ilgen, Karl Koberstein, Carl Steinhart, and Eduard Niese. Core members from Naumburg included Carl Peter Lepsius, Pinder, Krug, and Wachsmuth. For a list of presentations, see Bohley 2007: 235–237.

controversies. It has already been mentioned that Friedrich's father had strayed from his mother's approach to religion in favor of a variation known as the Awakening Movement. In fact, the tensions between these religious approaches were general and sometimes bitterly fought throughout Prussia. On the one hand, the sects appealed to different temperaments. The Rationalist persuasion, which had roots in the later decades of the preceding century, stressed the efficacy of practical virtues and assumed that the Deity expected humanity to make use of creation to promote harmony and happiness on earth. Erdmuthe Nietzsche was a firm adherent of this approach, as had been her husband, the practical and socially conscious Friedrich August Ludwig Nietzsche.[66] It is generally agreed by scholars, however, that their son Ludwig had begun to stray toward those of the opposed Awakened camp,[67] a movement which began to be propagated after Napoleon's defeat and which stressed the inevitability of sin and consequent dependence of humanity on God's grace. The Awakened took a more emotional approach to their faith and were known for their stress on sin and their consequent self-abasement and supplications for forgiveness.[68]

There was a political dimension to the controversy. Although the Awakened had been politically suspect for a time because they tended to question the official clergy and the government policies behind them,[69] a camarilla surrounding King Friedrich Wilhelm IV came strongly to support them.[70] Indeed, Naumburg had been one of the seedbeds of the movement, and Ernst Ludwig von Gerlach, one of its primary political architects, had worked (and been converted) while there in the 1820s, later espousing this faith to the new king. For these reasons Naumburg played an intrinsic role in the history of the Awakening movement.[71]

Meanwhile, tensions between the two approaches could be unpleasant, particularly since those in the Awakening movement were ardent proselytizers and in some cases didn't consider those of a rationalist or eclectic persuasion Christians at all.[72] Förster-Nietzsche records that Erdmuthe once returned from a visit to friends to remark, "I don't know what people want nowadays. We used to find joy in our own and other people's virtues,

---

[66] David Oehler seems also to be of this persuasion, as presumably was his wife. For Franziska, see n. 103.
[67] See Chapter 1, n. 41.
[68] For a paradigmatic sample of an "Awakened" text, see Goch 1994: 109.
[69] Clark 2004: 168–172. For detail, see Clark 1993: 42–44, 47, 55–57.   [70] Clark 1993: 58.
[71] Clark 1993: 44–45. Although Ludwig Gerlach was stationed in Naumburg at the time, his conversion was effected by practitioners in nearby Bad Sulza. Pernet 1989: 53–56.
[72] Pernet 1989: 54–55; Rosmiarek et al. 2003: 342–343.

Half an orphan

but now they take joy in their own and other people's sins. The more sinful, the better."[73] This complaint, while sometimes construed as an expression of personal taste or of good social form,[74] in fact reflects a sectarian outlook. Erdmuthe was not temperate; if she had been so, her son would not have needed to hide his views. Her comments rather asserted her own confessional allegiance and challenged its rival.[75] Far from expressing doctrinal laisser-faire, she was actively attacking one Christian sect and affirming another.[76]

Erdmuthe's chagrin must have been the more painful, since after the death of her son she had moved to Naumburg to resume old times and presumably to return to a place where she had once been happy. Some biographers speculate that she also hoped to raise her grandson in a spot where he would be exposed to the approach to the faith which Erdmuthe's brother, who had been preacher at the cathedral, had striven so hard to inculcate.[77] If so, she was disappointed. Times had changed, and during her absence a number of distinguished citizens had switched from the Rationalist to the Awakened persuasion, among them the prominent judge, Gottlieb Ernst Pinder, who was husband to one of Erdmuthe's closest friends.[78]

Erdmuthe's maiden name (Krause) had itself been a flashpoint in the struggle between these contingents. In the late 1830s an article by an Awakened hymnist arraigned the Naumburg hymnbook (introduced by Erdmuthe's beloved brother, among others) as one of the worst hymnals in the province.[79] Two Naumburg pastors took up the attack, decrying the book as damaging to faith and hostile to the Christian religion.[80] At least one of them was reassigned, and by the time of Erdmuthe's return to the town, the so-called "hymnbook controversy" seems to have abated. Nonetheless, the incident could not have been wholly forgotten, and the always socially conscious Erdmuthe must still have smarted at the aspersions cast on her beloved brother's choice of liturgical material, which,

---

[73] Förster-Nietzsche 1895: I, 65–66.   [74] Young 2010: 5.
[75] Goch 1994: 110. See also Goch 1994: 155 ff.
[76] Förster-Nietzsche treads lightly on this issue but acknowledges the confessional edge to Erdmuthe's complaint. Förster-Nietzsche 1912: 35–36.
[77] Bohley 1989: 381–386.
[78] Bohley 1989: 384–385. Lepsius by contrast rejected them forthrightly: "I need no grace, no reconciliation."
[79] The hymnist was Rudolf Stier. Pernet 1989: 58. Erdmuthe's brother, Johann Friedrich Krause, was one of four figures who instituted the hymnbook in 1806. Bohley 1989: 383.
[80] For the hymnbook controversy in general, including its use by Ludwig Nietzsche, see Pernet 1989: 58, and Bohley 1989: 383, 390–392.

48   The Making of Friedrich Nietzsche

indeed, was removed from use at the cathedral in 1856, just six years after her arrival and, significantly, the year of her death.[81] Nor can she have been wholly unaware that her own daughter, Rosalie, was inclined toward the new approach.[82]

As all this makes evident, Naumburg was by no means the homogeneous and placid town that it might appear on the surface. In addition to the religious tensions, at least two other sources of unrest, both political, would have troubled Nietzsche's childhood and forestalled easy certainties. First, as has been mentioned, only thirty-five years before the Nietzsches' arrival, the town had changed hands and been reassigned from the administration of its traditional masters to that of its traditional enemy. It would have been difficult for the public figures who had sworn loyalty to the Saxon king to forget these promises and to alter their allegiances overnight. It can reasonably be assumed that throughout Nietzsche's childhood he would have encountered older individuals who remembered former days and harbored misgivings concerning the comparatively new government in Berlin.[83]

This demoralization among the older ex-Saxons would be complemented by political disenchantment among the young. The Revolution of 1848 had ultimately failed in the German states, and this led the politically active citizenry to lose faith in both the left and right. The initial success of the revolution had undermined the conservative claim to divine sanction, while the inability of the people's government to hold onto gains suggested that the liberals were incapable of governing. As Ludwig August von Rochau, the man who made the word "*Realpolitik*" a byword, remarked of the liberals, "The castles that they built in the air have evaporated, the defenseless rights, whose theoretical recognition they achieved, have no more than an apparent effect on practice."[84] The general populace was accordingly adrift. Unable to believe in either side, they flailed for more than ten years, until a new chancellor, Otto von Bismarck, seized control. Meanwhile, the early- to mid-1850s,[85] the years after the abortive revolution and the period during when Friedrich was growing up, have been called a "decade of public failure and personal disappointments."[86] Friedrich himself put it more bluntly when, years afterwards, he asked, "When were the

---

[81] However, it was retained in other Naumburg venues until 1885. Bohley 1989: 383; Pernet 1989: 58.
[82] Such at least is the opinion of Pernet 1989: 33–35 and Bohley 1989: 388–389.   [83] Blue 2007.
[84] Quoted in Sheehan 1989: 854. Compare remarks made by Karl Biedermann (later Nietzsche's landlord): Bazillion 1990: 200–201.
[85] In the later fifties the pall somewhat lifted. Sheehan 1989: 861ff.
[86] Stern 1961: 3; Bergmann 1987: 12. Compare Schulze 1991: 79; Bazillion 1990: 208, 238; Green 2004: 72.

Half an orphan

Germans duller, more frightened, hypocritical, and sycophantic than during the fifties when I was a child?"[87] The answer may well have been "Never."

4

While all these social and cultural forces worked insensibly on the boy's frame of reference, a more direct influence was molding his outlook and values in the person of his mother, the single parent who remained. In the aftermath of Ludwig's death Franziska, like her son, seems to have turned inward. The events of the previous years – not just her husband's ordeal but the death of her beloved baby boy Joseph – had devastated her.[88] Just turned twenty-four years old when she moved to Naumburg, she found herself without means, her future apparently foreclosed, and with the responsibility of raising two small children without male assistance. It is telling that, shortly after arrival, she had to pray to God to stop her from grinding her teeth so she could sleep.[89] This temperamentally vibrant country girl, once known for her skill at the toboggan, now lived confined to the dark back rooms of her mother-in-law's home, her day circumscribed by maternal duties, which she would later describe to a nephew: "I had *nothing* to do but to care for the children, since Auguste and Mine [the maidservant] did the household chores. After I had put our small rooms in order each day and got the children, first Fritz and later little Liesbeth, ready for school, I sat at the sewing table for the last hours before the children again appeared, mostly reading aloud to my good mother-in-law."[90]

Isolated by household arrangements, Franziska would have been the lonelier since she seems to have known no one in the new town except persons associated with the Nietzsches, that is, people who would have seen her as a poor relation and accordingly an object of pity. On April 24, 1850, two weeks after the arrival in Naumburg she began to keep a journal,[91] a move which suggests the need to talk to someone, if only to a sheet of paper. It was also a resort to the written word which might not be expected from this uneducated young woman who was so patronized by her

---

[87] KSA XI: 209. Quoted (and differently translated) in Köhler 2002: 15.
[88] See Franziska's "prayer" to her late husband. Goch 1994: 152.   [89] Bohley 1987: 186.
[90] Franziska Nietzsche 1994: 34. Franziska: "There can be no question of *incisive* influence in [the children's] upbringing by the old, weak, dear grandmother, or the frightfully nervous Rosalie, or the very busy, heavenly good Auguste."
[91] Goch 1994: 210.

husband's family.[92] During her early association with the Nietzsches, however, Franziska sought to read and assimilate cultural and intellectual works well beyond the expectations of her family and original social class,[93] and perhaps the journal reflected this. If so, its origins were humble, its maintenance erratic. She began it in a notebook designed for housework and budget-keeping purposes[94] (she also made notes in three other booklets) and she herself construed its purpose as one of edification: "I have undertaken to keep a journal so as to maintain an account of every day spent as to whether it was a blessing to me and above all to write here everything that interested me."[95] The section explicitly labeled "Journal" ("*Tagebuch*") lasted only four pages, but she made entries elsewhere and liked to copy poems or household hints such as "Ways to Clean Glass," "Warning on Snuff," and "How Englishwomen Keep Their Beautiful Complexion."[96] The notebooks are also useful since they display Franziska trying to puzzle out a world familiar to her children but only distantly descried by her. To that extent she involuntarily disclosed the growing distance between herself and her son: "The poor boys must learn so much Hebrew, Greek, Latin, dead languages they're called, but of course the Bible is originally Greek and Hebrew, but it's been translated by many clever men like Luther and [others] from modern times, but each [student] will probably want to convince himself."[97]

If the lonely Franziska found one conversational partner in a sheet of paper, she found another in a chatty relationship with her God. Although raised in a parsonage, she showed little evidence of more than conventional piety during her childhood and early married years.[98] However, her husband's illness and the prospect of his death introduced her to new dimensions of spirituality. Five months before Ludwig's demise Franziska wrote a friend that she had only recently begun "to recognize and rightly cherish the need to have a loving, heavenly father."[99] With Ludwig's death, she began to treat her departed husband as her personal intermediary with God. As she wrote him one week after his burial, "Look down from afar, blessing and protecting your forsaken Franziska with her three children. Ask the dear Lord, my faithful Ludwig, that he allow you to be the good

---

[92] For patronization, see Goch 1994: 172.   [93] Oehler 1940: 58–59.
[94] Goch 1994: 379–380, n. 273.   [95] Journal entry, quoted in Goch 1994: 210.
[96] Goch 1994: 212.   [97] Goch 1994: 216. Franziska was a master of the run-on sentence.
[98] Martin Pernet stresses Franziska's upbringing in a parsonage. Pernet 1989: 27–28. Nonetheless, as she indicates in the letter to Emma Schenk, her spiritual outlook was transformed during the year of her husband's illness.
[99] Goch 1994: 148.

angel that leads me my whole life and therewith guides [us] that we might bring up our three children together, to the dear Lord's honor."[100] It is difficult to tell to what extent the bereft mother continued this practice of treating Ludwig as her "good angel," her conduit to heaven. However, there are indications that she continued to do so indefinitely,[101] and she certainly honored her departed husband to the end, visiting his gravesite when she could and holding up his saintly life as a model to her son.[102] She seems to have talked to Ludwig many mornings, thereby assuaging her loneliness and inventing a highly personal form of devotion. Such measures saved her from self-pity – by most accounts Franziska was resolutely cheerful in public – and although she went to church and actively supported a variety of religious organizations, she does not seem to have taken much interest in doctrinal disputes or congregational politics.[103]

It is sometimes asked why Franziska never remarried, since she was only in her mid-twenties and by all accounts attractive both in appearance and personality.[104] While the ultimate grounds for this reluctance lie hidden within her individual psychology, one reason seems evident enough. With Ludwig ever present in her thoughts and their children physically before her, she seems to have viewed the marital relationship, not as ended, but as merely left in her hands, a marriage sustained by one party alone.[105] In consequence, she bore the responsibility for raising their daughter and son as Ludwig would have wanted, and Franziska hardened herself to the task. If at Röcken she had been criticized as too lenient, in Naumburg she became strict and rigorous. Förster-Nietzsche would record, "We were never spoiled through blind motherly love. We found in our mother the sternest critic of our words and deeds. 'Who would tell you, if I didn't?' she would say."[106] One of Franziska's grand-nephews corroborates this view, stating that "We [children] had a holy terror of Aunt Fränzchen."[107] It is difficult to know whether the hitherto apparently gentle Franziska ruthlessly steeled herself to be a firm disciplinarian or if the need to be stern

---

[100] Goch 1994: 151. [101] Goch 1994: 151–153; Franziska Nietzsche 1994: 33.
[102] Bohley 1987: 185.
[103] Goch suggests that Franziska's religious philosophy (as opposed to liturgical practice) lay in viewing earthly life as a painful preparation for "the heavenly reunion" "toward which I long." Goch 1994: 162–163. It is difficult to align her either with the Rationalist or Awakened movements. Compare Pernet 1989: 11–12, 29–30; Goch 1994: 159–162; Bohley 1987: 189, 195.
[104] See, for example, the description given by Richard Oehler, admittedly an interested party, in Oehler 1940: 70–71.
[105] She frequently wrote that her deepest desire was to be reunited with her husband in heaven. Goch 1994: 162; Bohley 1987: 185, 186; and KGB II-6/1: 516.
[106] Quoted in Oehler 1940: 57.
[107] Hans Oehler, son of Franziska's brother, Theobald. Quoted in Oehler 1940: 58.

exposed a latent hardness in her character. Stricken as she was by the tragedy that had befallen her and the degrading terms of her current existence, her temperament may have harshened, with the children bearing the brunt of this change. This was certainly not how Franziska viewed herself: "I saw my motherly duties as the highest ideal of my existence," she wrote,[108] and it is undeniable that she sacrificed her early life in its service.

A number of Continental biographers have speculated that Franziska was an intrusive parent, scrutinizing her son's every action to ensure that it met her needs and ideals.[109] Goch, in particular, has suggested that Franziska's child-rearing practices were unhealthy and possibly even damaging to her children.[110] He cites a letter she sent her son which is remarkable in its specificity of command: "Be sure to take the umbrella in case it rains," she writes, "and if you ever should get wet, change clothes right away when you come home." She then specifies exactly which trousers and coat to wear each day and adds in a postscript, "Take this page with you. . . . put it in your desk, and read it from time to time . . . [since] these are *'codes of conduct.'*"[111] (Emphases in original.) It is difficult to evaluate Franziska's practices today since attitudes in her time were different and there is little hard evidence that can be brought to bear. Nonetheless, given her youth, vulnerability, inexperience as a mother, and the abruptness, drama, and torment of recent events, it would not be surprising if questionable family dynamics did not develop during Friedrich's post-toddler years.[112] As late as 1875, her brother, Edmund, would write that she should not "fall too much in love with" her children; otherwise, separation from them would hurt her too much and "might damage them psychologically."[113]

Despite her apparent sternness and the unquestionable grimness of her circumstances, Franziska publicly exuded the buoyancy and high spirits which remained a signal characteristic of her persona. A nephew wrote that both outwardly and temperamentally she gave the impression of "inexhaustible youthfulness,"[114] and Nietzsche's friend, Paul Deussen, recalled

---

[108] Franziska Nietzsche 1994: 33.
[109] Goch 1994: 167 ff. Kjaer 1990. See, for example, Kjaer's interpretation of letters that Franziska wrote her son during his early childhood. 53–58.
[110] See, for example, Goch 1994: 224–226, 252–255.
[111] Quoted in Goch 1994: 188–189. KGB I-1: 321–322.
[112] See, for example, Kjaer 1990. Kjaer assigns little direct blame to Franziska, although he certainly disapproves of some of her child-rearing practices. He does argue, however, that the son's relationship with the mother was pivotal and to a large extent damaging in his life.
[113] Goch 1994 382, n. 329.
[114] Richard Oehler, quoted in Goch 1994: 206. Perhaps the most sincere tribute to Franziska's inveterate cheerfulness lay in her son's accusation that she took life too lightly. KSAB II: 94.

that she was lively, cheerful, and a source of cheer for others.[115] She sang, she played games, and she carried the children on her back to their mattresses each night. They especially loved being thrown into the bedclothes and found the ritual so inexhaustible that she used to tell Friedrich, "If this continues, I'll still be carrying you to bed when you're a seminarian."[116] It is significant that she relaxed considerably when she visited her parents at Pobles, excursions which she and the children made at least twice a year and probably more often.[117] According to Förster-Nietzsche, visits to the fields and open air of the countryside allowed the three of them a sense of freedom and immersion in nature that was transformative for the entire family.[118]

While as ever, Förster-Nietzsche's account must be viewed with skepticism, it is probable that the children welcomed the excursions, particularly in view of Friedrich's dislike of Naumburg and his lifelong fondness for outdoor settings. Apparently their grandparents somewhat spoiled them (to Franziska's chagrin), and the boy and girl must have benefited when their mother lowered her guard and relaxed in ways she did not dare in Naumburg. Franziska would have welcomed a return to the world of her childhood and to people who did not look down upon her. She would also draw from her more worldly parents advice of a kind that she could not expect from the Nietzsches. She was concerned, for example, that Elisabeth read too much, behavior Franziska thought inappropriate for a girl, as it would undermine her later chances for marriage. Friedrich, as mentioned earlier, she found both too timid and, paradoxically, too independent in his thinking.[119] According to Förster-Nietzsche, David Oehler immensely admired his first grandchild's intelligence and opened his private library to the child. When Friedrich wasn't enjoying strolls through the countryside, he was immersed in his grandfather's books, a collection of a range and depth unknown on Erdmuthe's narrowly religious shelves.[120]

For heuristic purposes one might contrast the Oehler and Nietzsche families as distinct and competitive cultural worlds, both vying for the allegiance of Friedrich and Elisabeth. Certainly, there were tensions between the two families, as has already been seen in Ludwig's dislike for

---

[115] Deussen 1901: 15. Compare Gilman 1987: 18.   [116] Franziska Nietzsche 1994: 39.
[117] Pernet says that Friedrich visited Pobles at least seven times during holidays. Pernet 1989: 123, n. 13. Given that the boy left Röcken in 1850 and visited Pobles at least as late as 1859, this comes to less than once a year and is probably an underestimate.
[118] Förster-Nietzsche 1895: I, 56–57; Förster-Nietzsche 1912: 35–36.
[119] For timidity see Goch 1994: 179.
[120] For the ways Erdmuthe's literary sophistication was overstated by her grandchildren, see Goch 2000: 65–66, n. 135.

his in-laws; and the Nietzsches and Oehlers were sharply dissimilar in manners and policy. Whereas the Nietzsches were always decorous and tended to avoid conflict by retreating into silence[121] – one might recall Rosalie's passive-aggressive campaign to join the family at Röcken – the Oehler grandparents were gruff in manner and sharp in judgment. (One of Franziska's brothers described his mother as a powder keg.)[122] David Ernst Oehler had lifted himself from a pinched childhood as the son of weaver to become the pastor of this country village. His wife (the former Wilhelmine Hahn) had, by contrast, been raised in luxury and probably carried the authority of a woman who brought to her wedding a coach and carriage horse.[123] Yet just as her husband was moving up, so Wilhelmine had moved down. She was somewhat disabled, with one eye lost due to smallpox and a leg shortened because of a childhood accident.[124] These physical difficulties cannot have sweetened her disposition and probably limited her engagement possibilities within her own class. When at age twenty-one she wed the rising David Oehler, at least one member of her family viewed the match askance.[125] Despite this unpropitious crossing of classes, the relationship seems to have been happy, or at least stable, leading to eleven children and a thriving, if boisterous, household.

Contemporary memoirs and later research present David Oehler as a hospitable but fiercely private man, aware of his dignity as a minster yet hostile to religious pretense.[126] He was ambitious enough to procure his degree and wed Wilhelmine, but appreciative enough of country living that, having obtained his sinecure as a pastor, he made no effort to rise further. As an ardent family man he was the presiding male figure throughout Friedrich's childhood and probably the more assertive since the boy's father was dead and Franziska actively solicited his advice. Förster-Nietzsche presents him as shrewd and rather hardboiled. She also suggests that he was the complement (and, indeed, polar opposite) to her own father, who had been an enthusiastic idealist.[127] Shrewdness, however, has its limits, and David Oehler's advice, however informed and well meant, was inevitably limited by his own experience and vision. The possibility of certain ambitions was unknown to the Oehlers, as they had been unknown to Franziska until she married into the Nietzsche clan. It might be surmised that she stayed with the latter, not just from financial need but because she recognized that Ludwig's relatives offered her children wider social

[121] Bohley 1989: 388.   [122] Goch 1994: 86.
[123] For Oehler's introduction to the Hahn family, see Oehler 2002: 277.   [124] Goch 1994: 86
[125] Such is Goch's view, at least. Goch 1994: 84.
[126] See Pernet 1989: 45–48; Goch 1994: 69–83; Oehler 2002.   [127] Förster-Nietzsche 1912: 9–30.

possibilities and more distinguished careers than the country Oehlers could envision. This difference in outlook would come to the fore when choosing one of Friedrich's schools.

Quite apart from the vistas awakened by his grandfather's books, the trips to Pobles ensured that Friedrich would never forget his past. The landscape of the countryside would constitute an alternative to Naumburg, each venue bringing out the benefits and limitations of the other. Both town and country might be provincial, but by shuttling between the two the boy would enjoy a wider perspective than either could provide alone. In visiting the country, he not only returned to the world in which he had been born, but the children and mother would visit nearby Röcken with its churchyard and Ludwig's grave, a site on which Franziska had planted a rosebush and that she treated almost as a religious shrine.[128]

Restorative as were the loose discipline and refreshment in nature that the family enjoyed at Pobles, they inevitably had to return to Naumburg and to the pious, dark house with its hush suitable to the conservative and ever more frail Erdmuthe. Here they would resume their constrained, silent existence and, in the children's case, return to school.[129] While none of them probably welcomed their return to order, they surely recognized and to an extent embraced its benefits. They might lack the anchorage of a male representative in its professional structure, but Erdmuthe had compensated this disadvantage by leveraging her formidable connections. Not only was she good friends with Caroline Pinder, widow of Ernst Gottlieb Pinder, one of the city fathers, but she had been close to both the first and second wives of Carl Peter Lepsius, son of Johann August Lepsius, who had himself been Naumburg's mayor and the Landrat, the regional chief executive and the *quondam* most powerful man in the area.[130] She could thus bring her grandchildren to the attention of persons very high up, if not at the pinnacle of local society.

Franziska herself was invited to tea in these exalted circles and apparently treated appreciatively enough that she came to feel comfortable during visits.[131] In the process she must have taken their measure and, for all her oppression by the Nietzsches, she recognized the benefits of their superior

---

[128] For the rosebush, planted in the summer of 1850 with Friedrich at her side, see Schmidt 1991–1994 III: 536, n. 33.
[129] A few months before she turned eight, Elisabeth was enrolled in a school run by a Mme Paraski. Prior to this she had received instruction from a tutor. For a full account of her schooling, see Rosmiarek *et al.* 2003: 348. Carol Diethe provides valuable background on the actual instruction she received. Diethe 2003: 17–21.
[130] Ebers 1969: ch. 1. [131] Oehler 1940: 73.

status both for herself and for her children.[132] She might love her family of birth, but Franziska knew that her beloved husband had disapproved of them, and she would have watched with satisfaction as Friedrich (and to a lesser extent Elisabeth) were socially integrated into some of Naumburg's leading families. She must have urged them to assimilate to the requirements of upper society and to share its advantages. On this, the Nietzsches, Franziska, and the Naumburg citizenry were united. Every advantage of social conformity would have been impressed on the children and the consequences made clear if they should fail.

[132] When Franziska initially met her future husband, the first thing she noticed was his fine clothing. See also the abovementioned efforts by Franziska to cultivate herself through reading.

CHAPTER 3

The discovery of writing

I do not know any other way of associating with great tasks than play.[1]

I

In the preceding chapter Friedrich Nietzsche was presented as a well-behaved boy, who met the expectations of others, but only because he himself approved the deed and not because some authority figure said so.[2] This rather passive-aggressive form of obedience had two consequences. Friedrich really was well-behaved, as report cards show: he repeatedly received the highest grades in deportment.[3] However, teachers might suspect that he was making fun of them, and according to his sister this in fact happened.[4] His consciousness of always being right may also have been reflected in a dignified bearing which seems to have been distinctive to him all his life and which was already evident in these early years. In a letter to her brother, Elisabeth remarked that as a boy he had been "as dignified as a grandfather." Friedrich himself recalled that he had behaved "with the dignified bearing of a complete Philistine."[5] Apart from expressing the boy's genuine sobriety, such a carriage could also serve as a defense against mockery and from claims made by teachers, mothers, and peers. Like the pause to think, it gave him a zone of inviolability within which he could reflect before responding.

Nonetheless, Friedrich was still indentured to rules – he did as he was told – and this sustained obedience rendered him essentially passive and immobile. Fortunately, as he aged, he developed new modes of coping; and this chapter will examine strategies through which he managed to voice opinions without affronting the local authorities. The achievement was of incalculable importance for his future. It allowed him to preserve and

---
[1] EH, "Clever," 10; KSA VI: 297. [2] See Chapter 2, Section 2. [3] Brobjer 1999: 308.
[4] Förster-Nietzsche 1912: 102. This occurred in Schulpforte. [5] KGB I-3: 68; KGW I-3: 191.

strengthen his resistance to the status quo, to exult in the enunciation of his own views and thereby, so to speak, to let the genie out of the bottle, yet to preserve his acceptability in society.

One would think that the boy's sobriety would be underwritten by religion, and Förster-Nietzsche tells several anecdotes which dramatize his piety.[6] The biographer has only her word for these, but during Friedrich's first years at Naumburg it is not unlikely that – demoralized as he was by so many changes – he would turn to the one source of spiritual continuity that he could rely upon, the "eternal" teachings of a socially approved church. It is striking, however, that in his memoirs Friedrich says virtually nothing about personal participation in prayer or services, nor does he mention a single religious book he read or a church figure who influenced him. Indeed, were it not for one oblique sentence in his 1858 autobiography, readers would never know that he was destined for the ministry at all.[7] Not only does he never state this except for the one time mentioned, but several documents created during his childhood suggest decidedly irreligious tendencies. One might compare, for example, a childhood drawing with a sketch made by his father, who was also bound for the clergy. Ludwig Nietzsche's picture, already mentioned in the first chapter, shows a man brandishing a stick while standing beside a Bible near which is written, "One must reverence the word of God."[8] Friedrich, by contrast, depicted the funeral of what looks like a turkey. The bird, with bald head and protruding legs, is laid out on a bier or altar marked with crosses, while a mourner weeps copiously into a handkerchief.[9] The tone is burlesque, even sacrilegious, and the onlooker can only guess that the Naumburg boy was allowed far greater latitude than his father. Nor was this his only deviation from propriety. During this same period he produced three poems which are difficult to interpret but which include passages which appear to be scatological and sexual.[10]

For all his air of dignity, then, a suppressed side of Friedrich Nietzsche was beginning to surface, and a change in school catalyzed its emergence. In Easter 1853,[11] when the boy was eight, he was moved from the burgher

---

[6] Förster-Nietzsche 1912: 32–34.
[7] KGW I-1: 310. His family and friends, however, frequently voice this assumption: KGB I-1: 308; Oehler 1940: 66; Förster-Nietzsche 1895: I, 32; 1912: 42.
[8] See Chapter 1, n 16.
[9] Ludwig's drawing is discussed in Goch 2000: 30–31, and he provides a reproduction: 89. A copy of Friedrich's sketch appears in Benders *et al.* 2000: 21.
[10] KGW I-1: 6–8. Psychoanalytically inclined biographers have been much exercised by these. Schmidt 1991–1994 I/II: 175–179, 654–659, 745–750. Köhler 2002: 20–21.
[11] Date given by Bohley 1987: 167. Confirmed by Hödl 2009: 133.

The discovery of writing

school to a private facility with the magniloquent title, "Institute with the goal of thorough preparation for the Gymnasium and other higher learning institutions." Consisting of at least two grades with a faculty of six, this "Institute" was effectively a preparatory school run by Carl Moritz Weber, a comparatively young man of thirty-one, who was a clergyman in training.[12] Weber catered to well-to-do children, so instruction at his institution was benignly conveyed, discipline tactfully applied, and the subjects of instruction tilted toward higher education and specifically the Gymnasium.

The impact of the change can hardly be overestimated. After nearly three years' exile in a questionable school, Friedrich at last belonged to a student body which would consist of children of his own social class, that is, children likely to be welcomed in his family's home. The instruction he received was further more intellectually sophisticated and thus more relevant to someone who would continue in school.[13] It is here as well that the boy seems first to have awakened to the joys of companionship. It was the school's policy to provide field trips, and throughout the year but particularly during summer, the teaching staff-sponsored excursions to local sites such as the Rudelsburg, a nearby medieval fortress.[14] Recollecting that the entire student body often took part, Friedrich remarked, "Such a shared hike is always very exhilarating; patriotic songs resounded, humorous games were played, and when the path lay through a wood, we decked ourselves with greenery und branches. The mountains rang with the wild noise of the rioters" as they played at being knights and imitated on a small scale "the carousing of the Middle Ages." One need only recall a previous account of Friedrich's return from school – his grim and lonely march through the rain – to recognize the transformative nature of these communal hikes.

It was in this gleeful atmosphere that Friedrich bonded with Wilhelm Pinder and Gustav Krug, grandsons to Caroline Pinder, Erdmuthe's friend. Friedrich had probably met the two when he first arrived in Naumburg, and he certainly knew them before attending the Weber Institute. Nonetheless, it took years for reciprocal friendship to develop, and it was amid the festive atmosphere of this easygoing school that affection warmed and the boys became inseparable. There is no evidence

---

[12] Brobjer states that Weber's Institute limited itself to two grades (Brobjer 1999: 303, n. 8), and school records indicate that Nietzsche indeed left at Easter 1855, that is, two years after he began. However, he did not enter the Cathedral Gymnasium until October of that year, which leaves a six-month gap in his education. See Hödl 2009: 133–134, n. 331 vs. Pernet 1989: 60, and KGB I-4: 38.
[13] The Institute would introduce him to Latin and Greek. KGW I-1: 289. [14] KGW I-1: 289.

that Friedrich had ever had a friend before, and this was probably the first time he had access to intimacy outside the home and away from the immediate control of Franziska. He would also be encountering children who, having the benefit of excellent educations, could introduce him into the mysteries of the arts, a development of incalculable value to this aesthetically sensitive and talented boy. Although both were his age (Wilhelm three-and-a-half months older, Gustav one month younger), the cousins were quite different in interests and temperament. Wilhelm Pinder was a keen admirer of literature and an excellent student. He had a sickly constitution – he was often ill, sometimes seriously so – and in photographs he exhibits a gentle but cool demeanor, suggesting the elegant bearing of a born patrician.[15] Gustav Krug, more high-strung and quick-tempered, was already a skilled violinist and precocious composer. (Friedrich wrote, "If someone snatched [music] from him, it would rob him of half his soul.")[16] The boy was, however, a mediocre student, and school records indicate that Wilhelm usually made the best marks of the three, Gustav the worst, and Friedrich average or below, falling near Gustav. (The two boys often sat together, placement in classes being a function of grades.)[17]

The two native Naumburg boys lived with their families in a shared, distinguished residence that opened directly onto the marketplace. Friedrich would spend many hours here, and inevitably he would come under the spell of the boys' fathers. Both men worked in the legal profession, but Gustav Adolph Krug was also a major patron of the local music scene as well as an amateur pianist and composer.[18] Biographers write that he knew Robert and Clara Schumann, and he certainly arranged for Felix Mendelssohn to be Gustav's godfather.[19] While he was religious and later inclined to those who were Awakened, he does not seem to have been so committed as his brother-in-law.[20] Eduard Pinder, by contrast, was actively religious and almost certainly of the Awakened sect.[21] He was also an advocate of city beautification and a principal instigator of the restoration of the town's famous cathedral, a project not to be completed until 1878. It is important to

---

[15] Wilhelm's sickliness began in infancy. See Rosmiarek *et al.* 2003: 320.   [16] KGW I-1: 293.

[17] Brobjer 1999: 305, 307, 308, 314. Brobjer notes that Nietzsche's grades for his final two terms are no longer available, but he suggests that there is little reason to believe that he improved. Nietzsche himself acknowledges that he generally sat near Gustav, a bad sign. KGW I-1: 293.

[18] Pernet 1989: 56–57. See also Bohley 1987: 190–191.

[19] Pernet 1990: 491–492, 495. A biographer of Clara Schumann could find no indication that the pianist knew Krug. (Private communication.) As for Mendelssohn, the composer could not attend the christening and sent a proxy to represent him.

[20] Pernet 1990: 493.   [21] Pernet 1989: 52–53. See also Bohley 1987: 189–190.

note that if Friedrich's own home held itself somewhat aloof from the Awakened approach to Christianity, the home of his friends was steeped in that outlook. Meanwhile, Förster-Nietzsche indicates that Eduard Pinder had a penchant for literature.[22] This does not seem to have been one of his great passions, but as a member of the cultured classes, he would undoubtedly have been familiar with at least the so-called "Weimar classics."[23] Friedrich remembered Pinder's literary instruction gratefully.[24]

On his own side, Friedrich found in his acceptance by the Pinder-Krug boys a human connection which by his own account transfigured his life. In an early memoir he frankly describes his dislike for the town, and, invoking Gustav and Wilhelm, concedes, "Without [friendship] I might perhaps never have felt at home in Naumburg."[25] This declaration overstates the facts. Friedrich was never to like Naumburg, and not even intimacy with Gustav and Wilhelm could overcome his ingrained distaste. As a tribute to friendship, however, the statement rings true and indicates how transformative he found these human relationships. According to Förster-Nietzsche, one of his friends (and probably both) acknowledged similar esteem. At age thirteen Wilhelm referred to his first encounter with Friedrich as "one of the most important events of my life" and called him "the best and the most faithful friend of my life."[26]

Yet Friedrich still held something back. One would think that, having discovered a lifeline to Naumburg society, he would assimilate its values as fervently as he had hitherto kept these at bay. In fact a kind of artistic irony would come to his rescue; and he would discover a third approach which would allow him to recognize values without yielding to them uncritically. He could embrace his friends yet recognize a difference.

2

When he later considered the conditions necessary for friendship, Friedrich specified that "true friendship is built above all through common joys and sorrows, for only when the life experiences of one touch the other, do the souls unite; and the closer the outward connection, the firmer will be the inner."[27] He does not specify what these communal "life

---

[22] Förster-Nietzsche 1912: I, 78.
[23] During this period of political nationalism, a suitable literature was being canonized, with Goethe and Schiller at its center. Mandelkow 1990: 181–196.
[24] KGW I-1: 294.   [25] KGW I-1: 295.
[26] Quoted in Förster-Nietzsche 1912: 27. The document she cites is missing. Hödl 2009: 137, n. 341.
[27] KGW I-1: 288.

experiences" might be, and the term sounds rather grand, as if nothing less than heart-rending tragedy might qualify. In fact the binding experience for ten-year-old Friedrich and his two friends turned out to be vicarious participation in a conflict half a continent away.

The Crimean War began ostensibly through religious disagreements, namely, which European country had "sovereign authority" to represent Christians living in the lands of the Ottoman Turks. France claimed to protect the Catholics, while Russia asserted its right to defend the Orthodox. While the religious issue was serious in itself and inspired considerable pro-war fever among participating peoples, the geopolitical issues were rather Napoleon III's desire to cultivate domestic support and what was perceived as a Russian drive for territorial expansion.

Thus, the war, which was officially declared in March 1854, was largely a proxy affair with France and Britain abetting the Ottoman Empire in its bid to stop the Russian advance.[28] The boys' support for Russia probably reflected Prussia's alignment with that country during the Napoleonic years, as well as a general hatred of the French.[29] More surprising was the passion that they brought to this conflict, which did not involve their own nation directly at all. For perhaps the first time in his life Friedrich was allowed to show aggression, and he brought to it an enthusiasm amply evident in his notebooks.[30] Each of the boys kept an individual booklet which they called "Stratagems,"[31] and Friedrich researched military terms, drew forts, ships, maps, and cannons, and apparently played at destroying enemy vessels.[32] He also devised board games,[33] with elegantly drawn playing fields inscribed with associated gains and penalties, such as, "Dispensary. Lose four turns."[34] These activities were by no means limited to the page. The three boys were much exercised by the plight of Sebastopol, the besieged port on the Black Sea, and they found some earth, dug a basin in the shape of the harbor, and filled it with water. Mock forts were built, and they put paper boats into the water, which they subsequently bombarded with little cannon balls made of pitch, sulfur, and saltpeter.[35] Noteworthy here is not just the inventiveness that he and his friends brought to these activities, but the discipline and elaborate

---

[28] See Figes 2010; Rich 1985; Goldfrank 1994.
[29] Compare Förster-Nietzsche 1895: I, 60. For the *Grossfürstin*, see Goch 2000: 288, n. 42.
[30] Kjaer 1990: 89–90.   [31] "*Kriegslisten*." KGW I-1: 290.
[32] Several structures in his depictions are obliterated by the sorts of heavy scribbles children make when annihilating an object with crayon or pencil.
[33] Förster-Nietzsche counts 17. Förster-Nietzsche 1912: I, 43.   [34] KGW I-1: 97.
[35] KGW I-1: 290.

preparation that such games required. Friedrich's Crimean War notations fill ninety-seven pages of the published version of his Naumburg journals (nearly one-third of its 311 pages) and were produced over the course of a year. These researches were self-prescribed – no teacher or parent supervised – and they may have given him a first taste for the possibilities of independent inquiry.[36]

On September 9, 1855, the city of Sebastopol fell. A clearly upset Gustav brought the news, and the boys erupted in rage at the incompetence of the Russian defense.[37] The treaty would not be signed for another year, but the winning side was no longer in doubt, and the games lost their savor and came to an end. Yet childhood imagination and the need for play could not be suppressed. One month later, in October 1855,[38] the boys moved from Herr Weber's Institute to the Cathedral Gymnasium, where immersion in Latin and Greek redirected their attention to the mythology of the ancient gods. Soon Friedrich, Wilhelm, and Gustav were impersonating classical figures with the same gusto that they had brought to the travails of Sebastopol. There might be no more cannons or forts, but there were probably swords and, if we are to believe Förster-Nietzsche, spears. She claims that Friedrich threw one of these with such inspired disregard for the consequences that it pierced the foot of Wilhelm's younger sister, Gretchen. "Greek" games were henceforth suspended in the Pinder-Krug household.[39]

Regardless whether such a ban on physical assault existed, the boys lifted their activities to a higher plane. The Crimean phase had immediately resulted in only one literary production, an incomplete tribute to Sebastopol composed after the surrender.[40] The Graeco-Roman adventure, by contrast, inspired at least two plays, several historical charts, and Friedrich's first systematic attempt to write poems in a series.[41] One play, called "The Gods on Olympus," was co-written by Friedrich and Wilhelm and – according to both Förster-Nietzsche and her mother – performed with mishaps before the Pinder-Krug families.[42] While the text for that production is lost, German commentators believe that it reworked parts of

---

[36] Kjaer 1990: 91.   [37] KGW I-1: 303.
[38] Pernet 1989: 60. The date is controversial. Bohley 1987: 167; Hödl 2009: 133; and Brobjer 1999: 304 are in agreement. However, see Schlechta 1956: 131, n. 79.
[39] Förster-Nietzsche 1895: I, 48.
[40] KGW I-1: 103. By February 1856 at latest, Friedrich would write a proper poem on this subject: KGW I-1: 124–125.
[41] See his plans for a series of poems based on ancient Greek history. KGW I-1: 132–134.
[42] Förster-Nietzsche 1895: I, 46–47. Franziska confirms the performance and indicates that it occurred on February 8, 1856, that is, four months after the boys entered the Gymnasium. KGB I-4: 38.

an earlier script, "*Der Geprüfte*" ("The tested one"), which does survive.[43] "The tested one" is almost certainly the boys' first classical play, and it dramatizes the Ovidian story of Philemon and Baucis as reconfigured by a couple of eleven-year-olds. In this play Jupiter disguises himself as a beggar and visits the hut of a mortal, Sirenius. There the god finds himself so well received that, after consultation with fellow deities, he proposes to confer immortality on the unsuspecting human. Sirenius doubly proves his mettle: by offering hospitality to Jupiter, and by throwing himself into the sea at divine behest. He then asks that his father, mother, and little sister live with him in new semi-divine state, although whether they too receive demigodhood is unclear.[44] (The co-authors seem to have elided Greek Olympus and the Christian Heaven.)

It does not take a trained psychiatrist to see that the play's dynamics – a young man made immortal by the gods, who elevates his parents and sister in turn – might reflect the wish fulfillment of at least one of the fledgling writers.[45] Nor would Friedrich have necessarily limited this fantasy to a piece of paper. The hero's family includes a sister named "Elisabeth," who in performance was presumably played by Elisabeth herself.[46] This raises an issue integral to the biography of any artistic or intellectual figure. A play, even a childhood work like "The tested one," appears to be a self-sufficient and autonomous work of art, that is, an artifact to be deciphered on its own terms without reference to biographical background. Authors, if considered at all, are conceived to be impersonal mediums who effectively disappear in the light of their product. Yet such a view of artistic creation is not without difficulties. The case of "The tested one" is unusual in that it offers an egregious act of wish-fulfillment. Nonetheless, Friedrich's personal interests and values would probably filter into other writings, as when he later devoted a dozen poems to meditations on his father's grave or even when he created happy celebrations of nature at certain times of the year. As Nietzsche was to write years later, "The characters an artist creates are not the artist himself, but obviously the series of characters to which he devotes himself with innermost love does indeed say something about the artist himself."[47]

---

[43] Hödl 2009: 98–105, presents a perspicuous discussion of the evidence.
[44] The text can be found in KGW I-1: 105–108.
[45] Although the play was ostensibly written by both Friedrich and Wilhelm, the extant text is entirely in Friedrich's hand. Schmidt 1991–1994 II: 800.
[46] For cast lists see KGW I-1: 110. Compare Franziska's description in a letter. KGB I-4: 38. Hermann Josef Schmidt has paid significant attention to this subject. Schmidt 1991–1994 II: 799–802, 924, 948, 955. For his interpretation of "*Der Geprüfte*" as psychodrama, see 916–953.
[47] UO IV: 2. Translation by Richard T. Gray. KSA I: 437–438.

One might compare such artistry to the playfulness of the boys' Crimean games. A genuine war provided the occasion and factual boundaries of their imaginary forays. Within these limits they devised actions, played games, imitated events imaginary and otherwise, thereby inspiring yet keener interest in the factual situation on the ground. Actuality and imagination reinforced one another in constant interplay, sometimes directly, as when a new fact – a newly appointed general or the capitulation of a city – had to be incorporated into fantasies; while at other times the games and realities ran on parallel planes that rarely intersected, as in the board games. The same is evident in Friedrich's first play. Jupiter never actually visited the boy, much less offered him immortality, but he clearly felt worthy of such distinctions, and he translated this into a scenario which was both independent of and redolent of actual concerns. So it would be with his early literary efforts. As will be shown, Friedrich, occasionally at least, used writing to reconstitute his issues in a different, imaginary dimension. By doing so, he learned to play with them and somewhat to master their implications without having to engage in explicit, publicly actionable deeds of revolt.[48] The arts would allow him a reprieve from disturbing realities but also a way to understand, internalize, and thereby to come to terms with them. This would prove particularly evident in his poems.

3

Friedrich's incorporation into the Pinder and Krug families ended much of his isolation and allowed him to soften his initial rejection of Naumburg and to come to terms with its values. He appeared to have assimilated at last to a world he had previously held at bay. If this were so, his story would be at an end, and he would have grown up to be a comparatively conventional good citizen, as was the fate of his friends. Instead, Friedrich went underground in a new way. He apparently no longer blurted out personal opinions in public. Instead, he developed a private retreat where he could nurture and cultivate ideas unencumbered by the forces of public order. His first advance had been the plays he wrote with Wilhelm. At about the same time – the final months of 1855 – he broke new ground by composing poems, a development which arguably figures among the most important events in his life.

---

[48] Kjaer 1990: 91.

While Friedrich had personal reasons for exploring the written word, as was shown in the ways his values expressed themselves in "The tested one," his literary activities were also underwritten by social and familial considerations. He was the member of a social class that defined itself partly by its sensitivity to art and by its articulate and persuasive powers of speech.[49] Children of the cultivated classes were often expected to turn out verses, and they would offer these as gifts at birthdays, christenings, weddings, and holidays. Such occasional poems served a function similar to that performed in a later century by greeting cards. Like the latter, the poems were ephemeral, suited to the event, and not expected to be immoderately sincere or original.[50] In fact, a sheaf of poems for New Year's, presented when Friedrich was eight, includes a preprinted cover page where children could enter their names, an indication that the practice had become so widespread that title pages could be sold in shops.[51]

In Friedrich's family this cultural predisposition was further underwritten by Franziska, who had watched distribution of gifts at the Pinders one Christmas and been impressed by a family tradition.[52] It may be recalled that she had taught the children to read phonetically, by showing how words rhymed and associating these vocal parallelisms with patterns in the written word.[53] At the Pinders she had heard the presentation of each gift accompanied by a rhyme (such as "This gift from the *tree* / Comes from *me*"),[54] and she encouraged her children to do the same, slipping a rhyme into Elisabeth's hand before she uncovered a gift, then allowing her to improvise on her own.[55] As the mother would recall, this custom of couplets instilled gift distributions with a singular magic and charm.

Such an insistence on improvised rhymes was separate from the call to present full-blown poems. Both requirements, however, would sensitize the children to the opportunities inherent in such heightened speech. Given this social and family conditioning, then, it would be anachronistic to see Friedrich's early literary productions as necessarily precocious signs of incipient genius. He was more or less compelled to write verse, and by the age of seven, at latest, he would be persuaded to recite occasional poems (largely scripted by relatives) as presents for Franziska, Rosalie, and

---

[49] For more on the *Gebildeten* see Chapter 2, Section 3.
[50] For more on the very young Nietzsche's literary influences, see Goch 1995b.   [51] Kjaer 1990: 60.
[52] Franziska Nietzsche 1994: 37. See also Hödl 2009: 98 n.
[53] Chapter 2, Section 2. Franziska Nietzsche 1994: 35.
[54] Notebook entry cited in Goch 1994: 214. See also her reminiscence decades later in a letter to her nephew: Franziska Nietzsche 1994: 35–37. Franziska explicitly connected these later rhymes with those she had used to teach the children how to read. Franziska Nietzsche 1994: 36, 35.
[55] Franziska mentions only Elisabeth, but presumably Friedrich was encouraged to do the same.

Erdmuthe.[56] Sometimes these were accompanied by gifts, such as a basket of flowers. On one occasion, a more intimate gesture was offered, as shown in the following, one of the first poems which Friedrich wrote by himself:

> I bring a little gift to you.
> It isn't much, but let that be.
> The things I have, you know, are few,
> So not very much can come from me.

In ensuing verses, he imagines a list of gifts that he would like to offer his mother: the best in life, health, and joy. However, since these are blessings which only God can bestow, he considers what lies within his limited capacity:

> I love you so much, I'd like to squeeze you.
> But I'd better not. It might not please you.
> I'd like to give you something more
> But that's what the final verse is for.
>
> You possibly would like to know
> What I want you to share.
> I'd like to give you a kiss, and so
> I'll give you one right here.[57]

This poem probably had a touching effect when performed, and Franziska could recite the lines "I love you so much, I'd like to squeeze you / But I'd better not. It might not please you" to the end of her days.[58] Yet this was not the only poem her son presented. It was rather the first (after an introduction) in a collection of nine pieces which he delivered as a gift on February 2, 1856, her thirtieth birthday.[59] Friedrich had recently turned eleven, and his mother claimed that he wrote the entire collection by himself.[60] If so, her pride was justified, for the quality is significant for a first try, and since this was not a skill learned overnight, the boy had almost certainly been practicing for months.[61]

This endeavor, which he would sustain and extend over the next three years, suggests that he had awakened to some new and fundamental source of vision. He certainly wasn't writing just for his mother. Once past the birthday greetings, the poems in this sheaf introduced imagery and themes that would surface repeatedly during his youth and sometimes reverberate

---

[56] See Goch 2000: 355–356; Schmidt 1991–1994 II: 842. For examples of later, ghost-written poems, see Goch 1994: 175–177.
[57] KGW I-1: 115–116.   [58] Franziska Nietzsche 1994: 39; Oehler 1940: 61.   [59] Goch 1994: 177.
[60] BAW I: 460.
[61] In his first autobiography Nietzsche would date several of these to 1855. KGW I-1: 308.

well beyond. His point of departure might be some tale from Greece or commonplace of the Middle Ages, but the themes that he touched and elaborated – nostalgia, a sense of loss, and the need to direct one's life actively – were peculiarly his own.

In this initial collection, for example, three out of nine poems (excluding the introduction) deal with ships encountering storms, a striking feature, for the scenario of the embattled mariner struggling to reach port would remain a stock figure of his poetic vocabulary in Naumburg and well into the future.[62] As one poem dramatizes:

> O woe to the ship, when by waves overweighed
> It finds itself too long delayed.
> And no longer able to reach its goal,
> It runs itself blindly into the shoal.
>
> Now caught by the swell of the huge waves' might
> And thrown against the cliff walls' height
> It breaks in pieces and loses its crew,
> Such ships that disaster has claimed as its due.[63]

One might wonder why this boy, who lived landlocked in a placid town, was so gripped by visions of imperiled ships and violent storms. Naval events incident to the siege of Sebastopol had perhaps seized his imagination; and sailors at sea were a common metaphor in church literature, where the soul was construed as beset by storms in its desire to reach harbor in Christ.[64] Beyond these abstract sources the boy seems to have been genuinely thrilled by wild weather.[65] "Storms always made the greatest impression on me," he wrote, excusing his joy in mayhem by ascribing it to piety. "The thunder crackling for miles around and the bright flashing lightning increased my reverence before God."[66] While one can appreciate the appeal such violent weather had to a pre-pubescent boy, what is striking is that over time he turned from the storm to the endangered sailor and the latter's efforts to elude dangers through determination and guile.

This first sheaf of poems set a double precedent. Friedrich would submit collections to his mother on her next two birthdays as well.[67] Beyond that, he continued to explore this breakthrough, trying to extend both his vision and

---

[62] See Large 1995, especially pp. 163–167 on Columbus and 171–174 on ships and the call of open seas.
[63] KGW I-1: 117. [64] Hödl 2009: 110–111 also makes these points.
[65] In addition to the poems about the sea, one piece deals with an electrical storm which terrifies a city.
[66] KGW I-1: 288.
[67] This practice seems to have been limited to his stay in Naumburg. Once Nietzsche removed to Schulpforte, he ceased (with one exception) giving birthday collections to his mother.

the adequacy of its expression. One should not take his determination for granted. Poetry could have been just another pastime that he entertained before proceeding to another interest, as he had with board games, theater and drawing.[68] Instead, this first collection seems to have awakened him to powers that he found inscrutably exciting. Not all the poems he wrote were successful, and some seem technical exercises practiced by someone honing skills.[69] These failed poems indicate more clearly than inspired works that Friedrich *worked* at poetry, that he did not wait for inspiration to strike but kept to his task doggedly, like a pianist practicing scales. Symptomatically, he kept lists, recording the poems he had written, and wondering as the inventory of his achievements swelled in an accumulating hoard.[70]

These literary advances did not come easily, and the boy states in a memoir that he often stayed up well past midnight laboring over schoolwork and poems.[71] While such claims should be treated skeptically – he had to be awake at five and could scarcely sustain such a regimen for long – the statement probably reflects at least occasional long evenings and suggests considerable dedication, not to mention stamina, in a pre-adolescent. If one inquires as to motive, it is best to start with the obvious. Grinding away late at night, he recovered the solitude which so often eluded him in Naumburg. Further, through writing he discovered that isolation could be positive – not just a relief from human intrusion, but a resource through which he could explore personal concerns, as these emerged through themes, images, and unexpected turns of phrase. Above all, the poetry produced when alone allowed him a permanent and unlimited arena of self-exploration. From early childhood he had nursed unorthodox tendencies which troubled his mother and were probably taboo at school. Now he could release these without fear of reproach or concern that they might be banned. The spirit of aggressive inquiry which up to now had expressed itself only piecemeal and provisionally had at last found a stable outlet and one that allowed extended development.

4

While many of Friedrich's poems – salutes to nature and hymns to the Creator – were likely to gladden the hearts of devout family members,

---

[68] It is difficult to know how much Friedrich drew, since the KGW editors have stated that his art work would be published in a later volume. Figl 1995a: 321–322. Nietzsche later dismisses painting and drawing as dilettantish hobbies which he practiced for a while. KGW I-3: 418.
[69] For an obvious example, see "The youthful years of Cyrus" in his first collection. KGW I-1: 120–122.
[70] KGW I-1: 257–258, 275.   [71] KGW I-1: 301.

others were less orthodox and suggested preoccupations well in advance of his years. Shortly after presenting the first collection Friedrich wrote a poem in four "cantos" complete with his own line count in the margins.[72] The sequence, which bears no title – he would later call it "The transience of happiness"[73] – recounts the progress of a "wanderer" who visits Greece, Egypt, and Nineveh, and reflects on the temporary nature of great triumphs.[74] Ever more oppressed by a past that he cannot live up to and which has itself expired, the wanderer succumbs to grief and a sense of futility, dying in a pit that he dug himself. Consistent in its tone of elegiac tribute and quite carefully structured, the poem invokes a theme that young Friedrich would revert to several times during childhood, the belief that glorious times were past and that the present age did not invite heroics.[75]

Friedrich was not finished with the Wanderer thematics. In 1857, when he was twelve, he wrote a new poem, which also dealt with a pilgrim and which introduced themes that might definitely have disturbed his devout mother.[76] Here, the protagonist was not an anonymous traveler but Alfonso, whom he here calls the Cid, hero of many Spanish legends and the subject of a hugely popular work by Herder.[77] Unlike the Wanderer, Alfonso dismisses the possibility that the old heroes could have been happy. Instead, troubled at heart, he vacates his palace and roams the local landscape, inquiring as to the nature of happiness. An old priest advises him that nobody can reach that state until after death. Alfonso listens courteously but, in a major deviation from Christian theology, reflects, "Not to be happy until after death / he cannot accept that." He consults some

---

[72] KGW I-1: 125–129. The numeration seems to have been important to him. Cantos Three and Four last exactly 50 lines each, an equality that cannot be an accident, particularly as the first two come to a total of 50 as well. In all, then, the poem encompasses 150 unrhymed lines of sustained narration.
[73] The title does not appear with the original poem. However, see KGW I-1: 291, 308.
[74] In "From my life" Nietzsche recalls that the Wanderer also visited Carthage. If so, this section has not survived. KGW I-1: 291.
[75] Cf. the poem at KGW I-1: 155, which ends, "*Ach die Ritterzeit ist hin.*" "Ah, the age of knights is gone."
[76] See n. 79.
[77] The Cid's first name was Rodrigo, and it is not known how Nietzsche came to call him Alfonso, although in some versions Alfonso is Rodrigo's brother. More interesting, the opening lines of Nietzsche's work reflect the opening verses of Herder's version, which present the thoughts, not of Rodrigo but of his father Don Diego. It is the latter, not the Cid, who has been publicly humiliated and contemplates the emptiness of his life. This displacement of the father's views onto the son is striking, particularly as Herder's own Rodrigo wastes no thoughts on philosophy but moves directly into action, killing the man who had disgraced the family. Schmidt devotes many pages to "Alfonso" and its variant. Schmidt 1991–1994 I: 239–269, 274–293. The interpretation presented in the text is largely indebted to Schmidt's analysis. However, the comparison with Herder's poem is original to the present book.

fishermen, then a hermit who lives in the mountains. The latter offers the counsel of "the Greek old wise men": not to call anyone happy until at death when it was clear that they had brought their lives to a successful close. Apparently this is the best response of all, and Alfonso presents the hermit a golden chain.[78] A work of impressive length – "Alfonso" is 126 lines long, only 24 less than the Wanderer series – the poem treats Christian counsel (given by the priest) as merely an option and rejects it in favor of advice given by the others. While the more favored suggestions are not directly irreligious, they are certainly not presented as Christian, and the hermit explicitly credits his view to the Greeks.[79]

These were not the only poems which skirt morally questionable issues. Hermann Josef Schmidt, who wrote a four-volume account of Nietzsche's writings up to the age of nineteen, has observed that during 1856 and 1857 Friedrich composed a number of pieces dealing with problematic parents who either sacrifice their children or inadvertently cause their death. In "Rinaldo," the healthy daughter of a sickly father mystically transfers her vitality to the older man, so that he is saved, she left drained of youth.[80] In "Andromeda," a king is forced to chain his daughter to a rock, leaving her a prey to a sea monster.[81] This theme of a child either being sacrificed or sacrificing herself – the victims are all daughters – is psychologically suggestive, both of a sense of injustice on behalf of the young but also of identification with the oppressed parents, who are always treated with compassion. It bears saying that Friedrich also wrote works in which sons (the offspring in this scenario are always male) arrive at the last minute to defend an elderly father from revolution or some other menace.[82] Different as these may appear on the surface, however, the poems of heroic sons and sacrificed daughters address similar concerns. The older generation needs saving; and it falls to the younger to rescue them.

As these (and other)[83] poems make clear, Friedrich possessed and expressed subversive and highly personal views from an early age. Equally striking, he liked to write poems in series, repeatedly examining characters, situations, and themes until they were momentarily exhausted. The

---

[78] KGW I-1: 175–180.
[79] "Alfonso" may have alarmed Friedrich's relatives. In a second version he was careful to include lines such as the following: "He learned about God from a wise man and experienced true happiness." KGW I-1: 185–187.
[80] KGW I-1: 182–185.
[81] KGW I-1: 130–131; 136–139. For other examples of this dynamic, see 150–153, 187–191.
[82] KGW I-1: 3–5, 227–230; I-2: 8–9.
[83] Schmidt pays particular attention to a series of poems on Medea's seduction of Jason, some of which feature erotic elements. KGW I-1: 246–248, 255, 262–264.

succession of seafarer poems has already been noted, as has the number of pieces dealing with problematic parents. Friedrich would later write a series of historical portraits, numerous meditations on his father's grave, and dozens of poems saluting nature. Schmidt suggests that this tendency to write parallel versions allowed him to examine themes in varying lights and so to ingest their meaning more richly and effectively.[84]

Schmidt's observation is suggestive and important. Writing allowed the boy to hold themes in suspension, subjecting them to literary permutations without reducing them to the formulae of final belief. Every time he repeated a scenario it came out differently. To that extent poetry functioned as an artistic and intellectual laboratory, a controlled haven in which he could submit topics to variation and record the results. His poems were not just isolated visitations of the muse. They were queries and responses, the exploration of a personal labyrinth that he conducted through the give and take of mind and page. In the process Friedrich extended his frontiers of awareness and also found agency when other means of protest seemed foreclosed.

---

[84] Schmidt calls Nietzsche's private writings his "permanent monologues" and speaks of their "inner logic." Schmidt 1991–1994 II: 574. For examples of this method in action, see Schmidt's treatment of sky imagery (sun and birds), II: 989–1072. For an account of Nietzsche's early writings as an effort to understand and resist his environment, see II: 1080–1081.

CHAPTER 4

The discovery of self

> [E]very human being contemplates his past life, because he must, because he cannot interrupt for one moment the connection with his past – and the more he himself acts, standing above mere contemplation of his changing self, and the further he looks back on this being, so much the more will he develop his life toward a higher norm.[1]

I

From the ages of five to ten, Friedrich Nietzsche's life was comparatively stable. He twice shifted schools but when he made friends he kept them, and the dwelling he had accepted with reluctance on that first day in Naumburg presumably came to seem "home." Yet as the years passed, the Nietzsche household was being unobtrusively transformed. Franziska might be relegated to the back rooms, but she had the health of a country girl, an advantage not granted her chronically sick in-laws. Erdmuthe was in her later seventies – frail enough that, according to Förster-Nietzsche, she had ceased to leave the house[2] – and Rosalie was persistently afflicted by "nerves." The ever industrious Auguste, who had been ill from childhood, fell quite sick during her Naumburg years and was eventually diagnosed with tuberculosis.[3] Her progressive deterioration would bring exhaustion, pain, and emotional and spiritual anguish. Despite these impediments, Auguste, "the heavenly good Auguste," as Franziska remembered her,[4] continued to keep the house in order, a determination to work in the face of debilitating illness that may have impressed her nephew, who would have health problems of his own. Yet even the most heroic self-sacrifice did not stay the advance of the disease. When in 1855 the children left for

---

[1] KGW I-3: 291.   [2] Förster-Nietzsche 1895: I, 26; Förster-Nietzsche 1912: 52.
[3] Goch 1994: 200. Friedrich recorded that a lobe of the lung had been destroyed. KGW I-1: 300.
[4] Goch 1994: 172.

summer vacation, the forty-year-old Auguste, knowing well she would never see them again, broke down in tears as she bade them goodbye. "That is the last time I saw her," Friedrich recalled,[5] and on August 2, 1855, with the children away, she died.

Auguste's death seems to have dealt Erdmuthe a mortal blow. In her long life she had lost two husbands and two sons. Now the daughter who had never left her side except for visits to relatives joined the men of Erdmuthe's life, and the mother found the loss irretrievable. In a memoir Friedrich states that the elderly woman frequently mourned, "My Auguste! My Auguste!" and predicted that she would herself shortly join the dead.[6] Franziska's journals corroborate this account. "[My mother-in-law] was ever more aware of the frailty of old age and said often, especially after dear Auguste's death, 'The dear lord will forgive me if I long for and express the wish to say goodbye. But let his will be done.'"[7] Nonetheless, the end seems to have arrived unexpectedly. In her narrative of the woman's final hours, Franziska records that her mother-in-law had been restless during the night. When Rosalie awoke shortly before dawn and found Erdmuthe suffering, she asked in alarm, "Mother, you're not going to die?" "Let me die, if that is God's will," the woman replied. A spasm of vomiting followed. She then slept, awakened, and eventually ceased to speak. Around 2 p.m. on April 3, 1856, Erdmuthe Krause Nietzsche joined her beloved daughter, the cause diagnosed by the presiding physician as brain- and lung-stroke.[8]

Rosalie and Franziska were left as the surviving adults. They would have to vacate the home – it was too large and expensive for their needs – and the question arose as to whether they would continue to share a household. Until now, Franziska's domestic arrangements had been dependent on her negligible financial resources. Erdmuthe, however, had left considerable sums to the children, and while the capital was theirs, Franziska was allowed to spend the interest. Her relations with her "frightfully nervous" sister-in-law had always been strained, and this inheritance gave her just enough money to live on her own.[9] Rosalie, who had just watched the last

---

[5] KGW I-1: 300.   [6] KGW I-1: 300.   [7] Goch 1994: 202.
[8] For Franziska's narrative of Erdmuthe's death and the aftermath, see Goch 1994: 200–203; for the medical diagnosis, 201.
[9] The interest would go to the children, not Franziska, once they came of age. See Goch 1994: 379, n. 272. See also Oehler 1940: 69–70. For other sources of income, including hand-me-downs and pensions from the two princesses, a one-time award from the Naumburg cathedral fund, a recalculation of Franziska's widow's pension, and room rentals in her home, see Goch 2000: 293, n. 51; Oehler 1940: 69, n. 1; and Goch 1994: 208–209, 378–379, n. 272. Her children would need no such charity but would inherit both capital and interest. In addition, Elisabeth received bequests from Auguste and Rosalie. Goch 1994: 379, n. 272.

of her immediate family die, was for the time to live alone, although she took a maid.[10] (She would later room with her half-sister, Friederike Daechsel.) Since religious activities were ever dear to her heart, she found a retreat in the vicinity of St. Wenceslas's church, and there participated in the ecclesiastical activities with such fervor and generosity that an altar cloth with her name was still visible in that church in the late 1960s.[11] Franziska meanwhile found an apartment with a garden and swing at the edge of the town near the Marien Gate.[12] There she settled with the children, and the nuclear family lived independently at last, released from the supervision of the Nietzsche clan. This is not to say that the Nietzsches were not a constant presence. Rosalie lived a short walk away as did two half-sisters of Ludwig (Friederike Nietzsche Daechsel and Lina Nietzsche). Further, Friedrich was still the ward of Bernhard Daechsel, Friederike's stepson, who wielded the final decision on financial matters.[13] Nonetheless, Franziska was herself an Oehler, and once she had sufficient room, she invited brothers, sisters, and eventually her mother to stay for weeks at a time in her home. As the Nietzsche clan aged, the young Oehlers would increasingly impinge on the household; and from this time forward it was Franziska's family, not that of the deceased Ludwig, which would loom ever larger in the children's upbringing.[14]

2

The two children agreed that they were quite happy in the new home where they particularly rejoiced in the natural light. There was also a garden where they could play, and Förster-Nietzsche later recalled, "Fritz and I lived in it from morning to night, swung in our swing, right up into the very tops of the trees, played the finest games, ate, drank and learnt our lessons beneath the shady branches."[15] Friedrich also remembered the garden with affection, recalling its bowers and fruit trees and the view from its window.[16] Perhaps he enjoyed himself too much, for his poetic

---

[10] See letter from Franziska in Oehler 1940: 66.
[11] Bohley 1989: 389. See also KGB III-4: 31, cited in Pernet 1989: 117, n. 11, 118, n. 17.
[12] This building was demolished during the nineteenth century. Schmidt 1991–1994 II: 898. Meanwhile, Friedrich saw the new apartment before the family moved in and described it in a letter dated April 27, 1856, that is, a little more than three weeks after Erdmuthe's death. The decision to procure a new apartment must have occurred fairly quickly. KSAB I: 6.
[13] For Daechsel as guardian, see Chapter 2, Section 2.
[14] After Friederike Daechsel's death in 1873, the Nietzsches seem to disappear from the life of Franziska and her two children.
[15] Förster-Nietzsche 1912: 61.   [16] KGW I-1: 301–302.

output fell drastically in the coming year. The collection of poems he presented his mother that February of 1857 was both weaker in quality and more ragged in finish than those of either 1856 or 1858; and, aside from "Alfonso" (the work discussed in the previous chapter), he seems to have written little of significance until 1858, when he more than made up for the hiatus.[17]

Perhaps the comparative dearth of poetry in 1857 reflected more demanding scholastic requirements. This was Friedrich's second year at the Cathedral Gymnasium, and standards here were clearly higher than those of the Weber Institute. As has already been mentioned, he wrote that he was getting no more than five or six hours of sleep a night at this time, and the long evenings of study appear to have taken their toll. He experienced serious headaches in his twelfth and thirteenth years, and during this time he apparently missed a number of days of classes because of illness. Ever industrious, he relates that when he was once absent from school due to headaches, he used the time to write a novella titled "Death and corruption."[18]

Friedrich may also have written less poetry in 1857 because this was the year in which he began seriously to compose music. The boy had received piano lessons earlier (it is difficult to determine the date) but he was perhaps too young to benefit at that time, for this instruction seems not to have excited much interest, and it was discontinued. In 1854,[19] however, inspired he said by a church performance of the Hallelujah Chorus from Händel's "Messiah" and probably Gustav's growing skill with the violin, Friedrich enthusiastically embraced music. Franziska encouraged this, and although she had already learned to play the piano as a girl,[20] she took lessons herself from a local cantor and passed her learning on to the boy.[21] When she moved to the new home by the Marien Gate, she purchased a new piano (the older one being given to Rosalie) and had her son taught by "the best teacher in Naumburg," a woman, who is never named.[22] At this point, Friedrich's musical interests and abilities seemed finally to bloom coherently and he began to make sustained progress.[23] Nonetheless, he

---

[17] Schmidt provides a helpful summary of the issues and possible explanations. Schmidt 1991–1994 II: 764–770.
[18] KGW I-1: 309–310. The document has disappeared.
[19] This date is given by Wilhelm Pinder in a reminiscence that is excerpted in Förster-Nietzsche 1895: I, 71. See also Pernet 1989: 62.
[20] Oehler 1940: 12–13. [21] Franziska Nietzsche 1994: 35–36.
[22] For accounts of Nietzsche's musical beginnings, see KGW I-3: 191–192; Franziska Nietzsche 1994: 35–36.
[23] KGW I-2: 262.

seems to have been impatient with instruction and to have tried to teach himself, with questionable results. His music teacher at the Cathedral Gymnasium found his musical pretensions insufferable – "He is an industrious composer, but also extremely vain and conceited," he reportedly said.[24] Nonetheless, Friedrich was sufficiently skilled that he could play four-hand Haydn sonatas with his mother for the Lepsius family,[25] and he began to compose, turning out a succession of pieces, some with grand titles such as "sonata," others described merely by their tempos (*"Maestoso adagio," "Allegro con brio"*).[26] It is striking that, as with poetry, the boy was no sooner smitten with a field than he tried to participate in it himself, an active approach which probably allowed him to appreciate certain arts more immediately than the passive spectator.[27] These experiments could lead to dilettantism, however, a danger of which the boy would himself become aware.[28]

Tensions over Friedrich's educational future loomed from his tenth through his thirteenth year. As has already been mentioned, his move from the Weber Institute seems to have triggered an educational crisis in the Nietzsche household.[29] His grandfather, Franziska's brothers, and Erdmuthe herself (who was still alive at this time) all argued that the boy should be transferred to a school for orphans in the city of Halle, where he would receive a scholarship and be given the solid religious education appropriate to a future minister. One would think that the pious Franziska would have embraced this opportunity to place her son in a Pietist institution. Instead, quite unexpectedly and apparently for the first time in her life, she took a personal stand in the face of united authority (her father, brothers, even Erdmuthe) and refused to part with her son at so

---

[24] Pernet 1989: 63. Pernet gives no documentary evidence for this quote, but states that he had it directly (presumably privately) from Reiner Bohley. Pernet 1989: 133, n. 104.
[25] Franziska Nietzsche 1994: 36.
[26] Janz 1976: 324. Janz dates Nietzsche's first extant compositions tentatively to 1854, the year in which he was dazzled by Handel's "Messiah." However, the first sustained production of music occurs in 1857 and especially 1858. See Goch 1994: 177–178.
[27] The boy was not without models, however. Both Gustav and his father composed, and on at least one occasion, when he was ten, Friedrich heard string quartets by the elder Krug performed in concert. KGB I-4: 37–38.
[28] This concern would much preoccupy Nietzsche from his middle years in Schulpforte until well into his stay at Leipzig. See Chapter 5, Section 3.
[29] See Chapter 2, Section 2. This crisis almost certainly occurred in the spring or summer of 1855. This fits Franziska's claim that her son was ten. Goch 1994: 186. That date is also consistent with her son's claims that about this time he wrote his first poems. KGW I-1: 291. It is noteworthy that in October of that year he entered the Cathedral Gymnasium. Presumably if Franziska had not prevailed, he would never have entered that school at all but would have attended the school at Halle from the beginning.

young an age as ten. She seems to have stood up in particular to her father, who had made an arrangement with the school's director that the latter would let the family know as soon as an opening occurred. Decades later, just before she died, Franziska would still remember her firmness on this issue and how she had assured David Oehler that Fritz could eventually go to Pforta on a scholarship.[30]

For reasons which are not clear but which surely involved money – scholarships were always an issue – Franziska did not envision Friedrich as remaining at the Cathedral Gymnasium either.[31] At her own instigation but probably with Erdmuthe's help,[32] she began to explore securing a scholarship at Schulpforte, a nearby boarding school which had two advantages over the school at Halle. Schulpforte was located only 5 kilometers – a good walk – from Naumburg, and if her son studied there, Franziska could visit him regularly. Schulpforte also had a sterling academic reputation; its former students included Fichte, Ranke, the Schlegel brothers, and (notably for Naumburg) the archaeologist Richard Lepsius. Since the school offered five scholarships to Naumburg boys[33] and since Erdmuthe had been close friends with Lepsius's father's wives, Franziska was well positioned to lobby for Friedrich to receive one of these.[34] It is also possible that Franziska struck up an acquaintance with the wife of Robert Buddensieg, a teacher at Schulpforte whom Ludwig had known[35] and who was later Friedrich's tutor. If so, then Frau Buddensieg could certainly have provided helpful tactics and information. As for the boy's suitability for a scholarship, his grades were not exceptional, but Schulpforte (or "Pforta" as it was often known)[36] was dedicated to educating the children of deceased Prussian civil servants.[37] In that regard Friedrich amply qualified, his father having died in the service of the king. He would first have to prove his aptitude through a preliminary examination, and Franziska arranged for him to spend his summer holidays in 1857 taking classes specifically directed to training students for acceptance at Schulpforte.

---

[30] See Franziska Nietzsche 1994: 38–39.
[31] Hödl 2009: 133, n. 331, indicates that Franziska paid fees for Friedrich's attendance at the Cathedral Gymnasium.
[32] Goch 1994: 186.
[33] For the number of scholarships see Bohley 2007: 68, who cites a history by Karl Kirchner, the rector who preceded Karl Peter.
[34] The pull of the Lepsius family was conceivably substantial. Carl Peter Lepsius, Richard's father and the husband of Erdmuthe's friends, had been a significant force at Schulpforte and had supervised the school's final exams. Ebers 1969: 9.
[35] Pernet 1989: 116–117, n. 119.
[36] For the spelling of the various names of this school, see Chapter 5, n. 34.
[37] Brobjer 2001b: 325.

These were conducted by Gustav Adolf Osswald, a friend of the deceased Pastor Nietzsche, and it was during these coaching sessions that Friedrich first met Guido Meyer, a charismatic young man who would play a decisive role during his adolescence.[38]

Förster-Nietzsche would later describe her brother's acceptance at Schulpforte as unexpected and initiated by Schulpforte itself.[39] According to her the school administration learned of a model student in the area and offered a scholarship in order to secure him for their own institution. This view would be understandable in a fond sister, who, being twelve years old at the time, would have little knowledge of the facts; and it helped that she would later want her mother to receive as little credit as possible in the story of her son.[40] The sad effect is that many biographers have accepted her explanation and passed it on as truth.[41] On the contrary, as was just seen, Franziska was considering Schulpforte as early as 1855,[42] when Friedrich was only ten, and she not only opposed alternatives but clearly maneuvered to plant him there. (She also arranged for him to take the above mentioned preparatory classes.) As Reiner Bohley would bluntly state, "It was because of his mother that [Nietzsche] went to Schulpforte."[43] In any case, Schulpforte had no shortage of outstanding students, and if Friedrich came to their attention, it would not be because of his scholastic prowess, which was unremarkable, but because he had no father to provide for him, the man having died in service to the Prussian state.[44] (It would not hurt that families as prominent as the Lepsius, Pinders, and Krugs could suggest him in the first place and vouch for him afterward.) Accordingly, in the spring of 1857 inspectors from Schulpforte interviewed the boy and, as mentioned, during the summer of that year he attended the preparatory classes given by Gustav Adolf Osswald in nearby Kirchscheidungen. Had all gone well, he would have secured a scholarship at the beginning of the school year in October 1857, that is, shortly after completing the classes.

---

[38] Meyer himself disclosed this in a letter to Deussen, dated February 3, 1902. Quoted in Hödl 2009: 135–136. See Chapter 7, Section 5, for more on Meyer.
[39] Förster-Nietzsche 1895: I 89–90; Förster-Nietzsche 1912: 66–68.
[40] When Guido Meyer described the summer preparatory classes he shared with Friedrich, he indicated that his sister knew the facts and was deliberately suppressing them. Hödl 2009: 136.
[41] Hayman 1980: 27; Young 2010: 21.
[42] Schmidt cites entries in her notebooks in 1855 and 1856 which indicate that well-to-do local advisors (both *Stadträtin*) recommended Pforta. One of these indicated that she should inquire about scholarships. Schmidt 1991–1994 II: 225, 249, n. 185. It is also suggestive that a letter from Pastor Osswald's daughter Selma, written as early as 1852, assumes that the boy would eventually attend Schulpforte. KGB I-1: 308.
[43] Bohley 1987: 194.   [44] Brobjer 2001b: 325.

In fact, the Nietzsches had to wait until one of the scholarships allotted to Naumburg became available, either because a holder graduated or left school for some other reason.[45] This apparently did not occur until October 1858.[46] For a full year, then, the boy was suspended in academic limbo, an insecurity which was to induce considerable anxiety in Friedrich.[47]

3

If Friedrich left little record of poems composed in 1857, in 1858 he produced more than those of the two previous years combined. The new poems register as well a new level of quality and with it the first traces of that sardonicism so often associated with the later Nietzsche. In one piece he imagines himself riding the hippogriff and sailing majestically through the heavens – "Carry me on godlike wings," he enjoins – only to discover as he issues from this enchantment: "Ah! I sat upon a molehill / and the divine horse was a bat."[48] In this case the shift of tone is exploited for grimly humorous reasons, but the careful reader will approach other poems written this year with caution. Their tone too is sometimes at variance with the theme, and the boy may not always say directly what he means. As an example, he presented his mother with a poem describing a storm from which a town's inhabitants flee.[49] "Erbarmen!" ("Mercy!") they cry, and at one level the piece clearly depicts the might of God. Yet Friedrich himself delighted in storms, and the depiction of those terrified adults scampering in terror from a phenomenon which he personally enjoyed sounds suspiciously like mockery.[50] If attitudinal ambivalence qualifies the affect of many of these poems, however, it is an ambivalence which suggests complexity within the poet himself. In another piece presented to his mother on her birthday (February 2, 1858), Friedrich reprises another beloved theme, that of the ship afloat on the sea. Here, as is appropriate in a piece offered to his pious mother, he proceeds allegorically to match the components of a voyage, one by one, to various elements of Christian doctrine:

---

[45] Schmidt 1991–1994 III: 218, indicates that this would not occur before Easter, 1858.
[46] Nietzsche took the place vacated by Richard Wachsmuth. Schmidt 2001: 77.
[47] Friedrich included an apostrophe to Schulpforte in the sheaf of poems he presented to his mother on February 2, 1858, her birthday. KGW I-1: 221–222. This was probably not a spontaneous topic but represented interest in the school he knew he would eventually attend.
[48] KGW I-1: 214. [49] KGW I-1: 220–221.
[50] For a discussion of Friedrich's wonder at storms, see Chapter 3, Section 3.

The discovery of self

Skipper's song

The world is like the sea,
The human like the ship,
But that which sits at the steering wheel
And guides the vessel's trip

That is the good conscience
One carries in one's breast
In order that we feel and know
What's wrong and what is best.

The winds that billow through the sails
And through the mastheads blow
These are the will of God
Through which all beings flow.

A ship that's unequipped with masts
And unsupplied with sails
Would find itself propelled about
And on the wild sea flail

And soon it would break to pieces
Against a dark cliff's might
And quickly sink into the sea
In endless, lightless night.

But beware, for there appears
An island to your view
So lovely that you might think
Only bliss could here ensue.

But that is a false mirage
A fantasy of your mind
Try as you will to reach it,
The isle you'll never find.

Seek not to wander from the path
Nor from the goal to stray
Or dangers will beset you
And you will lose your way.

You must have a destination.
Diverge and you will be
Driven forward by the waves
Until you drown in the sea.

But if you land in harbor,
The port for which you steered,

Then you will find calm
And happiness be ever yours.[51]

This poem operates on multiple levels, not all of them tonally coherent. Its pious moralizing, which probably gladdened the heart of Franziska, sits ill at ease with the glibness of its allegory, as ship, steersman, tackle, winds, harbor, and island are ticked off, each finding its pat correlate in Christian doctrine. The repetitive commands and admonitions – "But beware," "You must not swerve" – seem likewise overdone, as though this boy just on the cusp of puberty were quietly mocking his vigilant mother. The final stanza, moreover, seems artistically flat and anticlimactic, nor can one believe that peace and calm were ardently desired by a boy who so clearly enjoyed the spectacle of sinking ships. At the same time the poem must have been sincerely meant insofar as its basic theme, that one must steer through life with resolution, squares with the purposefulness and sense of determination Wilhelm had noted in his friend. The future philosopher who decades later wrote, "Formula for my happiness: a yes, a no, a straight line, a *goal*,"[52] is amply in evidence here, and the poem can by no means be dismissed as insincere.[53]

Given the brisk confidence of "Skipper's song" it is noteworthy that Friedrich wrote one other sea-related piece in 1858 and that it differs radically both in form and attitude from the earlier work. In late spring or summer, 1858, the boy composed an intricately rhymed poem in pentameter octaves entitled "Colombo."[54] Here the famed explorer considers in monologue the futility of his passage so far and whether he has failed. At the beginning Columbus seems at the edge of despair. He has traveled for many days without result, and as another morning dawns, he expects further disappointment. Time is running out, and his courage is waning. In the third and final stanza, he sights birds which bring with them the promise of land, and he rouses himself with the reflection that success is near and spirit is all he needs. The poem ends with the expostulation, "Nur Muth, nur Muth." ("Courage alone, just courage!"), which sounds rousing enough but is qualified by the reflections of the earlier lines.

The subtle rhyme scheme of "Colombo" is intrinsic to its meaning and makes the poem difficult to translate. Earlier in the year, however, Friedrich had written a poem, "Two larks," which, in imagery and narrative drive, lends itself to a version in English. While it is not so complex in

---

[51] KGW I-1: 224–225.   [52] TI, Arrows and Epigrams, 44. Translation: Judith Norman.
[53] This treatment of the poem is largely a restatement of points made by Schmidt 1991–1994 I: 324–342.
[54] KGW I-1: 273–274.

attitude as "Columbus," "Two larks" certainly expresses ambivalence, not to mention raw poetic power, and it demonstrates the boy's growing recognition of the reach and complexity of human experience:

> Two larks
>
> I listened to two larks singing.
> They sang so bright and clear
> And flew in happy vaulting
> In the sky's heavenly air.
>
> The one drew near to the sun
> But blinded, shrank in fright,
> Yet often thought with wonder
> Of this foregone delight,
>
> For he dared not try a second time
> The flight toward that beam.
> He feared that its pursuit
> Would lead in the end to pain.
>
> The other, courageously driven,
> Hurtled directly toward the sun
> But closed his eyes in terror
> At the untried course he'd begun.
>
> He couldn't resist, however,
> He felt unconquerable desire
> To see the heavenly radiance
> And heedless of personal care
>
> He looked into the streaming sun
> Without cry of any kind
> In heavenly joy and wonder
> Until his eyes at last went blind.[55]

One can deliberate at length over the symbolism of this poem – whether the sun represents forbidden knowledge, philosophic insight, or as one researcher has argued, the dangers to the boy's eyes due to excessive reading.[56] However, the skill of the poet and the intensity of his imagination are vividly on display. The ambivalence, narrative drive, and statement of ecstatic commitment qualified by sober consideration of the implications, all reveal a great deal about the budding adolescent who composed it.

---

[55] KGW I-1: 259–260. At the close of the poem, following the period, the following succession of characters appears: "–??!!"
[56] Schmidt 1991–1994 I: 350–351. For other interpretations: Schmidt 1991–1994 II: 623, 663–671, 674–675, 990–1000.

Friedrich Nietzsche was beginning to come into his powers and in the process to wonder where he was headed.

4

Friedrich clearly found the year 1858 transitional. For a start, he was growing up poetically, moving from the facile if skillfully written "Skipper's song" to more measured and complex poems, particularly a series of monologues ("Colombo" being only one example) probably written towards the beginning of summer. Further, he was just entering adolescence, a transition which can be bewildering. His mother contributed to the instability. In late summer or early autumn of that same year she decided to move again, this time taking lodgings in the upper floor of a dwelling in Weingarten Street on the town's southeastern edge. While neither Friedrich nor his sister recorded their views, the change in homes would have proved another disruption in their already peripatetic life. They would lose their beloved garden, and the fact that neither so much as mentioned the move – particularly the usually positive Förster-Nietzsche – suggests that they had nothing good to say about it. Meanwhile, the looming possibility that Friedrich would receive a scholarship to Schulpforte and be uprooted from Naumburg altogether must have added to his sense of transience and induced a sense of instability. He began 1858 with a poem which opened, "Years rush by on mighty wings of time / So this year came also to its end."[57] Another poem began, "Alas, all my time is already gone . . . ."[58] and another "Protect, God, my home valley / Must I now leave you as well?"[59] Clearly the boy knew that the present was fleeting. Even some of his poems on seasons began on an elegiac note as he acknowledged that the season before is no more: "Winter comes now, autumn has left . . . ."[60] "Autumn has arrived / The little birds are gone . . . ".[61]

If in 1858 he was keenly aware of transience, he began to pit the precarious present against the comparative stability of the known past. As early as February 2 he wrote "Wohin?" ("Whither?"), one of his finest lyrics, on the subject of his father's grave, a theme which would surface repeatedly in years to come. It is as though, haunted by another imminent loss of home, a repeat of the trauma of his eviction from Röcken, the boy not only expressed anxiety at the fleeting nature of time but repeatedly

---

[57] KGW I-1: 211.   [58] KGW I-1: 271.   [59] KGW I-1: 249.   [60] KGW I-1: 216.
[61] KGW I-1, 249.

circled backward, reverting to his father's tomb as a stable marker and point of repair from which to chart later developments. It is unlikely that he had many conscious memories of his first days at Röcken, but during his frequent visits to his grandparents at Pobles he would have visited his natal village, a mere wagon ride away, and a sense of his beginnings there would be kept fresh. So during the changes of 1858 (and with the prospect of soon leaving Naumburg) his concern with transience led him to recall what for him must have been a primal loss, the departure from the hamlet where his father had lived and where he himself had spent his earliest days.

This unstable period ended in the autumn of 1858 when the scholarship was officially awarded. Very likely neither Franziska nor her son was surprised, for they would have known when one of the scholarships had been vacated, particularly if this occurred through so predictable an event as the previous recipient's graduation. Yet most human beings experience unexpected feelings when a scenario long envisioned at last becomes real; and one must assume that the Nietzsches were no exception. Friedrich would recognize that the moment he had anticipated all year had arrived: he was about to separate from city, family, and beloved friends, and he seems immediately to have sketched a poem which began, "Farewell, farewell, my homeland."[62] For Franziska this was the juncture she had dreaded since her son's graduation from the Weber Institute. While she had worked hard to ensure this very event, her home would now be emptier by one child, and she undoubtedly grieved. Elisabeth appears to have had the most overtly passionate response. The news arrived while she was visiting her grandfather's farm, and according to her account she found a private place, burst into sobs, and was ill for the rest of the day.[63] Like all her stories, this one must be regarded as suspect. Nonetheless, as an ardent reader who, because of her gender, would not be offered the same educational opportunities, and as a lonely child whose one stable companion was her brother Fritz, she must indeed have grieved. While Friedrich could offset his doubts with new hopes and Franziska could console herself with the satisfaction that she had completed her mission, Elisabeth experienced pure loss.

5

It was during this limbo preceding the arrival of his scholarship that Friedrich composed what is arguably the masterpiece of his childhood

[62] KGW I-1: 277.   [63] Förster-Nietzsche 1895: 91–93; 1912: 70–71.

years and certainly the work of most immediate interest to the biographer. As has already been discussed, he seems during his final year in Naumburg to have been oppressed by a sense of the transience of life. Toward the close of summer – almost certainly before he received confirmation of the scholarship – he became particularly alarmed that his past was already slipping away. "So much has vanished from my memory," he lamented, "and the little that I recall has probably been retained only through tradition." (282).[64] He therefore conceived a project to set down all that he could remember, and in two weeks he completed a memoir of his stays in Röcken and Naumburg, fixing in writing his assembled recollections. (281–311)

The work is quite long and it opens with a title which is a bit presumptuous for a thirteen-year-old (he would not turn fourteen until October):

> From My Life. –
> by
> F. W. Nietzsche
> I
> The Years of Youth. –
> 1844–1858.

It would appear that "F.W. Nietzsche" intended someday to be a major figure and was here getting the jump on his biographers. Having issued this pronouncement that he was worthy of having his life recorded, the young author offered in his first paragraph a short introduction in which he lamented the instability of memory, concluding, "The stream of years fly from my gaze like a wild dream." As a rearguard action against such dissolution he announced that he would record such recollections as remained and would do so plastically in the sense that he would not only write what he recalled but form these into pictures with light and shade. He may have forgotten dates. "Nonetheless, a few things remain bright and lively in my soul, and I will build these, together with the dark and gloomy, into a painting."

After this introduction, Friedrich's work opens, simply enough, with a description of Röcken and an account of Ludwig's death, both of these sensitively rendered. (282–287) He then embarks on a much longer presentation of events in Naumburg, as he recalls his arrival, describes each of his schools, gives a guided tour of the town, rhapsodizes over activities he enjoyed – swimming, skating, Christmas celebrations – and cites such

---

[64] All quotations from "From my life" are sourced in parentheses and refer to pages in KGW I-1.

desultory events as the king's visit to Naumburg and trips outside the city. By comparison with the opening section on Röcken, the Naumburg presentation seems diffuse and unfocused. Friedrich was new to prose, and the work lacks the instinctive sense of form which he brought to his poems.

Two themes recur throughout the narrative and help to knit it into a whole. Passages scattered about the text expound on his relationships with Wilhelm and Gustav: their respective characters, how the three became friends, the activities of their fathers, and the artistic pursuits they enjoyed together. Their sustained presence helps to make an otherwise wandering narrative more coherent. Second, Friedrich considers his own creative development. He is pleased with his musical accomplishments – he describes his progress at the piano and composition – and he writes at length about poetry, as he explains the difficulties of his early attempts and enunciates the requirements for a good poem. As the work proceeds, a sense of his growing expertise helps to create a sense of sustained discovery, thereby knitting the work's heterogeneous materials into a somewhat more cohesive whole. Incidentally, as mentioned earlier, at no point except at the close does he mention that he plans to enter the ministry nor does he evidence any personal interest in religion aside from that which might be expected of a contemporary boy. If any future profession is intimated, it is some artistic field, either literature or music.

Although, as mentioned, the accounts of friends and the author's artistic pursuits provide the surface continuities, the work also has a tacit third source of unity, the narrator, who is also the central subject. Slowly, the author comes to realize that the events of his history are not just accidental. Sometimes, at least, they are revelations of character, occasions for the truth about himself to emerge. Here, for example, is an account of Friedrich's conflicts with other boys at school, an experience that must have been painful at the time. "But already [during the first school days in Naumburg] my character was beginning to manifest itself. In early life I had seen much anguish and sorrow and was therefore not quite so merry and lively as children usually are. My schoolmates used to tease me over this seriousness, yet this happened, not just in the burgher school but later at the Institute and even in the Gymnasium. From childhood on, I sought solitude and was happiest when I could give myself to my own ways, undisturbed." (288) Few thirteen-year-olds would have described the process so dispassionately. Friedrich neither complains nor blames, and he even exonerates his teasers by portraying the conflict as one of temperamental difference in which he was the one who didn't fit. Yet he doesn't upbraid himself either. He merely observes from a distance, accepting the ordeal as an occasion for the revelation of character.

In this passage Friedrich actually offers two reasons for his difference from the other boys. On the one hand, certain events in the past – the death of his father and the subsequent tragedies that befell his family (the death of Joseph, the departure from Röcken) – plainly affected him and explain, he says, his more sorrowful demeanor as compared to his cheerful schoolmates. Yet he also says that he simply liked to be alone, a proclivity which would have estranged him from the boys regardless of previous experiences. In this case both factors – his response to the environment and intrinsic tendencies of his character – reinforce one another, accounting for his comparative isolation during his school years. In other cases, competing tendencies lead to the cessation of one in favor of the other. Thus Friedrich credits his friendship with Gustav and Wilhelm with overcoming his initial distaste for the town of Naumburg. "[W]ithout [friendship] Naumburg would perhaps never have seemed home to me," he said, adding significantly, "And so insofar as I gained living friends here, my stay here has also become precious to me, and it would be very painful for me to have to leave." (295)

Ultimately, intrinsic aspects of his personality and the responses to his environment (which may or may not be intrinsic) are ever in dynamic interplay, one sometimes overcoming or at least modifying the other. This is particularly evident when he addresses the arts. Discussing his attempts as a child to try out various forms of play (poetry, music, painting), he generalizes, "So in one's youth one gladly imitates whatever one likes. This spirit of imitation is particularly strong in children." Yet, as he notes, the particular field a person responds to will reflect individual temperament. Not all children awaken to the same inspirations, but each will imitate just the fields to which he or she is drawn by personal taste. "It is quite difficult for a youth who despises a poet or writer to imitate their way of doing things." (292)

As this and other observations accumulate, his ostensible chronicle of memories shifts meaning. What began as a narrative of past events becomes in effect a portrait of its author, who is, after all, the designated protagonist, engaging with the world that surrounds him. In writing his memoir Friedrich seems to have realized that he was not just passive under the impress of circumstances. He was rather responding and participating in ways which were distinctive and which displayed his own values and traits. His history was a reflection in which he could see himself portrayed; and in describing his interaction with events he was discovering an identity which he had heretofore known only subliminally. This was a revelation that he found very exciting indeed, and in his postscript he appended two paragraphs and a quatrain to consider the extent of his accomplishment:

> I have already experienced so much, happy and sad, enlivening and dispiriting, but God has led me safely through it all as does a father his weak little child. He has already laid on me much that is painful, but in all I reverently recognize his noble power that makes everything turn out well. I have firmly chosen to dedicate myself forever to his service. May the dear lord give me strength and fortitude for my intent and protect me on my life's path. Childlike, I trust in his grace: He will protect all of us, so that no disaster grieves us. But let his holy will be done. All that he gives, I will joyfully accept, happiness and misfortune, poverty and riches, and boldly look in the eye death itself, that which will unite us all someday in eternal joy and happiness. Yes, dear lord, let thy countenance shine on us forever! Amen!
>
> Thus I conclude my first booklet and I look back on it with joy. I have written it with great delight and did not tire in the process. It is just too wonderful afterwards to run one's first years of life before the soul and so to recognize the soul's development. I have told the whole truth here without poetizing or literary embellishment. In light of the work's length people will pardon me if I have now and then added something or will later add something. If only I could write quite a few more little volumes like this! (310–311)

Although directly juxtaposed, these two paragraphs differ strikingly in vocabulary and tone. The first, while probably sincere enough, is from a literary point of view formulaic. It is beautifully composed, yet virtually every line could have been taken from prayers and hymns that the boy had heard all his life. Conceptually, its effect is to present the boy's past as something external to himself, an inscrutable fate laid upon him by God. ("But let his holy will be done.") Life is something that happens to him.

A quite different outlook is dramatized in the second paragraph, which fairly crows in satisfaction and triumph. On the surface it treats almost exclusively his excitement over the booklet he has just written. He reflects on the physical artifact, which lies visibly before him. He considers his state when he wrote it and the more general reasons which led him to find the process edifying. And while he does not deny the fatality of life, he sounds far more active than acquiescent and recognizes within the vicissitudes of his past the soul's development, a process which is presumably far less contingent.

For all its difference, this second paragraph is intimately bound with its predecessor, for it is God (so prominent in the first) who creates and sustains the "soul" (Friedrich's term) whose depiction is celebrated in the second. Because of God he has an identity of which he had previously been only vaguely aware; and it is this identity which offers a fascination and security that he did not previously realize he had. Thus, the issues raised at the beginning of the memoir find an unexpected resolution. The piece had begun with the threat of persistent loss (the transience of memories) and the need to find a remedy (their transcription). Slowly the author has come to recognize that he has at his disposal a refuge of a different kind. In "run[ning] the first years of one's life past the soul" he begins to "recognize in them the soul's development." He is not just a collection of memories or a plaything at the mercy of events. He has a temperament, a character, which he here calls "soul" and will later designate "self." The world may be evanescent, but this companion endures, is able to grow, and will presumably accompany him in the future.

Still basking in this glorious vision he closes with a poem that he had actually written nine months earlier[65] but which acquires richer significance through its current placement:

> Life is a mirror.
> To recognize oneself in it
> Would seem to me the chief thing
> Toward which we should strive. (311)

This is the first occasion in his extant work that Friedrich Nietzsche apostrophizes "life," a theme that later would exercise him considerably. It is, of course, unclear just what he means by the term, "life" being a rather large and nebulous term. In this case he apparently means the specificities of *his* life, its events and his experiences, the sorts of episodes and themes that might be encompassed by a biography of the very kind he is writing. Yet the primary intent here is not to affirm "life," although that is implicit. It is rather "to recognize oneself in it," to decipher from its hieroglyphic the constraints and possibilities of personal recognition and development. Life is not just what happens to him, but also the individual way he ingests it and responds. To that extent life and self run in tandem – one is a reflection of the other – and for that very reason he can use this externalized image as a mirror of who he is. Incidentally, it is striking that this introspective and religious boy does not favor intuition and the examination of conscience as

---

[65] KGW I-1: 212.

sources of self-knowledge. Instead he seeks to understand the self through its actions on a larger stage. When Friedrich declares, "Life is a mirror," he suggests that, just as he can't see his face except by reflection, so he can't know who he is except by inspecting the events in his history. He is what his biography reveals.[66]

It should be observed that Nietzsche probably didn't come to this insight entirely on his own. By now he had been in the Gymnasium for three years and, as will be explained in the next chapter, the ideological fulcrum of that institution was *Bildung*, a word that now just means "education" in German but that in the late eighteenth and nineteenth centuries carried strong connotations of self-formation.[67] During Nietzsche's century educators taught that every self is an individual cluster of talents and energies which the person discovers through activity. The first task of education, then, was to awaken these possibilities, and the second, to coach the individual into wielding these into a coherent and vibrant human being. A fascination with individual self was at the center of Prussian education, and at the time of writing this autobiography, Nietzsche had doubtless heard this topic expounded on many occasions. This may have been the first time he applied those lessons; it was not the first time he encountered them.

Meanwhile, one might note that this section begins with religion and is throughout anchored in invocations of God, a pattern that cannot be ignored. Although the imputation has been made that the young Nietzsche showed little lively interest in either religion or the vocation which had been ordained for him, a religious underpinning nonetheless underwrites much that he says here.[68] Indeed, it is Christian faith which allows him to elide or simply not notice difficulties which a non-religious philosopher might fasten on immediately. Because Friedrich treats identity as a creation of God, he tends in effect to conceive the self as soul and thus to view it as autonomous and only incidentally influenced by family or environment, an assumption that more secularly oriented minds might query. In addition, his invocation of divine providence inspires hopes beyond what his present situation might warrant. He may be far more indentured to his environment and its influences, not to mention the vagaries of accident, than he realizes. Friedrich himself would address

---

[66] He does not explicitly reject soul-searching and introspective inquiry as resources here, of course. He merely recognizes the benefits of externalized inquiry and is too taken by the new possibility to even mention the alternatives.
[67] Vierhaus 1972.
[68] The religiosity displayed in this passage is virtually unparalleled in Nietzsche's prose writings.

these issues in adolescence when his faith in Christianity began to founder and the implications to dawn.[69] Meanwhile, he had glimpsed a project that would fascinate him from this point to the end of his youth: the desire to know who he was and how he might enact that self so as to make it register with maximal value.

---

[69] See Chapter 6, Sections 4, 6, and 7.

CHAPTER 5

Soul-building: the theory

Learning transforms us; it does what all nourishment does which doesn't merely sustain – as the physiologist knows.[1]

I

Before Friedrich Nietzsche enrolled at Schulpforte there is little evidence that he had any great interest in learning for its own sake. When the thirteen-year-old described his educational experiences at Naumburg, he mentioned socializing with friends but said nothing about ingesting knowledge, a primary function of schools. Nor, with the exception of his time at Herr Weber's, did he mention any of those academies with affection. He certainly had not enjoyed the burgher school, where he had been isolated and forlorn.[2] As for the Cathedral Gymnasium, he would write that he entered its rooms "with a secret shudder. The bleak classrooms, the strict and scholarly bearing of my teachers, the many more grown-up students, who looked down on me with contempt . . . all this made me timid and shy, and only slowly did I accustom myself to demand my place with more confidence and calm."[3] While Friedrich – or "Nietzsche," as he must now be called since this is how would be known at Schulpforte – was a dutiful boy and he aspired to do well in classes, he had not been conspicuously successful academically up to the present. It was only after arriving at Schulpforte that he awakened to the joys of learning and began to take scholarship seriously.

Such a shift would require a revolution in his attitudes, for he entered that institution with misgivings. As a sensitive child, who needed intimacy to be at ease, Nietzsche felt anxious when he was accepted as a boarding

---
[1] BGE: 231; KSA V: 170.
[2] In one autobiographical sketch, Nietzsche omits the burgher school altogether, giving the impression that his education began with Herr Weber's Institute. KGW I-2: 262.
[3] KGW I-2: 262.

student. He would now live at school twenty-four hours a day, and since 200 students and several dozen adults (teachers, wives, support staff)[4] occupied a space the size of a few city blocks, he would rarely be alone. He explicitly records that his mood was grim as he approached its walls on October 5, 1858, his first day at school. He had dreaded leaving his family and friends, and he was oppressed by the suspicion that he would soon lose his privacy. The hour was dawn, and as the institution emerged from the surrounding blackness, he reflected, "It seemed to me more a prison than an alma mater." The gate gave him a particular fright. The recently reconstructed entry included a hulking oriel and a tunnel bored through the main building through which students passed, leaving the world behind. As the thirteen-year-old sped through that corridor, he was terrified, and only afterwards did he find solace in prayer.[5]

Once inside the walls, he would be directed to take an entry exam, which involved translating a German text into Latin and fielding oral questions on Latin and Greek grammar and catechism, as well as a few queries on mathematics.[6] Thanks in part to his preparations at Kirchscheidungen the year before,[7] he passed, although he was put back a semester, a practice apparently not uncommon at that institution.[8] Having succeeded in his entry examination, Nietzsche's fears might have been somewhat allayed, for inside the gates he found that his beloved nature had not been left behind. A branch of the Saale River ran underground but was dammed in the so-called Millpond, and the boys would throw off their clothes and swim there in summer. As he had noted approvingly, the facility itself was superbly sited – set among broad meadows, while a gentle, wooded mountain known as the Knabenberg rose along its southern flank, setting off the landscape with its rounded silhouette. The combination of rural setting and ecclesiastical buildings – the facility had once been a

---

[4] The number of students was stable at 200, including 180 boarding students and 20 well-to-do internees, who housed with faculty. (Gersdorff and Wilamowitz were members of this privileged group.) The number of adults no doubt varied. Benders *et al.* 2000: 48, lists eight full professors, four adjunct professors, and three specialized instructors, plus one spiritual officer. (This does not include the physician.) Further, the full professors would have wives and often children; and there undoubtedly existed support staff in the way of handymen, gardeners, and cooks. It is therefore difficult to know how many non-students were on the premises during the daytime.
[5] KSAB I: 50.
[6] Heumann *et al.* 1994: 87. Deussen 1922: 62, indicates that Greek translation was involved as well, although according to Heumann, this was required only of potential upperclassmen.
[7] See Chapter 4, Section 2.
[8] See Förster-Nietzsche 1912: 73 vs. Brobjer 2001b: 326, n. 14. Among Nietzsche's acquaintances Paul Deussen was put back three semesters and Wilamowitz six months (initially a full year). Wilamowitz-Moellendorff 1928: 62.

Soul-building: the theory

cloister – might have reminded him of his beloved days at Röcken. He would probably have recoiled, however, from the air of monastic asceticism, which had not so much been eliminated as rechanneled into a totalitarian dedication to education. According to Förster-Nietzsche, a wall 12 feet high surrounded the facility, making every inhabitant a prisoner.

At Pforta Nietzsche could expect his life to be thoroughly regimented. His place in lines, his chair at dinner in the communal dining hall, and his seat in class would all be governed by protocols.[9] On his first day he would be given a bed in one of six sleeping halls, then assigned to one of fifteen rooms, where he would generally live with around a dozen other boys, forming under fortunate conditions a "family." In that same room he would be assigned a seat at a study table – two to four such desks per room – where he would study under the supervision of upperclassmen.[10] Similarly, although this description is disputed, the dining area would have fifteen tables (to correspond to the study rooms) with twelve seats to a table, where one would again be seated according to specific rules and calculations.[11] He would endure constant surveillance and be subject to the commands of upperclassmen. Entering Pforta was like joining an academic army where the professors were generals and selected students the officers and sergeants.

During his first days and throughout the first year he would have endured the indignities reserved for freshmen. Newcomers were expected to fetch barrels of water from the well and to sound the bell that punctuated the day.[12] Certain students described hazing ceremonies,[13] and in 1860 a parent would complain (among other matters) of *Pennalismus*, the German word for hazing.[14] However, that term has a long history in the German states, and the parent might have meant any domination of

---

[9] Schmidt 1991–1994 III: 143–146.
[10] For the number of sleeping quarters and tables, see Deussen 1922: 63. Schmidt says there were three to five desks per room. Schmidt 1991–1994 III: 142. In Governmental Inspector Karl Gustav Heiland's supervisory report he indicates that the maximum number of students in a room (*Alumnenstube*) would be sixteen, which seems high. Gilman 1979: 421. If 180 students were distributed in fifteen rooms, the number on average should be twelve.
[11] So Schmidt. However Heiland's report (reflecting conditions in 1859) indicates that meals were served at two long tables, seating ninety students each. Gilman 1979: 420.
[12] Wilamowitz-Moellendorff 1928: 68.
[13] Nietzsche never mentions hazing and may not have experienced any. However, see Wilamowitz-Moellendorff 1928: 68; Feldhoff 2008: 32; Gilman 1979: 419–420; and Heumann *et al.* 1994: 199–200.
[14] For a brief discussion of this incident, which was reported in the newspapers, see Bohley 2007: 74–76. For a separate summation and documents issued by investigating governmental inspectors, see Gilman 1979: 406–422.

younger by older boys, including ordinary disciplinary proceedings administered by student supervisors, a diffusion of authority common at Pforta. Regardless whether that privilege was abused, Nietzsche was unquestionably entering a male world – and one probably of unacknowledged violence – very different from the pious domicile he had shared with his mother and sister. Yet after his initial shock he seemed to like it or, at least, found the regimen not so bad as he feared. "Up to now I feel quite at ease," he wrote in his first letter home, adding, "But what does 'quite at ease' mean in a strange place?"[15] Five days later he predicted, "Just wait. I'll get homesick eventually."[16] A little over a month after arrival he found himself still trying to convince his mother that he missed her. "I almost believe that homesickness is coming over me. Now and then I feel signs of it."[17] In fact, there are no explicit indications that Nietzsche longed for his mother much at all. He was just turning fourteen, an age when adolescents tend to view families as an encumbrance, and Naumburg lay only three miles away. Since he was allowed two hours outside the walls every Sunday, he could meet his family in the village of Almrich, which lay midway between the town and the school. Within a month he was walking back and forth to Naumburg during these breaks so that he could choose himself whom he would visit.

If Franziska was not missed personally, her services were nonetheless indispensable. Nietzsche's letters abound with demands for necessities and conveniences such as eyeglasses, ink, knives, scissors, notebooks, chocolate, teaspoons, boots, and books. If Nietzsche did not himself confess to homesickness, the repeated and nearly frantic demands expressed in his letters suggest the unarticulated fear that his mother would not miss him either, that he would be forgotten. "*Don't forget my birthday!*" he writes (emphases his), as though this were likely.[18] Yet his anxiety is easy to understand. The departure from Naumburg and loved ones would revive memories of his traumatic expulsion from Röcken. Further, his mother changed residences on October 7, a week before his departure, moving from the house near the Marien Gate with its happy memories to the aforementioned new home at Weingarten Street in a quarter of town where he had never lived.[19] Most significantly, at the time of Nietzsche's relocation to Schulpforte, Franziska invited her nineteen-year-old brother Oscar to move in with her through the coming year, in effect replacing one adolescent with another. As it happened, Nietzsche very much liked Oscar

---

[15] KSAB I: 16.   [16] KSAB I: 20   [17] KSAB I: 29.   [18] KSAB I: 18.
[19] For the date of the move, see Rosmiarek *et al.* 2003: 323. Oscar moved in that same day.

and seemed to enjoy his company. Nonetheless, he cannot have avoided considering that the new boy was occupying a place previously taken by him; and thirteen-year-olds far more secure than Friedrich Nietzsche might have experienced misgivings under the circumstances.

Meanwhile, to move from Nietzsche's letters directed toward Franziska to those addressed to Wilhelm, is to enter a different universe. While with his mother he is commanding and brusque, he unburdens himself to Wilhelm with an affection and ease which displays more than any testimonial how much their friendship meant to him. While he tells Wilhelm too that he is not homesick, he adds, "You will not believe on the other hand how often I wish to be at your home in Naumburg ... The good times are over now, and I dare not think on them or I will grow sad."[20]

To friends and family alike, Nietzsche explains that he is overscheduled and overworked, frequently using this as an excuse for not having written. Some of this embrace of a heavy workload must have stemmed from boyish pride that he could withstand the pressure. Yet Nietzsche soon accommodated himself to Pforta's combination of discipline and structure, along with its local dramas. Popular literature on German-speaking boarding schools (the prototype being Robert Musil's *The confusions of the student Törless*) presents them as sadomasochistic hotbeds of bullying and sexual tension. There were apparently sexual antics at Pforta from time to time – not only is this acknowledged in official reports, but four boys were expelled in 1858 (the year of Nietzsche's arrival) for "a lewd act."[21] Bullying will be present wherever there are assemblages of boys, and one biographer has speculated that Nietzsche, who wrote home with surprising frequency of torn trousers, was himself (with his gentle manners and poor eyesight) a victim.[22] There is no documentary proof of this, however, and if true, Nietzsche never mentioned it. From the beginning, he seems to have accepted the ways of Pforta as given, and while he undoubtedly had difficulties with some of its aspects, he rarely complained.

He was hardly alone in his acquiescence. Other students apparently rose to the same challenges of structure, discipline, and force-fed education.[23] Yet Nietzsche's motives may have had a personal impetus. Pforta prided itself on operating *in loco parentis*, and a rector from the previous decade

---

[20] KSAB I: 24.
[21] Schmidt 1991–1994 III: 203–204. See Peter's report in Gilman 1979: 405. For more on sexual matters at Pforta, see Heumann *et al.* 1994: 202–204.
[22] Schmidt 1991–1994 III: 249–251.
[23] Wilamowitz-Moellendorff prized it, as is evident throughout his account. Wilamowitz-Moellendorff 1928: 72–73, 74.

had called the institution a "more than paternal home (*Vaterhaus*)."²⁴ As this term indicates, there was no doubt in anybody's mind which parent was being replaced. Pforta was specifically directed by the Prussian state to focus on boys whose fathers were either deceased or absent on foreign business.²⁵ Nietzsche need feel no misgivings for attending on a scholarship. Apparently half of his classmates enjoyed the same assistance.²⁶ Nor, for once in his life, need he feel isolated for being fatherless. In his first year approximately one-sixth of his classmates were missing a male parent.²⁷ Moreover, because the school controlled so many functions hitherto fulfilled by his mother, it appeared to offer the male instruction and guidance of which he had hitherto felt deprived. It is significant that in an autobiography composed after he had been at that institution two and a half years he concluded, "I can only wish that now and ever more in later times I might show myself to be a worthy *son* of Pforta."²⁸ (Emphasis added.)

Yet just as Nietzsche's paternal longings were being assuaged in one way, he suffered a blow in another. Friedrich Wilhelm IV, the monarch for whom he was named and whose birthday he shared, had suffered a stroke the previous year and in the view of his subjects (and apparently Nietzsche himself) had gone insane. On October 6, 1858, the day after Nietzsche's arrival at Pforta, the king was officially removed from his throne and his brother Wilhelm installed as regent.²⁹ All birthday celebrations for the king were canceled at the school. This had to have come as a blow to Nietzsche, if only as a dash of cold water thrown on his own birthday two weeks later (October 15). As a boy he had liked the holiday festivities which accompanied the day he shared with the king, and at least one biographer believes that he had viewed Friedrich Wilhelm as a symbolic parent.³⁰ Beyond this, the new student may have hoped that the pomp and ceremonies surrounding the common birthday would break the ice and serve to mark him as someone special to his schoolmates. Instead, what apparently was madness had taken a second paternal figure, a coincidence which could not fail to

---

²⁴ Quoted in Blunck 1953: 48.   ²⁵ Brobjer 2001b: 325.
²⁶ Brobjer 2001b: 325. See also Wilamowitz-Moellendorff 1928: 63.   ²⁷ Brobjer 2001b: 325.
²⁸ KGW I-2: 263.
²⁹ These events could not have appeared as abrupt as they are sometimes presented. The king had apparently suffered strokes in 1857, and a series of proposals and provisional arrangements preceded official announcement of the regency (October 7, 1858). Although Friedrich Wilhelm's illness was interpreted as madness, David Barclay, his principal biographer, regards this diagnosis as "certainly inaccurate" and construes the king's failures as due either to "a cerebral condition, probably advanced arteriosclerosis in the brain" or to Alzheimer's. Barclay 1995: 278–282.
³⁰ Ross 1980: 18–19.

impress him. Three years later he would write that his father succumbed to "an inflammation of the brain, its symptoms remarkably like the illness of the deceased king."[31]

Despite these disappointments, the boy made himself at home as best he could. He was used to fitting in, and he seems to have spent his first months at school acclimating himself to local customs and settling for an extended stay. He applied for the choir (which he would join officially a year later), and he paid for access to a piano. Above all, after a year of adjustment he began to study with an application he had previously reserved for poetry. He had not been a good student in the past, but he strove ardently to make himself a superlative one now. Ultimately and despite the dramatics of Nietzsche's first day, he found neither his hopes nor fears decisively confirmed during his first year at Schulpforte. He simply slipped into a new routine. Yet, as his determination to study shows, something new was awakened. Beneath the plod of daily life his priorities began gradually to shift, and upon graduation he would compare his stay at the school to his father's death as the second central event of his existence.[32] Ultimately, Schulpforte gave Nietzsche an educational model, and with it a myth, which would rescue him from childhood passivity and excite his imagination to the end of his conscious life.

2

Pforta was used to changing students' lives. That was its purpose, for by the mid-nineteenth century it conceived of education, less as a utilitarian aid to career, than as the development of the youthful soul. To that extent it had not strayed far from the institution's original intent. Founded in 1137 as a Cistercian monastery, it had been occupied by clerics for almost 400 years until they were evicted during the Reformation and the buildings converted into a school.[33] In the process the old name "St. Marien ad Portam" (Saint Mary at the Gate) was secularized to just Pforte ("gate" in German) or the incorrect but now established "Pforta," Schulpforte and Schulpforta being more formal designations.[34] If religion served as one pillar of the school's heritage, the Prussian army provided another, and the resident

---

[31] KGW I-2: 259.   [32] KGW I-3: 417–418.
[33] For the extraordinary continuity from its clerical beginnings to Nietzsche's time, see Pernet 1989: 67–69.
[34] Pahncke 1956: 55–64. This book will use "Schulpforte" and "Pforta." While inconsistent and (in the second case) etymologically incorrect, this usage reflects general practice. (The school today is generally known as Landesschule Pforta in Schulpforte.)

students were steeped in a culture of command and obedience.[35] However, Pforta's liberal faculty was not always in agreement with the very conservative government, and the school was frequently under investigation by suspicious administrators from Berlin.[36] The fusion of monastic austerity and Prussian militarism must have worked powerfully on the school's young charges. A rector from the decade before had aptly described it as "a self-enclosed school state,"[37] and even some parents were dismayed by the school's authoritarianism.[38]

The staff at Pforta took a dim view of idleness, and typical days began at 6 a.m. (5 a.m. in summer) with a run to the public washbowls, followed by services in the chapel, and a breakfast of rolls and milk – all accomplished within the first hour.[39] From then until students returned to bed at 9 p.m., virtually every minute of their day was dedicated to lectures, class preparation and review, meals, prayers, or athletic activities. Since the adults could hardly supervise so large a student body twenty-four hours a day, a system of rank diffused power to the students themselves. Seniors served as prefects in the dormitory rooms; others guided activities at the study tables, and the top students in each grade were responsible for assorted duties, such as maintaining order when no other supervisor was around. Such student empowerment along with the need to obey was thought to instill a sense of self-responsibility, which was certainly one of the desiderata at Pforta, where pedagogy did not limit itself to a curriculum found in books.

Traditional education, however, was not overlooked, and Pforta was regarded as one of the premier upper level schools in the German states.[40] Latin and, to a lesser extent, Greek formed the bedrock of the curriculum, and of the thirty-two hours per week devoted to classes in the freshman year, over half were spent on classical languages.[41] Not only was study of the ancients out of proportion numerically to other studies but, according to Wilamowitz, secondary subjects were often taught poorly and with little imagination.[42] It must be stressed that this emphasis on ancient languages,

---

[35] Goch writes that the school "with its strict discipline, its painfully exact, regulated daily schedule resembled a cadet academy, stamped with military spirit." Goch 1994: 185.
[36] Tensions between the Prussian government, which wished to standardize schools, and the Schulpforte leaders, who sought to preserve their institution's historic individuality, were chronic from the Prussian takeover onward. For what is arguably the government's endgame, although the editor doesn't call it that, see Gilman 1979: 406–426. See also Chapter 7, n. 44.
[37] Quoted in Blunck 1953: 49.   [38] Gilman 1979: 406. See also Pernet 1989: 69–73.
[39] KGW I-2: 101–102.
[40] Matthew Arnold compared Schulpforte to "the most renowned English schools." Quoted in Bergmann 1987: 19.
[41] Bohley 2007: 220–221.   [42] Wilamowitz-Moellendorff 1928: 74.

Soul-building: the theory

while not new, was newly conceived and by no means a passively received tradition inherited from the past. On the contrary, Enlightenment thinkers had regarded the study of Latin as moribund and had expected it to die out soon and to be replaced by studies in the vernacular.[43] (The study of Greek at the time was already limited to specialized fields.) That such "progress" did not occur was due to a remarkable irruption of quite new dynamics which few in the eighteenth century could have foreseen. Far from an age-old tradition, this new stress on Latin (and particularly Greek) dated only from 1809, and it reflected a vision which, while based on two Enlightenment figures (Rousseau, Kant), moved in directions that were arguably Romantic. The new pedagogy must be investigated now, for its influence on the young Nietzsche was fundamental.

During previous centuries education in the German states had been administered from a top-down perspective, children usually being considered either as blank slates to be inscribed with knowledge or as little savages to be disciplined into civility.[44] Both stances installed adults as dominant knowers to whom the child must conform. Slowly, a new conception of education began to reverse this relationship by assuming that the child and youth was in some sense autonomous and deserving of respect. Each resembled an organic seed with its own abilities and patterns of growth; and the task of education was less to trim all to the same cloth than to guide individuals as they developed their distinctive mix of talents.[45] The Swiss pedagogue Johann Heinrich Pestalozzi was the first to implement such an approach in the classroom, but as an ideal it has its roots in German Pietism,[46] and it was perhaps best expressed in a line from Rousseau's novel, *Emile*: "Plants are formed by cultivation, human beings by education."[47]

In German the standard word for education is *Bildung*, but the term has overtones of imposing form, whether from without (as in artistic creation) or from within (as in entelechy, whereby the organism develops according to interior design).[48] In the later decades of the eighteenth century it began

---

[43] Jeismann 1990: 323–324.
[44] Compare Sweet: "At [the time when Humboldt took charge] the typical elementary school throughout Germany was run along lines appropriate for a penal institution." Sweet 1980 II: 22. See also La Vopa 1980.
[45] See La Vopa 1990: 31.   [46] Sorkin 1987: 14–21; Vierhaus 1972: 510–511.
[47] "On façonne les plantes par la culture, et les hommes par l'éducation." Fourth paragraph of Book I of *Emile*. Quoted in Weil 1967: 42.
[48] Symptomatically, the term *Bildung* was used in the eighteenth century both in texts by Albrecht von Haller during the Preformation Controversy (biological) and in a translation from Shaftesbury (artistic). See Chapter 2, Section 3, for further discussion of this term.

to be used as a complement to *"Erziehung,"* (upbringing), *Bildung* suggesting something that could not be produced through instruction alone, but that required participation on the child's part and occurred as self-development.[49] Indeed, although Rousseau had invoked the analogy of a plant, certain theoreticians believed that this theory of natural growth must be complemented with a demand for animal intentionality and for personal responsibility. Individuals were not just plants; they were gardeners, their own gardeners, and they must tend and supervise their own development.[50] This new approach was distilled and disseminated by a number of major literary and philosophical figures (Herder, Schiller, Goethe, Fichte).[51] However, the man who most powerfully propagated this notion, and who inscribed it most effectively in the nineteenth-century psyche, was Wilhelm von Humboldt, who made *Bildung* virtually into a moral code and had the power to instill it in all Prussian youth.

Humboldt, the scion of minor nobility and older brother to the explorer Alexander, had been born in the pre-Napoleonic era and trained by particularly enterprising tutors. The growing boy came to dislike these preceptors and to hold himself responsible for his own moral and educational growth. "Nothing on earth is so important as the vital energy and many-sided development of the individual," he wrote. "The first law of true morality is therefore: Develop yourself."[52] Implicit here was the assumption that individuals were not a haphazard bundle of passions. Each was a unique organism, and one's lifelong task (which would extend far beyond the years of formal education) was to discover and enact one's particular blend of abilities and at the same time to discipline them into unity. Humboldt stressed activity – "Energy is the first and only virtue of humanity"[53] – because only through deeds could individuals ferret out their talents, bring them to fruition, and at the same time wield this sometimes unruly swarm of instincts and capacities into a coherent and unitary self. Human beings were here to create, not to enjoy themselves. "I consider the true aim of our life here on earth to be . . . the cultivation to the full of the talents with which we have been endowed."[54]

Although Humboldt's writings on education were little read during his lifetime, and most were not published until over a decade after his death, he was given an extraordinary opportunity to put his ideas into practice. In

---

[49] Vierhaus 1972: 509–511.
[50] This double heritage is much emphasized by Weil 1967, who associates the vegetative analogy with Rousseau, the supervisory with Shaftesbury. See also Sweet 1978 I: 52.
[51] Most notably Herder. See Vierhaus 1972: 515–517.   [52] Sweet 1978 I: 99.
[53] Sweet 1978 I: 110.   [54] Quoted in Sweet 1978 I: 51.

early 1809, less than three years after Prussia had effectively been conquered by Napoleon, he was put in charge of the nation's schools and allowed to reconfigure them along new foundations. It was a unique moment in history, and Humboldt's achievement, which involved setting standards for teachers,[55] reconfiguring the Gymnasium (the German equivalent of middle and high school), and virtually reinventing the university, was to last for over a century and a half and make Prussia's schools a model for numerous institutions elsewhere, including many in the United States.[56]

While Humboldt envisioned the Gymnasium and university as complementary institutions, they were by no means alike. The Gymnasium's task was to teach students how to learn by means of stern discipline and inexorable demands. The individuality of students might theoretically be respected, but the imposition of good working habits was regarded as essential to that stage of development. The university by contrast reversed this process. Graduates who had weathered the Gymnasium and received their graduating degree were now considered free adults who knew what they wanted. They were often in practice not required to attend classes at all and, in theory, they pursued knowledge for its own sake, serving as co-workers at the side of their professors. To put it simply, Gymnasium students were force-fed established knowledge; university students were expected to ferret out and extend knowledge for themselves.[57]

If the university represented the liberational aspect of education, the Gymnasium stood for its structured, disciplinary side, and it was here that the classical languages found their pedagogic place. Humboldt assumed that during adolescence, the point of education was less to learn content than to learn how to learn. The mastery of a difficult but circumscribed field of knowledge (in German a "*Wissenschaft*") such as Latin and Greek would teach students to discipline their time, mobilize their talents, and learn to work in a directed way so that demanding material could be thoroughly mastered.[58] Humboldt believed that speech represented the

---

[55] Humboldt used these examinations to undercut the previous dominance of teaching by often ignorant clergy. See Paulsen 1895: 78; Fallon 1980: 17–18, 39.
[56] For a simple and concise account in English of Humboldt's achievements see Fallon 1980: 16–19. For the influence of German institutions on those in the United States see Fallon 1980: 1–3, 51–52; Butler 1895: ix; Diehl 1978 passim; and Sweet 1980 II: 70.
[57] Paulsen 1895: 161–162. For a quotation from Humboldt in which he himself sums up this distinction, see Fallon 1980: 17.
[58] It should be stressed that the intent was not to learn something but to learn to learn. See Wilamowitz-Moellendorff 1928: 65, 72–73.

core of a culture,[59] and the study of Greek would, so to speak, force students to become Greeks themselves, to ingest and internalize the very essence of what was assumed to be a golden age of humanity. The process of this learning would itself induce personal development and force students to think for themselves, and, of course, it was hoped that by reading these mainstays of Western civilization students would recognize and develop their own talents and propensities, an individual efflorescence which was the essence of *Bildung*.[60] As to those who deplored devoting so much time to knowledge that was practically useless, Humboldt could reply that this was precisely the point. He mistrusted the Enlightenment ideal of self-sacrifice to one's profession and believed that any such self-suppression should occur only after one had discovered and exercised that self in the first place. To subject adolescent souls to training useful in a specific career would be to deform them. Their early education should stress *general* principles which would favor "the all-around development of the free individual personality"[61] and center on the ultimate model for humanity, the classical Greeks. Let individuals discover their individual interests and talents and to that extent enact their essential human essence; only then, with this mission accomplished, could they go to the university and pursue activities peculiar to more parochial professions.

For all this stress on the non-specific, Humboldt did admit one form of professional expertise into his curriculum, and it would be one that Nietzsche would struggle with for well over a decade. Humboldt had studied for years with the epochal philologist Friedrich August Wolf. When he advocated learning Greek, he had in mind the Wolfian approach which was both new and controversial. Wolf stressed the need for comprehensive study of the entire culture of antiquity, and this meant that students were expected to master quantities of factual material that had not seemed important until Wolf discerned their value. The sorts of detail that Wolf esteemed and that students were expected to ingest could seem petty indeed to neophytes (and even some professionals),[62] and the Wolfian approach to philology stressed exactly the sort of crabbed and specific information which the Humboldtian approach to education had supposedly wished to exclude. In other words, despite his ban on professional instruction, Humboldt made one exception, that of the quite specialized requirements of the trained

---

[59] Burrow 1969: xxviii; Humboldt 1960– II: 58–64. [60] Jeismann 1990: 326–331.
[61] Jarausch 1982: 83.
[62] For the reception of Wolfian methods at Schulpforte, see Paulsen 1885: 647. As a formerly Saxon school, Schulpforte had modeled itself on Hermannian principles.

philologist; and at least one historian has argued that this exception proved fatal to Humboldt's humanist project.[63]

Meanwhile, for all this emphasis on Humboldt and his ideals, the educational theory he sought to prescribe to Prussia schools was never really practical and could be implemented only in compromised forms. To that extent – and because the meaning of knowledge acquisition changed over the century, as will be shown in a later chapter[64] – an ideological dissonance was introduced into the system, troubling teachers and puzzling students. For a start, Humboldt held his post as chief of schools for a mere sixteen months, and many of the ideas and practices he supported were first suggested by others.[65] Further, like any new policies, his proposed innovations met considerable resistance, particularly from religious leaders and concerned parents, the first concerned about studying pagans, the second about the neglect of practical skills. In any case, the state itself revised its policies over the next century, sometimes bewildering Gymnasium instructors as they tried to reconcile these procedures to the *Bildung* ideal.[66] Indeed, there are those today who believe that the entire project of *Bildung* never really existed but was a myth trotted out for academic festivals but playing little role in everyday practice.[67] Certainly, Humboldt's vision had been diluted and bureaucratized by the time Nietzsche came under its influence, and it was increasingly displaying a shadow side.[68] Yet despite its failings and uneven implementation, the new approach to education was clearly superior to the models that had prevailed in the century before. It will therefore be seen that for all its authoritarianism and severity of discipline, education at Pforta was in intention benign. The school's rigor was strategic, its high standards designed to stimulate and inspire. Despite its Christian trappings, it never confused education with edification, and in fact the administration was repeatedly charged with neglecting religion.

The school's ideology would therefore have been highly attractive and seductive to the young Nietzsche. Its stress on self-development and "soul building" would have appealed both to his Christian upbringing and concerns about identity. If it appealed to religious notions of the soul, however, it also served as something of a Trojan horse, for the

---

[63] As Diehl dramatically summarizes, "In Humboldt's elevation of Wolf as the model for his new University of Berlin there is a kind of suicide of humanism, a humanism for which Nietzsche, the last philologist, mourned." Diehl 1978: x. For how and why Nietzsche might have done so, see Chapters 12 and 13.
[64] See Chapter 12, Section 2.
[65] For a skeptical yet appreciative presentation of Humboldt's contribution see Fallon 1980: 11–14, 27–28.
[66] See Jeismann 1990: 317–345.   [67] McClelland 1980: 21.   [68] See Chapter 12, Section 2.

Humboldtian ideal was essentially secular and, while not inimical to religion, did not demand any specific reference to God. The allure of this crypto-pagan vision would have been the more insidious because it was internalized almost subconsciously. For nineteenth-century German children, particularly those of Nietzsche's social class, the benefits of *Bildung* were part of the air they breathed, as implicit and taken for granted as the tenets of the Christian faith. As discussed earlier, the very class to which Nietzsche belonged would later be referred to as *Bildungsbürgertum*[69] (cultivated middle class), and it would have seemed his social duty to develop the self through immersion in the classics. The surprise is not that he would have embraced this ethos but that he managed to distance himself from it at all. Nietzsche would struggle with the meaning and uses of education all his life, but the initial terms of this inquiry were instilled at Pforta. Like Naumburg it would prove an environment which he could never fully escape.

3

Nietzsche spent six years at Schulpforte, only two less than he did at Naumburg, yet the situations were very different. In the town he had been a child who was expected to do as he was told. At boarding school he encountered even more regulation, but he no longer had his mother looking over his shoulder, a particularly intimate form of surveillance, which he may have wished to escape. For all his apparent docility, Nietzsche liked to have his way, and he seems to have believed that as the last surviving male in the family it fell to him to take charge of his own development. He therefore tended to play down his mother's role, a tactic probably made easier because of Franziska's reduced status among her in-laws. When he reviewed his life in his early twenties, he would write that, being fatherless, "the main points of my upbringing [*Erziehung*] had been left to me,"[70] a statement which might have amused the woman who reared him through early adolescence.

If Nietzsche's statement overlooks his mother's self-sacrificial contributions to his welfare, it does foreground an important truth. From an intellectual and artistic point of view he had long outgrown her powers of comprehension. After his humble and comparatively unassisted beginnings in a dark apartment and the burgher school, he had achieved formidable advances in both music and poetry and made himself an

---

[69] See Chapter 2, Section 3.   [70] KGW I–5: 52.

honored guest in the home of two of his town's more prestigious families. Soon he would turn his attention to intellectual matters and become an outstanding student. His mother might introduce him to these worlds, but she could not help him flourish there, and although his friends contributed, their assistance could not account for the quality of his achievements, which in the arts, at least, rivaled their own.[71] Nietzsche had himself to thank for the development of his talents, and perhaps for this reason he was proud to note that when transferring to Pforta, his mother allowed him veto power: he could have refused.[72]

That Franziska allowed her son final say on the transfer may explain why Nietzsche so readily embraced the school. If its rigors infringed on his freedom far more overtly than she ever did, he could at least remember that enrollment there had been his choice. He may have also hoped that one of the faculty might provide kinds of guidance that he had never received. If so, he was disappointed. As his sister rightly observed,[73] Nietzsche's teachers would have considered it unprofessional to take more than general interest in any particular student. The single possible exception was his tutor Robert Buddensieg, the faculty member whose specific duty it was to advise the boys under his care. Buddensieg, who was forty-one when Nietzsche first met him, was not only the school's assistant pastor but a clergyman far more enterprising and dutiful than the principal pastor, who was generally regarded as lax.[74] Most biographers portray Nietzsche as very fond of his tutor. While there is no reason to doubt this, there is little evidence that it is true either.[75] Judging from Nietzsche's notebooks and letters, he seems to have regarded the man as he did most adults, as one more authority figure whose existence he accepted with neither enthusiasm nor overt resistance. Nonetheless, Buddensieg was in charge of his care and would have been the first person he would approach when he needed assistance.

A far more stimulating companion for the boy was his prefect Oskar Krämer, a nineteen-year-old in his final year at the school, whom Nietzsche frequently took to Naumburg to visit his mother. Nietzsche seems both to have admired and genuinely liked Krämer, and the latter's name recurs repeatedly in his letters.[76] Unfortunately, this helpful young man graduated at the end of Nietzsche's first year, and he was replaced by

---

[71] "Rivaled" because to make a judgment, one would have to compare the poems and compositions written by Wilhelm and Gustav with those produced by Nietzsche.
[72] KGW I-2; 263.   [73] Förster-Nietzsche 1912: 102.
[74] Bohley 2007: 91–92, 94–97, 123–126, 166.   [75] See Chapter 7, Section 3.
[76] See his praise in his notebooks: KGW I-2: 99–100.

Richard Braune, whose appointment the boy initially protested. In one of his notebook entries Nietzsche indicates that Braune was despised by most of the student body, and Nietzsche feared that, as the latter's protégé, he would suffer a loss of prestige as well.[77] To his chagrin, however, Braune had asked Franziska's approval beforehand, and the mother, knowing nothing of student politics, gave the unpopular boy her blessing.[78] Braune was apparently Nietzsche's prefect for two years, until he graduated in the spring of 1861. Aside from Nietzsche's protests at the beginning of their relationship, there is no evidence of tension, and Nietzsche frequently brought Braune and his younger brother home to meet his mother. Nonetheless, it is unlikely that he responded with the respect and admiration he had awarded Krämer.

His tutor apart, Nietzsche seems to have had little personal contact with faculty, and the school's authoritarian culture did not encourage the nurturance he craved. Four years after graduation he would account for this in terms which show how much he longed for a paternal figure. "My father ... died all too soon; I lacked the strict and superior guidance of a masculine intellect. When as a boy I came to Schulpforte, I got to know only a surrogate for fatherly upbringing, the uniform discipline of a regulated school. But just this almost military coercion which, because it is supposed to work on the masses, treats the individual coolly and superficially, led me back to myself again."[79] Except for the reference to "the strict and superior guidance of a masculine intellect," an evaluation which might raise eyebrows in this century, Nietzsche's analysis seems insightful and just. It also explains why – however much he might admire Schulpforte – he was ultimately thrown back on his own resources. Bereft of family, friends, or even favorably disposed teachers, he must have been a grim boy indeed as he attended to his lessons and tried to apply himself to schoolwork in which at the beginning he had little genuine interest.

Amazingly, he did not fail but lifted himself from lackluster performance to exceptional achievements. This might not have been surprising had he been temperamentally inclined toward scholarship. Nietzsche's first inclinations, however, were toward poetry and music, and he would always chafe at the drudgery, impersonality, and dryness of imposed learning and research. A turning point in this regard occurred near the beginning of his

---

[77] KGW I-2: 119. There were two Braune brothers, Richard and Alexis. Nietzsche called them "Braune I" and "Braune II."
[78] Rosmiarek *et al.* 2003: 329–330.   [79] KGW I-5: 52.

second year at Pforta. In the months before, he had several times considered issues of personal discipline – whether it was better to take life lightly or to buckle down to duty and accomplish something worthwhile, and in general, how most effectively to use his school years.[80] His fifteenth birthday (October 15, 1859) impressed on him a sense of loss and vanishing opportunity: "Time goes like the roses of spring and pleasure like the foam of the brook," he wrote.[81] This was the theme which had inspired his first autobiography, and it was probably with anxiety that he turned to a gift from his Aunt Rosalie, a biography of Alexander von Humboldt, the recently deceased scientist, explorer, and Wilhelm's younger brother.[82] This book seems to have enflamed Nietzsche's imagination and inspired in him for the first time a love of learning for its own sake. "A general drive to knowledge, to universal learning has seized me," he recorded, adding, "Humboldt has awakened this feeling in me. May it be as enduring as my dedication to poetry!" He followed with a biographical sketch, describing the various "hobby horses" that had absorbed him in childhood, and he listed thirty-six subjects which have interested him since. At the close he exclaimed, "Great is the field of knowledge, endless the search for truth!" and, as a pious boy, he added, "And over everything religion, the fundament of all knowledge!"[83]

This ecstatic affirmation could have been a momentary effusion, a passing mood to which the boy did not return. Instead, Nietzsche held his course and six months later was made Primus (first in his class), an honor he would receive at least three (and probably four) more times at Pforta.[84] From this time forward, an abiding interest in scholarship vied with his joy in music and literature as the primary appetite of his youthful life. Eventually, this would introduce complications, for while poetry and music were compatible and even synergistic, the arts and scholarship did not cohabit quite so productively. It would take Nietzsche several years before he became aware of these implications, however, and in the interim he pursued his new passion in happy innocence, bringing his grades to the level of his abilities.[85]

---

[80] KGW I-2: 109–110, 125.   [81] KGW I-2: 134.   [82] Klencke 1851. See KSAB I: 82.
[83] KGW I-2: 134–136. Schmidt has analyzed this journal entry at length: Schmidt 1991–1994 III: 457–471.
[84] According to Schmidt, the number of students Nietzsche would have to surpass was nineteen. Schmidt 1991–1994 III: 486. Schmidt attributes the timing of this honor to Nietzsche's recognition that he must take his fate in his own hands after the death of his grandfather. For the number of times Nietzsche became Primus, see n. 89.
[85] For the rise in Nietzsche's grades, see Brobjer 1999: 311. Later Nietzsche would bewail that his early tendency to scatter his energies lasted until his fifteenth year, an age which corresponds with his reading of the Humboldt biography. KGW I-3: 418.

Interestingly, this new focus – perhaps because it introduced into his psyche fissures which did not exist before – awakened Nietzsche to the need for self-regulation. He was particularly troubled by one defect, a vice the more insidious since it masqueraded as a sterling virtue. This characteristic makes its first extended appearance in the journal entry just discussed. "A general drive to knowledge, to universal learning has seized me," he recorded, listing, as stated, thirty-six areas he found of interest. Inevitably when compiling that list, its sheer multiplicity began to perplex him. He was not sure how these subjects cohered, and he cast about for ways to organize them effectively. In subsequent years this "drive to ... universal learning" began to seem somewhat sinister, as though in pursuing so many subjects he was dispersing the self and frittering away time and opportunity like an educational dilettante. Accordingly, Nietzsche began to interpret his pursuit of multiple interests as a kind of intellectual dispersion which better supervision, the kind provided by a father, should have forestalled. Describing the consequences of Ludwig's death, he would write, "It was possibly a disadvantage that my entire development from then on was not overseen by a male eye, but that curiosity, maybe also a thirst for knowledge, introduced in the greatest disorder the most diverse educational subject matters ... bewildering a young intellect scarcely out of the nest, and, above all, jeopardizing the foundation of solid learning."[86] This concern would lead to one of the most significant decisions in his life.[87]

4

A "drive to ... universal learning" might seem questionable to Nietzsche, but it had its uses at school. As already mentioned, the new student took only a few months to emerge from anonymity and to impress his teachers. By Easter in his second school year, he was made Primus,[88] a title which indicates not just that he was academically at the top of his class but that he would be the one responsible for keeping order in his cohort when the teacher was away. In succeeding years he was to become Primus several more times[89] and to earn

---

[86] KGW I-3: 418.   [87] See Chapter 8, Section 5.
[88] Benders *et al* 2000: 65. Nietzsche himself never mentions this honor, which is odd, considering that on later occasions he writes a great deal about the duties to which his status obliges him.
[89] There is general consensus (with a few controversies) as to when Nietzsche was made Primus. See, for example, Brobjer 2001b: 328. Nietzsche's letters show him as receiving this honor in April 1860, October 1860, April 1861, then, after a year's gap, in October 1862. He was also clearly made Primus in April 1863 since he lost this position due to misbehavior. (See Chapter 7, Section 6.) These would correspond to his fourth, fifth, sixth, ninth, and tenth terms, which matches some but not all of Brobjer's suggestions. See also Hödl 2009: 145, n. 362.

Soul-building: the theory

three "firsts,"[90] grades so unusually high that several years could pass before they were duplicated. Teachers began to discuss him outside of class, and in his sixth year, an instructor could enthuse in private about one of his essays.[91]

Apart from these scholastic accomplishments and on the side, Nietzsche pursued his artistic ambitions, turning out lyrics, plays, and fiction as well as numerous musical works. If fellow students admired these activities, however, the faculty seems to have been silent. According to Wilamowitz, the school neglected the arts,[92] and Nietzsche's creative efforts appear to have created little stir among the masters. Since he probably identified these artistic achievements with his very sense of self, his initial enthusiasm for that institution began to falter. Six months after arrival, he gave way at last to homesickness and began to develop a passionate desire for the freedom of vacations and semester breaks. His first Easter vacation seems to have brought this to a head, and he wrote Wilhelm at their close, "You won't believe how terribly different it is when one's family and school are not in the same place. At the end of holidays you leave behind only pleasant relaxations and easygoing amusements. I, however, sever myself for a considerable time from house, family, and their joys to reenter an alien environment."[93] A year later, his wounds still unhealed, he would write, more poetically, "Our life at Pforta is nothing but constant remembrance and hope."[94]

As might be expected, homesickness played a role in poems written about this time, but in these Nietzsche goes straight to the point. Ultimately it is not Naumburg he misses, but the vanished world of Röcken, that largely imagined paradise, which now lay a decade behind. As has already been noted, many of Nietzsche's lyrics celebrate nature. Increasingly, however, forests, meadows, and the sounds of evening began to remind him of the countryside paternal household, the "father's house" (*Vaterhaus*), which was missing in his world. As summer neared and with it a visit to the Oehler household close to Röcken, the pace seemed to quicken and the *Vaterhaus* became more immediate and tangible: "Home! Home!" he cried, and he wrote, "My heart rushes jubilantly toward home."[95] Yet confrontation with the actual grave and rectory at Röcken seems to have left him unsatisfied, and he found himself driven back either to the woods and, more darkly, to the consideration that all

---

[90] The number of "firsts" Nietzsche received is unclear, but there seem to have been three: for essays on Mithradates and Cicero (KSAB I: 209) and for the Ermanarich study from 1863. Wilamowitz-Moellendorff 1928: 71.
[91] Gilman and Reichenbach 1981: 47. [92] Wilamowitz-Moellendorff 1928: 74, 66.
[93] KSAB I: 59. [94] KSAB I: 92. [95] KGW I-2: 77, 78.

human beings are inherently homeless and will remain so until they enter their true abode, heaven. Nietzsche was clearly becoming aware that feelings deeper than nostalgia lay behind this search for home.

Meanwhile, childhood is an evanescent state, and the world of Nietzsche's past was beginning to disappear. His family home was often occupied by relatives – and eventually strangers – as his mother began to rent out rooms. Elisabeth would soon relocate for several months to attend a girls' school in Dresden. To cap it all, an event occurred which put an end to an entire phase of boyhood. In August 1860, Franziska's father David Oehler had celebrated his seventy-second birthday at the family farm in Pobles. As mentioned, this was the occasion that apparently inspired so many poems about home and the *Vaterhaus*, and in a birthday poem Nietzsche explicitly saluted the recovery of his birthplace and "the otherwise vanished traces of childhood."[96] Such words would prove ironic, for that very autumn David Oehler fell ill, and on December 17, 1859, he died, apparently from influenza, forcing his family to vacate the premises.

His grandfather's death surely disturbed Nietzsche, if only because the man was probably the nearest to a father figure that he had known. His letters, however, are largely silent on the subject, and he may have shown his disturbance in a more indirect way.[97] Five days into January he found himself in the school infirmary with a severe cough, and he would remain there for nearly two weeks.[98] This was not his first visit to the sick ward, and he would become a familiar figure there during his years at Pforta. While the doctor could rarely come up with a satisfactory diagnosis, Nietzsche's chronic symptoms – rheumatism, chills, and excruciating headaches associated with his eyes – incapacitated him for weeks at a time. It is difficult to believe that Nietzsche's illness did not in this case have a psychogenic dimension. The administration at Pforta frowned on malingering, and Dr. Zimmermann, the resident physician, cast a practiced eye on boys who reported to the infirmary. Nonetheless, illnesses to which the boy was in any case susceptible were likely to come crashing through in the aftermath of a psychological shock. Shortly after the putatively mad and deposed Friedrich Wilhelm IV died in January 1861, Nietzsche fell so ill with rheumatic fever that he was put in bed for nearly six weeks.[99]

Meanwhile, Pastor Oehler's death brought with it the same practical consequence that had followed on the death of Nietzsche's father eleven

---

[96] KGW I-2: 93–95.   [97] He mentions it only once, in KSAB I: 89.   [98] Volz 1990: 329.
[99] Volz 1990: 329.

years before. The rectory had to be vacated, the home relinquished. With the loss of the country house at Pobles, the Nietzsches lost as well easy access to Röcken, which lay a wagon ride away. This was the end of regular visits to Ludwig's grave, and the fifteen-year-old Nietzsche must have reflected that with his grandfather's death, he had lost his *Vaterhaus* a second time. There is a blank in his notebooks from February 1860 to the following August, and private thoughts during the spring are unknown. Of course, as Primus, Nietzsche was very busy, but he may also have been in the grips of a contradiction which he silently resolved. If Nietzsche did not so much as mention his grandfather's death in his notebooks, two entries register its effects. The first is almost comical and reflects a school assignment. At the very time he was losing his second rural home Nietzsche was asked to write an essay entitled, "Is it better to live in the city or the country?"[100] (He obviously preferred the second.) More significantly, he wrote five poems for his mother, whose birthday would take place on February 2, a little over a month after his grandfather's (her father's) death. The ultimate effect of this collection is double-edged, for although all the poems deal with sorrow and loss, some have a Christian happy ending whereas others are pitilessly insightful. The first poem begins:

> From afar, from afar
> Shine my life's stars
> And with sorrow-laden glance
> I look upon my former happiness.

From this sad beginning the boy conjures up an unconvincing happy ending, as he consoles himself with "eternal joys." But the poem does not stop with this cliché. Immediately following and just as it seems to have ended, Nietzsche undercuts its banality with an Orphean pendant that jars violently with all that preceded:

> I see Charon's bark swaying —
> With the strings of the golden lyre
> I call again those who have sunk beneath,
> And they come near and surround me
> With their magical light.
> I try to seize them – they turn pale
> And I must let them sink again –
> My hope has failed![101]

---

[100] KGW I-2: 179–180.
[101] KGW I-2: 180–181. This translation is clumsily literal and does not attempt to render the poetically indispensable rhyme structure.

The explicit invocation of pagan Hades might come as a surprise in this poem, coming as it does on the heels of an implicitly Christian vision of eternal peace. More disturbingly, Nietzsche moves from nostalgia to recognition of the finality of death. There will be no resurrection here and, failing that, there can be no relief through the contemplation of "eternal joys." Dead is dead: the conclusion is pitiless and to the point. ("My hope has failed!") It should be remembered that David Oehler was the fourth close family member to pass away in the fifteen years of the boy's existence and that three of these departures (those of Oehler, Ludwig, and Erdmuthe Nietzsche) had led directly to the loss of a home. Any path backward, any effort to recover the past, was therefore foreclosed. If notebook entries from February through July were still extant, it might be possible to follow Nietzsche's struggle with this revelation. Nonetheless, the result is clear. Only twice more while at Schulpforte would he write poems about his father's grave at Röcken.[102] With those exceptions, such thematics were now closed.

With this abandonment Nietzsche seems to have drawn a stern but creative corollary. If the futility of homesickness had just been revealed, then he could not go back and should consider that option closed. "I prefer the past to the present; but I believe in a better future," he would write;[103] and the struggle to devise a new path began to dominate his horizon. It is striking that in the aftermath of his grandfather's death, when he had been so ill and study must have been difficult, he again became Primus. However bitterly he may have regretted his incarceration at boarding school, he also recognized that he could learn and grow there. The world he had known was vanishing, and the way forward now seemed to lie with the kindly fathers at Schulpforte.

---

[102] KGW I-2: 225–226, 354–356. Nietzsche does address another poem to his father (324–325), but the tone is more prayerful than sentimental, and there is no mention of graves.
[103] KGW I-2: 444.

CHAPTER 6

The turn to naturalism

> *We intend to hold ourselves responsible for our existence; consequently we also want to submit to our being's true steersmen and not allow our life to seem a thoughtless accident.*[1]

I

It is easy to imagine Nietzsche as alone at Pforta. His shyness, his lack of athleticism, his cultivation of the arts and scholarship at the expense of more popular topics, must all have ensured that he would never be a social success or a paragon for the other boys. At the same time his letters and journal entries teem with the names of associates and casual friends, as might be expected in such tight and intimate circumstances. He lived with classmates twenty-four hours a day and under every condition from the intimacy of the dormitory to the intellectual spheres of the classroom and the shared activities of eating and athletics. Inevitably, he would bond with some of them provisionally and within a specific context. Nonetheless, if any of these relationships blossomed into sustained friendship, the memory has not been preserved. So far as is now known, during the first year and a half of his stay at Schulpforte Nietzsche's fellow students were at most companions.

Meanwhile, in the autumn of 1859 a student arrived who was new to the school but allowed to enter in the same grade as Nietzsche (second year). Paul Deussen had traveled from Prussian territory near the Rhine, a very different culture from Prussian Thuringia, and he was made to feel that difference. It is helpful to examine some of the ways he did not fit in, for they throw into relief the milieu in which Nietzsche was himself immersed and show that certain characteristics which might appear personal – a concern for decorum, a disdain for the nonchalant – may not have been personal to Nietzsche but expected behavior within his culture and class.

[1] UO III: 1; KSA I: 339.

115

For a start, the very terms of Deussen's entry were ignominious. He had been raised on what Thuringians considered the wrong catechism, that of Heidelberg, which was Calvinist, whereas the mostly Saxon and Thuringian boys of Pforta had been reared on the Lutheran. During his qualifying examination young Deussen's ignorance of the appropriate religious text so irritated Inspector Niese, the principal chaplain at Schulpforte, that he dismissed the boy contemptuously; and Deussen, who claimed that he had heretofore been at the top of the third year class, was remanded to the bottom of the second. Already hampered by this inauspicious entry, he alienated his classmates further by assuming the jokey bonhomie with which he had grown up on the Rhine. The Pforta boys did not appreciate this sense of humor, which they could only see as buffoonery, and they called him brazen and cheeky. (Symptomatically, when his class performed "A midsummer's night's dream," Deussen played Bottom, the play's principal clown.)[2] Although the newcomer's grades up to this time had been superlative, he now saw them plummet.[3] Academically demeaned, snubbed by his fellows, he wandered miserably, searching for footing in this deeply uncongenial environment.

Deussen writes that his initial hopes of making friends with Nietzsche were disappointed,[4] but eventually, the boys did grow closer, possibly because both felt alien at Schulpforte but also because both loved their studies. According to Deussen, a shared appreciation for the lyrics of Anacreon, as well as for the comparatively easy Greek in which they were written, united the pair, and they began to recite the poems aloud on shared walks. Eventually, they pledged friendship (and the right to address one another with the familiar "*du*") in a pact, sealed with the mutual taking of some snuff that Deussen had concealed in his trunk. Deussen suggests that the two boys clung to one another with the relief of outsiders who had at last found someone to talk to. "In those days at Pforta," he recalled, "we understood one another completely ... Often our thoughts would trail off into obscurity, and when words failed, we would look in one another's eyes and one would say to the other, 'We both understand.'" Deussen could sympathize with Nietzsche's isolation the more because he had suffered from it himself. "When I now contemplate the venerable pastors, teachers, doctors, officers, architects, etc., into which our comrades of that time developed" he wrote, "I can understand that most of them even then lacked

---

[2] Feldhoff 2008: 39.
[3] Deussen 1922: 62–63, 68. For simplicity the German school years, Untertertia, Obertertia, Untersecunda, etc. have been translated "first year," "second year," and so on.
[4] Deussen 1901: 3. For English translation, see Gilman 1987: 10.

the sensitivity to understand a Nietzsche. But what would have become of me without him, I find difficult to say."[5]

Touching as Deussen's remembrances may be, the association may have been more one-sided than he recalled. Of the two boys, Nietzsche was far less in need of companionship. Deussen had only Nietzsche as a friend, whereas the latter had Wilhelm and Gustav whom he saw frequently, and even at Pforta he was not quite the outcast that the Rhineland boy might be. Further, Deussen's family with its nurturance and comforts lay hundreds of kilometers away, whereas Nietzsche's was as close as half an hour's walk on Sundays. Significantly, Nietzsche scarcely mentions this putative friend either in journal entries or letters from Schulpforte with the exception of occasional lists of classmates and three bits of doggerel which mock him.[6] Further, although Nietzsche frequently invited fellow students to join him on his weekend jaunts, he seems never once to have introduced Deussen to his family or town friends until the end of their stay at Pforta, when he invited him to spend post-graduation time at his home. (Förster-Nietzsche seems unaware that the friendship began any earlier than her brother's final year at school.)[7] It is possible that Nietzsche, who was always sensitive to social tone, was embarrassed by Deussen's awkwardness. Also, he had interests that the other boy could not share. Deussen, for example, showed little interest in any of the arts except literature, and since these were close to Nietzsche's heart, the newer boy must have appeared limited to his friend, who continued to pine for his more sophisticated comrades in Naumburg.

In the summer of 1860 Nietzsche conceived a scheme that reunited him with Wilhelm and Gustav and contributed significantly to the cultural development of all three. During a visit to his Uncle Edmund in Gorenzen, where Wilhelm joined him, Nietzsche proposed that the two form a society

---

[5] Deussen 1901: 3–6, 9, 8. Modified from the English translation in Gilman 1987: 13–14.
[6] KGW I-2: 304–305, 341–344. The doggerel printed in KGW I-3: 76 was probably written for Deussen, although his name does not appear in it. For examples of apparently innocuous entries see KGW I-2: 311; KGW I-3: 20, 24.
[7] Förster-Nietzsche 1895: I, 175. Nietzsche seemed to have had distinct sets of friends at Pforta. Some (the Braunes, Krämer, Theodor Schenk) were formal or imposed (Schenk was the son of an old friend of Ludwig's), and these he introduced to his family. Others (Granier, Stöckert, Meyer) were much more intimate, as evidenced by an interchange of literary works. None of this second group seem to have been introduced to his family, possibly because all were rebellious and would have aroused the vigilant Franziska's concerns. Finally, Nietzsche had friends that were merely associates – young men with whom he was thrown together a great deal but to whom he appeared otherwise indifferent (Bodenstein, Hempel). The name Gersdorff does not surface at all in his Pforta papers, as scarcely does Deussen. By contrast, no name appears so frequently – or at times so significantly – as that of Georg Stöckert. See, for example, Hödl 1994b: 377. For more on Nietzsche's friends at Schulpforte, see Chapter 7, Section 5.

in which they would submit literary papers for one another's inspection and critique. After spirited discussion, which suggests that relationships among the boys were not always unclouded, the two agreed to extend their subject matter to musical projects, and Gustav was invited too. The club, which they named Germania, was basically what today might be called a cultural support group. Members pooled dues to purchase educational and artistic works, and each would contribute a monthly creative or scholarly piece that the others would critique. Germania might seem an unrealistic endeavor – three adolescent boys turning in a serious work written just for themselves every thirty days – but it is a tribute to the ambition and determination of all that it survived for four years and for the first twenty-one months worked as planned, all three boys (with occasional lapses) turning in significant creative or educational endeavors on schedule.[8]

2

If 1860 was largely a placid year for Nietzsche, the year following proved to be among the most pivotal of his youth. It opened with a political event. On January 2, the supposedly mad Friedrich Wilhelm IV died, and his brother succeeded officially to the throne as Wilhelm I. Since there had been a transitional period of a little over two years, the shift was less dramatic politically than it might have been. For Nietzsche, however, the loss must have been significant. Having shared the unfortunate king's name and birthday, he had been linked with that ruler throughout childhood, a connection foregrounded by Wilhelm as recently as October, when he wrote that when celebrating his birthday he should "occasionally remember your name- and birthday-brother, the poor king in Sans-Souci!"[9] With the departure of this sidelined monarch, there vanished the last of the father figures from Nietzsche's childhood. He does not mention the event in letters, but two weeks after the event he fell so sick that he was under medical supervision for nearly a month and a half (with occasional breaks). Towards the end of his stay in the dispensary he found the medical quarters crowded due to a number boys arriving with rubella, and he was granted permission to convalesce in Naumburg, presumably either to clear a bed or to avoid infection. During early 1861 an aura of

---

[8] The results are listed in KGW I-2: 480–483. After the first two years only Nietzsche continued to contribute.
[9] KGB I-1: 342.

mortality hung over the school, for after the epidemic of rubella, there followed an outbreak of measles, from which one student died. During the first three years of Nietzsche's stay, three students, including the rector's son, would succumb to various illnesses.[10]

These, however, were merely subsidiary, informing circumstances. For Nietzsche the greatest external event of 1861 occurred on March 10 when he underwent the sacrament of Confirmation, an event that had required six months of instruction in the catechism. As the ceremony neared, the sixteen-year-old received letters and gifts from relatives and from his father's friends, all of whom counseled him to follow the example bequeathed by his parentage and tradition. "May Confirmation lead you to become like your father," one wrote, while another effused, "You are the very image of your father and . . . you will certainly strive to become more and more like him." While such advice probably reflected the embarrassment of distant acquaintances trying to write to a boy they scarcely knew, the letters highlight the theme of identity, which, insofar as it calls for a declaration of lifelong commitment, is also the burden of Confirmation. Who was Friedrich Nietzsche, and to what extent did he really want to emulate the unknown, much mythologized Ludwig? An associated event would have raised similar issues. Confirmation called for a photograph to be taken. This is the first extant full portrait of Nietzsche and probably the first that he had ever seen; and for a self-conscious adolescent the effigy must have given rise to reflections, even if the picture was unflattering. Feet apart and leaning against a plinth, with right hand thrust inside his coat like Napoleon, he resembled countless adolescents caught transfixed in the ceremony of the yearbook photo. Nietzsche acknowledged the picture's homelier aspects in a letter to his mother and sister: "My stance is hunched, my feet somewhat crooked, and my hand looks like a dumpling." Despite such misgivings, he seemed more pleased than chagrinned and asked specifically who would receive a copy.[11]

Confirmation also raised the issue of Nietzsche's commitment to Christianity. According to Deussen his friend ardently embraced the religious aspects of the occasion, taking Communion and even Confession,[12] a rite repugnant to some Lutherans, including Deussen, who after one more attempt, elected never to repeat the process.[13]

---

[10] For outbreaks of rubella and measles: KSAB I: 147, 154, 157. For deaths: KSAB I: 120, 157, 186.
[11] KSAB I: 150.
[12] According to Pernet 1989: 142, n. 108, the requirement that students who receive Communion confess their sins beforehand was upheld until 1880. See Bohley 2007: 131–132.
[13] Deussen 1922: 74–75; Pernet 1989: 142, n. 108.

Deussen further records that the two boys seemed prey to a delirium of piety, which he conjured up powerfully years later. "As the confirmants walked to the altar in pairs to receive the consecration on their knees, Nietzsche and I, as closest friends, knelt side by side. I still remember very well the holy, ecstatic mood that filled us ... We would have been quite ready to die immediately to be with Christ, and all our thoughts, feelings and actions were irradiated with a superterrestial joy."[14]

Deussen recorded this forty years after the events, and he may have exaggerated his friend's religious fervor. Nietzsche himself scarcely mentions his Confirmation in letters, and when he does, it is in passing as one event among others. On the surface he seems to have given the ceremony no thought whatever. Nonetheless, one aspect of Nietzsche's Christianity makes Deussen's account credible. Nietzsche had never seemed interested in dogmatics and, unlike his father, never evidenced significant fear of God or concern that his personal behavior might be sinful. The one place Nietzsche addressed religion frequently and fervently was in music and poetry. While most of his verse dealing with religious themes seems more dutiful than convincing, such writing does evince a religious spell to which he was clearly susceptible. One might surmise that religion infected him in the very spheres to which he was most vulnerable – in the imagination and the arts. If he never speaks of dogma and rarely of personal adherence to religious principles, he seems to have found a place for Christian mythology exactly where it would most entrance him and in the way that Deussen describes in his memoir: as a spell, an imaginative transport, a rapture in which he gives himself up to a vision. Whether such imaginative delight was sufficient to sustain a lifelong faith is questionable, but Nietzsche could yield to it on occasion, and such effusions could have left impressions that were misleading. The state Deussen observed might be as evanescent as a dream.

3

The theme surfaces at this point because Deussen suggests that after Confirmation the faith of both adolescents began to weaken. Deussen suggested that this was due to their academic studies. "[Our fervor] was undermined unnoticeably by the excellent historical-critical method in which the older students were trained in Pforta, and which quite spontaneously was applied to the biblical field, for example when Steinhart in the

---

[14] Deussen 1901: 4. For English translation, see Gilman 1987: 10.

Hebrew class at sixth-year level explained the Forty-Fifth Psalm completely as a secular wedding song."[15] Such an account should be treated with caution. The Steinhart lecture occurred during Nietzsche's final year at Schulpforte, and his Confirmation took place during his third. Three years, a very long time in the life of an adolescent, intervened between one event and the other.

Further, although there is a surface plausibility to Deussen's statement, he does not explain why "the excellent historical-critical method" should have necessarily had a secularizing effect. Readers who today try to investigate the nature of this method will find that it was frequently invoked in the nineteenth century, but it seems to have had different meanings to different practitioners and is accordingly difficult to define.[16] Some scholars trace its origins as far back as the late Middle Ages,[17] but biblical research first became prominent and established in the Renaissance and Reformation. At that time scholars recognized that, however hallowed the scriptures' original inspiration, the texts must afterwards have been subject to the same vicissitudes suffered by any other book. Bibles too had been prey to mistakes made in copying and to the erroneous conflation of quite different documents, not to mention "corrections" made by well-meaning clerics. Accordingly, philologists took it upon themselves – often at personal cost, for their efforts were not always appreciated – to examine records and to produce superior texts. Inevitably they sometimes touched on sensitive matters, such as the authenticity of single sentences on which dogmatic structures had been built.[18] Their stress, however, was on ad hoc correction rather than broader matters of hermeneutics or systematics. During the early- to mid-eighteenth century, these efforts began slowly to be codified into principles, and a reliance on historical studies gained influence. One of the more important of these theorists, Johann August Ernesti, served as a mentor to Friedrich August Ludwig Nietzsche, the beleaguered superintendent with whom this book began. Long before the latter had raised his first family and married Erdmuthe, he had been a student of philology and studied with Ernesti. Later he had written a monograph concerning *2 Peter*,[19] in which he applied his teacher's principles. Thus, although Nietzsche seems not have been aware of it, the historical-critical method was part of his family heritage.

---

[15] Deussen 1901: 4. For English translation, see Gilman 1987: 11.
[16] This account is based on the following: Baird 1992; Frei 1974; Maier 1977; Neill 1964; Timpanaro 2005; Zimmermann 1967; Krentz 1975; Law 2012; Hahn and Wiker 2013.
[17] Hahn and Wiker 2013: 17–59; Law 2012: 26–32.
[18] The reference is to the Johannine Comma. Erdman 2005: 80–82.   [19] Pernet 1989: 38–40.

Beginning in the late eighteenth century, a new and more controversial approach gained ground. Noting that the Bible had been assembled somewhat haphazardly, Johann Salomo Semler drew a distinction between the word of God and scriptures. Not all books of the Bible qualified as revelation, he declared; some had been superadded. Semler himself is not so important in this very brief synopsis, for he introduced his reasoning into a carefully wrought theory of the uses and limits of religion and the primacy of Christ, thereby embedding philology in theological principles.[20] However, by appealing to historical rather than doctrinal standards when evaluating scripture, he opened the way for other philologists to take this practice further and in the process to distance themselves from the demands of the church.

Rather than describe the vicissitudes of this approach through the nineteenth century, it is best to pause and state that, viewed from outside philology, the historical-critical method was less important for how it worked positively than for what it excluded, namely, the invocation of miracles or divine guidance as principles of explanation. Practitioners of the method employed a thoroughgoing naturalism, removing from consideration any transcendent significance of the works in question. Needless to say, their representatives at Schulpforte still regarded these books as the word of God, and that is how they would present them to students. Nonetheless, the sheer professionalism of scholarly methods might introduce a skeptical distance, and this could make an attitude of reverence more difficult to maintain.

It bears saying that the reference to philological method comes from Deussen alone. In letters and journals written at the time Nietzsche never cites Biblical scholarship as affecting his faith, nor, with one signal exception which will be discussed at the end of this chapter, does he indicate that his religious beliefs wavered during this period.[21] Of course, one should not expect to find such things recorded in notebooks that could be seized and read by authorities and by his mother. Nonetheless, Deussen is surely right in at least one respect. Nietzsche did begin to question his religion in the aftermath of his Confirmation, if not before. If he left few explicit musings, the origin and development of the crisis is visible in a series of essays he composed in the spring of 1861 – composed, indeed, at the very time of his Confirmation. As will be seen, these point toward a general secularization

---

[20] Baird 1992 I: 117–127.
[21] In his later works Nietzsche does, of course, tend to regard the practice of philology as incompatible with religious attitudes. See UO II: 7; KSA I: 296–297. He makes no such suggestions prior to his departure for Basel, however.

of his outlook and a consequent insistence on naturalistic explanation. The historical-critical method, it appears, was neither overriding nor negligible; it was one of several approaches that nudged the budding scholar in a particular direction. Nietzsche's entire universe of explanation became naturalistic during 1861 and would continue in this tendency in the period that followed. If Steinhart's lecture in his senior year served as a symbolic capstone, it consummated a process begun long before.

4

Nietzsche's changing attitudes through the year are best charted through papers he turned in to classes and lectures he addressed to Germania. These come directly from his pen, and although such writings rarely treat Christianity directly, they focus on an issue that has religious implications and that replicates the problem posed by the historical-critical method. Throughout this period, Nietzsche considers the adequacy of naturalistic explanations, as opposed to those that invoke supernatural intervention.

Around March 5, 1861, that is, immediately before his Confirmation (March 10) and at the very time Deussen saw him as imbued with religious fervor, Nietzsche began a short anthropological essay called "Hunters and fishers" for his German class.[22] While the paper he submitted no longer exists, a draft is preserved, and in it he dwells at length on the cultural limitations of prehistoric communities, particularly those that lived by the activities in question. Nietzsche's account is brutal and cruel and recounts at length the barbarism of an era when, he speculates, a wife was a slave, a child a serf, and sons rejoiced when their fathers weakened so that they could take their place. (In the process, he says, they ate them.)[23] Yet as a subsequent essay will suggest, these gruesome details are secondary to a more fundamental consideration. What actually interests Nietzsche is how these early, brutal humans could find the inspiration and means to develop the arts and moral sophistication enjoyed by later generations when they were themselves so primitive. How could this be done through natural means alone and without divine intervention? No answer to this question is given in the essay.

Immediately after writing "Hunters and fishers" Nietzsche prepared a lecture for Germania entitled, "The childhood of peoples," a phrase taken from the earlier piece. This second essay is considerably longer, and the reader might suppose that it would develop and extend the themes of

---

[22] This essay can be dated to early March 1861. See KSAB I: 148.   [23] KGW I-2: 232–234.

"Hunters and fishers," and to an extent it does.[24] However, the question which lies implicit in "Hunters and fishers" – how did these primitive groups come to develop more sophisticated social, moral, and aesthetic systems? – is explicitly raised and dismissed in this work's opening paragraph. Here, Nietzsche acknowledges that he wants to avoid "dangerous speculations concerning religion and history" and that he is on uncertain ground theologically speaking.[25] As to the question itself – how brutalized human beings could develop more sophisticated cultures – he proposes two hypotheses. First, humans might originally have enjoyed a divinely endowed golden age and afterward declined into barbarism; in that case, any subsequent improvements would occur through memories of their prelapsarian state. Alternatively, one could believe that human beings somehow managed to improve their lot through their own unaided resources. This is the approach that is dangerous to religion, and the seventeen-year-old Nietzsche professes to find it implausible. Nonetheless, he does not so much reject it as put it in abeyance for the purposes of this paper. "It is neither part of my intention to decide this issue nor does it seem possible to simplify so problematic an issue. Enough. I opt for the first opinion, that human beings were at first provided with culture, that under the impress of world events and revolution they turned to barbarism, and partly then began to develop the first paths to civilization."[26] Thus, "The childhood of peoples" builds an assumption of divine endowment into its story from the beginning. What that opening paragraph makes plain, however, is that the earlier essay's exploration of a world unassisted by heavenly providence was not innocently produced. The young Nietzsche understood the religious implications and proceeded undeterred.[27]

This excursion into naturalistic explanation seems to have both disturbed and stimulated the boy. He may, of course, have tailored his presentations to meet the expectations of their designated audiences. It is unknown, for example, if the non-theistic "Hunters and fishers" was toned down in the version presented to his professors, or, correlatively, whether "The childhood of peoples" was given its religious framework because Nietzsche wished to reassure his more conservative friends. What does

---

[24] Nietzsche no longer limits himself to just those two occupational groups but considers such modes of life as shepherds, farmers (concerning whom Nietzsche would write an entire essay in 1863), and others.
[25] For an incisive exposition of this view's dangers for religion, see Strauss 1970 I: 47–48.
[26] KGW I-2: 235–243, especially 236–237.
[27] I owe this point to Hermann Josef Schmidt, Schmidt 1991–1994 III: 518 ff.

seem clear is that the boy found the non-theistic approach of "Hunters and fishers" sufficiently troubling that he struggled in subsequent papers to devise an alternative approach.

Within a month at most of writing these essays, Nietzsche commenced an autobiography, this too occasioned by a class assignment.[28] The final product is missing, but three drafts survive, and two of these must have proved sobering for this ardent self-improver.[29] In these he considers his own life in naturalistic terms, that is, he ponders what it might mean to remove the element of divine guidance. If so, can the teleological aspects of *Bildung* be upheld? Just as he asked how primitive hunters and fishers could improve if culturally and morally they were limited by their environment, so he wonders to what extent he is constricted by the world he inhabits. What if the implicit optimism of *Bildung* is an illusion and human beings grow haphazardly and at the mercy of the stimuli and depressants which their chance environment affords? What then happens to self-determination? In his 1858 autobiography he had treated his environment mostly as scenery, against which he displayed himself in action. What if the "scenery" were itself active and more causally efficacious than he realized?

In the first and by far the most speculative of the three sketches he conceives of the self as a seedbed which the environment nourishes almost by accident. Just as a plant may be warped by vagaries of the weather, so the human soul might be deformed by dependencies beyond its control. Here, like a good student of Humboldtian *Bildung*, Nietzsche conceives the self as a repository of tendencies which "externally effective circumstances" awaken. All sorts of environmental factors might serve to rouse or repress the unwitting soul and it was difficult to predict which would help and which hinder. "Favorable as well as unfortunate life conditions can therefore show themselves as both helpful and harmful, accordingly as various seeds of good and bad tendencies are awakened." Even supposedly positive nutrients, such as riches or fame, might excite disruptive longings which overwhelm other elements of character. Rich people could be undone by riches, vulnerable people by undeserved good luck. For all their supposed good fortune, certain souls, burdened by temptations they could not withstand, would find longings awakened "which laid waste to their joy

---

[28] As Bohley 1976: 311, indicates, this probably coincides with the class assignment, "Each tells his previous life." Nietzsche was clearly aware of the upcoming project by late April (KSAB I: 155). Mette states that the third and most conventional of the three "was presumably graded on 25 May 61." BAW I: 457.
[29] For the three versions, all entitled, "*Mein Lebenslauf*" (The course of my life), see KGW I-2: 255–263.

in life." It was bad enough that human beings seemed at the mercy of their environment; but worse, and especially disconcerting for someone who believed in *Bildung*, people themselves didn't always know what would help or hurt them.

Plainly the chance influence of environment is not necessarily positive, and Nietzsche goes on to wonder about the justice of this apparently capricious arrangement. In doing so, he considers the worst – that the highest aims of humanity might lie in the hands of a thoughtless and undiscriminating being (in effect, an evil god) – and dismisses this hypothesis as too awful to entertain. Nonetheless, he acknowledges that insofar as disturbing influences certainly do throw otherwise good individuals off balance, the latter are right to bewail their fate. At this point Nietzsche seems so perplexed by the implications of this discovery that he throws himself into rather extravagant and perhaps obfuscatory metaphysical speculations which, while interesting in themselves, rhetorically distract him from the issue at hand. What is clear in this sketch is that for him the naturalistic hypothesis implies injustice and he cannot accept the possibility that the universe is either unjust or indifferent. He is determined to find an alternative approach.

For the moment any such solution eludes him. In the second of the three autobiographical sketches, he foregoes metaphysics and addresses directly personal application of the scenario he found so upsetting. Again the focus is fixed less on the self than on the environment in which the self is awakened. "Only now," he writes, "do I recognize how many experiences have affected my development, and how heart and intellect have been formed under the influence of surrounding circumstances. For even though the main features of each person's character are, so to speak, inborn, so time and conditions train these bare seeds and stamp specific forms on them which through duration become firm and inextinguishable."[30] He identifies in his own world, so to speak, the plight of the hunters and fishers, of wandering primitives whose development seems at the mercy of environment and chance.

In fairness, Nietzsche does not emphasize the element of chance circumstances, even if contingency is everywhere implicit. What he does stress is that autobiographers must examine not only the self, that is, their own particular talents and tendencies, but they must also take account of the world they live in, which will awaken and feed certain of these tendencies, possibly to the detriment of others. In his own

---

[30] KGW I-2: 258.

autobiography he cites only the effect of the tragedy at Röcken. He may also have had more insidious, environmentally formative factors in mind, as would emerge in a lecture he would deliver later to Germania. For the moment, however, specific influences were not that important. What mattered was that such insidious and powerful influences existed at all. Nietzsche wanted to take charge of his life. Now he was forced to recognize that external forces of which he might scarcely be aware could impede his ability to act autonomously. He could no longer accept the thoughtless optimism implicit in his religious faith.

It would appear then that at this time Nietzsche was beginning to view the history of humanity, of his own life, and (according to Deussen) of the Bible itself, outside the framework of traditional Christianity. This does not necessarily mean that he had lost his religious faith; it did mean that this faith was challenged, a development with potential consequences in at least three areas. First, if he forfeited his childhood beliefs, he would lose such traditional advantages of religion as the stimulation of spiritual vision and the comfort of a ready-made ethical framework for living. Second, religion lay at the center of his family life, and quarrels and misunderstandings lay ahead if he deviated from the beliefs of his father and mother. Finally, it seems to have been assumed by everyone that he would eventually become a minister. If that vocation foundered, what would he do with his life instead?

Shortly after writing these essays, Nietzsche made a symptomatic turn musically. Up to now he had been absorbed in the composition of an oratorio dealing with the birth of Christ. As late as June 1861, three months after Confirmation, he had submitted another installment of this project to Germania. Then, abruptly, he stopped. Over the summer he took a tour of Franconia and parts of Bavaria, and on his return he presented a rather turgid composition entitled "Pain is the keynote of nature."[31] There is nothing about God in that title, and, more significantly, the Christmas oratorio was shelved and never mentioned again. Nietzsche continued to write musical works and poems on religious themes, but these were henceforward occasional pieces, rather like his lyric poems. Religion had become merely another subject matter to explore; it no longer enjoyed the primacy that it had held in the past.

It would be unusual for someone so intense and fixated as Nietzsche to lose such a bulwark as religion without replacing it with some other system of values, and in a sense he had already done so. If he recognized the

---

[31] For the dates of these works, see KGW I-2: 470–473, 480–483.

critique of religion as valid or at least as calling for response, then to that extent he already subscribed to the methods of academic scholarship on which that critique was founded. The budding schools of anthropologists and the philological inquirers into the Bible were alike in their mistrust of supernatural explanation, and insofar as the ardent student accepted their tutelage, he would cultivate such mistrust as well. As already mentioned, during the period from autumn 1858 to spring 1861 Nietzsche had moved from being a mediocre student to becoming one of the more signal prodigies of Schulpforte. His determination to excel scholastically was particularly evident that spring, for not only was he made Primus again but he composed an essay on Mithradates, the Bythnian king, that secured him a "first," a grade given only every several years.[32] Probably without even recognizing it until faced with the consequences, he had shifted allegiances. Scholarship could never replace religion in his eyes; it could provide neither the visionary inspiration nor the ethically resonant way of life offered by Christianity. Nonetheless Nietzsche had moved from a fundamentally religious orientation, where reliance on tradition, authority, and imaginative investment were primary, to a worldview that affirmed reason, evidence, and a preference for explanation through natural causes. The die was cast. It was just a matter of developing what already had been done and recognizing the consequences.

5

In one respect Nietzsche's new interest in scholarship affected even his imaginative life. In July 1861 he delivered a paper to Germania, exploring the heritage of a theme which he had been trying to turn into an epic poem since the preceding summer.[33] The historical basis of this study concerned Ermanarich, a chieftain who had ruled Gothic tribes on the eastern border of the Roman Empire during the fourth century CE. Ermanarich served Rome as a bulwark against other enemies but eventually found himself besieged by the Huns. When his kingdom collapsed and the enemy invaded, a massive number of his tribesmen fled the enemy and sought shelter behind Roman lines. This influx of terrified refugees so overwhelmed imperial resources that, in the eyes of some scholars, they contributed significantly to the eventual collapse of the Roman Empire.[34]

---

[32] For a discussion of this essay, see Müller 1994.   [33] KGW I-2: 274–284.
[34] See, for example, Gibbon's *History of the decline and fall of the Roman Empire*, ch. 26. The Gothic invasion eventually led to the disastrous Battle of Adrianople.

Nietzsche himself was less interested in Ermanarich's world-historical significance than in how he figured in epics and sagas. The kingdom's fall and the old man's death had become the subject of myth in at least two traditions, each with many variants, and it was these that excited his imagination. In the more mythological set, which associated the king with events in the *Nibelungenlied*, the old man married the beautiful Swanhilde, the much younger daughter of Gudrun and Sigurd (otherwise known as Siegfried). This young woman later fell in love with the king's own son, whereupon Ermanarich hanged the son and had Swanhilde trampled by wild horses. Her brothers later stabbed Ermanarich in revenge, and the old man died slowly as he watched his kingdom succumb to invaders.

Over the next four years Nietzsche was fascinated enough by this story to reimagine it in every genre available to him – writing poems, sketching plays, composing at least two scholarly essays on the subject (one of which he considered the finest paper he produced at Pforta), and attempting both a symphony and opera. Some of these efforts deal with the adventures of the revenge-seeking brothers, others with an intriguer named Bekka who plots Ermanarich's downfall. The most striking poems center on Ermanarich's crazed grief and guilt after he has killed his son, a frenzy of regret that drives him half-mad and leads to his death.[35] Given all this bloody melodrama, it is striking that Nietzsche's first extant consideration of this subject took the shape of a scholarly paper which he delivered to Germania. Nietzsche did not let the irony go unrecognized. "The result of these studies lies before me – not a tragedy, but a dry treatise," he acknowledged.[36] Scholarship had etherized even the appeal of gore.

6

The Ermanarich theme first appeared in Nietzsche's writings in the summer of 1861, that is, at the very time when he ceased work on his oratorio. For the next four years, the Gothic king was rarely far from his consciousness and figured frequently and at length in his notebooks. Meanwhile a second figure stole into his imagination so stealthily that it is impossible to discover exactly when Nietzsche became aware of him. What is indisputable is that at some time between the springs of 1861 and 1862, Nietzsche

---

[35] "*Ermanarichs Tod.*" KGW I-2: 370–375. Nietzsche read this at one of Pforta's anniversary festivals, and it enjoyed considerable success.
[36] KGW I-2: 275.

discovered the work of Ralph Waldo Emerson, a writer who inspired his first extant philosophical work and would stimulate him for the rest of his active life.

Nietzsche's introduction to Emerson appears not to have been through the famous *Essays*, although he was certainly aware of these, but through *The conduct of life*, a collection only recently published in English (1860) but already translated into German by the beginning of 1862. One should note that in German Emerson's title was rendered *Die Führung des Lebens*, already a catchphrase associated with *Bildung* in the nineteenth century, and this may have drawn Nietzsche's attention.[37] This late book of Emerson is noticeably darker in tone than his earlier work, and it is full of hard-bitten remarks which might surprise those who think of the author as oblivious to the more sinister side of life. Indeed, some are worthy of Schopenhauer, as for example, "The worst of charity is, that the lives you are asked to preserve are not worth preserving."[38] When reproached for such comments, Emerson countered that they were offset by his positive vision: "I dip my pen in the blackest of ink, because I am not afraid of falling into my inkpot."[39] In fact, despite his reputation as a starry-eyed optimist, he had always tried to ground his vision in recognition of the bare realities that everywhere surround human beings. Decrying the futility of those who try to situate houses according to their personal likes or ideals, he countered, "We say the cows laid out Boston," that is, one must take account of practical matters such as where the land is level and the weather propitious.[40]

Emerson's demand that readers face unpleasant truths is amply on view in "Fate," *The conduct of life*'s opening chapter, and a piece that much impressed young Nietzsche. In this meditation, Emerson considers the limits of voluntary action and argues that while human beings think they are free, they find themselves hedged on all sides by factors beyond their control. Try as they might, they are balked by the particulars of their individual body, the influence of ethnic and cultural inheritance, and the physical habitat they occupy. This straitjacket of apparently inalterable circumstances he calls "Fate," and he dwells colorfully and at length on how baffling, demeaning, and insuperable these limitations can be. "No picture of life can have any veracity that does not admit the odious facts. A

---

[37] Koselleck 1990. See especially 22–23.
[38] "Considerations by the way" in *The conduct of life*. Emerson 1983: 1081.
[39] Emerson 1983: "Worship," 1055.   [40] Emerson 1983: "Wealth," 1008.

man's power is hooped in by a necessity, which, by many experiments, he touches on every side, until he learns its arc." (952)[41]

The essay is by no means wholly negative. In Emerson's view some people engage fate in a kind of spiritual jujitsu that makes it work for rather than against them. Human beings cannot change the hand they are dealt, but they can play it to their advantage. Thus, instead of complaining about steam, they can put it to use to drive engines, just as they can manage floods through dams. (959) Indeed, insofar as humans are a product of their environment, they are suited to the world they inhabit, and their freedoms and necessities move hand in hand. For Emerson the soul is like a homing device, alert for opportunities favorable to its necessities. Some persons seem destined to build cities and – he cites various American pioneers – they establish a series of these as they travel. (964) Others are so obsessed by sexual desire that it is only a matter of time before they meet a willing partner and consummate the relationship. (947) Thus, human activity displays an intrinsic fit of individual and expression, wherein just this person performs just this action and the action is in turn an index to the being who carried it through. "The secret of the world is, the tie between person and event. Person makes event, and event person ... The event is the print of your form. It fits you like your skin." (962) Implicit here, although Emerson does not use the term, is the notion of an ever active unconscious. Human beings seek certain ends and shun others without quite knowing what they do, but the results reveal their desires better than any conscious statement.

To this rather mystical account of reciprocity between individual and fate ("Person makes event, and event person" (962)), which, as will be seen, the young Nietzsche was happy to accept, Emerson adds a response to Nietzsche's earlier conundrum: how was it possible for human cultures to advance? They did so, says Emerson, the same way Fulton did when he harnessed steam – by deploying the strictures of nature against itself so as to relieve its onerous pressures. This is how human beings rise to new cultural levels without divine assistance. Emerson lists with satisfaction the apparent obstacles that human beings have turned to their own use. "The mischievous torrent is taught to drudge for man: the wild beasts he makes useful for food, or dress, or labor." (959) By inventions such as these – and the author cites many more, evincing an esteem for technology that might prove controversial today – human beings have neutralized oppressive environments and even transformed them into positive benefits.

---

[41] Page numbers in parentheses refer to Emerson 1983.

For Emerson this slow recognition and mastery of limitation and circumstance functions as the master narrative of human history. "History is the action and reaction of these two, – Nature and Thought." (964) Not once in this account of cultural and practical progress does he mention religion or God, although he sometimes introduces teleological overtones and presents Nature as a directive creator. It is human resourcefulness in the face of problems which leads to civilization's advance.

In the end, Emerson's essay, "Fate" admirably summarizes the same interplay of obdurate reality and human determination which underwrites many of his more popular pieces. The implications are many, and their bearing on the impasses Nietzsche encountered in the anthropological and biographical works of 1861 is evident. In "Fate" Emerson specifies a means – the determination to transform onerous necessity into benefit – through which humanity could socially and practically evolve without either divine intervention or invocation of a prelapsarian state. Further, Emerson shows that immersion in a limited situation is not intrinsically a liability. Without it human beings could not live at all; and if their environment inhibits their vision, it also provides an occasion to exercise countervailing faculties and occasionally to surmount its limitations. Finally, Emerson introduced a sense of human beings as being unaware of their own desires and to that extent, although he does not use these terms, of their unconscious drives. Nietzsche was not slow to recognize the implications. He not only mentions Emerson, he incorporates direct quotations from "Fate" into his next major work, an intellectual manifesto he presented during his Easter break in 1862.[42]

7

That April[43] Nietzsche presented his first extant philosophical paper.[44] Entitled "Fate and history" and delivered as a lecture to Germania, it acknowledged doubts concerning Christianity, and it reframed themes that had troubled the author in his anthropological and autobiographical essays.[45] Further, it was addressed to Wilhelm and Gustav, and to that extent it registered a public as well as a private avowal. Once Nietzsche had made so impassioned a confession of his doubts concerning Christianity, he could not again play the pious and compliant churchgoer, at least before

---

[42] Examples: "The Turk, who believes his doom is written on the iron leaf in the moment" (944). "Ask Spurzheim, ask the doctors, ask Quetelet" (946)
[43] The month is disputable. The paper may have been delivered in March.
[44] In *Ecce homo* he claims to have written one other before this. See also KSA VIII: 505.
[45] KGW I-2: 431–437. English translation by George Stack in Ansell Pearson and Large 2006: 12–15.

his friends. Clearly the work was revolutionary in both intent and scope, and its ambitions and achievements make it too complex to analyze at length within the current context. The following discussion will limit itself to the ways the work addressed issues Nietzsche had encountered in the spring of 1861 and which he was now ready to resolve.

The lecture opens with a rather turgid statement of skepticism concerning religious belief. "If we could look on Christian doctrines and church history in a free and impartial way, we would have to express several views that challenge those that are generally accepted." The statement is exceedingly bold, but it is framed as a hypothetical ("If"), and Nietzsche no sooner asserts it than he takes it back, suggesting that neither he nor his listeners are capable of any such freedom or impartiality. They were raised Christian, and the weight and tendencies of that educational environment make it almost impossible for its recipients to see without bringing into play the very blinders they are trying to shed. As he expounds in a later paragraph, "We are so determined in our innermost being by the impressions of our childhood, the influence of our parents, our educations, that those deeply rooted prejudices are not so easily torn out by reasoning or mere will."[46] The reader may recall that in his autobiographical sketches Nietzsche had acknowledged "how heart and intellect have been formed under the influence of surrounding circumstances." Now he makes explicit what one of these "surrounding circumstances" might be. It is his Christian upbringing which has formed his character and intellect, and it is this same Christian upbringing which he finds himself struggling to reassess. In effect, Nietzsche is portraying Christianity as part of his Fate and to that extent something that he needs to inspect and possibly to transcend.

After an eloquent exposition of the difficult and intimidating nature of this enterprise, he turns to historical processes, which display themselves only partially to humans, although their full meaning is revealed to God. This rather long and metaphysical passage is of lesser interest here, except that Nietzsche invokes the bewilderment of humanity in terms very similar to those he had used the previous spring when he noted the weakness of human beings *vis-à-vis* the forces of environmental play. He has returned to the problems posed by the autobiographical sketches of 1861, but this time he is better prepared.

Nietzsche can now introduce an insight which he has picked up from Emerson. While human beings are subject to environmental events, they

---

[46] KGW I-2: 431, 433. Trans. George Stack in Ansell Pearson and Large 2006: 12, 13. The translation of the second quotation, "We are determined," has been slightly altered.

do not all respond in the same way. Each answers a situation according to the lights of individual character and particular interests. "What determines our happiness in life? Do we have to thank events whose whirlpool carries us away? Or is it not our temperament, as it were, the coloration of all events? Do we not encounter everything in the mirror of our personality?"[47] At one level Nietzsche is making the obvious point that human beings respond to situations individually and according to personal values. What will devastate one person will galvanize another; and what one finds enchanting will nauseate someone else. Less obvious (and less innocent) is a corollary he draws. When he implicitly dismisses the "whirlpool [which] carries us away," he in effect is saying that what proves decisive causally is less an event (the whirlpool) than how an individual receives it. Not everybody will be carried away, even by a whirlpool. Events (and by extension environment), he then explains, may provide the musical key (*Tonart*), the key signature, in which we lead our lives, but the strength or weakness of our response correlates, not with the power of the imposition (the event), but with the intensity of our reception. "And do not events provide, as it were, only the musical key of our lot while *the strength or weakness with which it affects us depends merely on our temperament*. Ask gifted physicians, Emerson says, how much temperament decides, and what it does not decide at all?" (Emphasis added.)

These last statements can be better understood if applied to an example which Nietzsche had given the year before in his autobiographical sketches. There he had posed the case of someone who could not rise above the temptations of riches and had succumbed to their enervating allure. At the time the situation was presented as though the native goodness of certain human beings was simply *overwhelmed* by forces which they could not withstand. In that particular environment (and in implicit comparison with more stalwart human beings) they proved to be weak. Nietzsche now questions this implicit scale according to which all human beings are lined up according to a single value, the degree of their moral fortitude. He argues that the force of their character and personal values has to be factored in as well. If someone yields to the appeal of riches, it is not necessarily because they are morally flaccid; they may be simply the sort of person who would respond in that way to riches. In other words, the environment didn't overwhelm; it offered a situation which the person would embrace or reject, depending on their needs and interests. To

---

[47] KGW I-2: 435. Trans. George Stack in Ansell Pearson and Large 2006: 14, here slightly altered.

paraphrase one clause in Nietzsche's penultimate sentence, one's "strength or weakness" in standing up to an event wasn't contingent on the force of the *event* so much as on the force of one's *response*. To that extent taste reigned supreme, and human beings had opened the gates to the lot that they seemed to receive. People were not at the mercy of events; rather the capacity of an event to affect them was at the mercy of their temperament, the individual way they responded.

Having happily embraced these axiological views, Nietzsche turned to metaphysics and wondered how any kind of freedom was possible in a world ruled by necessity. This account (which involved viewing freedom as a limiting case of necessity) will be skipped here in order to turn to and examine another paper, "Freedom of will and fate," a pendant to the lecture he gave to Germania.[48] This ancillary text is very different from "Fate and history." It is, for a start, less impassioned because not predicated on a religious crisis. Nonetheless, it elaborates portions of the earlier essay and serves as an extension of the statements just quoted. It may be recalled that Emerson believed that individuals and events are reciprocally determined. Human beings respond only to influences to which they are susceptible and to this extent they cooperate in the reception of pressures. Further, the soul is like a homing device and alert for opportunities favorable to its necessities. "Nature magically suits the man to his fortunes, by making these the fruit of his character." (963) By these and other statements Emerson suggests that the soul's sensitivity and receptivity to the world is at the same time an active appropriation of that world. Passivity and activity, limitation and freedom are mutually implied, and human beings are to that extent implicated in their situation. "[The individual] knows himself to be party to his current estate." (948)

It is to this aspect of Emerson's view that Nietzsche repairs in "Freedom of will and fate." There he affirms Emerson's claim that while the self can be beset by all sorts of causal events, the self can only internalize and respond to a limited range of phenomena, those which register on its sensorium. "Can a tone, in general, touch us if there is no corresponding string in us? Or, expressed differently, can we receive an impression in our brain if our brain is not already endowed with a receptivity for that purpose?"[49]

At this point Nietzsche makes a discovery that will henceforward underlie his theory of the self. First, he speculates (as Emerson does not) that the

---

[48] KGW I-2: 437–440. English translation by George Stack in Ansell Pearson and Large 2006: 16–17.
[49] KGW I-2: 439. Trans. George Stack in Ansell Pearson and Large 2006: 17.

difference between voluntary and fatal responses is reflected by the distinction we make between conscious and unconscious reception.[50] "Free will [indicates] the capacity to act consciously; whereas by fate we understand that we are led by unconscious acts." No sooner does he make this distinction, however, than he downplays its significance, arguing that conscious and unconscious motivations alike enact something more basic, the strivings of the individual soul. For Nietzsche there is nothing pejorative about the unconscious. It doesn't matter whether individuals know what they are doing, or whether actions are performed with or without the benefits of consciousness. In either case actions express the self and to that extent direct its fulfillment. "One often says about a successful act: I've hit upon this by accident. By no means need this always be true. The activity of the soul continues undiminished even if we do not observe it with the mind's eye," i.e., consciously.

Ultimately, Nietzsche emancipates individuals from being a passive link in a causal chain – from being a mere product of history – and envisions them as independently vibrant and responsive in the present. They need not overanalyze; they should rather feel their own powers, the directions in which they can best move forward, and proceed. His reasoning is not always clear, but his confidence is unmistakable; and he has evidently overcome the anxieties which unsettled him the previous spring. Meanwhile, he has placed all his bets on the self, a position not necessarily uncongenial to one raised in the Lutheran tradition of individual conscience. Where Nietzsche's (and Emerson's) approach strays from the Lutheran, however, lies in the active, vitalist, creational value that they (and certain Romantic forbearers) ascribe to the striving soul. For Nietzsche as will be seen, the latter is always developing. Like *Bildung*'s Faustian prototype, it is tirelessly engaged in realizing its possibilities. Further, since many of these activities are unconscious, it is fundamentally unknowable. Individuals cannot be sure who they are or where they are going; they can only be certain that they are in transit and that whatever they do reflects their yearnings, conscious or otherwise.

Meanwhile, if Emerson's approach accepted the Humboldtian account of *Bildung* in certain ways, it diverged in others, and the differences are important, for they would ultimately lead Nietzsche down paths not envisioned in his education. First, Humboldt had construed individuals as growing through their struggle with external factors, particularly the

---

[50] Needless to say, Emerson readily admitted notions analogous to those of non-conscious motives and thoughts. He just didn't use the *vocabulary* of "conscious" and "unconscious."

educational and social. Emerson would agree, but he introduced a rebellious, anti-authoritarian animus that is absent in his socially exalted predecessor. The American tended rather to emphasize the individual as *opposed* to society, a view that Humboldt would probably have found repellent and unsustainable.[51] Second, while Emerson and Humboldt both affirmed the individual, Emerson shifted the stress in a Romantic way that Humboldt, who retained aspects of the *Aufklärung*, probably would have rejected. Although Humboldt's texts are subject to varying interpretations, he tended to foreground the distinctive interests and talents of each human being. He emphasized individual *capacities*, not individuality in itself, which he saw as emerging through the effort to wield these forces into a unified and vibrant whole. One did not begin with individuality; one achieved it. Emerson shifted the emphasis, downplaying talents and affirming rather that every self was radically different practically from birth. One *began* as an individual, and although this gift could be denied, Emerson preached that it was inherently valuable and should be developed. Years later Nietzsche would write, "At bottom, every human being knows perfectly well that he lives in the world just once, as one of a kind, and that no coincidence, regardless how strange, will ever for a second time concoct out of this amazingly variegated diversity the unity that he is."[52] While that sentence owes a debt to the Enlightenment, it implicitly claims that the self *qua* self is inherently precious, non-negotiably distinctive, and embattled amid a leveling society. These views are far more Emersonian than Humboldtian (and they are, of course, worlds removed from Kant, who is also implicitly invoked in the paragraph in question); and they would put Nietzsche on a trajectory at odds with contemporary values. It would take him several years consciously to make this transition and he would do so definitively only when he felt embattled for other reasons.[53] Nonetheless, the seed was probably planted years before during his initial encounters with Emerson at Schulpforte.

Meanwhile and whatever Nietzsche's ideas might be in the future, his new orientation required new modes of behavior. He had already proposed to question Christianity; and although he assured friends that he found such a prospect intimidating, certain remarks later in "Fate and history" suggest that he didn't seem to mind criticizing Christianity at all.[54] As the

[51] Sorkin 1983. [52] UO III: 1. Translation by Richard T. Gray, slightly modified. KSA I: 337.
[53] See Chapter 13, Section 2.
[54] See, for example, the breezy aside, "However, observing the impression that such doubts make on the mind must surely be a contribution to one's own cultural history" KGW I-2: 433. Trans. George Stack in Ansell Pearson and Large 2006: 13.

next chapter will show, he had also begun to deviate from socially approved behavior. The two texts he produced at Easter ("Fate and history," "Freedom of will and fate") provided, as it were, patents of intellectual emancipation, which he could use to justify the journey he had already begun. It is time now to observe these attempts at self-liberation and how they squared with his philosophic strategy.

CHAPTER 7

The underworld of Pforta

[The] tone of youth [is] too loud.[1]

I

In "Fate and history" Nietzsche had stressed the difficulties faced by anyone trying to free the self from a Christian upbringing. Yet despite his announcement of the dangers ahead, he no sooner proposed this project than he embarked upon it himself. A willingness to reconsider his faith is amply evident in the draft of a letter that he wrote to Wilhelm and Gustav one month after delivering his lecture.[2] The original letter, which was inscribed in a notebook, is lost, and readers are left with a sketch which unfortunately begins mid-thought. It is not difficult to reconstruct the missing context, however, for the extant words clearly flow from a position stated earlier in "Freedom of will and fate." There, Nietzsche had implicitly cited Emerson's claim that Turks, Arabs, and Persians were fearless because they believed that the day of their death was foreordained. Since they would die (or not) whatever they did, they might as well take risks. To this Nietzsche responded, "We find that people who believe in fate are distinguished by force and strength of will; whereas women and men who ... let things go as they will (since 'God has made everything good'), allow themselves to be led in a degrading way by circumstances."[3]

This sentence probably shocked its intended audience, for it expressed contempt for one of the pillars of contemporary Pietism, the belief that Christians should accept misfortunes as manifestations of divine providence ("Let his will be done"). Nietzsche's new letter apparently repeated this rejection of divine providence, for he continued:

---

[1] KSA VIII: 337.   [2] KSAB I: 201–202.
[3] KGW I-2: 438. Trans. George Stack (slightly altered) in Ansell Pearson and Large 2006: 16.

Only a Christian outlook can produce this kind of world weariness; it is very foreign to the fatalist. It is nothing but a pretext of the weak, a renunciation of one's own strength resolutely to make one's lot oneself. When we first recognize that we are responsible to ourselves, that a reproach for a deficient spirit in life can be attributed only to us, not to some higher powers, only then will the basic ideas of Christianity lay aside their outward garments and enter marrow and blood.

Despite his obvious disdain for Christians who invoke divine providence to excuse inaction, Nietzsche does not directly attack Christianity itself. He seeks rather to redefine it, disparaging modern representatives in favor of an older, truer faith, "the basic ideas of Christianity," which apparently counseled "responsibility to ourselves," an expression he might have found in Emerson. However, a more local author underwrote most of this passage, as Nietzsche tacitly acknowledges in the paragraph which follows:

> Christianity is essentially a matter of the heart; not until it is incorporated in us, when it has become our very nature, is a human being a true Christian. *The principal teachings of Christianity express merely the basic truths of the human heart; they are symbols,* just as the highest must always be merely a symbol of something still higher. To be blessed by belief means no more than the old truth, that only the heart, not knowledge, can make us happy. That God became human, merely indicates that the human being should not seek blessedness in the infinite but ground its heaven on earth; *the illusion of the supernatural has placed the human spirit in a false relationship to the earthly world*: this was a consequence of the childhood of peoples. The glowing youthful soul of humanity accepts these ideas eagerly and darkly pronounces the secret that roots itself in both past and future, that God became human. *Humanity* will become manly through arduous doubts and battles; it *recognizes in itself "the beginning, the middle, the end of religion."* (Emphases added.)

Here, Nietzsche unmistakably discloses that he has come under the spell of Ludwig Feuerbach, the leftist Hegelian philosopher who so powerfully influenced the early Marx, Engels, and Wagner. (The most Feuerbachian remarks have been italicized; the final quotation is taken directly, although slightly abbreviated, from his *The essence of Christianity*, ch. 19.)[4] Since Nietzsche does not explain Feuerbach's positions but merely invokes them, it might help to summarize that philosopher's views. In essence, Feuerbach suggested that human beings created images of God as projections of their own human qualities. When they celebrated the generosity, compassion, or wrath of the Almighty, they were imputing to God their own capacity for

---

[4] KGB I-4: 192. Compare Feuerbach 1956: I, 298.

generosity, compassion, and rage. In short, Christians worshiped what they had put there themselves, and in the process they alienated themselves from their own powers, worshiping God and personally disowning the essence of their own humanity. Feuerbach advised that, instead of prostrating themselves to an idol that they had themselves conceived, Christians should look to themselves as human beings first and reconsider their values accordingly. This is effectively the position Nietzsche advocates in this letter, and it shows that he had somehow come into contact with Feuerbachian teachings.[5]

One would think that having produced these arraignments of current Christian practice (the two Easter documents, followed by the Feuerbach letter), Nietzsche would pursue the theme and write a series of essays describing his developing views on Christianity. In fact, no further texts of this kind are available from his time at Schulpforte. Nietzsche, of course, wrote other papers on Christianity while at school, but none of these seek to redefine its dogmas or to ponder it as an object of belief. Nonetheless, he seems not to have let his interrogation of religion die but instead pursued it silently to its conclusion. Years later he would recall, "As an atheist I never said grace before meals at Pforta," and he indicated that the teachers knew this and penalized him accordingly.[6] The phrase, "As an atheist ... at Pforta," shows unequivocally that – despite the fact that he left no paper trail – Nietzsche continued his emancipatory efforts and even brought them to a decisive close. Of course, he was recording that memory fifteen years after the events in question and he may have misreported. He certainly continued to observe most Christian ceremonies during his last year at Schulpforte, and he seemed to have retained some loyalty toward his early faith even during his first year at the university. Nonetheless, it is unlikely that Nietzsche's memorandum is a wholesale misrepresentation. Regardless whether he recorded his progress in documents, he clearly continued to pursue his inquiries after the spring of 1862, and he took them very far indeed, even if, perhaps, he did not wean himself from Christianity so decisively as he remembered.

Meanwhile, Nietzsche did not limit himself to exploring beliefs but expanded his ethical horizons as well, behaving in ways outside his earlier,

---

[5] By 1862 Feuerbach's reputation had long since entered decline. Kamenka 1969: 17. Nietzsche may have become acquainted with the man's views through his teachers or through Ortlepp. (See next section.) Certainly, he was sufficiently apprised to ask for two books by Feuerbach for his seventeenth birthday in 1861, six months before "Fate and history" and "Freedom of will and fate." This is the same list in which he requests Hase's *Das Leben Jesu*. KGW I-2: 307.
[6] KSA VIII: 608.

decorous limits. Between the summer of 1861, when he ceased to work on his oratorio, and the spring of 1863, when a mortifying event brought certain kinds of experimentation to an end, he repeatedly probed limits, exploring new cultural and ethical viewpoints in an attempt to put critical distance between himself and traditional beliefs. Such behavior is not unusual for adolescents, and some of Nietzsche's rebelliousness no doubt reflected activities typical for his age. Nonetheless, as his demand for self-responsibility indicates, he had given this natural process a theoretical and emancipatory meaning. The issue then arises: how could he explore effectively, since his school was self-enclosed and he had so little access to alternative scales of value? How was he to find forbidden authors and to investigate alternate modes of behavior when he did not know what these were?

2

Schulpforte is often presented as a sternly disciplined society, peopled by exemplary professors and by students trained to give their all to scholarship. Such a characterization represents Pforta's ideal of itself, and such aspirations were largely realized, at least during the administration of Karl Peter (the rector during Nietzsche's stay), who may have presided over a golden age.[7] Nonetheless, implementation of exalted visions was inevitably subject to the undertow of dissidence and human failure. Distinguished teachers could coast in their lectures. Adjunct professors, who were not allowed to marry and were paid low wages, often did not stay.[8] At least one instructor was thought to be alcoholic, and another of Nietzsche's professors killed himself three-and-a-half years after the young man's departure.[9] Students too were by no means always devoted to studies or respectful of their elders. If Nietzsche was seeking a way to extricate himself from his self-consciously well-behaved and perhaps philistine past, he found a resource to tap in what might be called the underworld of Pforta.

There were, for a start, the inevitable sexual undercurrents, which were already mentioned in the earlier chapter.[10] Also, as the boys aged, they were granted prerogatives deemed appropriate to their new dignity. Some of these were innocent: by their third year, for example, they were allowed to

---

[7] Heumann et al. 1994: 107. [8] Pernet 1989: 135, n. 27.
[9] For alcoholism, see Wilamowitz-Moellendorff 1928: 80–81. For the suicide, see KSAB II: 239. The professor in question, Julius Kretschmer, had been Deussen's tutor after Buddensieg's death. Feldhoff 2008: 38.
[10] Chapter 5, Section 1.

carry canes (although a brawl led to this privilege being rescinded). Others privileges were more problematic. Seniors, for example, were allowed to smoke cigars, to leave campus without permission, and in general to hold themselves exempt from any rules not covered in the protocols, official or traditional.[11] These policies obviously could lead to tensions. Boys of any age might participate in classroom insurrections, particularly when a professor showed vulnerability, as did the otherworldly Professor Carl Steinhart, who was known for his lack of control over students.[12] A scandalous revolt took place in Nietzsche's own classroom during his second year, and he recorded in his journal the rising tensions as the administration sought the ringleaders.[13] Unworldly teachers were not the only ones bullied. Older boys preyed on the younger, and many students were jealous of and took revenge on those who were thought to study too hard and thereby to be currying favor with the teachers.[14] Finally, there were cliques of many kinds at Schulpforte, as one might expect with any group of adolescents.

The most sustained and extracurricular influence on Nietzsche, however, may not have been his fellow students, but a man who entertained the boys during free hours and who encouraged sedition on the side. Schulpforte had, as it were, a resident ghost, a man endured on sufferance, perhaps because he was a Pforta graduate, a significant poet and translator, and a man who had met Goethe and corresponded with Robert Schumann. He seems further to have inspired respect, or at least appreciation. Two of the more distinguished Pforta professors supplied him funds,[15] and according to Deussen, he was popular with certain seniors. (Deussen clearly liked him, and he and Nietzsche took up a collection on the man's death.)[16] Unfortunately, Ernst Ortlepp, once a student of promise, had always been subject to erratic behavior, and the man had repeatedly run afoul of the censors both for blasphemous religious poems (one entitled "Our Father") and for poems celebrating revolutionary ideals. Subject to indigence and increasingly to alcohol abuse, he had been expelled from Leipzig in 1836 as *persona non grata*, and he had repeatedly spent time in jail. By the late 1850s and early 60s he was usually tipsy and

---

[11] Heumann *et al.* 1994: 196–198.   [12] Heumann *et al.* 1994: 115–116.
[13] KGW I-2: 107, 109, 114, 116.
[14] Nietzsche surely encountered this prejudice and, according to Deussen 1901: 4–5, he engaged in it at least once himself. For an English version, see Gilman 1987: 11.
[15] Carl Steinhart and Karl Keil gave Ortlepp money on occasion, and Keil apparently paid for his burial. Agthe *et al.* 2006: 55–56.
[16] Feldhoff 2008: 41.

something of a laughingstock. He had lived in Naumburg for a time, occupying a dwelling at 19 Weingarten, near 18 Weingarten where Franziska Nietzsche would move in 1858.[17] There, he was subject to public derision and was eventually sentenced to prison for staggering through the streets in tears, apparently followed by a "rat's tail" of mocking children. He then seems to have relocated to the vicinity of Almrich, where he was closer to Schulpforte and could entertain the students in taverns. It is impossible to know how intimately Nietzsche knew him, although both he and Wilhelm Pinder were certainly familiar with the man. What is certain is that Nietzsche encountered Ortlepp in the drinking houses of Almrich, where the roaming poet liked to hold forth to students from the school. Indeed, Nietzsche records that he and friends had been talking to him on the very day he died.[18]

Certain Nietzsche scholars in German-speaking countries have begun to see Nietzsche's acquaintance with Ortlepp as pivotal to his development.[19] As of now there does not seem to exist enough evidence to sustain this position. Nonetheless the older man's influence does seem plausible in at least one way. Limited as Nietzsche was by the strictures of Schulpforte, which did not teach authors regarded as politically suspect or bad for morals, he would have had difficulty discovering an alternative canon on his own.[20] Here, Ortlepp could have proved invaluable. According to Reiner Bohley, the man's favorite authors were Shakespeare, Laurence Sterne, Henry Fielding, Hölderlin, Byron, and above all Jean Paul.[21] If so, the coincidence is remarkable, for with the exception of Fielding, these were the authors Nietzsche prized over the course of his stay at Pforta. He was much taken with *Tristram Shandy* at the beginning of his second year, and around the same time he speculated that Jean Paul might become his favorite author.[22] During his final three years there, he became fascinated

---

[17] Agthe *et al.* 2006: 60–61, n. 27. 18 and 19 are the current house numbers. In terms of mid-nineteenth-century addresses, Franziska lived at 355, Ortlepp at 354 Weingarten. This supposed proximity is misleading, however. There is no evidence that Ortlepp lived there except in the year 1856, during which time the Nietzsches lived in the Neugasse and at the Marientor. But see Schmidt 2001: 317–319.

[18] KSAB I: 288.

[19] See Agthe *et al.* 2006; Bohley 2007: 188–190, 299–307; Schmidt 2001; Ross 1980: 73–74. For the opposition, see Hödl 1998: 440–445.

[20] Karl Robert Mandelkow argues that a canon centered on Goethe and Schiller and designed to exclude Jean Paul and others was created during the course of the nineteenth century and embraced by the *Bildungsbürger*. Mandelkow 1990: especially 184–185.

[21] Bohley 2007: 302. Bohley also repeatedly mentions Ortlepp's interest in Montaigne but never calls the latter a favorite author.

[22] For Sterne, see KGW I-2: 100, 101, 111, 133. For Jean Paul, see KGW I-2: 123.

by the works of Hölderlin, Shakespeare, and especially Byron, all specialties of Ortlepp, who had published translations of principal works by Byron and virtually all of Shakespeare's plays. Nietzsche had other motives to study Byron, as will be explained. Nonetheless, he may have owned Ortlepp's three-volume edition of Byron's works while at school, and it was certainly the one he used in the last decade of his life.[23] Inevitably, he would have viewed the man who recommended the poet – and through whose versions he was possibly reading them – with curiosity and perhaps esteem. This is not to say that Nietzsche's admiration for literary figures was in imitation of Ortlepp's. He had his own sensibility, tastes, and personal reasons for championing certain writers over others. And Shakespeare, of course, was an author not only approved by the school but integral to the curriculum. Nonetheless, Ortlepp's suggestions could lead him to investigate authors that he might otherwise not have encountered. During his six years at the school Nietzsche increasingly began to explore an alternative canon, and, coincidentally or not, most of these writers were personal favorites of Ernst Ortlepp.

The first striking case where Nietzsche investigated art outside the mainstream, however, began that pivotal March 1861 when he was confirmed and wrote "Hunters and fishers." Somehow he encountered and became fascinated with a set of Serbian poems, and he "translated" several, presenting them to Germania. (In fact, Nietzsche used extant German translations, apparently sometimes consulting the Serbian originals.)[24] His fascination with Ermanarich had a Slavic dimension,[25] and during his years at Pforta he composed two sets of "Hungarian sketches," as well as a "Hungarian march," "Gypsy dance," "*Edes Titok*," and a pair of Polish dances: "Mazurka" and "*Aus der Czarda*."[26] Eventually, he

---

[23] Nietzsche definitely owned a three-volume edition of Byron's works while as Pforta. KGW I-2: 443. Campioni *et al.* 2003: 165–166, indicates that the three-volume Ortlepp translation remained in his final book collection and was by far the most annotated of his editions of Byron. David Thatcher claims that Nietzsche used the eight-volume Adolf Böttger edition at school but that he used the Ortlepp version from 1880 onward. Thatcher 1974: 130, n. 2, 131. This seems puzzling, for in a list of his books made in 1862 (well after the Byron lecture) Nietzsche shows only two Byron sets in his personal collection: a three-volume set in German (presumably Ortlepp's) and a five-volume set in English. KGW I-2: 441–442. No eight-volume set appears. As for Shakespeare, Nietzsche seems to have used the Tieck-Schlegel translations at Pforta.
[24] KGW I-2: 243–252. While his two friends recognized the quality of Nietzsche's new works, they inquired how he had learned Serbian. See KGB I-1: 356–357, 359.
[25] Ermanarich ruled over territories that were later part of Eastern Europe. Discussing a tone poem entitled "Ermanarich," Nietzsche conceded that it was modeled on Liszt's "Hungaria," and that in it he had attempted "to grasp the world of feeling of a Slavic folk." He stated in the same note that there were no Germans or Goths, but only "Hungarian forms." KGW I-3: 4.
[26] Janz 1976: 325.

became fascinated by Sándor Petöfi, the Hungarian poet and a ringleader in the Revolution of 1848.[27] Indeed, one of Petöfi's poems is sometimes credited with setting the conflagration ablaze in that country; and the twenty-six-year-old writer, who participated avidly in the revolt, was last seen alive during its final convulsions.[28] Nietzsche, of course, was raised in a politically conservative household, which must have regarded the Revolution as an unqualified evil which had contributed to the collapse of his father. Nonetheless, he set several of Petöfi's lyrics to music and his enthusiasm for this incendiary upstart was sustained for at least four more years: as late as December 1864 he composed six songs based on texts by this poet.[29]

If Petöfi was politically suspect, Nietzsche soon confirmed his unorthodox bent by turning to a poet certain to disturb traditionalists. In the early summer of 1861, it was Wilhelm's turn to suggest a book for Germania to buy, and apparently Nietzsche lobbied for his friend to order a collection of poems by Friedrich Hölderlin. The purchase was putatively Wilhelm's, and it was he, not Nietzsche, who gave a lecture on Hölderlin to Germania.[30] Indeed, Pinder had indicated an interest in the poet as early as November 21, 1858, long before the name surfaced in Nietzsche's notebooks.[31] Nonetheless, Nietzsche did strongly support this later choice – and in the fall of 1861 he had this book with him at Schulpforte. He also himself owned a book which Thomas Brobjer describes as comprising "a biographical account, critique, and a large number of examples and quotations from Hölderlin's works and letters."[32] Nietzsche had left this at home when returning to school after holidays, but he arranged for it to be sent to him.[33]

Although he strongly championed Hölderlin publicly, he rarely (with one outstanding exception) mentions that poet in his notebooks, and there is little evidence that he read him extensively at Schulpforte. Nonetheless, his interest in the poet went sufficiently against the grain of contemporary

---

[27] Nietzsche indicates that he began reading Petöfi during the same period in which he was studying Emerson and writing "Fate and history," that is, in late winter and early spring 1862. KGW I-3: 3.
[28] Ortlepp was a deep admirer of Polish poetry and had published books on that subject. That enthusiasm may have extended to other lands in Eastern Europe. He was also a fervent proponent of the Revolution of 1848, and he may have planted the suggestion that Nietzsche read Petöfi.
[29] Janz 1976: 325. To further prove his East-European credentials Nietzsche set at the same time two songs based on texts by Pushkin. He had also composed a poem called "The Old Hungarian." KGW I-2: 452–453.
[30] See letters from Wilhelm and Gustav. KGB I-1: 360, 363. Nietzsche apparently suggested the purchase, but his letter is not extant. Wilhelm presented a lecture on Hölderlin to Germania in March, 1862. KGW I-2: 483.
[31] KGB I-1: 328. Cited in Brobjer 2001a: 400, n. 20.   [32] Brobjer 2001a: 399–400.
[33] See this chapter, Section 4.

public opinion that one must assume that Nietzsche found genuine inspiration and sustenance in the man's work.[34] In Hölderlin he would have discovered an almost religious commitment to classical Greek ideals – indeed, a determination to take them so seriously that contemporary German culture seemed by comparison shallow and dishonest. There are also strong Christian undertones in Hölderlin's work to which the young Nietzsche, however he might question that faith, would respond. He would further have encountered some of the supreme poems in the German language. Hölderlin was also, of course, a significant thinker, a friend of both Schelling and Hegel, and a major theoretician of the Romantic movement in Germany. Finally, Nietzsche may have been intrigued from a biographical point of view by similarities between his own and Hölderlin's background.[35]

Just as Nietzsche's literary tastes were changing, so he began to explore new music, and – given music's visceral appeal – it is likely that new tastes here would be at least as influential as those in the more evidently mediated language of poetry. During his Pforta years he was exposed to music several times a week, not just as listener but as performer. He sang in the school choir, both on Sundays and during ceremonies, and he sometimes toured the surrounding countryside with this group. Meanwhile, he continued to improvise at the piano. As might be expected at this school, his efforts at composition took a systematic turn; he studied a text on counterpoint by Johann Georg Albrechtsberger (Beethoven's early teacher) and turned out so many fugues that Gustav advised him to show restraint.[36]

Beginning in 1861, Nietzsche began to leave the terrain of his beloved classics – Beethoven and Haydn had always figured in his gift lists – and to explore music that was more contemporary. One would think that when venturing into mid-nineteenth-century territory he would turn to the most controversial of modern composers, the notorious Richard Wagner. His friend Gustav was already a passionate Wagnerian and gave four lectures on that composer's work to Germania, thereby making sure that his two friends were kept abreast of the man's progress. Nonetheless, Nietzsche was to prove wary of Wagner's music (but not necessarily of his writings) for several more years.[37] Instead, he was smitten with the compositions of Robert Schumann, a composer who was romantic in spirit and willing to

---

[34] Brobjer attributes extraordinary influence to Neumann's introduction to Hölderlin. Brobjer 2001a: 402.
[35] Brobjer 2001a: 402.
[36] KGB I-1: 355. For Nietzsche's fascination with Albrechtsberger, see KGW I-2: 474.
[37] See Chapter 14, Section 2.

experiment in form but more associated with the traditionalists. (His protégé, Johannes Brahms, would become a hero of the more conservative school.) Nietzsche wrote repeatedly and enthusiastically about Schumann's "*Paradies und die Peri,*" and he recommended that his sister learn the song cycle, "*Frauenliebe und -leben,*" an offer Elisabeth declined. And one might note that, supposedly like his father and the Prussian king and certainly like Hölderlin, Schumann had gone insane, a biographical detail that Nietzsche would have noticed.

3

So far, Nietzsche's explorations had seemed comparatively benign, an expression of curiosity rather than any active desire to rebel. The pursuit of new artists no doubt reflected restlessness, but he seems to have been casting about for new pathways rather than attempting revolt. The most signal shift had occurred midway through 1861 when, as mentioned, he abandoned his oratorio to write secular music, a decision which suggests a loosening of ties to Christianity. As was apparent in "Fate and history," written eight months later, his allegiance to religion must have been eroding throughout this period. Nonetheless, and for obvious reasons given the punitive climate within which he lived, there were few outward signs of a drift from faith.

Yet in August 1861 an event occurred which, however lamented at the time, would set him free from his principal anchor to orthodoxy at school. As mentioned earlier, Schulpforte was subject to unpredictable and sometimes fatal incursions of disease.[38] In early August Professor Buddensieg, the school's assistant pastor and Nietzsche's tutor, fell ill with rheumatic symptoms, and on August 20, he died. It is difficult to determine how devoted Nietzsche was to Buddensieg.[39] Those who claim the relationship was close tend to cite two letters Nietzsche wrote immediately after his death. This seems questionable, for what adolescents would not have expressed themselves dramatically when reporting the death of a long-term faculty advisor? It is more to the point that before the man's death Nietzsche's remarks had been blandly perfunctory – he doesn't pay him a single compliment or gesture of affection – and when he later recalled the

---

[38] See Chapter 6, Section 2.
[39] Nietzsche did keep a book of Buddensieg's sermons. Pernet 1989: 142, n. 103, 141, n. 94; Campioni *et al.* 2003: 677.

teachers who had influenced him at Pforta, he never once mentioned his first tutor.[40]

In the aftermath Nietzsche could have responded in a variety of ways. He might, for example, have seized the occasion to revert to orthodoxy, taking his tutor's death as an omen that his own deviations from faith had been misguided. If he had truly loved Buddensieg, he might have shown respect by trying to follow his values. In fact he seems to have interpreted the event in the opposite way, as an opportunity to slip the reins altogether and to begin taking steps that his former tutor would have abhorred. This recourse is already explicit in his letter home, when he announces the event. "We already knew yesterday that [Buddensieg] would not survive the night. The doctor predicted it. I don't know anything more specific about his end, and we can't ask. Ah, it is too painful! But – what God does is well done."[41] The abrupt and tonally awkward reversal of that final statement suggests at least a shade of mockery. (One should not forget his contempt for this attitude as expressed in "Freedom of will and fate.") Even more startling is the businesslike sentence which follows: "You're probably coming out for his burial; I must now have a new tutor and will speak with H.D. Heinze today or tomorrow about it." Thus, Nietzsche's first response, after announcing his instructor's death, is not to mourn but to propose his replacement – in this case Max Heinze, a comparatively recent arrival at Pforta – and to do so before Franziska has an opportunity to oppose him. (If she has objections, he writes, she should voice them as soon as possible. He also needs fresh laundry.)

Regardless of the propriety of Nietzsche's announcement, his decision for Heinze was significant. More worldly, ambitious, and intellectually successful than most of the school's professors (and certainly than the deceased Buddensieg), Heinze was eventually to leave the school to serve as tutor in the household of the Duke of Oldenburg and later to marry into the patrician Lepsius family.[42] Although a Naumburg native, he had majored in philosophy at the University of Leipzig and had published a thesis on the Stoics only three years before arriving at Schulpforte. He therefore brought to the seventeen-year-old Nietzsche a freshly minted expertise in philosophy – particularly ancient philosophy – that few of the other professors were likely to offer. Nor was this interest to be abandoned. Heinze would become a leading figure in the philosophical world during Nietzsche's lifetime, and the two would renew acquaintance and exchange letters in the final third of Nietzsche's public life. While such events lay in

---

[40] See, for example, KGW I-5: 53.   [41] KSAB I: 170.   [42] See KSAB I: 229, 260.

the future, their roots were already present in 1861 (Heinze would leave in the early spring of 1863) and Nietzsche's turn to philosophy as well as his own ambitions may have been whetted by Heinze's example. It is also relevant that whereas Buddensieg was not only pious but much valued by Franziska, who was close to his wife,[43] Heinze was a recent arrival and already moving in social circles largely closed to Nietzsche's mother (but not to Wilhelm and Gustav, who knew the man personally). With this choice Nietzsche took command of his own supervision. He also entered a new phase in his life, a transition from what might be called benign exploration to active revolt. It was in the immediate aftermath of Buddensieg's death that he began to devise, largely unguided, a way of behavior that might replace the meek and obedient upbringing associated with his mother and the world of the Church.

4

It was earlier suggested that certain professors at Pforta were prone to rest on their laurels and to relax into their sinecures.[44] Inspector Niese is generally regarded as a signal example of this tendency. Although he was ostensibly the spiritual guardian of the boys, he didn't even attend morning prayers, leaving most religious supervision to Buddensieg.[45] Other cases of lax instruction were less egregious and might be represented by Karl August Koberstein, probably the school's most prestigious professor, who had written a history of German literature that could be found on the shelves of households with pretensions to culture. (The Krugs owned two volumes.)[46] Indeed, Anton Springer, later one of Nietzsche's favorite professors at Bonn, declared him, "by far the most important literary historian of our time."[47] Koberstein himself had been rebellious in youth, but an injudicious remark on Martin Luther had nearly cost him his career.[48] Whatever his true views, he seems thereafter to have settled into quiet conformity, writing his magnum opus and guiding the

---

[43] KSAB I: 167, 172.
[44] Governmental authorities became quite critical of the Schulpforte teaching staff during Nietzsche's later years there. Gilman 1979: 422–426. They recommended, for example, that Koberstein be retired and Steinhart transferred. Whether this represented sage judgment or a political move on the part of those who wished to undermine Pforta's independence cannot be judged here. Most of the more prestigious members of the faculty either left or were transferred shortly after Nietzsche's departure.
[45] For criticisms of Niese, see Pernet 1989: 75–76 and especially 139, n. 72. See also Bohley 2007: 91–97; Gilman 1979: 410–411, 422–423.
[46] KGB I-1: 348.   [47] KSAB II: 55.   [48] Schmidt 1991–1994 III: 177, n. 92.

development of students. He was considered a distinguished elder at Pforta. During the interregnum between rectors before the arrival of Peter, he ran the school;[49] and he often presided at celebrations of German literature. In 1859 during a three-day festival honoring the centenary of Schiller's birth, Koberstein gave the keynote speech and coordinated the program, which was attended by most of the political dignitaries of Naumburg and surrounding towns.[50]

Koberstein had inspired affection and loyalty during his early years at Pforta – Otto Jahn, one of Nietzsche's future teachers, would remember him with reverence. However, he seems to have been perceived by the boys of Nietzsche's generation as a benign but ineffectual figurehead, knowledgeable but uninspiring.[51] Carl Gersdorff, one of Nietzsche's closest friends, regularly referred to him as "Fatty," and this seems to have been his nickname among the student body at large.[52] This attitude perhaps accounts for an essay that Nietzsche composed for this teacher late in 1861, two months after Buddensieg's death. In a school exercise he was asked to write a letter to a friend recommending his favorite poet.[53] The response that resulted was disrespectful in two ways. First, Nietzsche chose as his subject Friedrich Hölderlin, a man Schiller and Goethe had both regarded with misgivings, and whose irregular life and unconventional art could not have endeared him to the authorities. There is some controversy as to how esteemed Hölderlin was during Nietzsche's youth, but from Koberstein's disparaging remarks on Nietzsche's essay, it is clear that he, at least, was not an admirer.[54] Nietzsche, however, wrote a spirited defense of this author, citing in particular "Empedocles," *Hyperion*, and a number of individual poems.[55]

Nietzsche's essay was also disrespectful because he crafted it to deceive his professor. While the piece itself is eloquent and provides a fine example of literary advocacy, which, after all, was the point of the exercise, scholars – notably Thomas Brobjer on whose work the following account is based[56] – have discovered that his text leans considerably on and sometimes directly copies the book Nietzsche himself owned and which he asked his sister to

---

[49] Gilman 1979: 399. The previous rector, Karl Kirchner, had died and there was a pause before Peter was appointed and took over the reins.
[50] KSAB I: 84–85. See also KGW I-2: 175–177.
[51] See, for example, Wilamowitz-Moellendorff 1928: 77–78.
[52] See Gersdorff's letters, KGB I-3: 14, 26. For the student population in general, see Wilamowitz-Moellendorff 1928: 67.
[53] Bohley 1976: 312.
[54] For a discussion of Hölderlin's reputation at the time, see Brobjer 2001a: 401.
[55] KGW I-2: 338–341.   [56] Brobjer 2001a.

send from home.[57] This was probably not the first and certainly not the last time that Nietzsche could be accused of presenting someone else's text as his own.[58] While the subject of Nietzsche and plagiarism in general will not be discussed here, his appropriation of another's writing does in this case afford an opportunity to show how he explored certain strategies of self-liberation. It might be noted, for example, that the passages Nietzsche copied were of two kinds. Leaning on his unacknowledged source, he professes himself enraptured by the novel, *Hyperion*, a work not present in either his own or in Pinder's anthology and for that reason probably not read by Nietzsche at this time. On most occasions, however, he helped himself to fragments rather than whole sentences from his source, assimilating the copied text to his own rhythms and stances. In other words, rather than just regarding Nietzsche's plagiarism as an academic misdeed – and this writer has no wish to defend it – one might interpret it as emulative. He was lighting his torch from someone else's flame, a transmission of enthusiasm common in adolescence and interesting insofar as it demonstrates Nietzsche's willingness to take inspiration where he could find it, even if he did not acknowledge the debt.

As a result, the reader can surmise that he was reading neither William Neumann, the author in question,[59] nor Hölderlin, just for their literary skills. These were models he tried to incorporate and imitate, expanding his repertoire of value and behavior. This aspect of Nietzsche's reading is more evident in his espousal of Byron, an enthusiasm he first announces in autumn 1861, shortly after writing the Hölderlin essay. As already mentioned, Ortlepp's influence was probably in play. At this time, however, Diederich Volkmann, a twenty-three-year-old professor, had just been hired at Pforta and he offered private courses in English.[60] Nietzsche did not enroll, but some of his classmates studied under Volkmann, and an interest in English-speaking writers must have percolated through the dormitory. (It is noteworthy that Volkmann gave a speech on Byron to the *Literaria* in Naumburg.)[61] Thus, it is unlikely to have been accidental that in the very semester that Volkmann gave his initial presentations Nietzsche became interested in three English-speaking authors:

---

[57] Brobjer 2001a: 400–403. Aspects of this discovery had apparently been previously made by Geoffrey Waite. See Breazale 1989: 100, 103, n. 16.
[58] See Sommer 2000. See also Chapter 13, Section 4.
[59] "William Neumann" was a pseudonym for Arthur Friedrich Bussenius. Brobjer 2001a: 399, n. 14.
[60] Nietzsche was drawn to this instruction but did not participate at the time, possibly because he was already taking private lessons in Italian, from Koberstein, no less. Deussen indicates that Volkmann shortly dropped the English classes. Deussen 1922: 105.
[61] Bohley 2007: 236.

Shakespeare, whose plays his Aunt Rosalie had given him for his birthday; Byron, for whom he conceived a veritable passion; and Ralph Waldo Emerson, whose writings would inspire him for the rest of his life.

In December 1861, Nietzsche celebrated his fascination with Byron by lecturing to Germania on the poet's dramatic works.[62] He was clearly inspired by the romantic onrush of the poet's sensibility, comparing it to (among other things) "the stormy force of a fiery spirit, of a volcano, that ... tears loose destructive, glowing lava." Brooding adolescent that he was, he also recognized that "the unhappy poetry of *Weltschmerz* finds in Byron its origin and its most genial unfolding." Nietzsche seems particularly to have valued Byron's melancholy and his celebration of the darkness of life – he describes "Manfred" as "really an accumulation of thoughts of despair" – and this would have encouraged and validated his own tendency to melancholy and distrust of good cheer.

However, the most immediate and visible manifestation of Byron on the adolescent Nietzsche may have been the pose of heroic isolation as celebrated in *Don Juan* and "Manfred." In his lecture he celebrates Don Juan as "the poet's innermost being." Yet if the Spanish grandee incarnates the imperturbable moralist scrutinizing humanity from a stance of innate superiority, "Manfred" takes that same pose to an almost demonic level, and this was a play that Nietzsche not only admired greatly as a student but continued to find inspirational to the end of his productive life. Byron's epic drama depicts the final days of a proud hero who seeks redemption and death without ever quite surrendering his ego. Like several of that author's plays the piece contains sublime passages that teeter on the edge of the ludicrous. Manfred spends much of the piece rather impressively rousing spirits from the deep. Yet when a witch whom he has summoned dares to offer advice, he dismisses her on the grounds that he is the master – she came at his bidding – so why should he obey someone inferior?[63] (To which one might ask, why then did he summon her in the first place?) At the play's end when demons arrive to drag Manfred downward, he simply refuses to go, an option which apparently never occurred to his spiritual kinsman, Don Giovanni. "Back to thy hell!" he cries and – entirely on his own terms – expires.[64] No wonder that one monster is compelled to acknowledge, "Had he been one of us, he would have made / An awful Spirit."[65]

---

[62] KGW I-2: 344–350. [63] "Manfred," II, 2, ll. 157–159. [64] "Manfred," III, 4, l. 125,
[65] "Manfred," II, 4, ll. 161–162.

While admiration for "Manfred" was widespread throughout the nineteenth century, Nietzsche seemed to have been particularly taken with the play.[66] Certainly the hero's most prominent characteristics – despair, independence, pride, loneliness – mirror aspects of Nietzsche's own psychology. Beyond this, Manfred is conspicuously self-contained and self-controlled, sustained and propelled solely by the imperiousness of his will.[67] Nobody can get to him; and he may have provided just the model Nietzsche needed to assert his new values. In the past he had tended to affect a pose of saintliness, modeling himself on his father and other ministers. Now "the imitation of Christ" was replaced with "the imitation of Manfred," and Nietzsche began to evidence kinds of behavior which startled former friends and began to alarm the authorities.

5

As though recognizing that he was becoming someone new, Nietzsche ordered fresh photographs made of himself. In these images (taken in June, 1862) he seems quite a different person from the rather conventional figure in the portrait from the year before. He has shed boyhood and is now clearly a young man, and he wears his hair Byronically long so that it falls in a clump well below his collar.[68] The new pictures are close-ups, but instead of looking frontally into the camera, Nietzsche turns his head to one side so that the eyes, which look rather startled under the eyebrows when viewed face-on, are seen merely to lie slightly sunk in their sockets, gazing from beneath an orbital shelf. From these clean-shaven portraits it is clear that his brow and jaw are almost as decisive in his appearance as the mustache which he would commence a year later.[69] Nietzsche himself seems to have regarded these photos as unfortunate, but he gave copies to Franziska, Elisabeth, and Rosalie and reserved three others for friends at Pforta.[70] Symptomatically, he did not include Wilhelm or Gustav, and indeed their friendship seems to have cooled about this time. Germania was falling moribund and there is a fourteen-month gap in which not a single letter from Wilhelm survives.[71] Gustav continued to write, but his letters grew

---

[66] Thatcher examines Nietzsche's fascination with this play (and musical interpretations) at length in Thatcher 1974: 137–148.
[67] In the winter of 1880, Nietzsche would write of Manfred, "[He] gives nobody the right to punish, pardon, or pity him." KSA IX: 388.
[68] The Byronic long hair was apparently an anomaly at Pforta. Gilman 1987: 16.
[69] Raimund Granier mentions that Nietzsche began to grow his mustache while still at Pforta. Gilman 1987: 9.
[70] See KSAB I: 209–210, 211.   [71] Compare the dates on KGB I-1: 384, 404.

increasingly fawning and self-abnegating, as though he had come to recognize in Nietzsche a dangerous superior, to be placated, flattered, and feared.[72]

Aside from Deussen, it is difficult to determine to what extent Nietzsche had other friends at Pforta. He exchanged Byronic letters with the sardonic Raimund Granier, and occasionally Nietzsche appears to have been close to Georg Stöckert, an intelligent and sensitive young man, who would graduate a term before him and whom he would meet again in Bonn.[73] Towards the close of his Pforta years Nietzsche also seems to have made friends with Rudolf Buddensieg, a nephew of his departed tutor, and letters written after graduation suggest intimacy with Carl von Gersdorff, one of the boarders at Pforta.

Above all, Nietzsche began to associate with Guido Meyer, a boy described by Deussen as "handsome, likeable and witty, also an excellent cartoonist, but forever at odds with teachers and the school system."[74] Meyer had entered Pforta the same year as Nietzsche but had been placed a full grade ahead, an advance that Meyer himself attributed to the preparatory school he had attended with Nietzsche.[75] This intellectual promise went unfulfilled, and he was eventually put back to join the same class as his friend. Clearly Meyer was headed downward, and Nietzsche may have been drawn to him as a prototype of rebellion. Good-looking, charming, sardonic, and anti-authoritarian, Guido Meyer must have seemed as Byronic as anyone at Pforta could hope for; and he and Nietzsche, who had known one another since 1857, became good friends.

The alliance between Nietzsche and Meyer seems to have begun in the autumn of 1861, that is, during the middle of the great change described in the last chapter. Nietzsche had been unsettled by the revelations of the anthropological essays and their implications for autobiography, and Buddensieg had just died. At this time he began his moral experiments, discarding pious restraint, testing new kinds of behavior, and probably alarming Paul Deussen, who could not be expected to approve. Alliance with Meyer meant trouble for this old friend, who remained

---

[72] KGB I-1: 407–409, 409–411.
[73] For intimate exchanges between Nietzsche and Stöckert, see KGW I-3: 3, 52. Hödl associates certain passages in "Fate and history" with Stöckert, which, if confirmed, would make Stöckert significant indeed. Hödl 1994b: 377.
[74] Deussen 1901: 5.
[75] As explained in Chapter 4, both Meyer and Nietzsche had attended preparatory classes in the summer of 1857. Meyer had not qualified even for Untertertia (first year) on his first try at the exam, but when he reapplied after the summer classes, he was assigned to Obertertia (second year). See his letter to Deussen, quoted in Hödl 2009: 135–136.

unregenerately studious and was probably not so witty and certainly not so glamorous as his dandyish peers. (They called him "the cobbler.")[76] Unable to join his friend in his new patterns of behavior, he paid the price in torments which he has described at length.[77] Others thought that Deussen deserved his lot; and Nietzsche himself recorded their quarrels in a mock epic succession of Latin hexameters, which began, "*Cantabo musae*," and which made clear that Meyer would play a heroic role.[78] (The project was left unfinished.)

In Deussen's account of his humiliations at the hands of friends, he gives the impression that after many arguments, harmony was restored and he and Nietzsche resumed their old understanding.[79] In other words, he saw the latter's adventure with Meyer as an aberration, after which he returned to his senses. There is some truth in this. Nietzsche would eventually drop his obstreperous friends and concentrate on his studies. However, given the exact chain of events, it is difficult to see his alliance with Meyer as due just to peer pressure or the meretricious glamor of rebellious boys. A reconsideration of values was probably at work, and Nietzsche's shift in loyalties may have registered a strategic step in his effort to disengage himself from an education he had come to mistrust. Students who misbehaved offered values unacknowledged and therefore unassimilated by the strictures of Schulpforte; and it should come as no surprise that Nietzsche investigated their alternative at the very time he had seen through norms enjoined by the social authorities. Suspicious of one kind of morality, he may have turned to the other.

Meanwhile, despite Deussen's relief, the peace made between him and his friend was by no means a restoration to order but only a temporary truce. Instead, in the coming years Nietzsche would demean and patronize him with such regularity that one biographer has called him the philosopher's "whipping boy."[80] Perhaps, as was suggested earlier, the so-called friendship was from the beginning more one-sided than Deussen depicted.[81] This already fraught relationship, however, took a darker turn after the spring of 1861, when Nietzsche began to change. Deussen was probably not able (or willing) to accommodate the shift, yet he expected the friendship to continue. If so, he had fundamentally misunderstood Nietzsche. Years later the latter would write in a poem, "Nur wer sich wandelt, bleibt mit mir verwandt": ("Only those who change stay related

---

[76] KGW I-2: 342. Wolleck 2010: 58.   [77] Deussen 1901: 4–7; Gilman 1987: 11–13.
[78] KGW I-2: 341–344. Wolleck 2010: 57–62.
[79] Deussen 1901: 4–7. English version in Gilman 1987: 11–13.   [80] Ross 1980: 215.
[81] See Chapter 6, Section 1.

to me.")[82] This attitude seems to have been constant in his short life. He might undergo many swift and dramatic transformations, yet he always expected friends to follow; and when they did not, he tended to lose interest. Deussen was merely among the earlier casualties of this ruthless yet inevitable dynamic.

6

Nietzsche's rebellious activities were not limited to bullying Deussen or conniving with Meyer. A musical composition entitled "Satan rises out of Hell" was abandoned only because he found it difficult "to strike the exact Satanic note."[83] Eventually, he began to play billiards and even drink, a pastime which shocked the more conventional Gustav.[84] Along with these behavioral shifts came a change in bearing that troubled Heinze enough that he mentioned it to Franziska. Fellow students, he wrote, had begun to find Nietzsche vain, and he concurred with this judgment.[85] Certainly, an air of arrogant superiority is evident in a letter the boy sent to his mother that autumn. He had just been promoted to his fifth year, a significant ascent since he would gain many new privileges, and he had also just been made Primus after a year in which he had not qualified. He therefore let his mother know that "I have kept waiting for a letter in which I had hoped to find at least a few congratulations. Especially Saturday, when you knew that the promotion would take place." He then directed her to arrange a celebratory tea dance. "You know who I want invited. See that nothing is omitted."[86] Such directions read not as requests, but as commands, and they probably manifest a peremptory attitude on her son's part with which Franziska was wearily familiar.

These changes did not go unnoticed by the school authorities. Nietzsche seems not to have been Primus from October 1861, the time of the Hölderlin paper, until October 1862, the period under discussion here, and that is understandable, as his new behavior was probably not conducive to his studies.[87] By October, 1862, however, he had recovered his position, only to endanger it by a miscalculation. As Primus Nietzsche had to submit inventories of schoolroom furniture, and in some of these he manifested his new insouciance by introducing what he considered levity into his reports. The faculty was not amused and seem to have interpreted

---

[82] The poem is "*Aus hohen Bergen,*" which concludes *Beyond good and evil*. This translation is by Walter Kaufmann, who drew attention to the line.
[83] KGW I-3: 3. [84] KGB I-1: 386–387. [85] Benders *et al.* 2000: 89. [86] KSAB I: 224.
[87] For Nietzsche's terms as Primus, see Chapter 5, n. 89.

this as insolence. He was called before a synod of professors and sentenced to a week's suspension of off-campus privileges, three hours in a room of confinement (effectively, a cell), and a threat to revoke his status as Primus.[88] This seems a severe punishment for so minor an infraction, but apparently the faculty was alarmed by other misdemeanors as well. "In January," they wrote, "he forgot himself so completely as to try to deceive us by writing someone else's report."[89] This accusation was made in November, and January had been ten months before. It therefore appears that the authorities had noted a long-term pattern of insubordination on Nietzsche's part and wanted to put a halt to it permanently.

Nietzsche himself tried to brazen the affair out, delivering the news home with the salutation "*Liebe Leute*" ("Dear Folks").[90] (He omitted, however, any mention of the earlier forgery.) Franziska, had discovered the truth on her own but seems to have answered the letter with extraordinary gentleness, considering the transgression. "My dear Fritz," she wrote, "I would have expected more tact from you, but you must again endure the reproach of vanity, always doing something different from the others. I find the punishment appropriate, since it seems a terrible affront to permit oneself something like that with regard to your teachers. But please, be more careful in thought and action, always follow your inner better voice, and you will be protected from all *the restlessness and struggle that now grows in you* ... Write me soon, my dear son, but not with the salutation, 'Dear Folks.' You will yourself feel that something like that shouldn't be sent to your mother."[91] (Emphasis added.)

Nietzsche's reply offers insight into how he saw himself *vis-à-vis* the authorities at this time, and the relevant passage bears quotation in full:

> I have astoundingly plenty to do but find myself both physically and mentally better than ever. I am always in a cheerful mood and work with great relish. I can't understand why you can worry even a moment over the consequences of that story, since you have understood it correctly and have reproached me in the letter. I will certainly beware of further indiscretions. But that I should linger in a bad mood, that is out of the question. Let Heinze and others look there for what they want – I know what happened there and I am fully at ease in consequence. As said, I have rarely been in a better mood than now, my projects move forward well, my dealings are various and pleasant – and there can be no question of influence; for that I

---

[88] Benders *et al.* 2000: 91.   [89] Hödl 2009: 146.   [90] KSAB I: 225–226.
[91] KGB I-1: 388. It is possible, of course, that Franziska wrote another, stronger letter which is now missing, for her son was stung by her suggestion that his companions had exercised a bad influence on him, an accusation Franziska does not make here.

would first have to meet people whom I considered my superior. I find even the cold temperature pleasant – in short I feel quite good and have bad feelings toward no one, not even the teachers. Perhaps as teachers they could not understand the situation differently.[92]

Aside from the arguable arrogance of Nietzsche's statement on not having superiors, his response seems remarkably thoughtful and mature. He in no way sees himself as having done something wrong; he does see that he has made an error, a miscalculation in not taking account of the faculty's likely response; and he resolves not to do this again. He blames no one else for this, and although he is plainly irritated with Heinze, he does not seriously blame his teachers. He does complain of his mother's intervention – it is as though a little "Naumburg Virtue" has intruded into his own realm and had to be exorcised – but he sees himself as responsible for his actions and is determined not to feel guilty when guilt, a moral category, is invoked. He has made a mistake; that's all.

If, as Nietzsche so Byronically puts it, he had not met a superior person, he was nonetheless indentured to a superior force. Toward the beginning of 1863 he twice witnessed the fate of those who challenged the administration at Pforta. In early February a boy "who was generally much loved" was expelled,[93] and later that month his beloved Guido Meyer (who had made an impromptu excursion off campus) met the same fate and tearfully bade goodbye to his comrades. For Nietzsche it was "the saddest day of my life at Pforta."[94] Fortunately for him, the school did not seem to associate him with his unfortunate companion, for when classes resumed after the Easter break, Nietzsche was appointed to supervise and counsel a group of three other boys. Max Heinze had recently left the school, and Nietzsche chose as his new tutor, Hermann Kletschke, a thirty-three-year-old cleric who had replaced Buddensieg as the secondary spiritual leader at Pforta.

Nietzsche seems never to have been close to Kletschke, and there is no evidence that the new tutor had significant influence over him. On the contrary, for all the piety that Kletschke clearly sought to instill in his young charge (and his letters invariably appeal to Christian ethics) Nietzsche's rebelliousness was merely in abeyance. On Sunday, April 12, 1863, he joined a classmate at a railroad station tavern and drank four mugs of beer. According to Deussen, he was not used to alcohol and for that reason easily showed the effects.[95] During his return to campus, a professor noted the symptoms and brought him and the other student to the attention of the authorities. Again there was a secondary charge:

[92] KSAB I: 227.   [93] KSAB I: 230–231.   [94] KSAB I: 232.   [95] Deussen 1901: 10–11.

Nietzsche was not only accused of drunkenness but of being too "devil-may-care."[96] Accordingly, he was relieved of his status as Primus for the remainder of his time at Pforta.

This time Nietzsche did not try to dismiss the incident. "Dear Mother," his letter home began, "If I write to you today, it is about one of the most unpleasant and saddest incidents I have ever been responsible for. In fact I have misbehaved very badly, and I do not know whether you can or will forgive me ... Last Sunday I got drunk, and I have no excuse, except that I did not know how much I could take ... Through this affair I have spoilt the fairly good position I succeeded in winning for myself the previous term ... I do not need to give you any further assurances how seriously I will pull myself together, for now a lot depends on it."[97]

Nietzsche's regret was real. The drinking incident marks a turning point in his adolescent life. It is not clear, however, what motive was uppermost in his change of mind. Did he feel guilt, shame, mortification at losing his status at school? Did he truly repent the moral experiments of the previous two years? Or, more practically, was he afraid that he would meet Meyer's end and be expelled from the Gymnasium, a serious fate in nineteenth-century Prussia. Probably all these motives were operative, but Förster-Nietzsche suggests yet another which strikes to the heart of Nietzsche's character.[98] Throughout his life Nietzsche had a horror of losing dignity. For all his stress on honesty, he had an immense respect for image and good form. In surrendering to alcohol, he had lost self-control and thereby betrayed not only himself but the model provided by his principal hero. He had failed to live up to the principles of his beloved Lord Byron: Manfred would never have gotten drunk.

---

[96] Quoted in Hödl 2009: 146, n. 365.   [97] KSAB I: 236–237.
[98] Förster-Nietzsche 1912: 105–106.

CHAPTER 8

The lottery

People choose *their career when they're not yet capable of choosing.*[1]

I

The letter announcing his disgrace was one of the first from Nietzsche to Franziska that does not sound dutiful and glib. Throughout his Pforta years he had treated his mother as a menial source of supplies, and his occasional testimonials of affection tended to be formulaic and uninspired, crafted to keep her lulled and incurious. The anodyne tone of Nietzsche's correspondence was perhaps necessary, since quarrels had begun to mar his visits home. An unknown disagreement disturbed his Easter vacation in 1861 just after his Confirmation,[2] and the following Easter (1862) he seriously offended his aunts.[3] According to Förster-Nietzsche, yet another controversy had erupted around Christmas, 1861. Towards the end of November (three months after Buddensieg's death and at the time he was discovering Byron) Friedrich had drawn up a list of books and music that his sister might wish for Christmas. Here, in addition to Schumann's "*Frauenliebe und -leben,*" he recommended that she ask for two works by the theologian, Karl Hase, his *Church history* and *The Life of Jesus.*[4] Förster-Nietzsche says that the latter suggestion "roused my mother and Aunt Rosalie (who was an authority on dogma) to a positive storm of indignation,"[5] and apparently the books did not lie under the tree that Christmas. It bears saying that this story has been questioned, and it cannot be true as stated.[6] However, Friedrich's

---

[1] KSA VIII: 20. [2] KSAB I: 154–155. [3] KSAB I: 204.
[4] KSAB I: 188. Nietzsche noted the price of Hase's *Dogmatik* in his notebooks: KGW I-2: 298. He requested Hase's *Das Leben Jesu* for himself in a birthday list. KGW I-2: 307.
[5] Förster-Nietzsche 1912: 89–90.
[6] Pernet observes that Franziska was not even home at this time and that Rosalie would not have found Hase's book intrinsically objectionable, since it was recommended by Friedrich August Wenkel, preacher at St. Wencelas. Pernet 1989: 81–82.

literary choices do seem to have been controversial, for even Gustav was shocked. In his Christmas list that same year to this friend, Nietzsche had asked for an unnamed book of which the latter said, "I have heard something of the title and am really alarmed by it, since I have heard of problems and other terrible things about it."[7] Gustav was neither so naïve as Franziska nor so religious as Rosalie. If he found Friedrich's choice problematic, then the boy's reading fell well outside the range of Naumburg respectability.

Nietzsche's misfortune seems to have brought these tensions to a head and momentarily restored peace, for he recognized that he was more dependent on the ministrations of family than he realized. He needed in particular his mother's understanding and forgiveness, qualities that could be in short supply with the rigid Franziska. Apparently she responded with sufficient charity and compassion that the tone of their relationship changed for the remainder of his time at Pforta. The peremptory tone of his earlier correspondence relaxed, and his letters become, occasionally at least, open acts of communication in which he exhibited real interest in how she would respond.[8]

Several of these letters issue from the sick ward for, given Nietzsche's history, his inevitable reaction to the crisis was to fall ill. A little over a week after the event, he entered the infirmary where severe hoarseness and a bad cold led to leeches being applied to his neck.[9] Two weeks later he reported a discharge from his ears and ulcers behind them. "It is absolutely the most painful illness I've had," he wrote Franziska;[10] and he had trouble hearing and seeing. He complained of having nothing interesting to read in the infirmary and regretted that he could not play the piano: "Everything seems dead to me when I don't hear music."[11] Instead he spent the time sleeping and thinking about his future, for he knew that he would soon be asked to specialize. At the age of fourteen he had listed the many fields that interested him and been unable to regard any as definitive. Now he was eighteen and no closer to a decision. Heretofore, he had coasted, perhaps taking for granted that he would eventually become a minister. As that profession came to seem increasingly unsuitable, he was confronted with an urgent need to address realities and to make a decision. He broached this to his mother, perhaps preparing her for developments she would not approve. "How easily one lets oneself be swept away," he wrote, "by a momentary preference, an old family tradition [sic], or some odd wish, so that the choice

---

[7] KGB I-1: 374.   [8] See, for example, KSAB I: 238.   [9] KSAB I: 238.   [10] KSAB I: 241.
[11] KSAB I: 238.

of profession becomes a lottery." Worse, he would have to give up some of his interests. "But which will be the unlucky ones that get thrown overboard? Perhaps my favorite children!"[12]

As his reference to "an old family tradition" indicates, Nietzsche was reconsidering his future as a minister. No documents confirm this, just as (with the single exception already noted), none confirm that he was destined to be a clergyman in the first place.[13] Nonetheless, his family and friends had taken this profession as a given, and insofar as it offered spiritual vision and appealed to his verbal abilities, it seemed a good fit for his talents. A refusal of so preordained a career would require a strong will and probably a willingness to inflict pain. Further, it would bring in its train a host of new anxieties. If he was not to become a minister, what profession would he choose instead?

Under the best of circumstances, Nietzsche would have found the selection of an alternate career difficult. He had no obvious vocation for any field but the one he now wanted to discard. He would shortly rule out becoming a writer or musician, and that seemed to leave only philology, a field that he had drifted into through an accident of education and which he had certainly not actively chosen. Beyond that, the once aspiring poet and composer recoiled from this austere profession. He would spend much of the summer taking notes on Emerson, focusing on the decidedly anti-academic essay "Beauty" from *The conduct of life*.[14] Early in that chapter Emerson laments that scientific methods of study inevitably alienate researchers from the very nature they affect to love. The more they investigate, the more estranged they become from the glory which first inspired them. (As he put it elsewhere in the book, "The naturalist is led *from* the road by the whole distance of his fancied advance." (1099)) Although the essay concentrates on natural scientists, much of its criticism is applicable to academics, and Emerson makes a cruel remark which Nietzsche could hardly overlook: "What manner of man does science make? The boy is not attracted. He says, I do not wish to be such a kind of man as my professor is." (1100)[15]

If, in the aftermath of disgrace, Nietzsche wrote in a new tone to his mother, he ceased almost entirely to write to his friends, apparently neglecting even to wish Wilhelm a happy birthday.[16] His conduct toward Guido

---

[12] KSAB I: 239–240.   [13] See Chapter 4, Section 5.
[14] Nietzsche made extensive notes on this essay. KGW I-3: 180–182. See also 227–228.
[15] See Section 3.
[16] With the exception of the sketch for the impersonal "Feuerbach Letter" from April 1862, not a single letter from Friedrich to his friends survives between August 21, 1861 (just before Buddensieg's death) and June 1864, a period of nearly three years. While letters were surely written and lost, a break must

Meyer is particularly telling. He had clearly been devoted to Meyer – he had given the latter the only copies of several of his poems[17] – and he deeply mourned the boy's departure. Yet although other schoolmates, some far less intimate with this black sheep than Nietzsche, kept track of the expelled boy's fate, Nietzsche passively severed the relationship by neglecting to answer his letters. He received at least two pleas from Meyer. In the first, the unfortunate boy describes his lack of success in enrolling in other schools, the bitterness of his disappointed parents, and the pain of having himself to blame for losing the paradise of friendship he had enjoyed at Pforta. He wants to believe that he has not been forgotten and concludes, "A letter! A letter!" adding that he'd like a photograph of Nietzsche if one is available.[18] Apparently, Nietzsche did not reply. A second letter, sent two months later, begins, "Dear God, why haven't I received a letter from you yet, from you, whose letters I would most like to read. Have you already forgotten?"[19]

Nietzsche had not forgotten – that he kept these letters speaks for itself. He had changed, however, and one consequence of that change seems to have been a severance from all friends except Paul Deussen. Even Wilhelm and Gustav did not survive this retrenchment. Relations with these childhood chums had been cool for some time, as suggested by their long-term lack of contribution to Germania.[20] But in the summer of 1863, Nietzsche made a presentation that they would probably not forget. From the beginning it had been the boys' custom to criticize one another's work, and in the process they were sometimes (in Förster-Nietzsche's words) "more or less driven to discourtesy."[21] In June Nietzsche presented two papers. One was untitled but devoted to Gustav's submissions and the other was called, "The poetical achievements of W. Pinder."[22] In the first, he briefly disparaged Gustav's work; in the second, he savaged that of his quondam friend, Wilhelm, stating, for example, that Wilhelm could not credibly write of love because he had never experienced it. This may have been chosen as Germania's last meeting. Alternatively Nietzsche himself may have administered the *coup de grâce*. In either case the group was dissolved.

It is difficult to know what turned Nietzsche against his associates. In May of 1863, just after the drinking incident and about the time he received

have occurred at some point, for Nietzsche failed even to say goodbye to his friends when they left for the university. KGB I-1: 416.
[17] KGW I-4: 89.   [18] KGB I-1: 401.   [19] KGB I-1: 401.
[20] Neither Wilhelm nor Gustav made any contributions after April 1862. KGW I-2: 470–471, 480–483.
[21] Förster-Nietzsche 1912: 92.   [22] KGW I-3: 135–142.

Guido Meyer's first letter, he wrote an essay on Shakespeare's "Julius Caesar" in which he interpreted the work as a tragedy of betrayed friendship.[23] In the play Brutus famously assassinates his dearest friend Caesar, a deed to which, as Nietzsche stresses, he is seduced by Cassius, although the murder may also represent his true desire. Meanwhile, Cassius, who is astute in political maneuvers, so values the other's nobility that he concedes to his friend even when the latter makes high-minded misjudgments which prove disastrous to their cause. Both men betray themselves at the behest of the other and in the process display their most profound weaknesses. Yet both conceive themselves ultimately betrayed by their friend in turn, Brutus when Cassius takes bribes, Cassius when Brutus accuses him of defalcation.[24] As an insight into the dynamics of the play the essay is both penetrating and appears to be original. It is no less significant from a biographical point of view. Nietzsche's topic was a class assignment but the timing was providential. He was required by the theme to take the point of view of Cassius, but whether he saw himself as "the noblest Roman of them all" or the man who swore loyalty only to find himself rebuffed must remain unknown. He certainly looked at friendship and saw it as potentially tragic, concluding, "A friendship of this kind, that weighs both down with error and guilt and leads both to ruin, has, nonetheless, something endlessly touching about it."

2

If Nietzsche's personal life had its joys and despairs, he seems never to have allowed it to incapacitate him for effective action. In the aftermath of his disgrace, he needed not only to repair his academic standing but to regain the respect of those who believed in him, including his mother and Hermann Kletschke, the tutor who had replaced Max Heinze.[25] Accordingly, Nietzsche spent the summer holidays of 1863 industriously reading and taking notes on such literary topics as the *Nibelungenlied*, the Roman satirists (Persius and Juvenal), the *New Testament*, and the essay "Beauty" by Emerson.[26] Having seen these projects through, he returned for the autumn semester in excellent spirits. He liked to be productive and in a letter home he reveals much about how he conceived happiness.

---

[23] KGW I-3: 115–122.   [24] Bohley 1976: 313.   [25] See Chapter 7, Section 6.
[26] KGW I-3: 144–145. At the close of 1863 Nietzsche made a list with Emerson named "most read" at the top. KGW I-3: 299.

Whatever the obstacles, he stays active, he remarks and adds, "The clockworks are in motion and whir along."[27]

Given the recent revolution in his life and the huge decisions impending, it was characteristic of Nietzsche to review his life and in mid-September, he wrote "My life," apparently his first self-portrait since the troubling attempts in the spring of 1861.[28] While he again opens with a sketch of environmental context, he now brings to bear the discoveries of the Easter essays; and he compares attempts to picture the biography and character of a person with efforts to depict a landscape. In both cases the more dramatic features leap to the eye – rock formations in the latter case and dramatic events in the former. Excessive attention to such striking features can mislead. "We ought not to be guided by chance events, the gifts of fortune, the changing external eventualities which arise from conflicting external circumstances, when, like mountain peaks, they first leap to the eye." Far more important than the picturesque rocks is the vegetation – organic, living creatures which develop on their own terms, heedless of the turmoil about them. "It is precisely those little events and inner occurrences we believe we have to neglect which in their totality reveal the individual character most clearly; they grow organically out of the nature of the man, while the former appear only in inorganic connection with him." The stress on "inner occurrences" and "individual character" as well as the expression "they grow organically out of the nature of the man," should remind the reader of the discovery Nietzsche made in Emerson. No two people respond identically to the same situations. As he had written in "Fate and history," human beings are not after all whirled about by the vagaries of events. Individual temperament colors the way they receive these, and "we ... encounter everything in the mirror of our personality." It was character, not events, which should draw the attention of the biographer.

It is not clear that this approach entirely answers the objections Nietzsche had devised in 1861. There he had worried that surrounding circumstances in the form of bad nutrition and violent weather could alter and deform the passive plant. Surely no plant, no matter how defiantly it responds to poor conditions, could overcome the absence of indispensable resources. However, in 1863 Nietzsche argues for the agency of the "plant" in two ways. First, as just stated, he emphasizes the powers of individuality

---

[27] KSAB I: 253.
[28] KGW I-3: 189–192. English version by R.J. Hollingdale in Ansell Pearson and Large 2006: 18–20. One comma has been changed to a semicolon.

and the subtle ways creatures absorb nature in order to thrive. Further, although this is unclear, he seems also to find comfort in the exigencies of genus and species, the ways vegetation is compelled to produce and express the kind of plant it was born to be. It is through such inherent determination that they "grow organically out of [their] nature." Whatever the exact course of Nietzsche's reasoning, which is difficult to follow, it is beyond dispute that he has returned to the image of the human being as vegetation and that he believes he has resolved the objections he made before. He has also restored to character the primacy it enjoyed in the biography from 1858. One's character is at least as important as one's life history, and it is the development of this individual seed, not the external events of life, which most concern the autobiographer.[29]

After this very long prologue (a full third of the overall text), Nietzsche turns to the autobiography proper, beginning as ever with the events in Röcken and proceeding to his development in Naumburg. As for Schulpforte, he stresses here the ways it brought focus to his hitherto scattered and erratic devotion to learning and the arts. "I contained the wisdom of several lexicons, every possible inclination awoke in me, I wrote poems and tragedies ... tormented myself with the composition of complete orchestral scores, and ... was in danger of becoming a real muddle-head and fantasist. It was thus beneficial ... to devote oneself for six years to a greater concentration of one's forces and to directing them to firm goals."[30] He closes the autobiography with language resonantly reminiscent of his attempt in 1858. There he had stated, looking over his life, "God has led me safely through it all as does a father his weak little child."[31] Now – with God conspicuously unmentioned – he writes, "events have up to now led me along like a child." In both cases he means to express gratitude for the way his character has been led to develop, but he now indicates that whereas he has hitherto been comparatively passive, he intends to make a change. "Perhaps it is time to seize the reins of events oneself and step out into life."

3

This was a year of hard decisions, and Nietzsche did not spare himself. As he would later acknowledge, "Only in the final time of my life at Pforta and

---

[29] Nietzsche also used these paragraphs comparing portraiture to landscape depiction in a different essay. KGW I-3: 193–196.
[30] In the original this final sentence begins a new paragraph.
[31] KGW I-1: 310. See Chapter 4, Section 5.

in full self-knowledge did I give up all artistic plans for life."³² In other words he cast a cold eye on his musical compositions and creative writing and recognized that he lacked the talent and commitment to make a career of them. This did not stop him from continuing to produce poems and music, and he still played the piano. If he ever entertained illusions of making these his profession, however, he abandoned them now. This renunciation would have left him the more baffled with regard to the choice of a career. Although he had not made a public announcement of apostasy and could backslide in public – he took Confession again in his senior year – he had surely questioned Christianity too acutely in the past to seriously consider becoming a minister.

At this point Nietzsche rather creatively considered a new criterion for his selection. Possibly recalling Emerson's jibe that students did not want to grow up to be like their teachers, he reversed the claim. He admired his teachers, and he decided that certain philologists in his vicinity – Steinhart, Corssen, Keil, Koberstein, and Peter – spoke well enough for their profession that he would adopt it himself.³³ This decision entailed a farewell to dreams of artistic fruition, but his choice was perhaps made easier (surely it was reinforced) by the ignominious end of a certain poet. During the spring of 1864 Ernst Ortlepp fell into a ditch and broke his neck. He had almost certainly been drunk – Nietzsche had met him in a tavern earlier in the afternoon – and an editorial in the Naumburg paper suggested that he died a suicide. Nietzsche described the funeral, although he surely did not attend (the obsequies were unannounced and held privately);³⁴ and his account is monotone and void of affect. Nonetheless, the implications of this end would have proved disquieting for a student envisioning the arts as a career.

Spurred by a need to be practical, Nietzsche reached new heights of scholarship. In the autumn he was involved on an exceptionally ambitious project, a thorough examination of the sources for the Ermanarich saga. He seems to have taken pleasure in the necessary hard work and wrote his mother, "In general I swim pleasantly in my studies and live very well like a fish in its element."³⁵ The completed paper seemed to him his only production at Pforta with which he was "almost satisfied";³⁶ and Koberstein, the professor who had been bemused by Nietzsche's essay on Hölderlin, praised it enthusiastically in private.³⁷ Possibly Nietzsche used

---

[32] KGW I-5: 52–53.   [33] KGW I-5: 46.   [34] For specifics on the funeral, see Feldhoff 2008: 41.
[35] KSAB I: 265.
[36] For the essay see KGW I-3: 239–269. For Nietzsche's evaluation see KGW I-3: 419.
[37] Gilman and Reichenbach 1981: 47.

the Ermanarich project to train himself for a severe task which lay ahead. Students at Pforta were encouraged to write a senior paper on a suitable theme.[38] Nietzsche and Deussen both chose to comply, and the Naumburg boy fixed on Theognis, an elegiac poet who flourished in the sixth century B.C. and was possibly from Megara, a city-state west of Athens.[39]

To this day scholars have little reliable knowledge concerning this figure, who was much esteemed by the Greeks of the Golden Age but has since come to seem minor.[40] He appears to have been an aristocrat who – due to some political upheaval (either the triumph of a despot or a popular uprising) – lost his lands and went into exile. His poems lament the arrival of new values that he regards as debased, and he celebrates the virtues of the aristocratic world that is passing away. Though considered primarily a moralist by his Greek admirers, Theognis hardly fits the ascetic image associated with that figure today. Many of his lines were probably drinking songs, written for the accompaniment of the flute,[41] and they seem largely addressed to a young man, Kyrnos, whom the poet alternately desires, flatters, and upbraids for his wandering eye. Few of the values Theognis esteems (friendship, loyalty) seem central in the modern era, and during Nietzsche's time many would deplore his appetite for vengeance and his esteem for a two-tier caste system in which the nobility are inherently worthy, while the other classes are despised.

Nietzsche's personal attitudes toward Theognis are difficult to determine. He rarely describes him as an individual and when he does, he tends to be dismissive, comparing him to a Prussian Junker. Nonetheless, Nietzsche often hid his ultimate esteem behind a captious demeanor, and that may have been the case here.[42] Certainly, his choice of the poet forced him to engage with a preceptor of a very different value system from that in which he was raised; and the experience must have appealed to him. Theognis would appear at least three more times in his work – as the subject of a presentation at the university, the central figure in his first published paper, and as a representative of archaic Greek values in *On the genealogy of morals*.[43] Meanwhile, the dissertation allows the reader to see the future professor in action as he tried for the first time to engage in that

---

[38] This practice is described and praised in the Heiland report, published in Gilman 1979: 414. See also Heumann *et al.* 1994: 133–137; and Deussen 1901: 11.
[39] According to Förster-Nietzsche 1895: I, 185, this topic was suggested by Diederich Volkmann. For text, see KGW I-3: 420–463.
[40] See Figueira and Nagy 1985: *passim*.   [41] Bowra 1960: 141.
[42] For a review of various positions taken by scholars *vis-à-vis* Nietzsche's interest in Theognis, see Wolleck 2010: 286–288. For an edition of Theognis' work, see Gerber 1999.
[43] See GM I: 5.

quintessential philological task, the squaring of several incommensurables. The ancients disagreed about virtually every aspect of Theognis' corpus and biography. Some identified him as a citizen of the Megara near Athens. There was also a Megara in Sicily, however, and other authorities claimed he came from there.[44] Moreover, of the 1,389 lines ascribed to Theognis, some (and possibly many) were spurious. Many of the passages later considered morally repugnant were particularly disputed, and Nietzsche himself would later attribute them tentatively to Christian copyists eager to malign this model of pagan rectitude. Such validation or rejection of lines or passages was not just a matter of aesthetics, for scholars could not use the texts as historical evidence until their authenticity was established,[45] and so they would go back and forth, testing questionable lines against known history and questionable history against plausible lines in search of a credible fit.

In his essay, Nietzsche addressed several such issues, assessing the evidence and making an informed judgment. He balanced opinion on Theognis' native city, for example, by assuming that he was born in the mainland Megara but fled to Sicily and its Megara during his exile.[46] This careful comparison of texts and weighing of evidence, as opposed to indulging in pet views, went to the heart of the philological enterprise, which had served as a model for scholarship earlier in the century. This was why practitioners considered themselves "*Wissenschaftlich,*" a word usually translated "scientific" but which encompasses both the natural sciences and scholarship. Under the Humboldtian dispensation, *Wissenschaft* had other functions besides the establishment of knowledge. Students were expected to expand their horizons and to extend their range of comprehension in order to master a subject matter. In other words it was expected that in this encounter of individual and field, the individual would grow. Nietzsche had no doubt experienced the pleasures and satisfactions of such enlarged mastery in his earlier papers, but he explicitly expressed this in the close to his Ermanarich project which he completed the December before. In that paper's final paragraph he recorded his satisfaction at having occupied himself with a series of thoughts and then having put them together consistently. He further associated this activity with the sense of also having "lived into" the ancient saga, that is, of growing imaginatively to a comprehension which engaged its grandeur and complexity.[47] This

---

[44] The Suda and Plato claimed that Theognis came from Sicily. Edmunds 1931: 166–169. Other Greeks took the Greek mainland option (169–171). This controversy remains undecided. Figueira and Nagy 1985: 3, 123–124.
[45] Figueira and Nagy 1985: 112.　　[46] KGW I-3, 422–423, 429–430; Wolleck 2010: 241 and 248.
[47] KGW I-3: 269.

experience had been so pleasant, Nietzsche recorded, that he regretted coming to its end, and he completed the paragraph by thanking his sources, particularly the Brothers Grimm. His final words in the Theognis project are more troubled, for he was aware that he had not succeeded in solving certain problems to his satisfaction. Nonetheless, he presumably experienced considerable satisfaction at completing the work, particularly as this lengthy dissertation (sixty-four pages) was written in Latin. The Theognis paper was his final scholarly production at Pforta, that school which he had entered with so much trepidation six years before; and it shows the enormous distance he had traveled since.

4

Meanwhile, something anomalous and not directly related to scholarship happened to Nietzsche about four months before he began the actual writing of his paper.[48] It may be recalled that from his first autobiography onward he had assumed that one could know the self only externally, by observing its actions.[49] In none of these narratives had he tried to consult his thoughts or feelings, to understand the self through introspection. During the Easter holidays of his final year at Pforta he at last made such an attempt, observing moods rather than activities. The occasion was apparently unusual. He had just bade farewell to an unnamed friend, and his feelings were turbulent as he tried to come to terms with the loss. Yet he does not center his essay either on the friend or specifically identified feelings. Rather he treats the occasion abstractly, observing the interplay of forces as thoughts and emotions combine to form moods and the moods in turn induce dynamics of their own.

The resultant essay, "On moods," begins with Nietzsche poised over a sheet of paper and bewildered by the many thoughts which demand to be recorded.[50] Trying to make sense of these, he finds that two groups vie for attention: certain fresh, tempestuous ideas (which he describes as "effervescent like new wine") and riper, more clearly discriminating thoughts which he likens to "an old master who surveys the strivings of the youthful world with an equivocal eye." These two varieties of ideas appear to be at odds, and Nietzsche speculates that his emotional state is conditioned by

---

[48] Nietzsche identifies the date as the first of his Easter holidays, which would probably make it March 23, 1864. He worked on Theognis that July.
[49] See Chapter 4, Section 5.
[50] KGW I-3: 371–374, 379–380. The English translation by Graham Parkes (reprinted in Ansell Pearson and Large 2006: 21–23) combines these entries. Parkes' translation is used here with minor changes.

the tensions between these camps and that "the current situation of the conflict is what we call 'mood.'" Such moods are not capricious, for the psyche mobilizes certain thoughts at the expense of others, following its own needs. Yet their production is also accidental insofar as the thoughts which underlie them often derive from chance impressions drawn from the external environment. Thus our moods always reflect our personal psyche but can never be wholly under psychic control.

Nietzsche finds it apt that the spell under which he is currently writing is itself conducive to examination of his theme: "Let us admit it: I am writing about moods, insofar as I am right now *in* a certain mood; and it is fortunate that I am just in the mood for describing moods." Profiting from this accident, he considers the many activities which preceded his arrival at his desk that evening, particularly a painful parting and repeated playing of Liszt's "Consolations," a set of compositions which seemed to reflect and complement that pain. Yet this initial mood proves transitory, for new elements stream into the psyche and Nietzsche's state of mind shifts accordingly. "But look! Here comes a friend, there a book is opening . . . Already new guests are streaming in from all sides into the open house." The wondering observer welcomes these ceaseless dynamics, and when he considers how new ingredients enter the mix, he compares them to new lodgers settling into a boarding house and consorting (sometimes uneasily) with the previous occupants. He then contemplates the many ways ideas, impressions, and feelings coalesce, disintegrate, and struggle with one another. The will seems often to sleep, but the drives and longings are always awake; and sometimes when he listens he overhears "the hum and buzzing of . . . wild factions, as if there were a rushing through the air as when a thought or an eagle flies to the sun."

Throughout this examination Nietzsche stresses the plurality and instability of inner experience, and one might expect such a discovery to alarm him. Under the influence of Byron he had fervently admired self-control, yet he recognized now that a wild and unpredictable ferment underlay the most ordinary acts of consciousness. How could such unruly interplay be subject to command? Yet far from being dismayed by this discovery, he finds himself heartened by its promise of renewal and responsiveness to the new.

He also explores the relevance of these discoveries to his views in "Fate and history." Thus he observes that vulnerable as the soul might seem to the contagion of environment, it is in fact protected by its own *cordon sanitaire*: "Anything the soul cannot reflect simply does not touch it . . . the soul is touched only by what it wants." (Or, as he had put this in the earlier lecture, "Can a tone, in general, touch us if there is no corresponding string in us?")[51] Meanwhile, he recognizes that the soul's deeper awakenings are not dependent on any single object within the environment. Rather it follows and is transfigured by needs of its own. If he has loved and lost one treasured activity or person, another might arrive in their place and awaken still deeper responses: "That which is perhaps now your whole happiness or your entire sorrow may soon turn out to be only the vestment of a yet deeper feeling, and will thus disappear when the greater thing comes." Thrilled by such "marvelous variations of a tempestuous soul," he finds himself already recovered from his initial chagrin over "a painful experience that had to do with a parting or a not-parting." He is renewed by the evening's changes and recognizes, "I no longer love as I loved some weeks ago; I am no longer this moment in the mood I was in as I began to write." This is clearly thrilling and he reaches for instruments to record the result: "Away with the paper: take a new sheet, and now pen quickly scribble, ink – quick – here!"

In a separate entry – probably written that same night as his call for new paper and a fresh start suggests – he records a dramatic sense of renewal he feels in response to the evening and to a lightning storm which is building outside. Both the main paper and this addendum suggest that the painful experience of losing the friend serves as the originary and immediate impetus for these investigations. Nonetheless, that relationship has been ended, and Nietzsche is ecstatic at the prospect of moving forward into newer, larger possibilities. Biographically, this triggering farewell is resistant to examination, for Nietzsche mentions the lost human connection only obliquely. We do not know who this person is. Autobiographically, he envisions a new approach to self-definition, one that is based less on the narration of acts and more on the contemplation of his psychic interior. As it turns out, this new possibility was stillborn and would not be pursued, possibly because he could not recover the mood that, as he had explained, encouraged him to examine moods. Instead, he would become increasingly uneasy about introspection, concerned that it was unreliable and even counterproductive.[52]

5

Once the Theognis essay was done, graduation loomed, and whatever his field of concentration might be, Nietzsche had joined Deussen in a decision to attend the University of Bonn. The school had an excellent

---

[51] See Chapter 6, Section 7. [52] See Afterword, Section 1.

philology department and Bonn lay close to Deussen's family home.[53] Wilhelm and Gustav had themselves chosen the University of Heidelberg and, since they graduated six months before Nietzsche, they urged him to join them, citing the joy of many parties and the plenitude of attractive women.[54] Apparently this prospect did not appeal to Nietzsche, and he responded in a frigid tone, asking for a particularly recondite book on Theognis.[55] Bonn and Heidelberg might be comparatively close geographically, but he would never visit his two companions in the year ahead.[56]

Although his family seems not to have realized it, Nietzsche's choice of Bonn evidenced a lack of interest in the ministry. One of his aunts' brothers-in-law, Rudolf Schenkel, had written the inquiring youth that if he wanted to major in theology, he should definitely choose the University of Leipzig over that of Bonn.[57] Nietzsche nonetheless opted for the latter. He had apparently confided his doubts to his tutor, and Kletschke had suggested that he choose a double major, theology and philology.[58] This temporizing suggestion probably reflected ambivalence in Nietzsche himself.[59] As his poems demonstrate, he still viewed religion with nostalgia, and he was probably willing to give it a final chance. Nonetheless, his true interests were indicated not just by his choice of university but by his grades. Students envisioning a future in the ministry took Hebrew classes at Schulpforte, and Nietzsche had studied that subject for four years.[60] When he took his final exams, however, he received an "Unsatisfactory" in that language, a grade of both symbolic and practical importance. He had still not told his family of his growing apostasy, but barring some unexpected epiphany, his effective decision was long behind him.

At the time he must have been oppressed with the well-founded concern that he might not graduate. Before leaving Schulpforte he had to pass a series of examinations administered by the state. Prussia was wary of creating an "academic proletariat," a surplus of students to available jobs,[61] and it allowed no one to attend its universities without the *Abitur*, a certification awarded only after they passed a barrage of tests. While

---

[53] For other reasons Pforta students went to Bonn, see Benne 2005: 51–53.
[54] KGB I-1: 418–421. Gustav wrote as well: 421–423.   [55] KSAB I: 282–283.
[56] Nietzsche also suggests that financial issues preclude him from enrolling at Heidelberg. Pernet 1989: 145, n. 154.
[57] KGB I-4: 14. Schenkel and Steinhart also warned him that philology was taught badly at Leipzig. KSAB II: 81.
[58] KGB I-4: 15.   [59] Pernet 1989: 83–84.
[60] All years except Unter- and Obertertia. Bohley 1976: 304.
[61] The term "Akademisches Proletariat" was apparently coined by Metternich. Vierhaus 1972: 543.

Nietzsche would be prepared for most of these, he had misgivings considering his mathematics examination. That subject had always been his weak point, as it had been his father's.[62] However, in contrast to the dogged Ludwig, who studied and passed his tests,[63] Nietzsche seems scarcely to have tried.[64] This did not endear him to his mathematics instructor, a man of high competence whom he had once esteemed,[65] and when the boy received an Unsatisfactory grade on his final exam in this subject, it seemed that all his other successes would not save him. Deussen records an intense evening during which his friend confessed the extent of his dread, for Nietzsche seems to have feared the worst.[66] Fortunately and for unknown reasons, although there are legends,[67] the Schulpforte synod elected to override this lapse, and Nietzsche was cleared to take his degree.

The graduation took place on September 7, 1864, a day of considerable ceremony. A high point of the festivities involved addresses by the graduates themselves. Called one by one to the lectern, they were permitted to address the assembled students and faculty as long as they wished, a remarkable privilege of which few took advantage, for, according to Nietzsche, most were too moved to utter more than a few phrases.[68] It is unknown what he himself said, although he could have read it from the page. His senior essay had included yet another autobiography, and since it is easily the most thoughtfully considered and carefully written essay of this kind that he had produced up to the present, he may have called upon it during his farewell.[69]

The work began with a salute to Schulpforte and an assurance that in this essay he would foreground what he learned there. Nietzsche then repaired to early childhood and remarked that his father had laid "the germ of the serious [and] thoughtfulness in my soul." Nonetheless, as he explained, the man's death deprived him of male supervision, and the poor learning habits he subsequently developed had led him to accumulate multiple and disorderly stores of knowledge. The arts presented a particularly sad example of amateurism gone awry. He had composed music at the age of nine, for example, "if one can call composing the efforts of an excited child to put consonant and sequential notes on paper." He also wrote

---

[62] Goch 2000: 33, 117–118.   [63] Goch 2000: 182–183.
[64] Even Förster-Nietzsche acknowledges this. See Förster-Nietzsche 1895: I, 188.   [65] KSAB I: 34.
[66] Deussen 1901: 15.
[67] Förster-Nietzsche attributes her brother's graduation to a dramatic confrontation in the Schulpforte synod. She further claims that she received this highly confidential information from Diederich Volkmann. However, she tells this story only in her second biography, which was published after Volkmann was dead and unable to respond. Förster-Nietzsche 1912: 116–117.
[68] KSAB I: 53.   [69] KGW I-3: 417–419.

"dreadful poems," and (as he confessed with evident horror), "I even drew and painted."

At Pforta, by contrast, he learned to embrace restriction and to master some specific field thoroughly and from the ground up. His musical compositions benefited from this new sense of focus as did his devotion to various Greek authors. Yet in his address Nietzsche was careful not to commit himself to any particular field – least of all to religion, which is never mentioned in any way. Rather than specify any subject matter, he affirmed rather the methodology through which they were best ingested. He had "learned to learn" and thereby overcome the educational handicap brought on through his father's early death. The occasion was dramatic and Nietzsche played his readers skillfully, ending with an operatic vow. Now that he was on the point of going to the university, he would embrace as law the need to combat dilettantism and in its place to seek mastery over one specific field.[70] "In my fight with the one and pursuit of the other, I hope to emerge victorious."

He thereby threw down a gauntlet toward himself and his inability to concentrate. Yet, as frequently happens with resolutions, he overlooked a problem. In this dramatic vow Nietzsche never specified the field on which he would focus his heroic endeavors. Would it be theology, philology, or some other subject? He seems to have assumed that the topic didn't matter. He would pursue it stalwartly regardless. Yet hidden within this ambition lay the confession that he didn't like any subject enough to devote his life to it. He wanted the discipline of commitment without the commitment itself. As will be seen, this is exactly what Nietzsche would do. He would take a field and pursue it with an energy and determination which impressed others and pleased himself. Yet the day would come when he discovered that he didn't really care about the field he had specialized in, and what would he do then? He would have to answer this when the inevitable occurred.

Meanwhile, Nietzsche's presentation done, he no doubt surrendered to the festivities at hand.[71] After the boys' speeches, a valedictory poem was read, the rector delivered an oration and, intermittently, the choir sang songs of farewell. The point of graduation was to leave, however, and Pforta had woven this necessity into the ceremony itself. Once the various

---

[70] Nietzsche would confirm this ambition at least as late as 1868. See KGW I-5: 42.
[71] The following account is based on three descriptions: by Nietzsche in a letter (KSAB I: 53), by Nietzsche in his notebooks (KGW I-2: 132) and by Heumann in his history (Heumann *et al.* 1994: 176–177). A drawing of Pforta graduates in their carriage, included in Heumann's book, has also been consulted.

addresses were completed, the students adjourned outdoors and waited until the horns of postilions sounded and one or more coaches garlanded with flowers drew up. As the undergraduates cheered, the departing alumni stowed their luggage and ducked inside. The horns then sounded anew, the coachmen snapped their reins, and the horses stepped forward, dragging the wagon from the walled school-state into the world at large.

CHAPTER 9

Soul-building: the practice

Freedom tricks you a lot.[1]

I

Until the age of twenty Nietzsche thrived through a sort of split consciousness scarcely distinguishable from hypocrisy. He had doubts concerning Christianity but had not told his mother. He mistrusted the authorities yet followed their orders. He nursed his reservations but did as he was told. As a child he had little choice but to pretend, and his occasional revolts – quarrels with his mother, delinquency at Schulpforta – had been painful to all concerned. More positively, self-censorship allowed him to keep the support he needed to excel at school. So long as his actions were guided by authorities, his life had a built-in plot line, and he matured with minimal social friction from well-behaved boy into an academically promising youth.

All this changed with graduation from Schulpforte when, for the first time, he was exposed to the vagaries of undirected living. Overnight, his usual sources of guidance and protection were withdrawn, and he was left vulnerable to events that he would have to address through inexperienced judgment. Further, his habit of yielding to authority now proved a liability since it left him unversed in the practice of actually implementing his desires. Theoretically, he was independent and could enact his ambitions, but outside the realm of pen and paper he was not versed in turning values into realities.

The transition was the more difficult because Nietzsche was removed so far from mother and family. Although he apparently chose to attend the University of Bonn because of the prestige of its philology department,[2] he was surely aware of its considerable distance from home. His new school

[1] KSAB II: 67.   [2] KGW I-5: 41.

lay over 300 kilometers distant from Naumburg and to get there he had to travel from a region near the present Czech Republic to an area near the edge of Belgium. Beguiled as he was by dreams of continuing the successes of Schulpforte, it probably never occurred to him that by moving such a distance he was cutting a lifeline. Instead, he diverted himself in the company of his friend, Paul Deussen, who had stayed with Nietzsche's family after graduation so that they could make the journey together.

Rather than head directly for Bonn, the boys stopped off to visit some of Deussen's relatives, first in the city of Elberfeld (now part of Wuppertal) and then at Oberdreis, a village east of Bonn, where Nietzsche celebrated his twentieth birthday. They then took a ferry down the Rhine to their final destination, where he and Deussen were forced by high rents to take separate quarters. Nietzsche located an upper flat on the Bonngasse, a lane that led to the town's central marketplace, and his letters from his new household brim with the wonder of a young person living for the first time on his own. He happily reports that he has just bought an oil lamp, and he enthuses over a coffee-maker which his mother has sent.[3] He also counts costs. Virtually every letter home touches on what he termed "the money issue" and how he found Bonn far more expensive than expected. The first report posted from his new address is studded with figures (the price of laundry, heat, and meals) as he struggles to convince the frugal Franziska to send a larger allowance.[4]

To his dismay, Nietzsche's new home turned out to be more alien than the twenty-year-old might expect. Bonn in those days was merely a town, but its population was a third larger than Naumburg's and considerably more cosmopolitan.[5] Further, Bonn had been the dwelling place of the Catholic bishop-electors, most of them Hapsburgs, who ruled nearby Cologne, and its architecture included the Electoral and Poppelsdorf Palaces, royal houses of a grandeur and opulence unknown in the province Nietzsche had left behind. The bishop-electors were eventually swept away by the French occupation, but their heritage remained: if Bonn was merely a town, it was a town turned up a notch, a former bedroom community for princes. It was also strongly Catholic – four of every five inhabitants were of that faith[6] – and when Nietzsche looked out his window, he could see a Jesuit church.[7] Although the town lay under the jurisdiction of Protestant Prussia, its more traditional religion was treated with delicate respect as a

---

[3] KSAB II: 16.   [4] KSAB II: 11–13.
[5] This history of Bonn is principally derived from van Rey 2001, chs. 6 through 10.
[6] Pernet 1989: 101.   [7] KSAB II: 18. Compare Wilamowitz-Moellendorff 1928: 84.

powder keg that nobody wanted jarred. Thus, as Nietzsche reported to his aunts, the university observed Catholic holidays, but Reformation Day (October 31) was ignored.[8] On the other hand, Catholics were aware that a preponderance of certain university jobs went to Protestants,[9] and tensions between the faiths tended to be high.[10] All would be aware that, as a noted historian has stated, "Bonn, unlike [the University of] Berlin, was a sort of outpost of Prussian *Wissenschaft* in a predominately Catholic and heavily populated province. Its creation was an outright act of state, as important to the Prussianization of the Rhineland as the posting of troops."[11]

If his new town proved disappointing, Nietzsche could probably find correspondingly little comfort in his scholastic situation. As agreed with Kletschke, he chose a double major, theology and philology, a temporizing measure which pleased neither him nor his family.[12] Both his mother and Aunt Rosalie were understandably troubled by this competing allegiance and wondered why he would burden himself with an extra field of study.[13] Nietzsche must have chafed as well, for this double concentration made it impossible to execute the vow he had made at Pforta, to focus his resources on one field alone.

During their initial days he and Deussen made the rounds of various departments, meeting such professors as Heinrich von Sybel (a renowned historian and politician) and the popular art historian, Anton Springer, whose lectures Nietzsche liked so much that his mother took alarm.[14] Since Nietzsche's focus was surreptitiously on philology, he probably invested particular hopes in Otto Jahn and Friedrich Ritschl, two of the more distinguished professors of classics in the German states. Both were excellent Latinists and had made important though not epochal contributions in their field.[15] Jahn, the quieter and more sensitive, was a widower and, being unmarried, had more time for students. A political activist, he had lost his job at the University of Leipzig in the aftermath of 1848 and had

---

[8] KSAB II: 27.   [9] Pernet 1989: 90.
[10] At least three of Nietzsche's teachers – Schlottmann, Krafft, and von Sybel – tended to be critical of Catholics. Konstantin Schlottmann in particular had caused a minor scandal in 1861 with the publication of an attack on that church. Pernet 1989: 90–92.
[11] McClelland 1980: 146.
[12] Nietzsche listed both majors on the appropriate form. University protocols did not permit this, and only theology was entered on his records. Pernet 1989: 144, n. 149.
[13] KGB I-3: 9.   [14] KGB I-3: 21.
[15] Ritschl was best known for his work on Plautus, Jahn on the satirists, Juvenal and Persius. However, both were wide-ranging. Among numerous other achievements Ritschl wrote a major work on Latin inscriptions. Jahn did solid work on a variety of subjects, ranging from vases to the importance of archeological evidence. For a sense of his range and prolificity, see the bibliography of his writings in Müller 1991: 45–87.

gone without employment for five years until hired at Bonn.[16] Like Nietzsche, he was drawn to both scholarship and music and had recently published an influential life of Mozart, the first to bring philological expertise to the art of biography, and a work that would not be superseded until the following century.[17]

In contrast to the more private Jahn, Friedrich Ritschl was outgoing and very much a political animal.[18] In particular, he was versed in the manipulation of administrative structures and skilled in advancing the careers of protégés. Ritschl could be extraordinarily generous to his pupils, and he significantly furthered the career of Jacob Bernays, an important figure in Greek studies, who as an unconverted Jew was not permitted to hold a professorship at Prussian universities.[19] Jahn himself owed his job to Ritschl's enterprise, for Ritschl single-handedly arranged his appointment, not bothering to inform his co-chair, who was away on a trip.[20] This impolitic act had repercussions which would last for decades and must be mentioned here for reasons that will be clear later. First, it offended the co-chair Friedrich Gottlieb Welcker[21] and led to an awkwardness between himself and Ritschl which was never fully resolved. It also angered Jahn, who felt put in a false position and was too mortified to show Ritschl the gratitude the latter thought as his due. The resultant coolness between the two, reinforced by their different personalities, led to a permanent estrangement.[22] Indeed, a public and probably painful confirmation of Jahn's hostility had occurred a mere six months before Nietzsche's arrival. On May 6, 1864, Ritschl celebrated his twenty-fifth anniversary at the University of Bonn, and Jahn failed to appear.[23]

Meanwhile, Deussen and Nietzsche, knowing nothing of such matters, tendered letters of introduction from Schulpforte and encountered a tepid reception from both men. Deussen's account does not mention a third letter, which would prove prophetic. Addressed to Karl Schaarschmidt, a professor of philosophy, the sender first recommended Deussen, then

---

[16] This biography is largely drawn from Müller 1990 and 1991.
[17] Müller 1990: 233. The *Köchel-Verzeichnis* is dedicated to Jahn.
[18] As of October 1872, thirty-six university professors and thirty-eight Gymnasium directors came from the Ritschlean school. See Ribbeck 1969 II: 337. See also Benne 2005: 48, n. 75.
[19] See Bollack 1998 and Glucker *et al.* 1996.   [20] Ribbeck 1969 II: 333–334, 336.
[21] Nietzsche knew some of Welcker's work well, for the man was frequently cited in his Pforta essay on Theognis. Welcker was regarded as "hopelessly anachronistic" by the time that Nietzsche arrived in Bonn. Benne 2005: 54.
[22] The preceding is based on Vogt 1990, Müller 1990, and Gildersleeve 1884. Ribbeck makes clear that Ritschl was increasingly put on the defensive by political and student adherents of Jahn. Ribbeck 1969 II: 342, 344–346.
[23] Herter 1975: 651.

remarked of Nietzsche, "The other ... is a deep, thoughtful creature, and enthusiastic about philosophy, particularly the Platonic, to which he is already quite devoted ... Under your guidance he will joyfully turn to philosophy, for that is where his deepest drive leads."[24] Deussen leaves no record of Schaarschmidt's response, except to indicate that he was the only professor who truly welcomed the two.[25] Nietzsche concurred, recording that the professor "has treated us with the most exquisite friendliness,"[26] and he attributed this to the letter. Over the coming year Schaarschmidt, who had himself attended Schulpforte and who at this time was basking in the aftermath of having published "a pathbreaking monograph" on John of Salisbury,[27] invited Nietzsche at least twice to dinner, attended festivities in which the young man took part, and would eventually introduce him to "the highest society in Bonn."[28] It would seem that the professor was watching over this potential protégé, and successfully so, since Nietzsche eventually became a pupil, taking two courses in philosophy under his instruction. Apparently Schaarschmidt recognized that if Nietzsche's declared fields were philology and theology, philosophy beckoned as a silent competitor.[29]

In accordance with his double major, Nietzsche signed up not only for two philology classes (one on Plato's *Symposium*) but two in theology. He also took two classes on the history of art under Springer and one on politics from von Sybel. A course load of seven classes was impractical, particularly as he would be busy with extracurricular interests, and the workload proved overwhelming. It quickly became clear that, for all Nietzsche's talent and ambition, things were not going well. Beyond his scholastic difficulties – his failure to impress any professors but Schaarschmidt and his inability to decide on a major – he was experiencing the effects of the sink-or-swim ethos that was built into his country's university system. Entry to Prussian higher education was very different from its institutional parallel in, say, the United States. In the latter country, students' first college years seemed a natural extension of high school: freshmen took regular exams, received grades, and had much of the curriculum imposed by administrative policy.[30] In Prussia, these external structures were deliberately withdrawn. Students could study what they wanted, they were rarely monitored to ensure that they showed up for

---

[24] KGB I-4: 338. The sender was Carl Steinhart. The text concerning Deussen is available in Feldhoff 2008: 49.
[25] Deussen 1901: 20. Translated in Gilman 1987: 21.   [26] KSAB II: 18.   [27] Bezold 1920: 479.
[28] KSAB II: 46.   [29] For more on Schaarschmidt see Emden 2008: 22–23.
[30] For a comparison of the American college to the German Gymnasium, see Butler 1895: xiv–xvi.

classes, and they were given neither tests nor grades. Instead, having presumably "learned how to learn" at the Gymnasium, they were expected to use their new freedom to develop their own compass and to set their course through a self-imposed and self-disciplined pursuit of knowledge. At a Prussian university, one didn't *receive* an education, one accomplished it oneself; and the school system assured this by suspending students in a disciplinary vacuum. As one historian remarked, "After [the student] has matriculated, and has given his hand to the rector in token of his promise to obey the laws of the university, no official inquires about him for several years; he is left entirely to his own devices."[31]

Such an approach, while meant to instill independence, could prove disorienting to newcomers, particularly if they had few practical skills to begin with. As an American educator has noted, "The contrast between the narrowness of the Gymnasium and the broad freedom of the university is very sharp, and many a university student loses his balance entirely, or wastes much precious time and force, in adjusting himself to his totally new surroundings."[32] Suddenly, Nietzsche began to realize that Schulpforte had in some ways left him ill prepared for adulthood. He would recall, "how exceedingly well instructed, yet how badly raised, a pupil of such a royal school is when he goes to the university. He has thought out a lot for himself but he now lacks the skill to express these thoughts. He has not yet experienced any of the cultivating influences of women; he fancies he knows life from books and tradition, yet everything appears to him strange and unpleasant."[33] He had always been wary of institutions, so this should not have surprised him; but to be so suddenly thrust on his own – and to discover an unexpected lack of expertise – must have proved alarming. He would remember his disorientation years later when, in his lecture series, "On the future of our educational institutions," he vented anger and frustrations which date from this time.[34]

2

Finding himself rootless and ignorant in a new city, Nietzsche, together with Deussen, sought out former classmates and found that a host of these had joined a fraternity called Franconia. On October 23,[35] the

---

[31] Paulsen 1895: 77. For more on the differences between the Gymnasium and university see Chapter 5, Section 2.
[32] Butler 1895: xix.
[33] KGW I-5: 47, 54. Wilamowitz corroborates this: Wilamowitz-Moellendorff 1928: 73.
[34] KSA I: 737–747.   [35] Per Wilhelm Metterhausen. See KGB I-4: 333.

Sunday after their arrival, the two young men were invited to a tavern and given a recruitment pitch by Georg Stöckert, their former dorm-mate at Pforta. Drinks were surely served, and the bar setting would have encouraged camaraderie and group dynamics. By the day's end Nietzsche, Deussen, and six others had signed up as pledges. The recruiter no doubt stressed what the neophytes needed to hear – that the fraternity promised continuity, community, and enlightenment on the local scene. Given the tavern setting, he probably did not need to describe the more roughhewn aspects of the fraternity – that they were notoriously rowdy and associated with drinking, fencing, and all kinds of festivity. Frat boys got together nightly with their pipes to vie in beer contests, speeches, and song.

This is not to claim that all fraternities were alike. Nietzsche joined what was known as a *Burschenschaft*, as opposed to a *Corps*.[36] The latter emphasized dueling and appealed to the military and nobility. The *Burschenschaften*, by contrast, were drawn from the middle class and had begun life in 1815 as a liberal, patriotic society demanding restraints on the absolutist government. Indeed, originally they discouraged duels, gambling, and excessive debts, and they even promulgated a policy of chastity in an effort to demonstrate that they were more mature and responsible than students from an earlier generation.[37] If the *Burschenschaften* sought to emancipate themselves from the dissolute behavior of earlier times, they were also committed to political reform. In 1817 they staged a bonfire in which, among other articles, literature defending monarchy was thrown into the flames. In 1819 one of their members assassinated August von Kotzebue (the cousin of Erdmuthe Nietzsche's first husband),[38] an event of grave importance since it led to the notorious Carlsbad Decrees, through which the German states were subjected to draconian laws. The *Burschenschaften* were banned for a time,[39] but they always maintained an underground existence as secret societies and were eventually permitted to reappear with the proviso that they no longer pose much danger.[40] By the year Nietzsche enrolled, the institution appears to have mellowed into

---

[36] The following treatment is taken mainly from Weber 1986, but also Elias 1996; Gladen 1986; Howitt 1969; Jarausch 1984; Paulsen 1895: 190–193, and Hart 1874: 69–70. There existed other forms of fraternity besides the *Burschenschaften* and *Corps*, but they are not relevant here.
[37] Jarausch 1974: 538.   [38] See Chapter 1, n. 22.
[39] The initial suppression of the *Burschenschaften* in 1818 was fortified in the early 1830s because of a rebellion in Frankfurt. Jarausch 1974: 541–542.
[40] For a description of how the *Burschenschaften*, including Franconia, led a surreptitious existence, then resurfaced in the early 1840s, see Bezold 1920: 413–416.

just another jolly student organization, one still theoretically devoted to liberal politics but mostly providing a patriotic cover for horseplay.[41]

Pledging seems a curious choice for a young man who tended to dislike groups, was not used to alcohol, and whose taste for Schumann made it unlikely that he would be beguiled by drunken songfests. In letters to his mother, Nietzsche explains that many members were from Schulpforte and of a scholarly bent.[42] He seems to have thought that he and others of similar ambitions could convert the fraternity into a heartier version of Germania, the intellectual society he had formed earlier with the Pinder-Krug cousins. Throughout his youth he would yearn to found all-male study groups, and during the coming year he would do his best to convert Franconia into such an institution.[43] Whatever his motivations, they were strong enough that he made considerable effort to live up to Franconia's standards. He stayed up late drinking, paying the price in hangovers, went on communal tours of the countryside, and wrote a skit entitled "The Franconians in heaven." Eventually he would deliver a lecture on German political poets to the members, thereby offering a link between his own interests (poetry) and those of the *Burschenschaft* (politics).

Since Nietzsche spent nearly a year with this organization, it might be explained that its members drank and dueled "by the book," that is, in accord with intricate traditions and protocols. The amount of beer a student consumed, for example, was not a private choice. When members assembled in the tavern, a leader (and various empowered subordinates) would order the entire group to empty their mugs, thus ensuring that descent into beery oblivion was not only communal but universal.[44] Duels too were not the dangerous battles subsequently depicted in films, although accidents happened. Deadly duels in the sense of life-threatening responses to serious insults were unusual, illegal, conducted in privacy, and covered up in secrecy. Fraternity members engaged rather in what were called *Mensurs*, extremely formal and rule-bound fencing matches. Sabers were blunted at the ends and the combatants muffled themselves in protective breast cushions, arm wrappings, thick scarves around the throat, and goggles without glasses, making them look, as one said, "like a pair of

---

[41] Literature on the *Burschenschaften* in the 1860s is less available, probably because they had ceased to be of political significance. The characterization given in the text is based on statements by Nietzsche, Deussen, and Gersdorff as well as Jarausch 1974: 543.
[42] KSAB II: 14.
[43] In letters Nietzsche mentions efforts by himself and associates to reform Franconia. See, for example, KSAB II: 71. Compare Ross 1980: 103.
[44] Hart 1874: 139–141.

submarine divers in armor."[45] *Mensurs* were illegal too but only in theory. So long as participants did not flaunt their combats, the universities tended to overlook them. These could, nonetheless, be frightening and were definitely regarded as a test, not only of skill but character. Nietzsche himself engaged in one *Mensur*, a rather brave act considering his physical ungainliness and poor eyesight. According to Deussen he acquitted himself honorably, receiving a permanent scar on the nose.[46]

Under his parents' influence, Deussen soon dropped his membership. As he later recalled, "Neither Nietzsche nor I could take much pleasure in [the fraternity] ... We found the mandatory drinking bouts on the tavern evenings disgusting ... and when on almost all Sunday evenings we had to skip lectures, no matter how interesting they might be, in order to watch the Franconians and Alemanians slashing their faces in a faraway barn outside the city, we really could not enjoy that either."[47] While this negative characterization reflects not only Deussen's but Nietzsche's later view, it does not accord with the latter's attitude at the time. He stayed with Franconia from October 1864 until October 1865 and praised it repeatedly in his letters. To his skeptical mother he wrote that, "Life in the organization is thoroughly disciplined and active. A parliamentary tone is strictly applied."[48] To his younger sister he extolled the spirituality of communal sprees: "The festival yesterday was delightful and elevating ... On such evenings of drink, there reigns a general uplift of souls. It's not the mere conviviality of the beer table."[49] Proud of his membership (and perhaps constrained by rules), he added a fraternity insignia with a flourish to his signature in letters, its symbol followed by an exclamation point. When, as late as two months before he left Bonn, he considered resigning in order to save money, he pleaded with his mother to spare him this step: "I beg you as hard as I can to provide enough funds that I can remain in the fraternity, if possible."[50] Most striking of all, although it falls outside this book's periodization, Nietzsche would later praise the *Burschenschaften* publicly as the heroic, most salutary organization within the current university system.[51]

---

[45] Hart 1874: 74.   [46] Deussen 1901: 22–23. Translation in Gilman 1987: 22–23.
[47] Deussen 1901: 21–22. Translation in Gilman 1987: 22. Deussen's claim that duels superseded lectures on Sunday nights is incorrect. Krafft's lectures took place that very evening, and Nietzsche's notes on these still exist. Pernet 1989: 147, n. 32.
[48] KSAB II: 21.   [49] KSAB II: 23.
[50] KSAB II: 59. This letter was written on May 29, 1865, only two months before Nietzsche left Bonn, so his regard for the fraternity lasted virtually to the end.
[51] KSA I: 748 ff.

Nonetheless, Nietzsche and Franconia cannot have been an easy fit. He acknowledged to his mother that his fraternity brothers found him "weird" (a *Kauz*) and a "pain" (*Quälgeist*).[52] They also called him "the red rooster," a name that suggests not only self-importance but that he turned red when singing. (His face tended to flush when he exercised.)[53] In a photo made at the time, the brotherhood sits assembled around a beer keg, and the general membership stares stalwartly into the camera. Nietzsche practically alone averts his head, his fingers pressed theatrically to his temples as though he were nursing a headache. This implicit disdain cannot have been easy to live with, and in the photo the other boys pretend to ignore him, showing not the least awareness that one in their midst is, highly ostentatiously, not joining the fun.

3

Carousing with Franconia was not Nietzsche's only distraction from study. Living for the first time in an area where major cultural opportunities were available – Cologne lay a mere 25 kilometers away – he went frequently to the theater and concert hall. (His notebooks indicate that he attended close to thirty performances in his first six months alone.)[54] He also signed up for the community chorus – Nietzsche sang bass[55] – with which he would perform Händel's "Judas Maccabaeus" and "Israel in Egypt," as well as Mozart's "Requiem."[56] Perhaps inspired by so much ambient music, he returned to composition and produced twelve songs,[57] compositions that he prized enough to submit them to the choirmaster for criticism. The latter observed that Nietzsche needed lessons in counterpoint, advice probably unwelcome to this young man who had always been impatient of musical instruction and certainly could not afford a teacher now.[58] What is interesting here is that, caught between theology and philology and apparently not very enthused about either, he reached out to music, as though to try one last time to envision this as his career. His mother seems to have recognized this, for in one of her letters she goes out of her way to state how relieved Gustav's father had been that, for all his love of music, he had never majored in the arts but had turned to more profitable fields of endeavor.[59] Nietzsche does not seem to have replied to this gambit, but shortly after the choirmaster's verdict he did ship back his rented piano,

---

[52] KSAB II: 43.   [53] Deussen 1901: 10. Compare Förster-Nietzsche 1912: 82.
[54] KGW I-4: 16–17.   [55] Ross 1980: 97.   [56] Pernet 1989: 102.   [57] KGW I-4: 89–90.
[58] KSAB II: 40. Compare Ross 1980: 97–98.   [59] KGB I-3: 21.

ostensibly to save money, and in the coming year he wrote only isolated pieces, some unfinished. An entry in his journals indicates that he gave up poetry as well: "No more desire to compose, terrible poems. End."[60] Apparently he was now making the sacrifice he had been unable to take at Schulpforte. He bade farewell to any dreams of a career in the arts, and although he occasionally produced a poem or song, he held fast to this resolution for over a decade.

Meanwhile, he was de facto majoring in theology, and although he had been aware how problematic were certain Christian positions, he may have still sensed the appeal of a faith which had provided edification during childhood and which his mother (and implicitly his dead father) counted on him to embrace. Also, since Protestantism was embattled in Bonn, he may have felt the tug of distant loyalty and a desire to come to its defense. He did join the student wing of the local Gustav Adolf Missionary Society and even became its secretary. He would deliver a quite orthodox lecture to this group and remain a member until his final days in Bonn, possibly because he could not resign as secretary until his term was completed. Such loyalty did not extend to his theology classes. He wrote that he was disappointed in the one,[61] and he gave up attending the other, apparently because its time slot competed with the art history lectures delivered by Springer.[62]

Caught academically between theology and philology, and bewitched alternately by Franconia, music, and philosophy (not to mention art history and theater), Nietzsche must have been overwhelmed in his first term. Here was his old enemy from the past – the temptation to dissipate his energies in too many directions – reappearing just when he thought it vanquished; and by December the stress was beginning to build. This would be his first Christmas without his mother and sister and, since Paul's entire family was converging on the Deussen home, there would be no room there for Nietzsche. Through December his letters home grew more frequent (seven, all told, vs. one in November) and they became more wistful and yearning. As a present for Elisabeth, he sent the songs he had written, and he clearly expected gifts in return (specifically an edition of Aeschylus or a copy of the piano reduction of Schumann's "Manfred Overture").[63] These did not arrive until the 25th itself, and Nietzsche, who had experienced a mournful Christmas Eve, was ecstatic with relief and joy. Inside he found homemade food, gifts made in his fraternity colors, and above all, the piano score to the "Manfred Overture," a present

[60] KGW I-4: 63. [61] KGB I-4: 15. [62] Pernet 1989: 86. [63] KSAB II: 21.

from Aunt Rosalie. A fraternity brother visited that afternoon, and the two ran through the four-hand work together.[64]

If Christmas proved ultimately happy, the week following brought a "devilish" toothache, the first sickness to strike Nietzsche at Bonn and an ominous sign for someone so prone to illness as himself. He sent a somewhat bad-tempered letter home and wrote that the pain had prevented him from composing his customary New Year's poem for his family. Nevertheless, the holiday did not go unremarked. In the same letter Nietzsche wrote, "I love New Year's Eves and birthdays, for they give us hours ... when the soul stands still and can survey a phase of its own development ... In such hours," he added ominously, "decisive resolutions are born."[65]

He knew that he must resume his own path,[66] and in a piece entitled "A New Year's Eve dream,"[67] he let his subconscious sink into this insight and find a response. In this complex fantasy a figure which represents the dying year is besieged by apparitions, all of which have found it disappointing. Suddenly, a disembodied voice erupts to chide those who complain – "[W]hat have *you* done?" – and it announces that if the apparitions are to get what they hope, they must first perform what the gods require. At this moment the cry of "Happy New Year!" rings from the street, and the vision dispels, leaving Nietzsche to ponder its meaning.

Nietzsche makes no comment on this narrative, which is considerably more complex than presented here. It is hard not to view the dying figure not only as the moribund year but as Nietzsche himself, lying discouraged in his own bed. It is he who has proved a disappointment, and the shadows are his own surface opinions which clash and posture, only to be dispersed by the superior revelation at the end. And where does the latter's redemptory wisdom come from? Readers familiar with Byron will recognize that the dream's spectral voices and oracular declarations are reminiscent of "Manfred," the play that so powerfully affected Nietzsche in adolescence, and which had just, so to speak, paid him a visit, reminding him of forgotten ideals and promises not kept. He had just spent the week playing Schumann's musical interpretation of the work, and his dream seems to recast his situation in Byronic terms, asking in effect, "What would Manfred do?" If so, Nietzsche, who admired that hero's fierce independence, knew the correct response. He must see to his own deliverance.

---

[64] KSAB II: 31–32. [65] KSAB II: 34. [66] KSAB II: 34. [67] KGW I-4: 7–8. Emphasis added.

4

Nietzsche could – and possibly did – diagnose for himself the reasons for his bafflement. As he had recognized at Schulpforte, the Christian religion was subtly entwined not only with his vision of the world but with his emotions and the ideals that served as his guides. That childhood resource had now been withdrawn, and he had not yet found a worldview to replace it. The obvious alternative lay in the very ideals that led him to reject religion in the first place, and it might help to define what these were. Nietzsche never argued at this time that Christianity could be proved false – that he had, as it were, some infallible criterion by which to discredit it. His claims always turned on culture and the interpretive structures it imposed. Had he been raised differently, he would have believed differently. That in a nutshell was the insight he had stressed in "Fate and history," and he would foreground it again in a letter he would shortly write to his sister. In both documents, however, he introduced a second factor, one based on character. Knowing that one's attitudes toward Christianity are a reflection of upbringing, one could accept it anyway, since after all there existed no positive reason to regard it as false; or one could reject it, since there is no positive reason to regard it as true. The choice a person made – and either was theoretically defensible once the effect of environment was recognized – might be logically capricious but was no gratuitous leap of faith. Rather a person's decision would reflect individual character and temperament. It was not that the believers or skeptics possessed superior grounds for their decisions, although Christians might have some implausible claims to defend. Religious belief could not be argued. Human beings made choices based on the kind of person that they were.

One would think that this approach would make Nietzsche respectful of those who took a stance other than his own. The opposite seems to have been the case. Although he does not make an argument for this during his youth, he was an ardent proselytizer and clearly believed that those who did not make the same decision as himself were of lower character and somehow deficient in qualities that he was pleased to possess.[68] Nonetheless, the stress on individuality shows the path that Nietzsche would have to take. If one's character was so central to one's being that it could direct the metaphysical and ethical principles by which one lived; if, at the same time, its expressions were often a reflection of – and to that extent

---

[68] One might compare his rather unforgiving dismissal in Leipzig of those who did not share his esteem for Schopenhauer.

undermined by – cultural inheritance from the past; then the way forward lay through self-discovery, self-enactment, and the careful disengagement of self from attitudes that did not belong to it. It was not enough to embrace what was his own; he would also have to disown those aspects of his cultural inheritance which compromised his values and therefore impeded development. One could hardly find a better example of such blockage than his current situation when he was enlisting in a field alien to his vital beliefs, and for little other reason than that his family and upbringing made it seem inconceivable that he could embark on any other.

It was not just Nietzsche's family, of course, that was pushing him into the clergy. Nietzsche's stress on self underestimated the complexity of the human psyche and of his psyche in particular. He had asserted at the beginning of "Fate and history" that a person's values and ways of thinking were so subtly bound up with upbringing that to disengage was almost prohibitively difficult; and he appeared to be experiencing just this tension during his year at Bonn. It was easy to backslide, and in later books he would describe the long shadow of religion – how deeply it imprinted itself on those raised under its influence and how difficult could be the effort to awaken oneself from its spell.[69] Nietzsche had been extremely pious as a child, and in the confused state of post-adolescence he must often have felt the grip of convictions he had thought dead. Now thanks to Emerson and the ideal of *Bildung* he had found in a metaphysic of self the belief in an autonomous and guiding individuality that must find expression or die. If religion stood in the way, it must go.

The New Year's crisis seems to have roused him to action. On January 10, he wrote his Aunt Rosalie that although he had slept until 8 a.m. during his first term at Bonn, he was now rising at 6.[70] 6 a.m. was the standard wake-up hour at Schulpforte during winter, and Nietzsche may have been trying to recreate the discipline and structure that that school had imposed by force. It was shortly after this that he decided to return the rented piano and forego the composition of both music and poems, significant renunciations, which suggest that he was psychically cleaning house.[71]

One must now consider those religion classes which were causing Nietzsche such perplexity. During his first term, Nietzsche had been taking one course on the *Gospel according to John* and another on the history of the early Church. The instructor for the latter, Wilhelm Ludwig Krafft, was

---

[69] Compare, for example, his complaint that Strauss had divested himself of Christian belief but not Christian morality (UO I); or his aphorism on the shadows of Buddha (GS: 108).
[70] KSAB II: 36.   [71] KSAB II: 40, 41, 75.

comparatively orthodox, but the field had been fraught with tension since at least the 1840s when the so-called "Tübingen School" had attempted to treat the emergence of the Christian Church as a historical subject like any other. Members of that group disdained such explanations as miraculous interventions or the guiding hand of God, interpreting the early days of a Christian church through the lens of individual ambitions and social dynamics. This caused considerable distress among more orthodox church historians, who were able to reject some of the Tübingen School's views as clearly false.[72] However, the group's call to study the establishment of the early church from a strictly historical point of view presented a challenge not easily repudiated. Krafft faced this dilemma frankly, bringing Ferdinand Christian Baur, the school's leader, to Nietzsche's attention.[73]

It was also apparently Krafft's class that persuaded Nietzsche to read the notorious David Friedrich Strauss.[74] Nietzsche was already aware of that author, as was virtually everyone in the German states, for the latter had managed to create single-handedly what was arguably the greatest scandal in nineteenth-century German Christian studies. In 1835 he published *The life of Jesus, critically examined*, a work that summed up and refuted much of the theological work of the preceding century and in the process introduced new concerns. Over recent decades scholars had repeatedly examined contradictions in the New Testament. Religious writers had also become uncomfortable with the notion of miracles, interruptions of the natural order which seemed difficult to sustain in an age of science. Theologians had divided into those who were willing to accept the miraculous at face value – Krafft and Schlottmann were of this persuasion – and those who sought to explain these away by resorting to non-supernatural accounts. Strauss's *The life of Jesus* cleared the playing ground by rejecting both approaches and repeatedly performing three operations. Strauss exposed the contradictions and implausibilities in the gospels. He then showed that both those who invoked miracles (the "supranaturalists," as they were called) and those who sought to supplant these with natural explanations (the "rationalists") were alike forced to introduce absurdities. Finally (and this occasioned the greatest scandal), he argued that all these scholars had erred in assuming that the gospels recorded historical truths. In fact, Strauss claimed, the stories in the gospels were largely a cluster of

---

[72] Baur, for example, had made the unsustainable claim that a conflict between Pauline and more traditional Jewish versions of Christianity had persisted to the end of the second century.
[73] This account is greatly indebted to Harris 1975. For a much shorter (and significantly different) account, see Beiser 2014: 24–25. For Nietzsche's views on Baur, see KGW I-4: 367–368.
[74] Figl 1984: 89.

myths invoked to associate Jesus with well-known tropes concerning the Jewish messiah. Far from being historical, much less eye-witness records, the gospels constituted an assemblage of resonant, extant stories thrown together in a plausible narrative. They were no more factual accounts than the *Iliad* or *Odyssey*, and although there existed historically accurate kernels in the gospels, most of their texts were a kind of mythic poetry.[75]

The German clergy (and the governments which supported them) reeled at such heresy. Strauss quickly lost his university position, and at the age of twenty-seven he found his professional life effectively ended. While the man might suffer, his book achieved a wide readership and went through several editions. Prior to Nietzsche's arrival in Bonn, Strauss had already published four of these, none of which the young man seems to have read. In 1864, however, the author issued a radically new version, *The life of Jesus, reworked for the German people*. As its title indicates, this edition was designed to be popular in the sense that it was not directed toward theologians but to thoughtful members of the general public.[76] It was also radically different in form, engaging less in the Hegelian see-saw of balancing between schools. Instead, it presented its theses straightforwardly as a lecturer might rattle off facts. One might compare the earlier book to a detective story, which poses a mystery and shows how it was resolved, and the later to a police brief, which eliminates the guesswork and summarizes exactly what transpired.[77] If the later book is simpler, it also sacrifices the sense of intellectual enterprise, dramatic tension, and play which makes the first so spirited and stimulating. For these reasons and others, the 1864 version is sometimes regarded as an inferior work,[78] and it may have influenced Nietzsche less by its inherent power than through his own receptivity. He was ready for a change, and the book gave him a push.

Nietzsche never indicated that Strauss's book had anything to do with his rejection of Christianity. On the contrary, he had conceived and worked through doubts as early as 1861 and 1862, long before the year (1865) in which he finally read that work. In any case, he based his critique of Christianity on culturally enforced mores, not the historical authority of the gospels. It would appear that the man's scandalous book served mostly as a catalyst, allowing him to mobilize his concerns and come to a decision that he had long postponed. He would brandish it as a weapon on his next

---

[75] This presentation is based on a reading of the fourth edition of Strauss's book in the Eliot translation as well as the German 1864 edition. See also Harris 1973, Neill 1964, and Law 2012: 58–62.
[76] Strauss 2005: xi–xii.
[77] Note Strauss's own comparison to the analytic and synthetic methods. Strauss 2005 I: 159–161.
[78] Schweitzer 1960: 194–195.

visit home, and while the book may not have occasioned his apostasy, it certainly smoothed the way to a public declaration.

5

On February 2, a mere month after New Year, Nietzsche wrote a double-edged letter to his mother on the occasion of her birthday. On the surface, it was lighthearted and casual as though offering no more than an update on recent events. Nonetheless, the bantering tone was twice interrupted by extraordinary announcements. Near the beginning, he abruptly declared that he would leave Bonn at the end of the school year: the town was simply too expensive. Toward the end, he declared that he had chosen philology as his major, a decision that must have stunned his family. Aunt Rosalie had already expressed strong doubts at his choice of a double major.[79] Nietzsche now acknowledged the justice of these concerns but moved to the opposite conclusion. "My turn to philology is decisive," he wrote Franziska. "To study both is to do things by halves."[80]

Franziska's reply has disappeared. It will be remembered, however, that after Ludwig's death, she had taken refuge in religion and assumed that her husband's profession would be followed by their son. That assumption had now received a mortal blow; and the announcement came in a birthday letter, no less. Very likely she could not quite believe it, and she may have taken comfort in the knowledge that the Easter holidays were fast approaching. Her son would return home for the first time in six months, and she may have assumed that she could then persuade him to change his mind.

This Easter visit loomed large in the ensuing correspondence, as Franziska and Elisabeth on one hand, and Nietzsche on the other, dreamed of their fond reunion and how happy it would be. Mother and daughter had missed their son and brother badly. At Christmas, Franziska wrote that she would spend it in a nearby city, "for to stay here is almost impossible without you."[81] As for Elisabeth, she had begun to discover in her brother's absence that her friendships with Naumburg's upper crust were more shallow than she had realized. Neither she nor her mother were invited to several social events (including a dance hosted by the Pinders), and she was both surprised and hurt by her exclusion. Franziska had counseled, "Don't count too much on friendship; rank and class prevail," but the adolescent Elisabeth's ability to profit from such advice seems to have been

[79] KGB I-3: 9.   [80] KSAB II: 38–40.   [81] KGB I-3: 20.

limited, particularly when at the same time she had an eye inflammation and was apparently recovering from a romantic rebuff. Her brother, who rarely took his sister's stories seriously, ridiculed her pain, telling her in so many words "to get over it" and to view the situation as humorously as he did.[82] Such advice was not well received, and Franziska reported that Elisabeth was "terribly hurt" by this letter. She also noted that during her son's absence and under the pressure of these social and romantic snubs, her daughter had grown serious in a way that alarmed her. She therefore begged Nietzsche to be more respectful of Elisabeth's feelings. "She feels your absence very much, so write *cheerfully*, well, lovingly and sincerely, my dear son. Do your duty, spend little money ... Your letters are our hearts' light and sun."[83] (Emphasis Franziska's.)

Although these interchanges had taken place shortly before Christmas, they give some idea of the situation Nietzsche left behind and the welcome he would receive on his return. When in mid-March the young man took the long journey back across the German states to Naumburg, he found himself greeted by an adoring family who admired his good looks and new maturity.[84] The reunion might have been paradisiacal, except that Nietzsche brought a copy of Strauss's notorious book,[85] and he apparently showed it to Elisabeth, suggesting that she give up Christianity as well. According to his sister, he also refused to take Communion. If her story is correct, then the truth of his turn against religion was visible for all to see, and for Franziska it must have seemed like the end of a world. However, again according to Förster-Nietzsche, relief arrived from an unexpected quarter. Aunt Rosalie observed that every great theologian had moments of doubt and perhaps one should temporarily avoid discussion until they returned to the fold.[86] If Rosalie Nietzsche really said this, then her advice was less diplomatic than it seems and would hit close to home. In the late 1850s Edmund Oehler, Franziska's brother and a minister whom Nietzsche often visited, had despaired of his vocation and taken leave of the ministry, working as a mechanic in Merseburg. He would eventually return to his pulpit, his faith fortified by his relapse, but the memory would linger, and it was surely this man Rosalie had in mind by her surprising suggestion.[87] Whether this comparison of brother and son comforted Franziska – or indeed whether it happened at all – is difficult to know. She did resign

---

[82] KSAB II: 19   [83] All quotes from KGB I-3: 18–20.   [84] Förster-Nietzsche 1912: 133–134.
[85] Strauss heads the list of books he planned to take on his holidays. See KGW I-4: 50.
[86] Förster-Nietzsche 1912: 135.
[87] Pernet 1989: 124, n. 24. Nietzsche must have been aware of this. See KSAB I: 86 and Franziska's brief reference to it, quoted in Goch 1994: 258. See also Goch 1994: 366, n. 126.

herself to reality and informed Friedrich that he could believe whatever seemed right to his conscience, so long as he kept his opinions to himself. She asked, however, that he refrain from discussing religion with Elisabeth.

To an extent it was too late. If Franziska found peace in acceptance, Elisabeth was thrown into spiritual turmoil. She had always believed in her brother, but little in her limited education prepared her for the abyss he offered with the book of Strauss. She consulted both Edmund and another uncle who was also a minister, and she was reassured by both as to the truth of Christianity. Fortified by their advice, she imparted her doubts in a letter.[88] Nietzsche responded in two ways. In July he would send his sister a German translation of *Thoughts on life* by Henry Ward Beecher, the American Abolitionist (and Harriet Beecher Stowe's brother), inscribing it, "Dear Liesbeth, Take this book as an answer to the 'religious' lines of your last letter."[89] First, however, he wrote a long, good-humored, and firm reply. Whereas Elisabeth had argued, "It is much easier not to believe a great deal than the reverse,"[90] he countered that, when it came to the faith of one's forbearers, this was not so. "Is it really so difficult simply to accept everything in which one has been brought up, which has gradually become deeply rooted in oneself . . . ? Is that more difficult than to take new paths, struggling against habituation, uncertain of one's independent course, amid frequent vacillations of the heart?"[91] As in the past he stressed the extent to which beliefs are conditioned culturally and not therefore reliable as an argument for a more comprehensive truth: "If we had believed since youth that all salvation came not from Jesus but from another – say, from Mohammed – is it not certain that we would have enjoyed the same blessings?" Ultimately, he appealed to a difference in temperaments. "Here the ways of humanity divide. If you want to achieve peace of mind and happiness, then have faith; if you want to be a disciple of truth, then search."[92]

Nietzsche's reply to Elisabeth is probably the best-known single letter he ever wrote[93] and is usually treated as a passionate declaration of his own, more secular values. In fact, the positions he takes are rather old, having changed little since he outlined them three years before in "Fate and history." Indeed, the statement, "Here the ways of humanity divide," is a gloss on Emerson, who had written, "God offers to every mind its choice between truth and repose. Take which you please, – you can never have

---

[88] For Elisabeth's letter, see KGB I-3: 43–47.   [89] Campioni *et al.* 2003: 138.   [90] KGB I-3: 44.
[91] KSAB II: 60. Translation by Christopher Middleton, slightly modified.   [92] KSAB II: 61.
[93] For an English version see Middleton 1969: 6–10.

both."[94] One might note the non-moral nature of this observation. Neither Emerson nor Nietzsche say that we *should* demand truth; it is not the requirement of some code. Rather whether we demand it reflects the nature of our character. Some will insist and some will not, depending on their temperament.

If the ideas were not new, the simplicity and directness of Nietzsche's presentation were worlds apart from the convoluted arguments of "Fate and history." These were no longer theoretical but vital principles, and they demanded action. The difference shows how far he had come during his first nine months at Bonn. He had broken the logjam of familial self-censorship and done so in the light of his own values and judgment. He could now in his eyes dedicate himself to the pursuit of truth, a stimulating and heroic ideal, which was further underwritten by the tradition of scholarship to which he belonged. For once, all his values seemed aligned.

6

Nietzsche could not have chosen a worse moment to major in philology at the University of Bonn. Even as he was making his decision, a scandal was brewing that would hobble that department for a decade to come. Philology had, of course, been known for infighting since at least the Renaissance, when one renowned scholar tried to assassinate another for scoffing at his Latin.[95] The brouhaha which erupted at Bonn, however, was exceptional by any standard. One American scholar called it, "as bitter a feud as ever stirred the philological world"[96] and was moved to write, "I do not yield to any one in admiration of German learning ... but the more I have seen of the arrogance, the jealousy, the hateful maneuvering, the shameful backbiting ... which a closer knowledge of the professor's life in Germany reveals, the more glad am I to live [elsewhere]."[97]

The professor in question (Basil Gildersleeve) was referring to the following.[98] It will be recalled that Otto Jahn and Friedrich Ritschl, the two current leading professors of the department, were outwardly civil but privately mistrustful. Beginning in 1863, Jahn began to arrange for another professor, Hermann Sauppe, a renowned Graecist, to be appointed to the philological faculty at Bonn. Since Jahn feared that Ritschl would object

---

[94] "Intellect." Emerson 1983: 425.
[95] Pfeiffer 1976 II: 34. Poggio Bracciolini tried to murder Lorenzo Valla.
[96] Gildersleeve 1884: 340.   [97] Gildersleeve 1884: 354.
[98] This account is based on the following sources: Ribbeck 1969; Bezold 1920; Herter 1975; Hübinger 1964; and Müller 1990.

and knew he could not match the latter's political skills, he maneuvered behind his colleague's back, leaving other faculty members out of consideration as well.[99] It helped that he was politically backed by two powerful associates: Wilhelm Beseler, Jahn's cousin, a representative of the Prussian government at the university,[100] and Justus Olhausen, a childhood friend, who reported directly to the minister responsible for education in Berlin. Jahn thus operated, not just as an individual, but in collusion with two men who were personally favorable to him and who wielded enormous governmental influence over the school.

There is no need to go into the details of Jahn's actions beyond giving the end results. In late January, 1865, the government acceded and Jahn's choice was approved. Less than a week later, Jahn received word that Sauppe had changed his mind, electing to stay at his current post and thereby leaving his sponsor in the lurch. Further, Ritschl and other faculty were alerted to the subterfuge, and the failed appointment was announced in the newspapers, embarrassing Ritschl, since the implication was that he was soon to retire because of illness. Jahn was now exposed as less than straightforward, and tensions between him and Ritschl must have become significantly more strained.

The incident might have ended here with Ritschl's darker fears realized but with no further harm done. Unfortunately, two protégés of Ritschl, one of them a future son-in-law, accused Jahn of chicanery and consequently faced disciplinary hearings. Ritschl happened to be dean and in charge of legal proceedings, and under his auspices, although not at his direct behest, his future son-in-law was judged guilty but given no sentence. (The second protégé lost his *venia legendi*, his right to teach.) This verdict electrified his opponents, who accused him of rigging the system. Now it was Ritschl, rather than Jahn, who became the object of judicial scrutiny. A series of regrettable incidents followed, as Jahn's powerful friends arranged for his opponent to be repeatedly reprimanded and demeaned. Because so many documents and ostensibly secret proceedings were leaked to newspapers – and not only in Bonn but in Cologne, Elberfeld, Berlin, Weimar, and Augsburg[101] – the general public, students

---

[99] For a discussion of how the selection and presentation of suitable candidates for professorial appointments were supposed to proceed and how they were often circumvented by the Prussian government, see McClelland 1980: 182–187.

[100] Beseler's actual title was Curator, a position that does not exist in English-speaking universities and so cannot be translated. For descriptions of this official's powers see Paulsen 1895: 93–94; Fallon 1980: 35.

[101] Bezold 1920: 506–507.

Soul-building: the practice

included, were kept abreast of these mortifying developments; and groups divided into those favorable to Ritschl (the Ritschlianer) and Jahn (the Janitscharer). The issue was even raised in Parliament, Ritschl's treatment being seen by some liberals as a stick with which to beat the Bismarckean government.[102] The parliamentarians may have been the more astute, for while the quarrel is often depicted as a spat between the two professors – and of course it began that way – it evolved into something different, a quarrel between those who supported university independence and those who favored government supervision.[103] Beseler in particular, who had already clashed with and humiliated Ritschl, was ruthless in his prosecution, and he so demeaned the eminent professor that the latter vowed never to work for the Prussian state again.[104]

Ritschl's position deserves stress because it has implications for the future of Friedrich Nietzsche. The university in which Ritschl had flourished and whose ideals he would later try to inculcate in the much younger man was slowly changing and becoming a different institution – one more practical and useful to the state but in the process abandoning and even actively expunging the ideals of an earlier generation, which was in any case dying out. Ritschl's expulsion may have been an accident, the result of various cabals and individual bad judgments, but it also reflected a historical trend, one that boded ill for the young man who had just decided to major in philology and thereby in theory to commit himself to the university for life.[105]

This larger, political context would not be discernible for years, although Ritschl saw it clearly enough. Instead, the affair was sensationalized and trivialized as a petty fight between two major scholars and therefore, as another philologist recalled, "the saddest chapter in the history of our discipline in the nineteenth century."[106] Although the politicians (Olhausen and particularly Beseler) had triumphed, the Bonn department was compromised for some time. Ritschl departed to start fresh at the University of Leipzig, while the conscientious Jahn, stricken with grief at his own part in the affair, remained in an attempt to assure conformity and healing. He persisted in teaching and continued to be popular with the students, most of whose support (including Nietzsche's)[107] he received.

---

[102] Bezold 1920: 510 and Hübinger 1964 provide the best political treatment of the controversy.
[103] Bezold 1920: 507.   [104] Ribbeck 1969 II: 364.
[105] Some have argued that the fight between Ritschl and Jahn reflected different approaches to philology or opposing political views. Anthony Jensen strongly rejects the first view and disputes the second. Jensen 2013: 45, 50 and 50, n. 75. The evidence indicates that he is correct.
[106] Alfred Körte. Quoted in Calder 1991: 198.
[107] KSAB II: 56. Two of Nietzsche's favorite teachers, von Sybel and Springer, strongly supported Jahn.

Nonetheless, Otto Jahn seems never to have recovered from these events, and a student would write of him, "He was a broken man. Only his work kept him alive."[108] A later chronicler records more tellingly, "After 1866 he heard no more music."[109] Already suffering from pulmonary disease (probably cancer), Jahn would die a mere four years later, leaving behind students still angry at what they considered his unjust fate. One of these would seek revenge.[110]

All of this was occurring during the months just before and after Nietzsche's Easter vacation. Throughout the process he attended lectures by both men and he wrote a paper under Jahn's supervision.[111] Thanks to the newspapers and the indignant responses of students the departmental drama was hard to ignore, and he must have been present to view all the humiliation and damage inflicted on both professors. Yet amazingly, he does not mention any of this until a letter written May 3.[112] There, he tells Franziska that Ritschl had received permission to leave, a statement made so casually and without explanation that it can only mean that he had explained the situation verbally at Easter. (Of course, his mother may have read the newspapers too.)

To some extent Nietzsche may have been insulated from departmental events by his extreme youth and his personal problems. Nonetheless, having given so much time and energy to scholarship during his short life, he probably considered the professors substitute parents, a secular source of the values that he no longer found in Franziska and religion. To see the sanctum of scholarship riven and its practitioners discredited must have unnerved him. He needed stable institutions, and one of the most august and self-confident had dissolved in scandal before his eyes.

This collapse was the more unfortunate since, unusually for him, Nietzsche was unstable himself. Earlier, he had found it difficult to choose a major. After embracing philology he could no longer use that excuse, yet his bad habits persisted; the only shift he made was to drop theology classes. Thus in his second term he took one class under Jahn, another from Ritschl, two from Schaarschmidt, one from Springer, and one from Karl Joseph Simrock on the medieval poet, Walther von der Vogelweide. That would be six courses, only one less than from the preceding term, and

---

[108] Wilamowitz-Moellendorff 1928: 85. [109] Bezold 1920: 511.
[110] The reference, of course, is to Wilamowitz, who became a disciple of Jahn and would attack Nietzsche eight years later.
[111] This paper was the basis for Nietzsche's later publication on the Danaelied of Simonides.
[112] KSAB II: 49. Nietzsche discussed the entire affair with Ritschl at some point, as he explains to Gersdorff. KSAB II: 75.

they would be in four different subjects: philology, philosophy, art history, and literature. Further, he continued to fail in his efforts to control his finances. When he had first arrived in Bonn, he had briskly drawn up a budget and made great signs of showing that he knew all about managing money. Yet mysteriously he was always in arrears, and his relatives back home were not pleased. Nietzsche was insulted that Franziska did not understand how very expensive life was at Bonn. She in turn must have raised her eyebrows when he mentioned weekly forays to the local concert halls and opera houses. It was all very nice that he had heard Adelina Patti and Clara Schumann and had seen Karl August Devrient in "Wallenstein," but where did he get the funds for these excursions? And what about that carousing with the fraternity? It may be remembered that Franziska's adult life had been largely blighted by poverty, and although her more rigorous letters have disappeared, she apparently reproved her son with a directness which he found insulting. It can therefore hardly have helped when he poetically informed her, "The money vanishes, 'like flowers in the field and ripples in the stream.'"[113]

Nietzsche could take comfort that his financial plight was by no means unusual in the fraternity. Most members had found their way to a pawnshop,[114] an indignity that he was apparently spared. They further borrowed so extensively both from one another and from tradespeople that eventually they had to lurk and take backstreets to homes and local pubs lest they be subject to hard words and the threat of legal action from their creditors.[115] That Nietzsche's plight was shared would prove less consoling as the year wore on, for he and Franconia were increasingly at odds. He was mocked by members for his devotion to study. He also failed to share his fellow members' political sympathies, a divergence which seems to have led to his final disenchantment with that institution. In early summer the fraternity decided to adopt the red-black-and-gold tricolor associated with revolutionary ideals.[116] Nietzsche apparently deplored this choice, and it cannot have been pleasant for him to wear them publicly. For the first time he began to make deprecating comments in his letters. He was dismayed by his erstwhile brothers' "beery materialism"[117] and naïve political posturing. He reported that three fraternities had recently held a convention at which

---

[113] KSAB II: 50. [114] Hermann Mushacke was reduced to this indignity. KGB I-4: 17.
[115] Local townspeople stalked delinquents for payment because they could not appeal to civil authorities for redress when students were involved. Hart 1874: 315–316.
[116] KSAB II: 59, 67. Franconia's original colors were white, red, and gold. KSAB II: 15. Max Eyffert reports seeing the new caps on June 3, 1865. BAW III: 407.
[117] KSAB II: 55.

there was considerable boasting: "Yay! What happiness! Yay! What hasn't the fraternity done! Yay! Aren't we the future of Germany, the seed ground of German parliaments!" He concluded, "As Juvenal says, sometimes it is hard not to write satire."[118]

With his world collapsing about him, Nietzsche turned to friendship but not particularly to his old companion, Deussen. A diary kept by an acquaintance indicates that the latter remained part of the Nietzsche circle, but only tangentially.[119] This is unsurprising, since Franconia's membership and activities were central to Nietzsche's social life in Bonn, whereas Deussen had long since withdrawn from membership. Further, their friendship had taken a painful turn. Like his friend, Deussen found himself demoralized at Bonn – "The first year at the university was truly damaging for me," he would write – but unlike Nietzsche, he was unable to rouse himself to decisive action.[120] Nietzsche upbraided him, apparently with considerable vigor, and Deussen began to find their relationship lacerating. Speaking of his erstwhile friend, he wrote, "It was though I were enslaved by a demonic power, and my admiration for him was like a kind of pain."[121] Nietzsche, quite unlike Deussen, did not dwell on losses, and he turned instead to Hermann Mushacke, a fraternity brother who was the son of a Gymnasium teacher in Berlin. This young man was apparently hospitable and entertaining; the aforementioned diary indicates that he and Nietzsche frequently spent the evening in Mushacke's lodgings. When the latter's parents arrived for a visit, young Mushacke probably introduced them to his new friend.

Nietzsche also conducted an extensive correspondence with Carl von Gersdorff, scion of a recently ennobled family in the Oberlausitz, an area to the east of Dresden. Gersdorff had been a younger student at Schulpforte, and while Nietzsche does not mention Gersdorff in his writings at Pforta, the latter had been much taken with Nietzsche's piano improvisations while there, and subsequent letters suggest that their relationship had been warmer than the documentary evidence indicates. "Close relationships with one or two friends are a necessity to me," Nietzsche wrote him. "So long as I have these, I can take the remaining as a kind of side dish, some as pepper and salt, others as sugar, others as nothing."[122] Gersdorff apparently fell into the category of "close relationships," and he became so important to Nietzsche that when the younger man elected to transfer to the

[118] KSAB II: 66–67.   [119] See Eyffert's journal. BAW III: 403–414.
[120] KGB I–4: 70. In the same letter Deussen indicates that Nietzsche found him "limited" and fretted that he did not apply himself with sufficient energy and focus.
[121] Quoted in Feldhoff 2008: 54.   [122] KSAB II: 55.

University of Leipzig, Nietzsche chose to enroll there too.[123] He had already decided to leave Bonn but had been unsure where to study next. The chance to be with Gersdorff apparently tipped the scales, but Leipzig beckoned for other reasons too. It had a thriving arts scene and was situated near Naumburg, so he could easily visit his family.[124] Above all, Ritschl was moving to Leipzig as well, as Nietzsche announced in the very same letter. Although Nietzsche had specifically been warned against studying philology at Leipzig because the program there was so poor, Ritschl's presence was bound to be transformative: "That makes the philosophical faculty in Leipzig the most significant in Germany."[125]

7

Nietzsche had decided to leave Bonn during the mid-August holidays. He actually left on August 9. As the date with all its finality approached, he came down with "rheumatism," a term which in those days could refer to pains not just of the joints but of other organs,[126] and which in this case affected his arms, neck, back, and teeth, and also occasioned headaches. Even a stay at Bad Ems, a spa which he visited with Deussen, did not avail. This persistent pain can hardly have improved his mood, and he began to see much about him in a negative light. He turned decisively against the fraternity, holding it henceforward in contempt. He also had nothing good to say about Bonn, and he equally berated the town's Catholics for their processions and statues and its upper classes for their formal demeanor, which he found inhibiting.[127]

His stay in Bonn came to seem a blunder, which he would deplore for years to come. Yet Nietzsche seldom encountered a misfortune from which he did not extract a little gold. He later realized that the year at Bonn had yielded one clear benefit: he had learned a great deal about himself, presumably by so often violating his own nature.[128] "I was still too timidly wrapped up in myself, and I had not the strength to play an independent part amid all the influences that surrounded me then," he would record. "Everything obtruded upon me, and I could not succeed in dominating my environment."[129] Instead, he received his values second hand, a subservience uncharacteristic of him either in the past or future.

---

[123] KSAB II: 56. [124] KSAB II: 58, 65.
[125] KSAB II: 56. In German universities the "philosophical" faculty consisted not just of philosophy but of most subject matters other than theology, law, and medicine.
[126] Volz 1990: 151. [127] KSAB II: 65. [128] KSAB II: 81. [129] KGW I-4: 507.

Two situations had challenged him throughout the year. The first was the fraternity, of which his mother disapproved and concerning which Nietzsche himself increasingly had reservations. As he would write Mushacke:

> That I remained in the fraternity for the final summer semester seems to me frankly a faux pas ... By doing so, I violated my principle not to devote myself any longer to things or human beings once I had come to know them.
> Something like that punishes itself. I am annoyed with myself. This feeling has somewhat ruined the summer for me and has even darkened my objective judgment of the fraternity ... Here, my friend, I must always think gratefully of you; how often with you and with you alone have I lost the fretful mood that usually held sway over me. Therefore, my pleasant memories of Bonn enjoyments are always bound up with your image.[130]

The final sentences are important. In a later paragraph from the same letter, Nietzsche attributes his emancipation from dependency to his friendship with Mushacke: "In my estimation the greatest profit of the year is that I have learned better to understand myself. And, not least, that I have won an intimately sharing friend. *For me these necessarily go together.* That I with my complex inner conflicts, with my throwaway, often frivolous judgments, could draw such a dear human being as you, sometimes surprises me, but I hope for the same reasons."[131] (Emphasis added.) The italicized statement is striking because – in contrast to Nietzsche's usual stance as an unregenerate individualist – it acknowledges that self-growth and human relationships run parallel and can be mutually reinforcing. Of course, Nietzsche being Nietzsche, he could not make such a confession without retreating, and he no sooner conceded his regard for his friend than he somewhat took it back, continuing, "and only in moments when the spirit negates everything do I wonder if my friend Mushacke knows me only too little."

The fraternity apart, the focal drama of Nietzsche's year lay in his need to choose a field of concentration. He rose to the challenge enough to discard theology and to confirm this rejection by rejecting Christianity before his family. Although he was able to uphold this disavowal, he was less successful in embracing a positive path: his decision for philology did not allow him to focus his powers any better the second term than he had the first. Perhaps, as he would later acknowledge, he already recognized

---

[130] KSAB II: 79–80.
[131] In the original the sentence beginning, "These necessarily," starts a new paragraph.

that he was not a born philologist and that the dry and self-mortifying ways of academic scholarship were ill-suited to his talents and temperament. Meanwhile, philosophy beckoned as a distracting third way. During his first term he had attended Jahn's seminar on the *Symposium*, ostensibly a class in philology but one with philosophic implications. The following semester he took Schaarschmidt's lectures on Plato and attended his course on the history of philosophy, the latter a survey course extending from the Pre-Socratics to Kant, possibly including Schopenhauer's criticisms of the latter.[132] Throughout the year, he also studied a book[133] that Thomas Brobjer has identified as Carl Fortlage's *Genetic history of philosophy since Kant*.[134] Nietzsche does not reveal how extensively he read Fortlage, but he certainly consulted him during the autumn. At Easter six months later, he was still engaged with this *Genetic history*, for he listed it an item to pack for his trip to Naumburg. In short, throughout his time at Bonn Nietzsche studied philosophy on the side, underwriting the observation his old teacher had made: "[Philosophy] is where his deepest drive leads."

It must be said that Nietzsche may have been too hard on himself when he berated himself for failing in his first year. Some educators considered such indecisiveness and false steps as built into the system and an inherent part of the educational process. *Bildung* had, as it were, its centrifugal and centripetal aspects. The Gymnasium in theory fed potentially disruptive drives by awakening unexpected interests and talents; these, however, were kept in check through the external confines of strict discipline. At the university such safeguards were withdrawn. Students were now given almost total freedom and expected somehow to wield multiple interests and abilities into vibrant but coherent order. They were asked, in effect, to take responsibility for themselves. This was no easy accomplishment to achieve at such a young age, and undergraduates often "went to the dogs"[135] in the process. As Friedrich Paulsen, later the reigning authority on the German educational system, said, using language that reflected the gender arrangements of the time:

---

[132] See Chapter 10, Section 3.
[133] Letter to Kletschke. KGB I-4: 15. Nietzsche here mentions a book on "the history of philosophy since Kant." The letter is dated October 31, 1864. If Brobjer is correct that the book is Fortlage's, then Nietzsche carried it about for the better part of a year.
[134] Fortlage 1852. Cited in Brobjer 2008: 46. As the title indicates, Fortlage's book is wholly post-Kantian in orientation and begins with Fichte, whom Fortlage considers a pinnacle in the field. The book then extends through Schelling, Hegel and their contemporaries, not excepting Arthur Schopenhauer, who is allotted 17 pages. See KGW I-4: 37, 50. In the latter Nietzsche indicates he will take the book to Naumburg for the Easter holidays.
[135] Jarausch 1982: 240. The quotation comes from a translation from Paulsen.

> Only in the midst of freedom ... can one learn what use to make of freedom, how to commune with oneself and govern oneself. True, it is a dangerous school, but there is no other. One may go astray, and many do so; nay, most men go astray for a longer or shorter time, until they discover what is right and suited to them. But no one who has not strayed at his own risk, and found again the right way by his own efforts, has gained any experience of great importance.[136]

He closed with a citation from Rousseau, "We must risk boys if we would gain men."[137] In other words, what Nietzsche construed as a personal failure was for educators part of the plan.[138]

Not himself privy to Paulsen's wisdom and frustrated by his own inability to succeed, Nietzsche passed his final hours in Bonn with Hermann Mushacke and Paul Deussen.[139] Mushacke, although momentarily confined to Bonn by unpaid debts, would eventually accompany his friend to Leipzig. Deussen, although equally dissatisfied with educational opportunities in Bonn, would remain at that university for another nine months, after which he would transfer to the theological school at Tübingen, a move of which his Naumburg companion sternly disapproved. Nietzsche never hesitated to tell his friends when he believed they had strayed from the right path, and he may have imparted some of this good advice that evening. As the three students stood by the steamer which would carry one of them away, Deussen was prey to mixed feelings. The two had spent six intimate years together, from their formal bonding over snuff, through the crises of Nietzsche's last years at Schulpforte, to the bumpy months at Bonn. Now they were separating, and Deussen felt a wave of loneliness pass over him. However, he confessed, "I also breathed a sigh of relief, like one from whom a heavy pressure is removed. Nietzsche's personality had exerted a strong influence during the six years of our life together. He had always shown a sincere interest in my situation, but also a tendency to correct, criticize, and occasionally torment me."[140] Despite frequent entreaties from his friend, he would not visit Nietzsche a single time during the following three-and-a-half years, even when he lived in Berlin, less than a day's journey away. Indeed, with the exception of one overnight stay made by Nietzsche under duress, the two men would not

---

[136] Paulsen 1895: 207–208.   [137] Paulsen 1895: 209.
[138] Nietzsche's views on this subject are most extensively presented toward the end of his lecture series, "On the future of our educational institutions." KSA I: 737–747. Unfortunately, this passage does not lend itself to brief quotation.
[139] According to Deussen, at least. Nietzsche mentions only Mushacke's presence that evening. See KGW I-4: 507.
[140] Deussen 1901: 26.

meet again for another seven years, and even then their encounter was ultimately abrasive.[141]

As for Nietzsche, he felt no ambivalence whatever. In Bonn he had yielded to timidity and paid the price in fecklessness, and he could not wait for the steamer to bear him away. As the boat pulled from shore, he "stood on board the steamship in the damp, rainy night and watched the few lights which marked the river bank at Bonn slowly vanish." In his judgment, "Everything gave me a sense of flight."[142]

---

[141] Deussen 1901: 85. For the overnight stay, see Chapter 12, Section 4.   [142] KGW I-4: 508, 507.

CHAPTER 10

The fourth cycle

If someone does not have a good father, he should get himself one. It's more reasonable for a son to adopt a father than the opposite, for he knows far more clearly what he needs.[1]

I

Nietzsche left Bonn baffled, somewhat beaten, and still recovering from illness. His first move was to convalesce, and a train ride across the German states deposited him in Naumburg where his family awaited. In the quiet and decorous setting of this provincial town, he basked in their admiration and began to pick up the pieces of his life. His year in Bonn had been no grand failure. It had, however, bruised his pride and certainly did not meet the high expectations he envisioned for his life. Nietzsche wrote steaming letters to his friend, Hermann Mushacke, decrying what he saw as his own feckless behavior during the year and deploring the fraternity, which had wasted his time and involved him in low company.[2] Such fulminations may have masked anxiety, for leaving Bonn had not inherently resolved Nietzsche's problems. He had merely taken flight, an act of useless escapism unless he learned from the experience.

Meanwhile, he could scarcely have chosen a more restorative path than to return to his childhood home. His health improved almost immediately, and he reported that although he had looked ill on arrival, his mother soon fattened him up.[3] He spent nearly two months in that picturesque but sedate town, surrendering to what he called "the quiet and abandonment of a provincial city."[4] There he played the piano, enjoyed what for him was light reading (mostly secondary works by David Friedrich Strauss), and rose at five each day to enjoy the clear, blue days of late summer.[5]

---

[1] KSA VIII: 334. Compare HAH I: 381.   [2] KSAB II: 79–80.   [3] KSAB II: 82.   [4] KSAB II: 85.
[5] KSAB II: 82, 85.

This is not to say that there were no awkward moments. As late as October 16, Nietzsche's guardian had to ask, "What amount is still required to wind up your Bonn affairs?"[6] and Nietzsche's frugal mother weighed in on this sensitive subject as well. A mere two weeks after arriving in Naumburg, Nietzsche received a letter from Mushacke. The latter could not leave Bonn without paying his bills and had already pawned his silver watch. Desperate for funds, he reminded his friend that Nietzsche had borrowed two silver groschen in the past. Could he pay it back now?[7] In what must have been one of the most humiliating letters he ever wrote, Nietzsche confessed that he could not repay because he did not dare tell his mother that he had more debts. He would have to leave his friend stranded.[8] The resourceful Mushacke was not aggrieved and quickly found the money elsewhere. Nonetheless, the interchange demonstrates how demoralized Nietzsche was on his return and how powerless he must have felt.

During this time Nietzsche probably wrote an autobiographical account of his previous year, which has been lost.[9] He certainly composed the notes for it,[10] and if he didn't follow through, this would be the only period of his youth that he did not so memorialize. Regardless whether he wrote such a complete memoir, however, he certainly reviewed his stay in Bonn and drew two morals. First, as already mentioned, his membership in the fraternity had been a "faux pas," and he would probably be wise to resign. Second, the best antidote to drifting was to immerse himself in "continuous, thoroughgoing work."[11] Accordingly, he began a new essay on Theognis, the archaic Greek poet who had been the subject of his graduation thesis at Schulpforte. In fact, Nietzsche had already recommenced work on this topic during his spring and summer at Bonn,[12] but he now turned to it with the energizing intent of using it to procure entrance to the philological seminar at Leipzig. In particular he tried to identify the source of spurious additions made to the original texts. "Theognis has been abominably mishandled," he wrote Mushacke. "With critical shears and following a lengthy, methodical thread, I clip from him daily a few patches of tinsel."[13]

---

[6] KGB I-3: 59. [7] KGB I-4: 17. [8] KSAB II: 79.
[9] He burned some poems in Leipzig and probably destroyed an entire notebook. KGW I-4: 516.
[10] KGW I-4: 62–64. [11] KSAB II: 80.
[12] KGW I-4: 45. Nietzsche was working on Theognis as early as Easter, 1865. KGW I-4: 50. See also KGW I-4: 64.
[13] KSAB II: 81. Adapted from a translation in Porter 2000a.

His Schulpforte paper on Theognis had also been written in Naumburg, and this amalgam of scholarship and domesticity – working at his desk while his mother and sister quietly cared for his needs – probably awakened memories that hastened his convalescence. He found the presence of his family so healing, in fact, that for a time he hoped that his mother and sister might move with him to Leipzig. This possibility had been broached in early August before he left Bonn, and Nietzsche acclaimed it an "absolutely blissful idea!"[14] According to Förster-Nietzsche, Franziska vetoed the relocation on the grounds that her son should establish independence on his own.[15] If so, her concern is easy to understand. Very few male undergraduates would welcome the news that their mother and sister were joining them at school, and Nietzsche's enthusiasm suggests that he had yet to sever ties with home. Nonetheless, and despite Förster-Nietzsche's claim, Franziska had more immediately practical reasons for demurring. She probably had little intention of pulling up stakes in a town where she had lived for fourteen years in order to follow this prodigal for a mere three or four years to Leipzig.

Yet if her son had turned unexpectedly clinging, this may have reflected his mother's own difficulty in letting go. A letter Nietzsche would shortly write Franziska shows remarkable insight into their mutual needs. She had apparently accused him of being ungrateful for the homemade gifts she had sent. Nietzsche penitently responded that he would rather have a woolen sock from Franziska than a province from a king. A mere monarch could not possibly act from such heartfelt motives, he wrote, whereas "[a mother] consecrates everything through her love and would like to make every gift into an amulet for her son."[16] While this comparison was no doubt offered as a sop to his mother's hurt feelings, it suggests a doubly poignant truth. Franziska cared for her son with a devotion which was at times unintelligent but would ultimately prove absolute. The amulet metaphor exactly captures the compound of affection, concern, and helpless yearning with which she sent him into a world she did not understand. Meanwhile, Nietzsche's response suggests that he too needed that amulet – that the clothes he wore (which Franziska would continue to wash until he was twenty-four, sending them back and forth by train)[17] carried with them the spell of her love and commitment. They were a way to make her affection portable.

---

[14] KSAB II: 77.   [15] Förster-Nietzsche 1912: 148. See KSAB II: 82.   [16] KSAB II: 92.
[17] KSAB II: 333.

Nonetheless, Nietzsche could not remain in Naumburg long, nor did he wish to. At first, he seemed content with the joys of family life, but he soon took off to visit his Uncle Edmund in Gorenzen,[18] a village isolated on a mountaintop where he had spent several vacations as an adolescent. Sustained exposure to provincial activities had begun to wear on his nerves. He had just returned from the small but cosmopolitan town of Bonn, and his home grounds did not fare well in the comparison. He mocked the local amateur theater, and he compared his stay in Naumburg to immersion in rich autumn days – placid but boring.[19] Hermann Mushacke had invited him to join his own family in Berlin, and the young man accepted without hesitation, even though it meant that he would spend his twenty-first birthday away from his family. When he was ill, Franziska and Elisabeth would be his first point of repair. When he was well, he could not wait to get away. On October 1, 1865, he left for the Prussian capital.

2

Nietzsche's high spirits did not survive the trip to Berlin. He had never visited that city before and should have been thrilled. Instead, he was moody and sardonic, and he withdrew in a silent and patently rude glower when he and Mushacke encountered some Franconia brothers at the theater and were invited afterward to their fraternity drinking establishment. Nietzsche's sulks may have been due to the city itself – as a nature lover, he was rarely drawn to the metropolis – but his spirits may also have been affected by Hermann's saturnine father, Eduard. The elder Mushacke combined scholarly authority – he edited various academic almanacs and yearbooks – with the seductive intimacy of being the parent of Nietzsche's beloved friend. He also had apparently been acquainted with certain philosophers who flourished in the 1840s and afterward. As a result, the young man celebrating his twenty-first birthday listened credulously as the older man imparted "his insights concerning the administration of higher education, his scorn of Jewish Berlin, and his memories from the era of the Young Hegelians." Since Nietzsche sums up these views as "the completely pessimistic atmosphere of a man who has seen much behind the scenes," one can assume that few of these "insights" reflected well on either higher education, the Jews, or the "Young Hegelians," a group of comparatively left-leaning philosophers which included, among others, Ludwig Feuerbach, David Friedrich Strauss, and Max Stirner. As Nietzsche himself

---

[18] KGW I-4: 90.   [19] KSAB II: 86.

acknowledged, the elder Mushacke inducted him into a bleaker world. "At that time I learned to like seeing the dark side of things when – through no fault of my own, as I thought – dark things happened to me."[20]

If Nietzsche was impressed by the elder Mushacke's philosophical and social views, he had an opportunity to apply them when, on October 17, 1865, he and his friend descended at a train station in Leipzig. Unlike sedentary Naumburg or Bonn, that city had thrived as a mercantile center for nearly a millennium and was known for the trade fairs that the city had hosted since at least the twelfth century. During the 1830s to 1860s with the advent of railroads and the introduction of the Prussian Custom Union, the first seeds of the Industrial Revolution had come to Germany, and the citizens of Leipzig moved to seize their share of the wealth. Although the city was far from the behemoth it would become in another decade, its population grew 37 percent between 1860 and 1870[21] to around 100,000,[22] and in the process it encroached on and swallowed its neighbors, ballooning in size with little civic control over the resulting social problems.[23] Meanwhile, a true proletariat had evolved. On May 23, 1863, a little more than two years before Nietzsche's arrival, Ferdinand Lassalle and others founded the first labor union in the German states in Leipzig.[24]

Nietzsche was insulated from many of the city's more noisome social problems because he spent most of his days and evenings in the educational and cultural centers of the city. Safely distant from the factories and slums, lay the Thomaskirche, where Bach had once composed and where Nietzsche, who had joined the Riedel choral society, frequently sang. Nietzsche also attended concerts at the Gewandhaus and heard lectures at the university itself, which had recently celebrated its 450th anniversary. All these, as well as most of the coffee houses he frequented, were within the formerly walled "old" city. By 1865 these fortifications had been replaced by a perimeter of trees and gardens, but within their cincture time stood comparatively still. Only when Nietzsche went home in the evenings was he exposed to the destabilizing spell of the new economy.

On October 17, the day of their arrival, Nietzsche and Mushacke made a brief search and rented quarters in the Blumengasse, a site located slightly to the east of the old city and a fifteen-minute stroll from school. Nietzsche

---

[20] KGW I-4: 509. Translation by David F. Tinsley, somewhat modified. Nietzsche had almost certainly met the elder Mushacke and his wife previously in late July. BAW III: 413. He would retain a book by Eduard Mushacke to the end of his life. Campioni *et al.* 2003: 402.
[21] Heise 2000: 16.   [22] Green 2001: 29. Compare Heise 2000: 16.
[23] See Heise 2000: 17 for some specifics.
[24] For more on Leipzig at this time, see Legrelle 1866 and Bazillion 1990.

took rooms on the top floor and was disposed to like his apartment at first. He records that his landlord was a second-hand bookseller, a profession that probably spoke in the man's favor. However, Nietzsche's statement was apparently not quite correct, for while his landlord, a man named Rohn, undoubtedly sold books, this seems at best to have been a secondary source of income. (There is no record of his bookshop, and the Leipzig *Addressbuch* of 1865 lists him as a helper in the market.)[25] Meanwhile, the room Nietzsche rented lay in a separate structure to the main building's rear, and he entered through a garden, probably a precious relief in this boisterous city. As the last positive touch, his good friend, Mushacke, found accommodations in the building next door.[26]

Nietzsche was under the impression that he and his companion enrolled at the university on the hundredth anniversary of Goethe's own registration. As two biographers have discovered, he was off by a day.[27] Nonetheless, the apparent coincidence seemed a good omen, and he hoped that the university would someday celebrate the hundredth anniversary of his own enrollment, a fantasy that did not come to pass.[28] He was not pleased by the caliber of his schoolmates, whom he found "dwarflike and apparently dumb"[29] – clearly inferior to the dashing young men with whom he had enjoyed such colorful experiences in Bonn. Although Nietzsche's contempt may have been influenced by Prussian pride, he may nonetheless have been right – at least with regard to newly registrant philologists. The university's forte was law, and the repute of its philology department poor.[30] Of the 163 students who enrolled during that first school year, 66 applied to law school, 22 to philology, and one lone soul registered in philosophy.[31] Ulf Heise has suggested that with their large numbers and prestige, the law students would muscle out students in other disciplines, and as will be seen, Nietzsche would not be happy until he found comrades in his own field.

Meanwhile, his bad mood from Berlin failed to lift, partly due to an accident. He had left some belongings behind in Bonn, and although his former landlord packed and forwarded them, they arrived so late that the young man began to think them lost forever. Worse, the luggage that his mother had ostensibly dispatched from Naumburg disappeared altogether.

---

[25] Heise 2000: 17–18.
[26] Nietzsche's address was No. 4, that of Mushacke 3B. Heise 2000: 13, 16.
[27] Ross 1980: 114 and Heise 2000: 11 ff, are correct. For a discussion of the issues, see Blue 2012: 368–369.
[28] Heise 2000: 11. Nietzsche was unpopular in the GDR.   [29] KSAB II: 88.
[30] Ribbeck 1969 II: 392.   [31] Heise 2000: 20.

The unexpected loss of one's possessions would have upset anyone. For Nietzsche this struck to the heart of his new plans. He had longed desperately to transcend the drift and lack of concentration that afflicted him at Bonn and to instead immerse himself in study and hard work. Yet all his tools – the indispensable reference works, his own manuscripts, and, incidentally, his household goods and clothes – had vanished. In particular, the Theognis paper which he had prepared to qualify him for the philological seminar now seemed irrecoverably lost. No matter how much work he had done, he had to watch as October 21, the date for student submissions, came and passed while he stood by with nothing to show. "The wretched railroads, the wretched shipping agents," he ranted. "I am angry with the whole world."[32] Although the missing trunk did eventually appear, a mere two weeks late, Nietzsche's joy in its arrival did not begin to match the intensity of his despair when it turned up missing. He had in the meantime lost the opportunity to participate in the seminar, and as will be discussed below, he had found new reasons to let his spirits darken.

On arrival in Leipzig, Nietzsche returned almost immediately to the fastidious standards of friendship that had guided his childhood and adolescence. He professed nothing but regret for his participation in the fraternity, and on his second day in town he wrote a supercilious letter, asking Franconia to strike him from its rolls.[33] (They gladly obliged.)[34] Although in the following months he spent several hours a day in coffeehouses, he confined his company largely to Mushacke, Gersdorff, and Rudolf Schenkel, ostensibly a cousin, but not related by blood at all, being the brother-in-law to one of Franziska's sisters. As Nietzsche attests and as Schenkel's letters show, Rudolf was merry, flirtatious, an avid dancer, and quite allergic to philosophy – not the kind of person likely to enjoy Nietzsche's favor. In fact, the two were compatible enough to socialize, travel together, and even live for a time in nearby apartments. Nietzsche might deplore Schenkel's aversion to philosophy, and Schenkel might opine that Nietzsche was "a miserable hiker,"[35] but Schenkel remained a presence in the latter's life throughout his first stay in the city, no doubt gladdening the heart of the family-centered Franziska.

Nietzsche's disgruntlement during the weeks in Berlin and his first month in Leipzig may have been due to a grim recognition. Despite his determination to take charge of his life, he was still essentially adrift. Virtually nothing in his present life corresponded with a passionately held desire. He was not at Leipzig because he liked the city. He had landed

[32] KSAB II: 89.   [33] KSAB II: 88–89.   [34] Deussen 1901: 24.   [35] KGB I-4: 463.

The fourth cycle 215

there as an alternative after rejecting Bonn. He did not care particularly for philology. He simply could not think of a more practical major. Even his companion, Hermann Mushacke, might appear less a friend than a simulacrum, a placeholder between Paul Deussen and the next soul mate, who would not appear for several more years. Everything supposedly essential in Nietzsche's life was ersatz except for his bitterness and a chronically bad mood.

All his life Nietzsche would heed the whispers of passing time, and he did not let his twenty-first birthday go unremarked. He had celebrated it with the Mushackes in Berlin, and two weeks later he reminded his Naumburg aunts (Rosalie and Friederike) that the entire body renews itself completely every seven years; his birthday had registered the third turn of the wheel. "But what will happen to me in this fourth cycle of seven years? All must be decided within it. Once it's gone, the human being must be complete, the entire structure irreproachable. We can then merely bedeck it, not reconstruct it."[36] This was a theory of character that put heavy pressure on the very young man. He had to make changes but was unsure what these should be.

Whatever good cheer Nietzsche had mustered on arrival now deserted him, and he began to see his apartment as the rather dreary and semi-proletarian housing which it probably was. "It is a very sad Sunday afternoon," he wrote his mother that autumn. "The rain drops gently on the zinc roof that runs under my two windows. Many people live about me, and I can see into their apartments. Nothing but hideous faces. And in the gardens that extend to my left and right everything is yellow, mummylike, and desolate. That is now my world."[37]

3

With a perspicacity unusual for a twenty-one-year-old, Nietzsche seems to have grasped the exact nature of his predicament. He needed to find a way of life that was true to his own nature. He had failed at Bonn because he had yielded to the influence of others. A similar failure would likely ensue unless he took stock of his own values and insisted on seeing them through. This called for a return to the search for self-definition that had so preoccupied him during adolescence, and he began doggedly to identify the ideals and activities that corresponded to his needs. "From morning till

---

[36] KSAB II: 93.   [37] KSAB II: 89. In Nietzsche's text the final sentence begins a new paragraph.

evening," he recorded of this time, "I strove to fashion a life that fit me as my own."[38]

While in the midst of this struggle (and within two weeks of his arrival in Leipzig), he paid a visit to the bookstore operated by his landlord. There, he took a volume from the shelf, opened it, and found himself entranced. "I cannot say what demon whispered to me: 'Take this book home with you,'" he wrote. "It occurred in any case despite my usual custom of not rushing into book purchases."[39] On this occasion he overrode the inhibition, hurried to his apartment with his treasure, threw himself into a corner of the sofa, and gave himself up to its spell. The author was Arthur Schopenhauer, the book, *The world as will and representation*; and the reader, Friedrich Nietzsche, seems to have consumed it as voraciously as if it were written expressly for him.[40]

Although in his reminiscences Nietzsche gives the impression that his encounter with Schopenhauer was wholly an accident, he was certainly familiar with the name and probably some of the man's central doctrines before he read his book. Fortlage's history of modern philosophy, which Nietzsche owned and presumably at least scanned in Bonn, devoted an entire section to Schopenhauer's philosophy, and Schaarschmidt's class on the history of philosophy seems to have ended with mention of Schopenhauer's critique of Kant, as suggested by Nietzsche's own notes.[41] Deussen further indicates that while at Bonn both men were familiar with the man's reputation, although they "rarely" mentioned him.[42] Finally Schopenhauer's fame was by now so widespread among the German public that it seems implausible that Nietzsche wouldn't be familiar with at least his general outlook. If he had never read the man's work, he was nonetheless primed to receive it.

At this point some acquaintance with Schopenhauer's philosophy is indispensable if the reader is to understand what Nietzsche found there. From the outset, however, two caveats are in order. First, the characterization which follows is intended only to convey some of the positions and implications of his principal work and is obviously no substitute for engagement with Schopenhauer's texts. Second, before one can even begin to address his views, one must engage with the work of Immanuel Kant, the modern philosopher whom he most honored and whose disciple – a somewhat obstreperous disciple – he considered himself to be.

---

[38] KGW I-4: 513.   [39] KGW I-4: 513.   [40] UO III: 2; KSA I: 346.
[41] See Figl 2007: 185–188, for cautious discussion of the issue.   [42] Deussen 1901: 25–26.

Kant found himself puzzled that human beings could know the world at all. How could there be such a fit between limited creatures and reality that they could not only understand the world about them but be able to make timeless judgments about it? Why should human experience and the reality it ostensibly confronted match so seamlessly that mathematicians could expect their theorems and physicists their laws to hold throughout the universe? To explain this, Kant hypothesized (and by his own lights proved) that human beings could know the world because in perceiving it they ingested the data in ways that they could internalize and order. Experience was never passively "given." Rather, Kant suggested, human beings used certain forms of sensibility (space, time) and coordinating categories (unity and plurality, cause and effect, among others) to create a coherent experience and to arrange the data in ways that they could comprehend. They could understand the world because, so to speak, they recreated it on their own terms.

Kant's hypothesis was ingenious, but it entailed a metaphysical dilemma. He had thrown new light on certain structures of experience and explained how the latter could be both varied and reliably predictable. He had done so, however, by drawing an invisible boundary between what he called the phenomenal world, that is, the world as structured by human cognitive faculties, and (to use an improper but heuristically useful expression) the world as it actually was, a reality beyond human ken. On the one side lay the world of representation, the world human beings found intelligible because to some extent they had created it themselves. Yet there also existed, Kant believed, a dimension which many people would call ultimate reality but of which they could have no determinate knowledge, for it was not assimilable to the ways in which they ordered experience. Kant called this extra-experiential world the thing in itself, and he strongly discouraged attempts to speculate about it. Humanity could understand and explore the world presented to them through the interplay of intellect and senses, he declared, but they could not go beyond that without engaging in metaphysical absurdities. However, as is often the case with forbidden things, Kant had no sooner issued this injunction than contemporary philosophers began to push against it, directing their attention in the very direction he deplored.

In 1818 at the age of thirty, Arthur Schopenhauer entered the fray. He had read Kant at the university and studied under one of latter's more penetrating critics (Gottlob Ernst Schulze).[43] At first Schopenhauer was

---

[43] Schulze had published *Aenesidemus*, a damaging critique of Reinhold, and therefore of Kant. Henrich 2003: 147–153.

somewhat resistant to Kant's theories, but eventually he found many of them illuminating and true. On one point, however, he disagreed in the strongest terms. Schopenhauer decided that the thing in itself was not so alien or distant after all. It was as close, immediate, and intimate as our physical body. Consider, said Schopenhauer, that our body is given to us in two ways. On the one hand we can physically see it: we observe our elbow resting on a table or look in a mirror and notice that our hair needs combing.[44] To that extent our body is part of observable reality, part of what he and Kant would call the world of representation, "an object among objects." (100)[45] However, said Schopenhauer, we are also aware of our body as a vehicle of our will, that is, as the expression of an often vaguely sensed but constantly present complex of longings and distastes that often issue in actions within the world at large. We want a sip of coffee, and we see our hand reach for the cup; a bookcase falls and we leap out of its way. Schopenhauer urged us to see everything we do as expressing this connection of inner attitude and external stance. "The action of the body is nothing but the act of will objectified, i.e., translated into perception." (100) Indeed, our body expresses our will even when we seem to be impassive, for we always have emotions and these are inextricable from bodies, as shown by the grosser emotions: when we are suffused by anger, for example, or transfixed by sexual desire, or obsessed with the need to eat or drink. As he states more generally, "[E]very vehement and excessive movement of the will, in other words, every emotion, agitates the body and its inner workings directly and immediately, and disturbs the course of its vital functions." (101)

Schopenhauer then returns to the two ways the body is given to us, two ways that we now recognize run parallel: reaching for coffee and seeing our arm reach for it are two sides of the same event or, to put it somewhat more generally, the stretch of my arm and the bodily desires it manifests are two aspects of a single reality. My will and my body are coordinate. Schopenhauer then proposes that if our body, seen externally as just another object in the world, is disclosed to be a manifestation of our will, then we should consider the possibility that other human beings are also expressions of the same sort of inner being. In other words, other human bodies, like ours, are expressions of will. Indeed, Schopenhauer goes further and asks readers to construe all that they see – not just other

---

[44] All examples given in this section are the author's and not Schopenhauer's.
[45] Schopenhauer 1969: I, 100. All page numbers given in parentheses refer to this edition and translation (E. F. J. Payne). Unless otherwise noted, references are to vol. I.

human beings but all living creatures and even the material furniture of nature (stones, sky, trees, soil) – as possessed of this double aspect. Their appearance in representation is also the expression (or, as Schopenhauer calls it, the "objectification") of will. Here, the philosopher is obviously expanding the meaning of "will" to encompass objects ruled by what scientists of his time would have called "force," that is, the sorts of cause and effect discussed by physicists. This is a significant move, the implications of which may not be immediately evident. By "force" Schopenhauer seems at first to mean mostly biological concepts such as the operation of stimuli and instincts. Eventually, it becomes clear that he also intends to replace such concepts in physics as action at a distance (gravity) and magnetism. This global extension of will to force allows him to interpret everything in the world as the expression of a dynamic monism. "It only remains for us to take the final step," he assures us and we too will "observe the powerful, irresistible impulse with which masses of water rush downwards, the persistence and determination with which the magnet always turns back to the North Pole, the keen desire with which iron flies to the magnet ... If we observe all this, it will not cost us a great effort of the imagination to recognize once more our own inner nature, even at so great a distance." (117–118)

This is the type of hypothesis that might give many readers pause. Nonetheless, it has imaginative appeal, and it was necessary if Schopenhauer was to sustain a pivotal thesis: all phenomenal reality was of a piece, the representation of a far more sinister underside. This stemmed from his second "correction" of Kant, his first being that we have ways of knowing which elude the structures of representation. It will be recalled that Kant had stipulated two kinds of reality, that of our representations (which he called the phenomenal world) and that of the thing in itself. Following this reasoning, Schopenhauer argued that we ourselves are both the knowing subject and thing in itself, and if we have this second mode of awareness, then this interior awareness of our body must somehow introduce awareness of the thing in itself as well, that is, the ultimate reality that grounds the world of representation.

This was a leap, and the implications were enormous. If will was the thing in itself, then it was not subject to the activities and rules that structured the world of representation. It could not be individual, for example, since it was not subject to the restrictions of space and time. Nor was the will subject to causality, for this was a governing principle limited to the world of representation. The will should not have been knowable either, at least not in the way we can cognize objects of sense experience. Schopenhauer, however, seems to have thought he avoided this impasse with the claim that we know the thing in itself, not objectively, but through "a subterranean passage, a secret alliance, which, as if by treachery, places us all at once in the fortress that could not be taken by attack from without. Precisely as such, the *thing in itself* can come into consciousness only quite directly, namely by *it itself being conscious of itself*" (II, 195; emphases Schopenhauer's.) Beyond that, we could understand the will through the spectacle of nature, for the latter was a manifestation of will and implicitly the will's self-portrait.

Under either guise the will seemed greedy, restless, and cruel. Within our psyche it manifested itself primarily through desire. We wanted things and would fight to get them. Yet once we attained the objects of our desire, they seldom satisfied and the pleasure of obtaining them did not last. We then desired something else. The will, in short, seemed not only demanding but insatiable. It would never give us peace. Further, because we shared the world with millions of other creatures, each of us contending for a limited supply of benefits, desire brought conflict, and conflict suffering and fear. This was true, not only of ourselves, but of the world at large. "Everywhere in nature," Schopenhauer writes, "we see contest, struggle, and the fluctuation of victory." (146) Each individual lives at the expense of another or (as he put it in his typically pungent way), "[T]he will-to-live generally feasts on itself, and is in different forms its own nourishment." (147) Cannibalism, metaphorical or otherwise, was the principle of life and development.

Since we were all manifestations of the one will, none of us was innocent. Certain of us might not have engaged in acts of overt cruelty ourselves (although we lived off plants and meat), but this did not exempt us from our origin in the fierce strivings of will. "Tormentor and tormented are one. The former is mistaken in thinking he does not share the torment, the latter in thinking he does not share the guilt." (354) Or, to put it more graphically: "In the fierceness and intensity of its desire [will] buries its teeth in its own flesh." (354)

Schopenhauer was ultimately a visionary, and he developed a horrific picture of phenomenal reality as one vast charnel house of cruelty and ceaseless retribution. We all lived in terror and we were all submerged in guilt. "If we want to know what human beings, morally considered, are worth as a whole and in general, let us consider their fate as a whole and in general. This fate is want, wretchedness, misery, lamentation, and death. Eternal justice prevails; if they were not as a whole contemptible, their fate as a whole would not be so melancholy. In this sense we can say that the world itself is the tribunal of the world." (352)

In the face of such misery and guilt, what redemption could be found? Schopenhauer held out a few, niggardly crumbs of solace. He devoted a full quarter of his book to the arts and declared that insofar as these were contemplative, they lifted us from the realm of self-interest and offered a respite from the ego. Certain forms of knowledge too offered self-transcendence. When we contemplated the object of knowledge disinterestedly, we experienced a temporary suspension from combat, restful but unsustainable. Such consolations were transitory and merely palliative. The true solution began when we recognized that other individuals were, like ourselves, caught in the throes of will and suffering. Rendered compassionate by seeing ourselves in others, we resolved to inflict no further suffering and to relieve such as already existed. "The will now turns away from life; it shudders at the pleasure in which it recognizes the affirmation of life." (379) Since our very essence, the will, produces the futile cruelty that surrounds us, our only solution is to deny the will, that is, the source of life itself. The self now embraces asceticism, the deliberate renunciation of pleasure, and does its best to disengage from all desire, starting with sex.

There can be no conventionally happy ending to this withdrawal, and Schopenhauer did not shrink from the implications. We are products of the will and to forego it is to achieve, not happiness, but oblivion. When we cease to will, we cease to be altogether. "No will: no representation, no world." (411) Schopenhauer did not advocate suicide, for that represented a flight from pain and therefore an affirmation of desire. One was still caught in the will. Our only recourse was, so to speak, to rescind our own birthright by metaphorically ceasing to breathe, to forgo every desire and fear until we extinguished ourselves out of sheer apathy. This might sound empty, but the alternative was equally so. Schopenhauer, who was a keen reader of the Upanishads, closed his book with a meditation on nothingness, the good kind and the bad: "We fully acknowledge that what remains after the complete abolition of the will is, for all who are still full of the will, assuredly nothing. But also conversely, to those in whom the will has turned and denied itself, this very real world of ours with all its suns and galaxies, is – nothing." (412)

4

There can be little question that the encounter with Schopenhauer's book was one of the decisive experiences of Nietzsche's life. He would question its metaphysical aspects within a mere ten months, and a decade later he would declare his intellectual independence almost entirely. Nonetheless, his initial reading of that philosopher generated considerable enthusiasm, and he afterwards implemented those views so comprehensively that the experience can scarcely be overestimated. As already stated, Nietzsche seems to have burnt a notebook, so apart from a letter to his mother and an autobiographical account written two years later, it is difficult to know exactly how he responded at the time. In the autobiography, however, he recalled the bafflement, frustration, and anxiety that had haunted him since leaving Bonn, and he summarized, "I hung suspended in those days alone with certain painful experiences and disappointments ... Now imagine the effect in such circumstances of reading Schopenhauer's chief work ... Here I saw a mirror in which I beheld the world, life and my own nature in a terrifying grandeur ... Here I saw ... sickness and cure, exile and refuge, Hell and Heaven."[46]

Significantly, this account doesn't stress Schopenhauer's intellectual achievement so much as the magnificence of his vision – its "terrifying grandeur," its evocation of the sublime. Nietzsche's practical response is also noteworthy. He states that in the aftermath of reading *The world as will and representation* he berated himself in "bitter, unjust, and unrestrained" reproach and prescribed himself bodily penances. For fourteen days in a row he never went to bed before 2 a.m. and then rose exactly at 6.[47] Later he would admit, only "the seductions of life, of vanity, and enforced regular study" saved him from becoming ascetically unhinged. While Nietzsche relates all this with mild irony, its value must have been decisive at the time. He was in effect undergoing a conversion experience and, however humorously one may treat the external melodrama, he was thereby setting a gulf between his previous, ineffectual life and the fresh start he hoped to achieve at Leipzig.

Nietzsche soon relapsed from his ascetic practices (not with any evident remorse), but he replaced these with new habits and interests of which his master would approve. For the first time Nietzsche depicts himself as frequently disputing philosophy with friends, not so much in disagreement as in attempting communally to penetrate and appreciate the intricacies of his master's doctrines. Meanwhile, he would widen his philosophic horizons by reading, not only all of Schopenhauer, but works by Friedrich Albert Lange, Kuno Fischer, possibly Kant, and certainly Rudolf Haym. Of course, Nietzsche had read quite a bit of philosophy before but in a desultory fashion as shown by the influences to which he had been exposed:

---

[46] KGW I-4: 512–513.
[47] KGW I-4: 513–514. He tells his mother he awakes at 6:30 a.m. KSAB II: 96.

Christian apologetics, contemporary materialists, Feuerbach, Strauss, a few dialogues by Plato, and insights gleaned from the histories given by Schaarschmidt and Fortlage. This collection lacks unity and suggests proportionately little sense of commitment or opportunity for progress. By contrast, Nietzsche committed himself almost religiously to Schopenhauer, and even if he shortly saw through various aspects of his master, he did not shy from fundamental allegiance and single-minded investigation of his doctrines. Schopenhauer gave him a philosophic center of gravity, and the increasing sophistication he displays in both reading and letters suggests a confidence and burgeoning ability which he probably owed to development along a single path.

Although Nietzsche presents himself as being overwhelmed by Schopenhauer, he gives little sense that the latter invaded his soul violently, displacing old beliefs wholesale with new ones. On the contrary, Nietzsche probably responded because his predecessor's vision accorded so invitingly with his own. This may have been due to the crypto-Christianity inherent in Schopenhauer's vision. *The world as will and representation* might exhibit little love and no mercy, and God was conspicuously absent; yet the doctrines of human depravity, grace, and the wickedness of the world stood out the more prominently for the Deity's absence.[48] Intellectually too, Schopenhauer's views were remarkably consonant with those of the young Nietzsche. Space precludes close inspection of their similarities, but readers familiar with Schopenhauer's work will recognize that his distinction between the "intelligible" and "empirical" self ran remarkably parallel to Nietzsche's attempts to detect his native self amid the guise of its manifestations.[49] Schopenhauer also stressed the unconscious nature of motivation and action, a position Nietzsche had glimpsed as early as his first autobiography and decisively come to terms with through his readings of Emerson. As a result, for all the older man's self-proclaimed and imperious authority, his effect must have seemed gentle and reassuring. He displayed Nietzsche's insights on a grander stage and thereby endorsed their validity and inspired him to pursue them further. He told him, so to speak, that he has been right all along. This was the sanction that the beleaguered Nietzsche needed, and he used the man as a guide in other aspects of his life. As he would write nine years later, "When in my younger days I used to indulge my wishes to my heart's content, I thought that fate would relieve me of the terrible effort and duty of educating myself: at

---

[48] Compare HAH I: 26.
[49] Leiter 1998: 248–250 notes these resemblances between Nietzsche and Schopenhauer.

exactly the right moment I would find a philosopher to be my educator, a true philosopher whom I could obey without further reflection because I could trust him more than myself."[50] Arguably, he had found such a master in the autumn of 1865, and the spiritual security that the latter gave assured that his first terms in Leipzig would be far more satisfying and productive than his dissipated year at Bonn.

5

Friedrich Nietzsche was not the only new arrival in Leipzig. Friedrich Ritschl, the teacher whose battle with Otto Jahn had so troubled the philology department at Bonn, had also left that town and – determined never to work in Prussia again[51] – had just resettled in this Saxon metropolis. Ritschl was probably only marginally aware that his former student – a rather uncommitted freshman while at Bonn – had also transferred to Leipzig, but their shared transit was pivotal for Nietzsche. He had arguably chosen Leipzig because Gersdorff was about to enroll there, but he had also moved in order to study under Ritschl. As he well knew, German university professors were expected not just to teach but to mentor, and success in the system depended on establishing a bond with some powerful teacher. Nietzsche probably placed his hopes on Ritschl.

There must have seemed an immense social distance between the master professor arriving in triumph and the twenty-one-year-old student smarting from his recent failures. Both, however, had wounds to heal. Ritschl was fifty-nine years old and, apart from the humiliation and betrayal he had suffered at Bonn, he would have found the shift to a new venue daunting. Not only was he leaving a home where he had lived and taught for twenty-five years, but his health had been frail since childhood and now he could scarcely walk. Among other illnesses and disabilities – severe short-sightedness, lameness in his undergraduate years, chronic fevers, arthritis, a possible stroke at the age of twenty-six, and a polyp removed from his nose (which permanently altered his voice)[52] – he was prey to gout or podagra, and for ten years had been unable to wear shoes: he had to go everywhere in felt socks and slippers.[53] Although he could travel by train, he still had to traverse the stations, and his trip across the German states had been quite painful. He probably arrived with the more relief since his

---

[50] UO III: 2. Translation by Richard T. Gray. KSA I: 341–342.   [51] Ribbeck 1969 II: 372.
[52] Ribbeck 1969 I: 31–32, 77, 78, 79; II: 29.   [53] Ribbeck 1969 II: 322–325.

wife Sophie Ritschl had visited Leipzig beforehand and arranged a home which he found already furnished.

Once in Leipzig, the two men's experience had been quite different. Nietzsche lived opposite a safe manufacturer and looked out his window into proletarian houses. Ritschl received an audience with King Johann of Saxony, who would later sit in on his lectures.[54] Ministers and citizens committees offered honorary testimonials to the new professor, and Ritschl's inaugural lecture on October 25, 1865, drew a large audience, not just of academics but of local citizens and newspaper reporters, the latter disappointed because the speech was delivered in Latin.[55] Ritschl's address proved a stirring event for Nietzsche, who would recall, "Everyone was generally excited at the appearance of this renowned man whose conduct during the Bonn Affair had put his name in the newspapers and in every mouth. As a result the academic citizenry were fully in attendance but numberless non-students also stood to the rear." After most of the crowd had assembled, Ritschl himself arrived, dressed immaculately in a formal suit with a white bow tie, his otherwise flawless appearance set off by his felt slippers. Cheerful and excited, he waded into the crowd, reveling in congratulations until, as he moved back into the hall, he suddenly shouted, "Ah! Herr Nietzsche is here too!" and gave a wave of the hand. It was, the thrilled student recorded, his first happy experience in Leipzig.[56]

For a time these two men moved on separate planes. Ritschl settled into his new home and watched with care as his daughter planned marriage to a student who had defended him at Bonn. At work he tried to reform the philology department, which had been in decline since the death of the celebrated Gottfried Hermann.[57] Nietzsche, who because of the loss of his luggage had been ineligible to join Ritschl's seminar, bided his time by studying, attending concerts, touring local sites, and making trips with friends to Naumburg and the Saxon towns, Colditz and Grimma. Although he no longer had the fraternity to blame, he soon outspent his budget and had to plead with Franziska for an immediate loan.[58]

In early December Nietzsche had his chance. On return from a visit to Naumburg he found a note from Ritschl inviting him for tea in the latter's home. Upon arrival, he found other students in attendance, all apparently unsure why they had been summoned.[59] After food and civilities (in which Nietzsche made the acquaintance of Ritschl's wife Sophie and the

---

[54] KSAB II: 109.   [55] Heise 2000: 21–23.   [56] KGW I-4: 510–511.
[57] Ribbeck 1969 II: 392. Compare KSAB II: 81.   [58] KSAB II: 97.
[59] This event took place on December 4, 1865. Gilman and Reichenbach 1981: 65.

betrothed daughter Ida), he and the other young men were assembled and offered a proposition. Ritschl had initiated a philological society at Bonn and found it a useful venue in which students could present their own work to peers. He suggested that the men establish a similar organization at Leipzig.[60]

Nietzsche and three others canvassed promising candidates, and a preliminary organizational session led to the official first meeting on January 11, 1866. Nietzsche agreed to make a presentation, and the ill-fated Theognis paper which he had worked on in late summer (and which had been lost for a while in transition) was at last retrieved and read publicly. He presented it on January 18, and it was so well received that the highly flattered student took the liberty of giving a copy to Ritschl himself. Ritschl read it reluctantly but was impressed. A few days later he called Nietzsche into his office, quizzed him regarding his age, background, and intent, then confessed that he had never seen work by a third-semester student which was so strict in method and sure in its conjectures. If Nietzsche was willing to turn it into a small book, he would help with additional materials and – the promise was implicit – try to see that it was published.

As might be imagined, Nietzsche left this interview ecstatic. "My self-esteem went through the roof," he recorded; and when he later told friends of his good fortune, their praise enchanted him. "It was then that I was born a philologist."[61] For the next four months, he engaged in a frenzy of research, petitioning the Cathedral Gymnasium and Schulpforte for books on Theognis and pleading with friends and at least one academic in Berlin to find rare texts for him. These strenuous efforts were somewhat short-circuited when Ritschl discovered that two established researchers in Paris were about to publish a new edition of the poet. He compensated his student with a prospect almost as glorious: he would publish the rewritten paper in the highly prestigious *Rheinisches Museum*, a philological journal that Ritschl co-edited.

It is possible that so much praise and excitement distracted Nietzsche from a loss that might otherwise have depressed him. At the end of his first term at Leipzig, both his closest friends had decamped, Hermann Mushacke to return to Berlin and Carl von Gersdorff (whose choice of Leipzig had tipped the scales for Nietzsche in the first place) to pursue a military career. Nietzsche weathered what might have been a crisis with ease, possibly because he wasn't so close to these men as he had once been to Wilhelm Pinder or Paul Deussen. He seems to have transferred his social

[60] KSAB II: 100. [61] KGW I-4: 515.

ties to various members of the new Philological Society, joining them nightly for coffee, dinner, or the theater. Although he could be characteristically harsh about the members of that organization, it seems to have satisfied a dream that he had nursed since the dissolution of Germania. He again inhabited a setting where scholarship and friendship converged.

Meanwhile, Ritschl's championship of the Theognis paper was merely the first of many favors he conferred on his student. No sooner was that project completed than he proposed to Nietzsche (who was not yet twenty-two) that he prepare a lexicon for a distinguished professor's new edition of Aeschylus. This project fell through due to Nietzsche's disenchantment with both the work and the professor. However, when Ritschl heard that Nietzsche was interested in Diogenes Laertius, a third-century Greek whose compendium of philosophic texts and anecdotes was decisive in transmitting certain traditions, he encouraged him to continue. The department shortly announced a contest for the best paper on that figure, which may have been a fortunate coincidence but might also reflect an ethically questionable act of benevolence on the part of Nietzsche's benefactor.[62] In either case the older man kept his student occupied with projects that, while presumably of philological value, would also make his name known in the academic community and strengthen his commitment to the field.

In view of Nietzsche's later complaints about philology and laments that he was not drawn to the field by nature, one might question whether Ritschl's encouragement was healthy. Certainly his praise and support rescued Nietzsche from his momentary bewilderment, but it also led him down a path that was neither consonant with his temperament nor of genuine interest to him. Even when working on the abortive Theognis book, the twenty-one-year-old acknowledged that the project was beyond his abilities.[63] Of course, Ritschl's offers did not admit refusal and Nietzsche, as a student, had little practical choice. He had long since abandoned music and poetry, recognizing that he did not have the drive and talent to make them a success. "Philology," he wrote, "moved into the resultant gap."[64]

The puzzling question, however, is not why Nietzsche swallowed the bait but why Ritschl offered it in the first place. Arguably, he simply

---

[62] Compare KSAB II: 182–183 with KSAB II: 196.
[63] KSAB II: 145, 168. See also KSAB II: 171, where he speaks of Ritschl's "unmerited patronage." Finally, see KGW I-4: 520: "In doing so he tended somewhat to overstimulate each [student's] productive seam."
[64] KGW I-5: 53.

recognized the talent and brilliance that have secured Friedrich Nietzsche so many readers to the present day. Other factors, however, must have come into play. Ritschl liked to compare himself to the Pied Piper of Hamelin,[65] and he prided himself on his ability to inspire and lead talented men. Nietzsche must have seemed the sort of student he had specialized in all his life. Secondly, as Werner Ross has noted, the two had much in common, and Ritschl may have identified with young Nietzsche.[66] Both were sons of pastors, and (because of parental pressures) both had considered a double major (theology and philology) before deciding on the second.[67] Like Nietzsche, Ritschl was drawn to music,[68] although he was not nearly so talented, and both men were sickly but self-disciplined.[69] Thirdly, Ritschl was at a critical juncture in his life. Not only had he just left a long-established base at Bonn, but of his three children, all had already or were about to leave the nest.[70] As his home emptied, he may have found in this fatherless and intelligent student a filial replacement. Finally, it bears saying that Ritschl was a highly political animal and one inclined to be a kingmaker. He was accustomed to seeding philology departments with protégés who would preach his method throughout the German states, and Nietzsche must have looked like a safe bet.

Whatever his motivations, Ritschl provided just the sort of vigorous yet intelligent guidance that the young man needed. He was something of a battler – "Life means being a fighter," he liked to say[71] – and he was prone to express himself with a directness that Nietzsche sometimes found entertaining, sometimes rude. Nonetheless, Ritschl was fundamentally unpretentious and enjoyed making toothsome, if undiplomatic, sarcasms in Thuringian dialect.[72] He had a great love of rigor, a corresponding contempt for dilettantes, and such a passion for argument that during one discussion a gesture from his foot sent one of his white slippers sailing through the air.[73] Perhaps nothing says more about Ritschl and the students he inspired (Nietzsche included), than the appeal to idealism, duty, and self-development implicit in his standard exhortation: "When I sense in someone a talent that cannot emerge, then I give him – none too

---

[65] Ribbeck 1969 I: 284.   [66] Ross 1980: 121–122.   [67] Ribbeck 1969 I: 16.
[68] Ribbeck 1969 I: 79.
[69] As a young man Ritschl would rise at 5 a.m. in the morning and not go to bed until 11 p.m. or midnight, seven days a week. Ribbeck 1969 I: 40.
[70] One daughter was married, another engaged, and a son (who was just a year older than Nietzsche) would soon depart to work in New York.
[71] Ribbeck 1969 II: 459.   [72] Ribbeck 1969 II: 338.   [73] Ribbeck 1969 II: 400.

tenderly – advice to this end: 'You can, therefore you must.' Seldom does this fail me."[74]

Clearly the two men found their relationship satisfying, and the professor invited his protégé to visit his office twice a week. There over a glass of wine he would discourse – often with questionable frankness – on university policies, the peculiarities of fellow professors, and a host of issues that were probably none of Nietzsche's business but certainly made him feel part of the department.[75] He also integrated Nietzsche into his home, where other sides of the teacher would emerge. Nietzsche might have discovered, for example, that Ritschl liked to design gardens,[76] a hobby he may have recalled when he later used horticulture as one of his most important metaphors, just as, when he called himself a pied piper, he was almost certainly remembering his venerable instructor.[77]

While accommodating himself to this bourgeois house with its offer of domesticity, Nietzsche became acquainted with and increasingly attached to the professor's dutiful wife. Born Sophie Guttentag, the baptized daughter of a Jewish doctor in Breslau, Sophie Ritschl was not only of a different heritage than her husband but fifteen years younger, only slightly more than the age difference that had existed between Nietzsche's parents. She was also twenty-four years older than the young man, making her eligible as a mother figure. Following her husband's example, Sophie Ritschl too came to befriend his talented student, and when the middle-aged woman and very young man discovered a common interest – they both loved music – they began to play piano duets together.

This assimilation into his teacher's house might seem to cap Nietzsche's Leipzig journey from insecurity to stability and success. If he looked back – and he probably did, for he loved to review his life – he would have recognized and approved each step of his recovery after Bonn. Schopenhauer had given him a sense of spiritual foundation. Ritschl offered a practical path and a career. The Philological Society provided a ready source of suitable friends, and the household of his professor conferred a second family, inducting him into a more good-humored but disciplined world than any he had known. Only a passionate relationship – or, at least, an intense male friendship – was lacking, and that too was soon to come.

It would seem that he had what he wanted. Yet as so often in his early years Nietzsche was somewhat acting a role – that of the dutiful son or

---

[74] Ribbeck 1969 II: 284.   [75] KGW I-4: 519–520.   [76] Ribbeck 1969 II: 56, 391.
[77] For pied piper see GS: 340; BGE: 205; TI, Preface. For gardening see GS: 17, 290.

conscientious student who goes through the motions but keeps his true opinions concealed. While at one level he cultivated unity of purpose and effective action, he also knew that he lacked the *sine qua non* of professional integrity, a sense of identity with his field. Even as he actively built up a public career and gave every evidence of responsibility and weight, his intellect and skepticism were corrosively at work, eating at the foundations. Despite Ritschl's confidence, Nietzsche was like a top which spins upright in place but could at any moment go skittering across the floor.

CHAPTER II

"The end of the first act"

The truth is ugly. We have art, so that we do not perish from the truth.[1]

I

During the spring and early summer of 1866 Nietzsche labored intently on his Theognis book (shortly to be reduced to an article). He liked to work in Naumburg, which he called, "that comfortable backwater,"[2] and he spent most of March and half of April there during the Easter holidays, pursuing researches while his mother and sister saw to his needs.[3] He also enlisted the aid of two former teachers from Schulpforte: Wilhelm Corssen, who made the school library available, and Diederich Volkmann, whose knowledge of Byzantine Greek studies would assist Nietzsche over the next two years. Meanwhile, he read the newspapers with care. War seemed imminent, and the draft could take him from his studies at any time.

This was not the first military campaign to threaten Nietzsche during his youth. Previous hostilities, however, had centered on territories far from home and went unmentioned in his letters.[4] What now loomed was no limited conflict in proxy venues but something far more fearsome and with immediately tangible consequences: the direct collision of giants. Future historians would view the impending war as such a watershed that to this day many works on modern Germany end in 1866 with its immediate fallout.[5] Nietzsche was about to witness a redefinition of the German state.

---

[1] KSA XIII: 500.   [2] KSAB II: 214.   [3] Oehler 1940: 68–69.
[4] In 1859 Prussia had nearly joined a conflict between Austria and France over Italy, and in 1864 Prussia and Austria had battled Denmark in the Jutland.
[5] See, for example, Sheehan 1989, Schulze 1991, and Nipperdey 1996.

The conflict began through a geopolitical anomaly. During and after the Napoleonic Wars the number of German political units was reduced from 812 (the quantity of states, cities and territories included under the old Holy Roman Empire)[6] to 39.[7] When a new ideology of nationalism appeared, the question arose: why not lower the number further – to one? Leftists believed that the elimination of so many kings and lords was inherently desirable. Cultural enthusiasts found it painful that there should exist so much German art and literature with no corresponding political entity. Traders saw the benefits of a unitary economic unit. Encouraged by these and other constituencies, the ideal of a single state increasingly seized people's imaginations, and its implementation began to appear inevitable. It also became clear that such a country would have to be created under the aegis of either Austria or Prussia, a situation which heightened tensions between those rivals.

In 1866, Otto von Bismarck provoked war with Austria, effectively eliminating the German confederation in power and throwing the nation into chaos.[8] Thus, while the conflict that followed is known in English as the "Austro-Prussian War," it is more accurately described as the "German War." (It is actually called this in German-speaking countries and this is the title that Nietzsche used.)[9] Since Prussia did not allow any state of significance to remain neutral, the conflict became in effect a civil war, and Prussia had to defeat not only Austria but the military forces of that country's allies, including Saxony, Bavaria, Hannover, Electoral Hesse, and several other regions.

Bismarck had carefully expanded and modernized Prussian forces. Accordingly, when hostilities were declared (June 16), his armies almost immediately removed Hanover and Electoral Hesse from action. The seizure of Saxony was particularly vital because it controlled the passes through which Austria could enter the Prussian flatlands. Fortunately for Prussia, that country's army had moved to Bohemia to join the Austrian contingent, leaving its people undefended. It took the invaders only two days to reach Dresden, the Saxon capital, seizing Leipzig along the way.[10]

Thus it was that a certain young man studying at the local university found himself in the midst of occupational forces which, fortunately for him, were from his own country. Some associates were not so lucky. His

---

[6] Gagliardo 1980: 5; Simms 1998: 9; and Williamson 2005: 4, 15. Compare Brose 2013: 4, and Winkler 2006 I: 44.
[7] Williamson 2005: 14.
[8] The German Confederation was officially dissolved by the Peace of Prague.   [9] KGW I-4: 528.
[10] Wawro 1996: 77. For Saxony's options and policies, see Bazillion 1990: 343–347.

guardian could hear cannons during the Battle of Langensalza, in the aftermath of which the Hanoverian troops were defeated.[11] His sister reported that Naumburg was in a panic because of a reported advance of the Bavarians and had sent its public coffers to Magdeburg. (The rumor turned out to be false.)[12] Gersdorff worried that his family's estate, which lay near the Bohemian border, could fall prey to marauding soldiers.[13] Paul Deussen, who was studying in the Württemberg city of Tübingen found himself considered an enemy alien; and while he was not imprisoned, he was treated with suspicion and contempt.[14]

Plainly, this was not a war that one just followed in the newspapers. Threats abounded and, because communication was largely cut off, Nietzsche described himself as living on an island with erratic sources of information. He also wrote that he had difficulty in sending letters outside of Prussian territories, although this claim seems exaggerated, given how many letters he sent and received at the time. Indeed, Nietzsche was arguably the most secure member of his family, for he lived in what he called "the Prussian city of Leipzig" and was surrounded by a garrison of home troops.[15] Not yet drafted, although he frequently inquired as to his status, he observed the situation from a double point of view. On the one hand he was clearly pleased to see his countrymen occupy a region he had always thought inferior. Thus in his first letter home after Prussian occupation he acknowledged ambivalence over Bismarck's methods, then added that it didn't matter: "Our situation is quite simple. When a house burns, one doesn't first ask who caused it but puts it out. Prussia is on fire. Now it must be saved."[16]

At the same time Nietzsche's letters show him trying repeatedly to escape personal enmeshment and to rise to a less partisan vision. He did not aspire to be even-handed and to offer the Saxons sympathy. Rather he tried to forego allegiance altogether and to see the war aesthetically, as a performance in the theater. Thus, in a letter to Mushacke he compared recent events to a play which he watched in breathless suspense. "How lucky we are," he wrote his fellow civilian, "that up to now we can shout bravo and clap. I am meanwhile not sure that the drama could not turn into a tragedy for us. We too could also be called up to take over one of the numberless supernumerary roles."[17] He later presented the same analogy to Gersdorff, "I try for a few minutes to separate myself from consciousness of

---

[11] KGB I-3: 105. Daechsel also worried that the Saxons would "visit": 91. [12] KGB I-3: 113.
[13] KGB I-3: 87, 103.   [14] Deussen 1922: 90–91.   [15] KSAB II: 135.   [16] KSAB II: 135.
[17] KSAB II: 140–141.

the times and from subjective natural Prussian sympathies. Then I see a farcical play of the sort that history makes just once, *by no means moral* but quite beautiful and edifying for the onlooker."[18] (Emphasis added.)

One advantage this aesthetic stance provided was the chance to observe psychological dynamics, notably the chagrin of Saxons at being conquered. This was, after all, a war they had never wanted and in which they need not have been involved, since it directly concerned only Prussia and Austria. Now they found themselves occupied by arrogant Prussian troops, and, as one journalist remarked of the populace of Dresden, "They sulk, do what they have to, and wish the Prussians in hell."[19] Nietzsche thought this poor form and refused to understand why the country of his kinsmen – the Nietzsches were originally from Saxony and still had branches in that country – did not accept its defeat more gracefully. He was particularly annoyed that "their small minds continually cast mistrustful looks on our successes."[20]

Nietzsche was also fascinated by an apocalyptic sense that subterranean shifts long hidden had abruptly been revealed to view. "Haven't we the strange feeling as if an earthquake had made the ground, which seemed unshakeable, unsafe, as though history after years of solidity suddenly were put in motion and cast down numberless related conditions with its weight ... If we look back, we feel that the coming storm lay in our limbs. I don't mean that higher spectral powers have a hand in the game. Rather rotten buildings collapse with a crack merely because a child jars a column."[21]

Above all, Nietzsche pondered the figure of Bismarck, who had initiated this earthquake and had so deftly ridden it to its close. Nietzsche was himself careful to express pious chagrin at his leader's immorality, which, as a student of Schopenhauerean ethics, he was obliged to condemn. He also commented on Bismarck's paradoxical political position. Although the man represented a conservative government, his aim (creating a unitary state) and his means (which included demands for the abdication of hereditary rulers, including a king) were not just left-wing but considered by some to be "Bonapartist."[22] This view was seconded by no less an authority than Friedrich Engels, who remarked of Bismarck's moves, "If that wasn't revolutionary, then I don't know what the word means."[23] Nietzsche agreed, as is clear in a sardonic reference he made in a letter to his

---

[18] KSAB II: 159.   [19] Quoted and translated in Green 2001: 57.   [20] KSAB II: 138.
[21] KSAB II: 140.
[22] Compare the hostility directed against Bismarck from the right. Green 2004: 85.
[23] Quoted in Winkler 2006 I: 165.

mother.[24] Nonetheless, he wrote to Gersdorff that it was important to recognize that "Bismarck's game was exceedingly shrewd, that a policy that dares to go for broke can just as well be cursed as worshiped, [depending on its success]. But this time the success is there; what has been attained is great."[25]

This ambivalence concerning Bismarck, which during this period he mentions in every letter but one, represents a double allegiance within Nietzsche himself. He was a Schopenhauerean after all, and the latter's ethics were not so different from those associated with early Christianity, with particular stress on sympathy. This was certainly not Bismarck's way, yet Nietzsche admired him all the same. Here the invocation of earthquake and abrupt eruptions might be applied to his own psyche. When he talked of Bismarck a long-forgotten approach to ethical values was dislodged and emerged into view. During a Germania meeting in 1862 Nietzsche had scandalized Wilhelm Pinder with a lecture in which he praised Napoleon III for his willingness to override conventional morality in pursuit of a higher political good.[26] During the Prussian occupation of Leipzig, when even Nietzsche regarded Napoleon III as despicable, Wilhelm couldn't resist reminding him of that essay and asking implicitly what he thought of his French hero now?[27] Nietzsche did not take the bait, but he surely noticed Wilhelm's taunt, and he might have reflected that he had not so much changed his mind as redirected his esteem from a French to a Prussian statesman. Yet the current situation was more complex. In the year 1862 and aged seventeen, he had come fresh from reading Machiavelli's *The prince*, and he had applauded Napoleon III for reincarnating that sixteenth-century model. Now Prussia had a prince of its own, and Nietzsche had reasons to ask himself whether this was really what he wanted. Theoretically he could not approve, for the war in question had offered from start to finish a spectacle of undisguised cynicism – a process of duplicity, bullying, capricious violation of treaties, physical violence, and (in the eventual peace terms) ruthless acquisition and humiliating reprisals, all pursued without generosity, grace, or shows of respect.[28] At first, the populace at large had been largely undeceived. Not until the later days of the war did Prussians in general begin to rally around the much-despised leader. Yet at the close of this unedifying sequence of events, large sectors of the German-speaking public, both left and right, rose up to

---

[24] KSAB II: 135.   [25] KSAB II: 159.   [26] "*Napoleon III als Präsident.*" KGW I-2: 357–362.
[27] KGB I-3: 115.
[28] When the Prussians marched into Frankfurt, a city that had been free for several centuries, the local mayor hanged himself.

acclaim the war as an almost holy manifestation of historical destiny, an approval in which Nietzsche somewhat concurred. He surely felt bewildered at the inconsistency of these evaluations, as is indicated by his comment that a policy like Bismarck's could only be judged by the outcome. After studying history his entire life, he now saw it in action, and the discrepancy between public accounts and the realities he witnessed must have given him pause. Small wonder that he sought to elevate it from the practical to an aesthetic plane, as though he were watching "Henry V" or "Wallenstein," instead of participating in a brutal imposition of strength. He might have been thinking of the Saxons, the Prussians, but also of himself in the final revelation that he made to Wilhelm: "One can learn much in such times ... Above all, one observes how negligible is the power of thought."[29]

Eventually, the Austrians were defeated in the Battle of Königgrätz. The Prussians then moved slowly southward, much impaired by an epidemic of cholera, until by July 18, they were within 19 kilometers of Vienna. At this juncture France and Russia intervened, and the conflict that had been universally expected to last for months, if not years, earned the nickname, "The Seven Weeks War." Bismarck had achieved his goal. Austria, which had been part of Germany – arguably its center – for a millennium, was now effectively expelled; and it would be only five more years before Prussia seized full control.

One issue had been settled: if the German states were to unify, it would occur under Prussian auspices. Further, Prussia benefited enormously from the acquisition of new territory and the imposition of its authority. Yet virtually nobody believed the war had resolved the fundamental problem. Germany might be ready to unify, but it could not do so without the consent of the rest of Europe and particularly of France. This was unlikely to occur without further war, and many Germans bided their time in the happy prospect of settling scores with the nation which had humiliated them sixty years before. Nietzsche and his friends waited expectantly as the greatest political experience in their lives slowly moved forward. Gersdorff wrote, "[A]re we at the end of the first act of the great song and dance?"[30] For Nietzsche and others of his generation the question was purely rhetorical.

2

Sometime between mid-August and mid-September Nietzsche turned in a draft of his Theognis paper,[31] and for the first time in six months he could

---

[29] KSAB II: 138. [30] KGB I-3: 145. [31] KSAB II: 157.

enjoy some leisure. It was during this time that he turned to Friedrich Albert Lange's *The history of materialism and critique of its meaning for the present*, a book he must have found gripping, for by the end of August he had either finished it or read enough to quote generously from its pages. He immediately recommended it to Gersdorff and later to Mushacke.[32] Although he was afterward silent for a while concerning the book, he returned to its advocacy in 1868 when he again campaigned, praising it to Gersdorff,[33] importuning a former classmate (Heinrich Romundt)[34] to read it, and apparently loaning his own copy to another friend (Erwin Rohde).[35] Scholars debate the extent to which the book continued to inspire Nietzsche after 1869,[36] but the influence during his undergraduate years can scarcely be exaggerated.

Nietzsche does not explain how he chanced on the work, but Lange had once been Ritschl's student, and perhaps a remark by that professor drew his interest. Gersdorff had seen a copy on Rohn's bookshelves, so Nietzsche may have found it the same way he happened on Schopenhauer's masterwork.[37] The title alone would have intrigued him. During this age when science and technology were ascendant, books on materialism, usually with philosophic overtones, sold well and were earnestly discussed. (Nietzsche had considered the topic himself while at Schulpforte.) Four writers in particular – Ludwig Büchner, Carl Vogt, Jacob Moleschott, and Heinrich Czolbe – had captured the popular imagination, not just in Germany but abroad.[38] By the mid-1860s, the tide had somewhat turned, academically at least. The renowned chemist, Justus von Liebig, would refer to these materialist popularizers as "dilettantes," because their knowledge of the sciences was deficient. Meanwhile, Lange, who had a doctorate in philosophy, decided to treat the subject with greater sophistication than had been offered by its amateurish adherents. He also hoped to redeem philosophy, observing that while Büchner and his cohort lacked knowledge of chemistry, certain natural scientists who pontificated on philosophy knew little of the latter subject and could be termed dilettantes themselves.[39] As this even-handed irony suggests, Lange played few favorites. Materialism might be his target, but he

---

[32] KSAB II: 159–160, 184.
[33] KSAB II: 257–258. Gersdorff procured a copy and read parts. KGB I-3: 278.   [34] KGB I-3: 293.
[35] KGB I-3: 299.
[36] There were four editions of the book and critics disagree on which Nietzsche read in later years. See Salaquarda 1978 and Stack 1983.
[37] See KGB I-3: 146.
[38] Compare the remark by Carl Fortlage in 1857: "A new world view is settling itself into the minds of men. It goes about like a virus." Quoted in Gregory 1977: 10.
[39] Lange 1866: 320 ff.

was by no means disrespectful. His claim rather was that as a philosophic system, it had ultimately failed,[40] and even scientifically its theses had been superseded.[41]

Symptomatically, Lange's account opens with a statement that immediately redefines the issue. "Materialism is as old as philosophy but no older," he says,[42] and his point is that materialism is not just an attitude of hardheaded common sense, but rather a school of philosophy and specifically a system of metaphysics. Consequently, it should be viewed within the context of other metaphysical systems, and his first task is to examine the place of materialism within the history of philosophy. In the first edition of his work, the one Nietzsche read in Leipzig and the only version of interest here, Lange effectively begins with Democritus, who rejected final causes and who, building on Leucippus, devised the first extended theory of atoms in empty space. Lange then proceeds to such figures as Epicurus, Lucretius, Gassendi, Hobbes, la Mettrie, and d'Holbach and to such schools as the Sophists and the medieval Aristotelians, bringing his historical survey up to Hume and Kant. In this historical section Lange treats representatives of the materialistic outlook with considerable esteem, for he believes that methodologically their approach did little harm in the sciences and served as a prophylaxis against idealist views, most of which he considers flawed and counterproductive. Ultimately, he may find materialism limited in its imaginative range and mistaken in its metaphysical claims, but he believes it useful as "a maxim for scientific research."[43]

Although the title of Lange's book is usually shortened to *The history of materialism*, the actual heading – *The history of materialism and critique of its meaning for the present* – suggests a double purpose. Quite apart from presenting the school's origin and development, Lange explores its relevance for contemporary action and thought, and it is here that he explores the problematic nature of metaphysics in general. For Lange the decisive moment occurred with Kant's "Copernican Revolution," the view that instead of asking how human knowledge can conform to objects, we should ask how objects must conform to human knowledge.[44] "You can't get around Kant," Lange writes. "Here lies the beginning of the

---

[40] For examples of decisive rejection, see Lange 1866: 276, 371, 379, 499–500.
[41] See Lange 1866: 365, 371, 379, 483, 499–500.   [42] Lange 1866: 3.
[43] Lange 1866: 238. For a discussion of materialists' general insensibility to aesthetics and the spiritual, see 200–204. Gregory hypothesizes that the proposal of a maxim referred to the so-called "reductionists." Gregory 1977: 148.
[44] *Critique of pure reason*, B xvi. I have expressed the "Copernican Revolution" in Kant's terms. Lange, whose work is based largely on the *Prolegomena*, not the first *Critique*, explains it somewhat differently. See Lange 1866: 287 ff.

end for materialism, the catastrophe of the tragedy."[45] His admiration was not unconditioned. Vast tracts of the first *Critique*'s "Transcendental analytic" disappear unmentioned, as Lange reproaches his predecessor for trying to explore the production of the synthetic *a priori* through "pure thinking."[46] "Here the great man was as completely mistaken as any metaphysician has been."[47] Nonetheless, Lange applauds the Copernican Revolution itself. "The fact that we definitely [have] experience, is … conditioned by the organization of our powers of thought," he agrees; and he construes various logical operations as being "not only pre-experiential but … a condition of experience."[48] In other words, Lange does believe there are reliable *a priori* judgments, that is, judgments that are both universally and necessarily true. He just doesn't believe that these can be validated by logical proofs. They can be falsified, but their positive acceptance must always be provisional. (It should be noted for those familiar with Kant that except in his examination of Kant himself Lange does not distinguish between analytic and synthetic *a priori* propositions; all must submit to the trial of experience.)

If *a priori* propositions are so problematic, why believe that any are true? Lange finds the explanation in his own Copernican turn. Valid *a priori* statements reflect the structures through which we create experience and to that extent must always be true. Lange locates those structures in our "physical-psychological" organization, a notion he leaves undefined and largely uncharacterized in the first edition of his work.[49] He does provide examples of that organization in action, however, particularly in the field of physiology. Lange presents experiments in which the application of a stimulus is compared with the thresholds and forms through which a human being perceives them. At what frequencies and at what volume, for example, must tones be produced before a person can report hearing them? And further, what correlation exists between the sensuousness of the perceived "sound" and the kind and degree of the electronic event that "produced" it?

On the one hand Lange claims that these physiological experiments have exhibited life as a product of mechanical processes, exactly as the

---

[45] Lange 1866: 241.
[46] Lange never discusses the metaphysical or transcendental deductions, and the issue of apperception (except for a reference on p. 280) goes unmentioned. His footnotes, which refer exclusively to the *Prolegomena*, suggest that when writing his book he did not use *The critique of pure reason* at all.
[47] Lange 1866: 248.   [48] Lange 1866: 241.
[49] Lange scarcely fares better in the second edition. There, however, he adds a lengthy footnote in an attempt to characterize this notion. See Lange 1892: III, 193–195, n. 25.

materialists claimed. As the materialists did not at all predict, however, there is often little match between the occasioning events and the ways human faculties register them. In other words, there does not exist – and Lange argues that there cannot be – any one-to-one correlation between physiological cause and the corresponding "conscious" effect. Lange spends dozens of pages demonstrating the ways human sensations misalign with – and so misrepresent – the forces that occasion them. For a variety of reasons – the receptive limits of our sense organs, the incommensurability between external cause and sensational content, and the way sensations seem to modify themselves at a post-causal, pre-conscious level – the reality we actually inhabit does not and cannot coincide with the world we perceive. This carries numerous implications, some of which will be discussed below. Meanwhile, it is clear that thinkers need to be cautious when making wholesale judgments about the universe, as metaphysicians aspire to do. Human beings should recognize that any ontology which claims to hold universally and for all reality cannot be sustained, and this includes materialism with its assumption that reality is composed of matter and force.[50]

While materialism is certainly vulnerable to Lange's arguments, so is the philosophy of Arthur Schopenhauer. That philosopher too develops a system of metaphysics through the claim that he knows the nature of the thing in itself. As Nietzsche would argue two years later, this claim to be able to say anything about ultimate reality is not consistent even with that philosopher's own assumptions and certainly not with those of Kant as modified by Lange.[51] Lange does not himself specifically spell out the damage his findings do to Schopenhauer. He mentions the latter significantly only three times in the first edition of his book: once in the Foreword,[52] where he dismisses him as a retrograde figure, and later, where his comments are more perfunctory.[53] It is not difficult, however, to discern why Schopenhauer seemed regressive to him; and as will be seen, Nietzsche appears to have recognized the damage himself.[54]

---

[50] Since this is a book about Nietzsche, not Lange, I have considerably simplified Lange's account. In fact he declares materialism "finished," on multiple occasions and for various reasons, including but not limited to the following: (1) on pre-Kantian grounds, because the Sophistic stress on the primacy of sensation leads to the irrefutable Berkeleyan position; (2) through Kant, as explained in the text; (3) through physiological discoveries, as explained in the text; and (4) through the achievement of nineteenth-century French mathematicians, notably Gay-Lussac, Ampère, and Cauchy, who in various ways reduced the atom to extensionless magnitudes representing force-fields, thereby wholly removing its material, metaphysical aspect.

[51] See "On Schopenhauer," KGW I-4: 418–427.   [52] Lange 1866: v–vi.

[53] Lange 1866: 292, 298, 299.

[54] For a richer account of Lange's implicit refutation of Schopenhauer see my unpublished article, "Lange's consolation prize: Nietzsche's first criticisms of Schopenhauer" (on file with author).

One would think that the explicit dismissal of Schopenhauer in the Foreword and main text would offend Nietzsche, who tended to be touchy about criticisms of his idol. Lange, however, relents from wholesale condemnation in a surprising way. Having dealt a deathblow to metaphysics, or rather, having redelivered Kant's deathblow, a mortal wound from which the victim mysteriously failed to expire, he offers a generous consolation. "Metaphysics as science is self-deluding," he writes, "whereas it finds its true value in the architecture of concepts."[55] Lange argues that if we don't know the ultimate nature of reality, then nothing prevents us from speculating, so long as we make no dogmatic claims to truth. The need for imagination and uplift also appears to be part of human organization, and that need must be fulfilled. Metaphysics, art, and religion, all represent for Lange a necessary expression of human aspiration, and to that extent they demand respect. When metaphysics presents a vision of reality – a *vision*, with no claims to scientific truth – it provides uplift and inspiration and is not only to be encouraged but acclaimed. Lange often calls it a "poetry of concepts," and this association of metaphysics with the arts animates his language whenever this subject is touched. "Art is free, even in the realm of concepts," he declared. "Who will refute a movement by Beethoven, and who accuse Raphael's Madonna of a mistake?"[56]

Nietzsche was surely thrown into confusion when he first grasped the implications of Lange's book. Schopenhauer had been his spiritual linchpin for the preceding ten months, and the philosopher's values corresponded with those Nietzsche longed to embody at this time. Further, Schopenhauerean ideas were the common coin of exchange between Nietzsche and his friends, particularly Gersdorff and Mushacke. (To his annoyance Deussen declined to admire his new idol.)[57] What was Nietzsche to do now that this master had been refuted? Nothing observable, it appears. Certainly, he issued no retraction to anyone but Gersdorff. Instead, he grasped at Lange's consolation prize and quietly switched grounds from the truth of Schopenhauer's system to the edifying nature of his vision. "Lange believes," he wrote Gersdorff, "we should leave the philosopher free, assuming he can edify us. Art is free, even in the realm of concepts." Having begun to quote Lange (see above), he continued verbatim and closed with the observation. "You see that even within this strict, critical standpoint, our Schopenhauer remains standing, means almost more to us."[58]

---

[55] Lange 1866: v.   [56] Lange 1866: 269.
[57] KGB I-3: 110–111. Later, of course, Deussen would become a lifelong admirer of Schopenhauer.
[58] KSAB II: 160. Middleton 1969: 18, translation somewhat modified.

Much depends on that verb "means." Although Nietzsche might claim that nothing significant was lost philosophically, he had to make a rather large concession to keep within that "strict, critical standpoint." He would now read Schopenhauer the way liberal Christians read the Bible, finding consolation in its vision, but not taking its factual claims too literally. Nietzsche apparently studied Schopenhauer with similar reservations, silently eliding the metaphysics. A couple of years later he would write Deussen that:

> except for theologians, a few philosophy professors, and the vulgar, no one has any illusions here. The kingdom of metaphysics, and thereby the province of "absolute" truth is inevitably put on a level with poetry and religion. Whoever wants to know something contents themselves now with a conscious relativity of knowledge – as, for example, all known natural scientists. Metaphysics belongs then to a few people in the realm of temperamental need and is essentially edification; alternatively, it is art, namely that of the poetry of concepts; keep in mind, however, that metaphysics no more than religion or art has anything to do with the so-called "true in itself or being."[59]

Schopenhauer is not mentioned here, but he doesn't have to be. The truth claims implicit in *The world as will and representation* vanish rather similarly to those in poetry, through "the willing suspension of disbelief."[60]

It was earlier remarked that Lange's insistence upon the limits of experience carried significant implications. One was the invalidation of most metaphysical systems. Another was the redefinition and qualified revalidation of metaphysics as spiritual vision. A third must now be added, although it would take Nietzsche a year to internalize it. Since generalizations could only be derived from experience, they required positive confirmation of one kind or another – either through empirical inquiry in the natural sciences or through the establishment of facts in scholarship. The *Wissenschaften* (natural science and scholarship) deserved respect because they delivered sustainable, if qualified, propositional truths. What respect could the arts then command? As an individual, Lange immensely admired these; Schiller was his hero, and he closed his book with a twenty-page paean to the majesty of the arts and the benefits of their influence.[61] Nonetheless, the arts certainly didn't purport to establish facts, and Lange's book in effect shelved off activities associated with the

---

[59] KSAB II: 269.   [60] This expression, of course, is not Nietzsche's, but Coleridge's.
[61] For Schiller, see Lange 1866: v. For Lange's attempt to reconceive the function of the arts, see 539–557.

humanities from those considered scholarly and scientific. *Kunst* (art) and *Wissenschaft* were now exclusionary terms, and their divorce was hailed as a salutary advance in the discovery of truth. The consequences for humanism were arguably grievous. If edification and scholarship were severed, if advances in the sciences demanded the depersonalization of the practitioner rather than the latter's self-fulfillment through imaginative grasp, then the development of self through activity as envisioned by Humboldt, Goethe, and Schiller became highly problematic.

This shift will be examined in the following chapter. For the moment it is enough to note that in accepting Lange's views, Nietzsche was implicitly renouncing the ideals that had guided him through adolescence and that had eased his decision to choose philology as his career. Lange had no positive metaphysics to offer and could never provide a world of visionary splendor as had Schopenhauer. His point was rather that, with regard to truth, the visionary age was over. In accepting this view and in recognizing the *Wissenschaften* as sole arbiter of propositions concerning reality, Nietzsche was turning his back on the conservatism and idealism that had marked his youth. For years he had been outgrowing the provincial outlook of Naumburg with its shopkeepers, small manufacturers, and lawyers. Now he began to see beyond the intellectual legacy of Schulpforte as well. The Greeks, Romans, and great philosophers might be admired there, but his Gymnasium professors favored a humanist view of the classics and certainly did not see the natural sciences as decisive for the future of culture. Meanwhile, outside the Schulpfortean walls, history was being remade, a shift that must have been particularly evident in the commercial and manufacturing hubbub of Leipzig. In the summer of 1866 Nietzsche had seen the map of Germany redrawn. Now and in the immediate wake of that experience – his letter to Gersdorff was written during the week peace was signed – he discovered and allied himself with forerunners of the age to come. Lange had stated, "I would like to work in the direction of human progress."[62] When Nietzsche began to criticize philology, as he would shortly do, a fundamental complaint would be that it contributed little to "progress." He may have ceased to read Lange for a couple of years, but he was bringing the implications to bear in his daily practice. During those same two years Nietzsche cast an increasingly unsatisfied eye on his classical education and began to admire the sciences instead. Lange had awakened him, and he no longer needed his book's prodding to remind him of the need to change.

[62] Lange 1866: viii.

3

While Nietzsche was reading Lange, other events were afoot of which he took little heed. In the preceding summer, while he was still at Bonn, ships in the Mediterranean had delivered cholera, a disease borne through water and feces, from the Middle East to Odessa. A carrier brought it to Altenburg, whence it diffused through the Saxon river system to Leipzig, where the winter months put a temporary halt to its spread. With spring the infection resumed its progress, being picked up by the invading Prussian army, which carried it to Bavaria, Bohemia, and Austria.[63] Afterward, returning troops marched again through Saxony, infecting that country a second time.[64] Rumors, then outbreaks of the disease, had become ever more prominent from early spring through summer. By late August in 1866 when Nietzsche returned home for the holidays, three cities in his vicinity – Zeitz, Weissenfels, and particularly Halle – were badly infected. These formed a triangle with Naumburg in the center, and "[i]n Naumburg, where the privies and dung-heaps were offensive, and the pump-water bad," a doctor wrote, "the disease spread readily all over the town."[65] Franziska was already alarmed, for at the end of August she had visited Halle, an epicenter of the disease, where the Prussian army had bivouacked its wounded troops. Meanwhile, back in Naumburg her downstairs neighbor, a comb-maker named Lurgenstein, succumbed. Her daughter Elisabeth was already away, having gone to visit friends and relatives in southwestern Saxony. On September 15 Franziska decamped as well, taking her son to a hotel in nearby Bad Kösen. We do not know whether Rosalie and Friederike remained to brave out the epidemic (Lina had died in 1862), but in Sangerhausen to the north, Bernhard Daechsel, Nietzsche's guardian, wrote that four to six people had died on his street alone.[66]

Remarkably, Nietzsche mentioned little of this in letters, citing the Naumburg infestation rarely and usually only to explain his change of address.[67] His attention was largely fixed on reworking his Theognis paper and doing preparatory work for a lexicon for an edition of Aeschylus. While the cholera raged, he seems to have been quite happy in the hotel, welcoming the opportunity to work steadily with virtually no distraction.[68] Nonetheless, it is impossible that he would not be aware of the danger, particularly as there had been several deaths recently in his circle of

---

[63] After Königgrätz the Prussian army's advance was delayed by an outbreak of the disease.
[64] Peters and McClellan 1875: 648–651, 651–654.   [65] Quoted in Peters and McClellan 1875: 652.
[66] KGB I-3: 153.   [67] Exceptions: KSAB II: 154, 172.   [68] KSAB II: 176.

acquaintance, bringing mortality repeatedly to his attention. Three people he knew in Leipzig died from cholera, including Christian Weisse, a Hegelian in the philosophy department who is today best known as the mentor of Rudolf Lotze.[69] Beyond these Leipzig associates, Nietzsche experienced far closer losses. He had learned in August that two acquaintances, including his much-admired first prefect at Schulpforte Oskar Krämer had been killed in the war.[70] In May he received word that Hedwig Schmid, one of his Plauen half-aunts, had died, an event that occasioned a letter of condolence to her sister, Julie Opitz.[71] Then in August Julie passed away as well. At least seven acquaintances, friends, or relatives had vanished in the space of four months, not counting the neighbor downstairs or others that Nietzsche did not think to mention. While he seems not to have been close to either of his Plauen aunts, he had met both several times and visited them most recently just three years before.[72] He remembered them with great respect, as he acknowledged when writing a condolence letter to his aunt, Friederike. There, rather than dwell on death itself, he reflected that these departures meant that time was inexorably passing, leaving the younger generation ever more exposed and vulnerable. "Röcken has been taken from us, Pobles has become alien to us, and Plauen lives only in memory ... We young people remain ever more lonely in the present; the faithful protectors of the past slowly leave us."[73]

Such reflections complemented more positive comparisons of present and past. While at the hotel Nietzsche had found a Leipzig newspaper, and as he looked through its pages, he was struck by longing for that city where he had been so happy. As his birthday approached, he compared his situation in October 1866 with his state the previous October when he had just left Bonn.[74] In contrast to the ignominious failures of the year before, Nietzsche had in 1866 helped establish the Philological Society, been plucked from academic obscurity by Ritschl, written a paper soon to be published in one of the most prestigious philological journals in Germany, observed a war, discovered what for him was an epochal book (Lange's *History*), and was soon to be offered the opportunity to produce a fresh work of scholarship. All before he reached the age of twenty-two.

---

[69] Willey 1978: 41–43. Weisse also made important contributions to Biblical studies. Strauss 2005: 99–104; Law 2012: 63.
[70] KSAB II: 151.   [71] KSAB II: 130.
[72] KGW I-4: 86, 88. His sister records that they also went there in the summers of 1854 and 1857. Förster-Nietzsche 1895: I, 61.
[73] KSAB II: 149.   [74] KSAB II: 166, 171–172.

Yet if Nietzsche could take satisfaction in his advances, he recognized an undertow of time passing that gave his ambitions an almost hectic cast. As his letter to Friederike exhibited, he was ever alert to the leakage of time, and that autumn and early winter he faced his keenest loss in a decade. After so many deaths, his beloved Aunt Rosalie fell ill, and Nietzsche was now old enough to recognize the full extent of the impending loss. He had lived with Rosalie until his eleventh year, and in contrast to his mother, he seems to have had only positive feelings for his sometimes temperamental relative. Both at Schulpforte and then at Bonn he had written her regularly, and the letters to Rosalie were always affectionate and replete with the sorts of information (mostly church matters) he knew she would welcome. He described her to Mushacke as "next to my mother and sister, the most intimate and closest of my relatives," and he called her "irreplaceable." Now as her health took a turn downward, he wrote his mother, "I am very happy not to get a letter from you, which suggests that there is hope for Aunt Rosalie. If you find anything that brings her relief, give it to her in my name and at my expense."[75] Any hopes Nietzsche might have nursed proved illusory. Rosalie Nietzsche continued to decline and around 5 p.m. on January 3 of the new year (1867), she died in what was apparently considerable anguish. Nietzsche, who had been present, described her final hours to Mushacke, mentioning "a thoroughly painful sickroom and a hemorrhage several hours before her death. It was dusk. Snowflakes swirled outside. She sat bolt upright in bed and slowly death arrived with all its sad manifestations."[76]

Nietzsche left no record as to how he responded afterward to this event. However, a second incident allows a probable guess. Approximately ten days after Rosalie's agony he received a letter from Gersdorff in which the latter related in vivid detail the decline and death of his oldest brother Ernst. This young man of twenty-seven had been severely wounded at Königsgrätz but had entirely healed except for a now useless sword hand. Insisting on surgery for the hand as well, he withstood it and began to convalesce but felt so lively that he took a three-hour walk outdoors. This foray proved disastrous. Afterwards, he collapsed and the infection began to spread. His final hours were excruciating, and he asked his mother to leave so that she would not see what followed. Gersdorff remained to witness and was afterwards bereft. He had idolized his brother and used him as a model in difficult times. Now he poured out his grief and spiritual

---

[75] KSAB II: 187. [76] KSAB II: 194.

bafflement in a letter of over seven pages in which portrayed his brother's noble character and the horror of his death.[77]

Nietzsche responded with a sensitivity probably heightened by his own recent bereavement. The deaths were not the same, as he acknowledged. Rosalie had lived a full life; Ernst had been taken in his middle twenties. Nonetheless, he urged Gersdorff to try to find consolation in the works of Arthur Schopenhauer. If that man's eloquence provided solace, then this provided the ultimate proof of his wisdom and insight. If by contrast those reflections failed, than the philosopher's books should be rejected.[78]

The grieving Gersdorff responded with relief. "Of all the letters that I read during this difficult, tearful time, none made such a soothing impression on me as yours." Recognizing the superior comfort brought by Nietzsche (and Schopenhauer), Gersdorff contrasted their wholesome reflections with the comparatively stultifying answers of his religious family, which had only annoyed him.[79] Yet if Nietzsche's counsels proved effective, this surely reflected a consolation that he had already devised for himself. Since at least the age of thirteen when he wrote his first autobiography, "From my life," he had been acutely aware of the quick passage of time; his transit through a season of mortality had exposed afresh a wound with which he was long familiar. What was new here was the relief and perspective provided by Schopenhauer's vision. Nietzsche may have begun to question the man's metaphysics several months before, when he read Lange. Nonetheless, the redemptive majesty of the philosopher's vision seems now to have entered his psyche and sealed a loyalty which he might otherwise have outgrown. Although Nietzsche was quite capable of seeing the weaknesses in Schopenhauer's system, his gratitude and respect for the man would not waver for a decade, and one reason was evident in January 1867. Schopenhauer provided consolation and relief when he was badly in need.

---

[77] KGB I-3: 175–182. [78] KSAB II: 194–196. Translation in Middleton 1969: 19–20.
[79] KGB I-3: 183–185.

CHAPTER 12

An education in mistrust

I lack the talent to be loyal, and what is worse, not even the vanity to appear so.[1]

I

In the aftermath of his aunt's death Nietzsche returned to Leipzig and pursued his studies with his usual zeal. Immediately before Christmas he had made a discovery concerning Diogenes Laertius that he wanted to develop.[2] He was also scheduled to lecture to the Philological Society on February 1, and he needed to finish his presentation.[3] Sometime during these months he became that body's president and delivered an address.[4] Always in the background lay the pressure of his classwork and the sundry projects which he held in reserve.

It was in the midst of these varied and demanding philological tasks that he commenced what would become one of his richest and most enduring friendships. Now that Mushacke and Gersdorff had departed, Nietzsche's social circle in Leipzig consisted largely of fellow students with whom he could discuss classes and projects. These were colleagues, not friends in his demanding sense of the term. He might be personally close to a few of them – Heinrich Romundt and Rudolf Kleinpaul, in particular – but none seemed to be persons with whom he could share intimate understanding as he had with Pinder, Duessen, and Mushacke. He observed at the time to Gersdorff, "There are many kind and intelligent people [here] – Kleinpaul especially – but the time when I can quickly make friends is ... past."[5] Nietzsche was only twenty-one years old when he wrote this letter, hardly an age in which to be composing valedictories. Nonetheless, he was right

---

[1] KSA VIII: 501. [2] See KGW I-4: 397, 526.
[3] *"Die PINAKES der aristotelischen Schriften."* KGW I-4: 137–151. [4] KGW I-4: 154–156.
[5] KSAB II: 152.

248

An education in mistrust

that he was slow to form close relationships. It was not until nine months afterwards that one of his casual companions broke through his shell and released him from isolation.

Nietzsche must have been aware of Erwin Rohde, at least by sight, since the summer of 1865, when both had audited Ritschl's seminar at Bonn.[6] The two men had moved separately to Leipzig, and Rohde joined the Philological Society in mid-August 1866, although he and Nietzsche had begun to socialize the month before.[7] While the men were frequently together over the following months,[8] they seem not to have been close until March 1867, three months after Rosalie Nietzsche's death. Rohde records that they then had a breakthrough of sorts,[9] which deepened in June when they took horseback riding lessons together. The following months were among the personally richest in both men's lives.[10] "We led an amazing existence all summer," Rohde wrote, "as though in a wandering magic circle, not closed outwardly in an unfriendly way, but associating almost exclusively with one another."[11]

On the surface the two had much in common. Rohde too had been smitten with Schopenhauer, and the men shared with that philosopher a saturnine temperament and a skeptical view of the so-called pleasures of life. Both were emotionally labile – it was in defense against this instability that Nietzsche exerted so much discipline – but Rohde was perhaps more directly passionate, as his literary interests suggest. Whereas at the Gymnasium Nietzsche had investigated Ermanarich and Theognis, Rohde translated Catullus and wrote about Ovid's *Amores*, Plautus's erotics, and medieval love poetry.[12] When he joined the Philological Society at Leipzig, he again lectured on Catullus – hardly likely to be a favorite of Nietzsche,[13] whose taste in Latin poetry ran more to Horace and Juvenal.[14] Characteristically, of the two men, it was Rohde who described their friendship both more humbly and more extravagantly. He would confess to Nietzsche, "May [this letter], my dear friend, serve as a pledge of

---

[6] KSAB II: 140. Ribbeck 1969 II: 555–556.   [7] KSAB II: 140.   [8] KSAB II: 200–201.
[9] KGB I-3: 213. Rohde describes the period of friendship as lasting the previous "half-year." His letter is dated September 10, 1867, and six months before would be March, immediately after which Nietzsche announced to his friends the possibility of a Paris trip.
[10] Over a decade later, Rohde could still wistfully recall his friend's nightly improvisations at the piano. Cancik 1985: 447.
[11] KGB I-4: 475–476.   [12] Cancik 1985: 442.
[13] References to Catullus: KGW I-4: 41, 43, 45, 64; KGW I-5: 6; KSAB II: 250. He also bought an edition of Catullus in either 1867 or 1868 and had it bound in 1868. Campioni *et al.* 2003: 168.
[14] Nietzsche wrote an essay on Horace and another on the satirists while in Schulpforte. He was again considering a paper on Horace in 1868. KGW I-5: 19.

the unwavering love with which I always think on you. To you alone I owe the best hours of my life. I wish you could read in my heart how inwardly thankful I am to you for all you gave it. You have tapped in me the happy country of the purest friendship in which I, with a heart thirsty for love, glanced at earlier like a poor child in a lush garden."[15]

Nietzsche's account of their relationship, while heartfelt and appreciative, was considerably more reserved, sometimes to the point of being disingenuous. Thus, Rohde sees the two as having bonded in a fundamentally deeper way in March, and he is surely right, for in April Gersdorff indicates that Nietzsche has acknowledged the new friendship.[16] However, in a letter to Deussen on April 4, Nietzsche describes a plan to visit Paris – Rohde's idea[17] – without so much as mentioning the man who proposed the project and who would certainly be supposed to accompany him. He makes the same announcement (and same omission) to Gersdorff.[18] As late as July and after the riding lessons, he refers casually to Rohde as though he were just another friend, parallel with Kleinpaul;[19] and in an earlier letter to Franziska, Nietzsche misspells the name as "Rhode."[20] Although his friend dates the establishment of deep appreciation to the spring and speaks of the way the two sat, as it were, on a stool separately from their comrades,[21] Nietzsche expressly describes the process as more gradual and deliberate. "In a letter Rohde used an image that portrayed us as passing the final semester so to speak sitting on an isolated stool. That is completely right, but I surrendered only when the semester was over [in August]."[22]

If Nietzsche was restrained – and he makes no statement commensurate with the intensity of his friend's declarations – it may have been in part because Rohde could be socially abrasive. Nietzsche once described him to Gersdorff as "a very smart but also a contentious and obstinate person,"[23] and Gersdorff agreed, calling him "opinionated and stubborn."[24] Rohde himself conceded that his outward behavior could be alienating – at one point he expresses to Nietzsche "my gratitude for the heartfelt interest that you showed to a pigheaded and irritating person like me"[25] – and it may be that his interpersonal skills were impaired by an early experience that had

---

[15] KGB I-3: 321–322. [16] KGB I-3: 195. [17] KSAB II: 264. [18] KSAB II: 205, 212.
[19] KSAB II: 220. For Kleinpaul and Rohde, see KGB I-3: 245, 289. [20] KSAB II: 217.
[21] KGB I-3: 213.
[22] The "end of the semester" to which Nietzsche refers occurred officially on September 6, although he presumably means July 31, the end of their studies. By late August at latest, the two men separated, never to meet again except on visits. On Nietzsche's view then they were joined as true friends for three weeks.
[23] KSAB II: 158. [24] KGB I-3: 195. See also KGB I-3: 226.
[25] KGB I-3: 213. See also KGB I-4: 475–476.

thwarted his social development and left him permanently embittered. Nietzsche had certainly suffered as a boy, but he had been sheltered and perhaps comforted by his mother and other relations. Rohde, by contrast, seems to have regarded himself as fundamentally abandoned. Born to an upper-middle-class family in Hamburg, he was sent at the age of seven to a boarding school in Jena, over 300 kilometers away. There he was forced to remain until he was fourteen, an exile that Rohde regarded as painful and damaging. "We weren't raised, we were drilled," he said.[26] Eventually, he was recalled to Hamburg to attend the Johanneum – one of the more prestigious Gymnasien in the German states – but he never relinquished a grudge against his mother, whose brother, Matthias J. Schleiden,[27] had chosen the Jena institution. (His father died in 1866.) Years later he would take his daughter to visit her and write to his wife, "No child can thrive in [my mother's] vicinity. From the beginning, she has never really loved anyone but herself – not her husband with whom she later flirted – and not us, her children, at all."[28]

These were strong words, but they express a rancor and sense of disappointment that seem to have dogged Rohde to the end of his days[29] and were surely evident in Leipzig.[30] He cannot have been easy to live with, but Nietzsche saw past the surliness to what he considered the depth of feeling within. He would write of his friend, "Usually we were at one another's throats; indeed, there were an enormous number of things on which we clashed. As soon as the conversation took a turn toward depth, however, the dissonance in opinions fell silent, and there sounded a calm and full harmony."[31]

This "calm and full harmony" must have offered a spell of relief in the midst of his rather frantic philological activities, and it may have reminded Nietzsche that scholarship was not the only value that he honored. If so, he left no record. By contrast, there are abundant indications of another change that took place after March and that he explicitly associates with his new companion. Immediately before the reminiscence just quoted, he mentioned that he and Rohde specialized in different fields but that they had one ground in common professionally. "We were united only in irony

---

[26] Quoted in Blunck 1953: 166. Reprinted in Janz 1978 I: 208.
[27] Schleiden and Theodor Schwann were founders of modern cell theory. [28] Cancik 1985: 443.
[29] See Rohde's frequent complaints of undiagnosable ills (Cancik 1985: 459, 468), his dislike of changing mores (*passim*), and his regret every time he moved (461–462, 464, 466).
[30] When Rohde left, he wrote Nietzsche, "I will try to work a bit on the development of my talent for sociability." KGB I-3: 214.
[31] KGW I-4: 527.

and in mockery of philological manners and vanities."[32] This observation is amply borne out in his letters. On April 6, 1867, six days after the month in which Rohde described the two men as awakening to the possibility of serious friendship, Nietzsche wrote a letter to Gersdorff in which, for the first time ever, he sharply attacked philology.[33] From this point on, that is, from the time of his initial bonding with Rohde, he began to heap ridicule on his professional field and even to regret that he had chosen it. The resultant bitterness and self-laceration contrast vividly with the views expressed in letters written during earlier, happier years in Leipzig and suggest that the joy he found in his friendship with Rohde was offset by new anxieties. By demeaning philology Nietzsche was imperiling the very structures that had enabled his success – not just belief in his field but the moral regimen of discipline and focus which had brought so much stability and satisfaction. Yet if Rohde was the catalyst, he was not the cause. "Led by a sure instinct," Nietzsche says, he had gravitated to this new friend, and perhaps he chose Rohde exactly because he needed to distance himself from a discipline that he was beginning to find suspect. The resultant wrench may have been spiritually necessary, but it was also painful, and a partner in the endeavor would provide reassurance and relief.

2

It may be recalled that over the years Nietzsche had committed himself to philology at least three times: during his last months at Schulpforte, after rejecting theology at Bonn, and in Naumburg when he vowed to keep to his last in Leipzig. If his vows were renewed so frequently, one might surmise that his commitment was weak. In fact, Nietzsche's devotion to the field was more a pious wish than a reflex of intrinsic interest; it was not philology that he sought so much as a sense of purpose. He had stated this himself upon graduation from Schulpforte[34] and he stumbled upon this unpleasant truth again in the draft of a letter addressed to Deussen, written in September 1866. Paul had shown a tendency to relapse into theology, and Nietzsche sought to recall him to his earlier profession by insisting on the primacy of finding one's vocation. He began by portraying himself as in the forecourts of philology and vouchsafed glimpses of its "holy places."

---

[32] KGW I-4: 527.
[33] KSAB II: 209–210. Compare the gentler, "first" criticism, which Nietzsche made just three days before in a letter to Deussen (206).
[34] See the close of Chapter 8.

"The powerful and empowering feeling of a life's task appears soon enough to the true philologist," he intoned, an utterance that assumed that there *were* "true" philologists and that Nietzsche was one of them. He then observed, speaking of the compensations of philology *vis-à-vis* more remunerative occupations, "We shall not, dear Paul, depend upon a life insurance organization or a timely benefice. Truly, we both long to banish that sad state of affairs where the young spirit has found no path which it can healthily take." At this point his sentence trails off without so much as an end stop, perhaps because Nietzsche has just inadvertently made a confession.[35] "We both *long* to banish," he had written, using the present tense of the verb and thereby suggesting that he himself had not found any such predestined "path," certainly not with the irrevocability that he had projected.

In fact, Nietzsche was not a "true philologist" at all, as he would himself acknowledge in the future and as he must have known in 1866.[36] He might be a good one and he might enjoy its practice, but he hardly qualified as one who was "called" to that profession. Rather, as he would observe, he had chosen it as an interim measure which would bring discipline and order into his life. "I longed for a counterweight to the shifting and restless nature of my earlier inclinations, for a field [*Wissenschaft*] that could be advanced with cool sobriety, with logical iciness, with steady work, without the results directly touching the heart. All of this I then thought to find in philology."[37] His "calling" was not a "life's task," but a substitute for one, a pose that he tried to make good.

Such resort to the second best could not satisfy a person so ambitious as Friedrich Nietzsche, a man who longed to find in his profession "the most serious and most longingly envisioned goal of [his] life's wanderings."[38] He had been able to ignore this subterfuge up to now, but friendship with Rohde seems to have allowed him finally to address it. As he floundered, increasingly coming to recognize that he was on a path that did not suit his ambitions, he began seriously to disparage philology, recording a host of specific criticisms. The most subtle and varied of these appear in his notebooks and are too complex to summarize here.[39] In his letters, he addressed the issues more simply and distilled them to the following.

---

[35] KSAB II: 163. Nietzsche ends the draft with no period but merely the doleful repetition, "truly, we both long . . . "
[36] KGW I-5: 44–45.   [37] KGW I-5: 47.   [38] KGW I-5: 44.
[39] See, for example, KGW I-4: 397–398, 399, 470, 495–496; KGW I-5: 96–98. Some of these are difficult to separate from his notes on literary history, which in turn also have philological implications. See KGW I-4: 221–223, 223–225, 361–368, 394–396, 404–408, 534–537.

Students were overloaded with work and too stuffed with information to find either the time or distance to look freshly at the very literature they professed to admire.[40] Further, the entire field was moribund, having been overtaken by the natural sciences.[41] Finally, he began to take a sharp look at the mentor who, if he had not led him into this field, had certainly done his best to keep him there by assigning rewarding tasks.

Nietzsche had already been wary of his teacher's influence in Bonn and had written Mushacke, "I am much taken with self-development – and how easily one can be impressed by men like Ritschl and perhaps deflected to paths that lie far from one's own nature."[42] At Leipzig he had submitted to the professor's guidance (and gloried in his praise), yet his responses could be peevish. Ritschl had, on the one hand, published him, procured prestigious work, written to colleagues on his behalf, and provided him access to libraries of ancient manuscripts.[43] Nietzsche further liked him personally and could pay him extraordinary compliments. "He is the only man whose criticisms I gladly hear, for his judgments are so healthy and forceful, with so much sensitivity for the truth, that he is a kind of scholarly conscience to me,"[44] he would write. Yet in the spring of 1866 he could inform Mushacke, "[Ritschl] took it very badly when I postponed taking the seminar. Such people can be awfully arrogant."[45]

This was, of course, the very seminar that Nietzsche himself had so eagerly sought to join seven months earlier when he had worked on the Theognis paper in Naumburg. Since he had pursued membership so recently, it might be asked why he now rebuffed Ritschl on this delicate matter, a rejection that he himself acknowledged was ungrateful?[46] In one letter he complains that the seminar students were of inferior quality,[47] but his resistance probably also reflected his need for a buffer between himself and his sometimes importunate professor. Apparently, he kept to this resolve. A record of enrollment published by Otto Ribbeck indicates that neither Rohde nor Nietzsche ever formally joined the seminar.[48]

---

[40] These are presented most simply in a letter to Gersdorff, KSAB II: 209–210, written April 6, 1867, immediately after the March which Rohde cites as the beginning of his closer relationship with Nietzsche.
[41] For other extended criticisms of philology and its practitioners, see KSAB II: 283–284, 316, 320, and 328–329. For a particularly insightful investigation into why philology can never meet the standards of the natural sciences, see KGW I-5: 96–98.
[42] KSAB II: 81.   [43] KGW I-4: 524.   [44] KSAB II: 205.
[45] KSAB II: 127. See, however, remarks by Wilhelm Wisser, Gilman and Reichenbach 1981: 65–66.
[46] KSAB II: 168. Nietzsche is actually talking of the *Societät*, but it was composed of seminar students.
[47] KSAB II: 152. Again, Nietzsche is actually talking of the *Societät*.
[48] Ribbeck 1969 II: 555–556. Ribbeck lists both Nietzsche and Rohde as auditors in the philological seminar at Bonn. He lists neither student as enrolled in the seminar at Leipzig.

Eventually, Nietzsche became a member of the *Societät*,[49] an organization separate from although associated with the seminar, but relations between him and his sponsor must have been fraught from the beginning.

Nietzsche had other reasons for putting distance between himself and Ritschl. His charge of arrogance can be dismissed as a momentary outburst. Nietzsche expressly absolved Ritschl of this flaw, stating that he admired the man because he *lacked* the arrogance so frequently found in professors.[50] Nonetheless, Nietzsche had other and more lasting reservations. As noted in a previous chapter, he worried that Ritschl overrated his student's abilities and assigned tasks beyond his powers.[51] He also complained of his teacher's tactlessness, his distaste for philosophy, and his overestimation of philology.[52] Nietzsche was surely correct on the first point. Ritschl's rudeness was acknowledged even by Ribbeck and may explain some of the virulence directed against him at Bonn.[53] The complaints about the prejudice against philosophy and esteem for philology were also true, but Nietzsche's valuation – his assumption that these were flaws – deserves closer inspection. Ritschl's concerns over philosophy may partly have been based on his disdain for Hegel and the romantic idealists, a group in which he probably included Schopenhauer.[54] However, they probably reflected his high opinion of his own profession, a field in which, in his view, there could be no serious competitors.

The fact that the man highly esteemed his profession, however, was not, as Nietzsche implicitly represents it, a personal peculiarity or whim; it was intrinsic to his vision, and it probably influenced Nietzsche's choice of profession as well. Ritschl, born in 1806 and nearly forty years older than Nietzsche, had become a philologist during the late 1820s, a brief period in neo-humanism when earlier objections had been overridden and new ones had yet to be advanced. During this era an almost religious awe was attached to mastery of the Greek and Latin languages, a skill that was thought to put the reader in immediate contact with the models for all humanity. This implicit ethical aura supported and was in turn validated by one of the founding principles of the new pedagogy. When Humboldt reformed the educational system, he removed theologians and installed

---

[49] KSAB II: 182. For characterizations of the *Societät*, see KGB I-4: 424; Ribbeck 1969 II: 401–403; Blunck 1953: 150; and Janz 1978 I: 188–189.
[50] KSAB II: 205.   [51] See Chapter 10, n. 63.
[52] For tactlessness, see KSAB II: 341; for overestimation of his field and aversion to mixing philology and philosophy see KGW I-4: 520.
[53] Ribbeck 1969 II: 338–339.
[54] Anthony Jensen argues that Ritschl was not so much hostile to philosophy as to its Hegelian practitioners, among whom he would likely have included Schopenhauer. See Jensen 2013: 47.

classical philologists as instructors in the Gymnasien.[55] "Humanism was the new religion, philologists the new priests," as Friedrich Paulsen put it.[56] Not only were the latter made masters of the primary academic material; they saw themselves (and were seen by others) as the spiritual guides of coming generations, the molders of future German youth.[57]

Ritschl himself was a member of the so-called "second generation" of philology, a less romantic cohort. Also, as a rather hard-boiled character he would encourage students to pursue scholarly research, rather than to pose as missionaries of humanity.[58] Nonetheless, when Nietzsche complained that his teacher overrated his profession, he was probably recognizing two truths: first, that Ritschl thought too much of his own field to alloy it with another (philosophy), a sore point with the Schopenhauerean Nietzsche; and second, that his teacher retained vestiges of the older (and to Nietzsche outdated) reverence for philology as institutionalized by Humboldt. Indeed, for all the modernity of Ritschl's methods, which were undeniably on the cutting edge,[59] he was conservative as an academic, promoting values which had their roots in the Humboldtian revolution. As already seen, at Bonn in the 1860s he had defended corporate principles against government interference, a rearguard action during the Bismarck era. Earlier, he had objected when professors voted to remove the requirement that all thesis defenses be conducted in Latin.[60] Ritschl rightly observed that the only students to chafe under this restriction were the natural scientists, and he argued that to give in to their incapacity would fracture the unity of the university and convert the latter into a technical school. (Forty years later, Friedrich Paulsen, no friend of compulsory Latin and Greek, would concede that Ritschl was right.)[61] For all his willingness to forge new paths, he remained loyal to the vision of his own teachers, and he upheld these values against those who sought to dilute or defame them.

Nietzsche could be susceptible to the same quasi-religious esteem for philology, as could be seen in the letter cited earlier when he referred to the field's "holy places." Nonetheless, he had come of age much later than Ritschl, and he was the heir of developments which his master had held at

---

[55] Paulsen 1885: 569–570. For the Wolfian rationale in replacing Christian instruction with knowledge of the Greeks, see the same work, 535–539. This attitude has its roots in Herder, 520. For some of the sociological bases for the shift, see 593–596. For more on Herder's views, see Jeismann 1990: 321–322.
[56] Paulsen 1885: 591.
[57] For a rich discussion of this ethos and the tensions it induced, see Jeismann 1990. For the exalted views of themselves entertained by philologists, see Jeismann 1990: 339, n. 42. For the religious aspects of *Bildung*, see Koselleck 1990: 16–17, 24–25.
[58] Paulsen 1885: 675.   [59] Paulsen 1885: 674–675.   [60] Ribbeck 1969 II: 146.
[61] Paulsen 1885: 738.

bay. For example, religiously inflected attitudes toward the ancients and to the professors who taught them were still honored in Nietzsche's day, as they were at times by Nietzsche. Nonetheless, visceral belief in them had been undermined as the decades advanced. At the beginning of the century, adoration of the Greeks had been widespread and powerfully sustained by the reading public.[62] As time passed, the idealistic faith of the humanistic fathers began to wane, as did idealistic attitudes of any kind – noticeably after 1831, the year of Hegel's death, and decisively after the disappointments of 1848.[63] Politically, this transition led to esteem for *Realpolitik*, a term invented in the 1850s. Academically in the guise of the "research imperative," it led to a balkanization of faculties and enabled a positivist conception of knowledge.[64] This sense of disenchantment was particularly unfortunate for philology, since, as Anthony La Vopa has shown, the field required a transcendental vision if it was to override certain tensions inherent in its practice. Earlier in the century, weary scholars could refresh themselves with the comfort that they were advancing the entire human race. This consolation proved ever more tenuous as the decades wore on, and this posed a serious concern for teachers, who still ran the Gymnasien and were supposed to inspire and shape new generations.[65] As its redemptive vision lost its credibility, philology seemed left only with its more dispiriting side, its unglamorous, and ever more specialized investigation into languages that had long been extinct.[66]

This might be supposed to mean the end of the classical philologists' vision of themselves as sovereign benefactors of humanity. Yet many professionals, like Ritschl, refused to acknowledge a spiritual shift which they could only regard as a symptom of decline. Abandoned by the public, which no longer understood their ideals, they were left with an increasingly defensive faith, which they continued to uphold but which some students, themselves raised during a period of disenchantment, found empty and vainglorious. Thus, a young Egyptologist would remark of Ernst Curtius, brother to one of Nietzsche's Leipzig teachers, "When, with a jerk, he raised his eyes to the heavens and then spoke rapturously of 'the Greeks,' I simply could not take him seriously."[67] Yet these same later generations were still expected to expend grueling labor on behalf of ideals which no

---

[62] For the classical leanings of intellectuals and the reading public, see Paulsen 1885: 422–424, 514–530. For another treatment, see Vierhaus 1972: 518–519.
[63] Paulsen 1885: 671–673. He follows this with some of the problems this occasioned philologists, citing Ritschl in particular: 673–676. See also Lange 1866: 282, 292.
[64] Turner 1974: 530–531. Schnädelbach 1984: 27–30.   [65] Jeismann 1990.
[66] La Vopa 1990: 27–45.   [67] Quoted in Marchand 1996: 78.

longer compelled passionate belief. Thus, Nietzsche counseled Deussen to specialize on the use of the ablative in Ammianus Marcellinus, advice that even the industrious Deussen declined. ("I am not yet philologist enough [for that]," he replied.[68])

While the changes just described underwrote some of Nietzsche's misgivings concerning philology, the situation was actually worse and struck to the very heart of his educational ideals. Philology was not the only field to be transformed. As already discussed in the section on Lange, during the nineteenth century the very nature of what constituted knowledge and research slowly evolved, shifting from a stress on comprehensive structure to collections of positivistic facts.[69] This change arguably proved fatal to the neo-humanist vision.[70] Humboldt had conceived *Bildung* as intimately related to the exploration of fields of knowledge. By expanding their minds to accommodate and master – and later to extend – comprehensive fields of scholarship, students were expected to awaken and develop their own vital and creative powers.[71] This shifting yet systemically integrated object of knowledge that they pursued was covered by the term *Wissenschaft*, a word more fluid in meaning than today's translations ("scholarship," "science") can suggest.[72] For Humboldt and his neo-humanist followers, as Charles McClelland explains, "*Wissenschaft* and further discoveries emanating from it were the instrument, not the goal, of the scholar. The full development of the personality and of a supple, wide-ranging habit of clear, original thinking was the goal ... In no sense was *Wissenschaft* regarded as an alienated product of human endeavor. In whatever terms it was expressed – Fichte's search for absolute truth, Humboldt's 'devoting oneself to science,' or even the romantic poet's search for the elusive 'blue flower' – the *search* was paramount."[73]

Most of this visionary transfiguration was lost over the course of the century. No longer a comprehensive and dynamic system of learning, *Wissenschaft* became ever more specialized and positivistic,[74] the very sort

---

[68] KSAB II: 204; KGB I-3: 200–201.
[69] See Chapter 11, Section 2. For the transformation of *Wissenschaft*, see Schnädelbach 1984: 24–25, 27–29; Jarausch 1974: 547; McClelland 1980: 172–189. For an account of contributors to this transformation, see Turner 1974: especially 505–506. See also Sweet 1980 II: 70–71; Daum 2004: *passim*.
[70] According to Kocka 1989, specific and professional knowledge intruded upon and to an extent displaced general *Bildung* during the course of the century. Compare Helmholtz's claim that the age of the Renaissance man was over. Nicholls and Liebscher 2010: 89.
[71] For an eloquent account of *Bildung* as conceived by neo-humanists at the beginning of the century, see the description given by Friedrich Immanuel Niethammer. Bödeker 1989: 21.
[72] For a discussion of the difficulty in translating "*Wissenschaft*" into English, see Ringer 1969: 102–103.
[73] McClelland 1980: 125.   [74] Turner 1980a.

of "alienated product of human endeavor" from which Humboldt had recoiled.[75] Once knowledge was pinned down and isolated as a fact of the kind that could be disseminated in a lecture, it became the same sort of dead knowledge which humanists had abhorred in the dismal days of the previous century. *Wissenschaft* had hitherto been conceived, not as the sort of data that one might possess, but as a quest, an ongoing inquiry into the nature of things, where mere facts represented earlier conquests that one supplanted as one moved forward, developing one's spiritual resources in the process.[76] As *Wissenschaft* ceased to be a challenge to be met and became instead something objective to be known, the viability of *Bildung* changed as well. Knowledge was no longer expected to serve the student; the student was expected to serve knowledge; and any personal relation to a field of study was conceived to be extraneous and even suspect since it might imperil objectivity.[77] *Bildung* in the neo-humanist sense was much more difficult to pursue in this new world of learning. Nonetheless, the term was too useful as a hortatory watchword wholly to be abandoned. It became, as Karl-Ernst Jeismann puts it, "arrested as an ideological function,"[78] to be invoked in the sort of speeches that Nietzsche might have listened to raptly as a boy. *Bildung* became an inspirational flag to be waved, even if it could rarely be applied in practice, at least in the older sense of the term. As classical philology lost its ideal aura, the concept of self-development that it underwrote became attenuated as well, although the latter loss went unacknowledged. Such intellectual shifts were almost imperceptible because of the gradualness of the change, and most students probably did not recognize or care about the difference. Nietzsche, however, came of age late enough in time and he sufficiently valued the term's educational promise that he could not overlook the disparity. Slowly he came to believe that the ideals he had been fed through the years were spurious, and he expressed a rage born of misled innocence. He had truly believed the ideology offered by his masters.[79]

In an early letter to Deussen, for example, Nietzsche presented a vision of *Bildung* in the old-fashioned sense as he explained how devotion to a subject matter could induce maturity in the soul. Speaking of his Diogenes Laertius project, he wrote, "Every greater work, as you will also have found, has an ethical influence. The struggle to concentrate on a subject and to form it harmoniously is a stone that falls into the life of our souls; out of the

---

[75] Quoted in Schnädelbach 1984: 27. [76] See the quotation from Humboldt in Fallon 1980: 25.
[77] Nietzsche himself makes this observation. UO II: 6; KSA II: 293. [78] Jeismann 1990: 345.
[79] He was correspondingly anxious not to deceive the younger generation. See KSAB II: 329.

narrow circles wider ones will come."[80] This reciprocity of student and subject, the one developing as it mastered and extended the other, echoed the view that philologists subscribed to in the earlier half of the century. It also showed how committed one part of Nietzsche was to that ideal. By Nietzsche's time, however, classical philology had become so specialized and detailed that any such comprehensive vision was almost impossible to sustain. (Nietzsche's friend Heinrich Romundt had written his dissertation on the Greek root "leg-.") Further, *Bildung* could function only if one respected the field being studied. As knowledge came to seem cumulative rather than transformative, it lost much of its expansionary promise. When Nietzsche ceased to value the philological project, his reverence for its study would dissipate as well.

Nietzsche never made such a connection explicit. Nonetheless, after he bonded with Rohde, such elevated sentiments as he had communicated to Deussen were quietly shelved. A year and a half later, there would be no more talk of "ethical influence," at least with regard to scholarship. Instead, he would savagely write (again to Deussen), "Just believe me that the talents needed honorably to work as a philologist are *unbelievably* slight and that anyone, placed at the *right* spot, learns to turn his screw. Diligence above all, then knowledge, and thirdly method – that is the ABC of every productive philologist, assuming that someone *directs* him and *shows* him a *place*."[81] (Emphases in original.) Dynamic interplay of student and subject through which both were enriched was no longer in question. Knowledge had become information and learning a matter of mechanical ingestion. Thus, in the following month Nietzsche wrote, emphasizing alimentary engorgement: "Now ... I see up close the swarming philological brood of our times, where I must daily view the whole mole hustling, the full cheek pouches and the blind eyes, the joy at the captured worms and the indifference toward the true and urgent problems of life."[82]

One should bear in mind that these attitudes reflect Nietzsche's views at a specific juncture in his own life and at a particular moment in history. Although he continued to rail against philology during his early years, he came to view it more appreciatively as he matured;[83] and in any case, he was torn because he was loyal to the views of different historical eras. He did believe in *Bildung*, as did Ritschl, but with this difference. Ritschl could maintain his increasingly anachronistic values in good conscience because he was aware that times had changed; he simply refused to yield to them.

---

[80] KSAB II: 206.   [81] KSAB II: 316.   [82] KSAB II: 344.
[83] See, for example, the Preface to BGE.

Nietzsche was coming of age in historical mid-transit. He was therefore caught between the older vision and the new. He could not help but respect the traditional world that had formed him, but the modern world had formed him too and was in any case the era in which he would have to live. "Soyons de notre siècle!" ["Let's belong to our century!"] he exclaimed,[84] and as his championship of Lange had shown, this was a principle which he took seriously. In the coming year Nietzsche would find a way to escape this impasse; in the meantime, his demoralization and sense of grievance spoiled much of the pleasure he had taken in his field and in some ways proved self-destructive.

3

In 1867 Nietzsche had already achieved a great deal in his chosen profession, and he assumed that he was just beginning. These hopes would prove illusory. As he continued to critique philology, he began to lose interest in the topics and methods that could be approved by his academic peers. This shift would not be immediately evident because of the time lag between submission and publication. Nonetheless, one could argue that all Nietzsche's papers which appeared in print were either written during his student years or extended insights made during his time in Bonn or Leipzig.[85] In particular his first (and groundbreaking) paper on Diogenes Laertius, the work which is usually regarded as his signal contribution to philology,[86] now lay behind him.[87] Nietzsche might continue to make discoveries in his field, most notably in the area of Greek prosody,[88] but these efforts went unpublished. His public career was already past its peak and winding to a close.

Nobody knew this in 1867, and since the papers he produced were the focus of all his daily work, even during vacations, one might think that they would receive a great deal of scrutiny. In fact, Nietzsche's philological work

---

[84] KSAB II: 275, 329.
[85] Aside from the two installments of his Diogenes Laertius paper (and two addenda, written at Basel), Nietzsche would publish only his monograph on Simonides, which dated to work at Bonn, and two articles on the supposed contest between Homer and Hesiod, a theme he had addressed twice in lectures at Leipzig. Nietzsche would also complete a few book reviews, all written in Leipzig. For Simonides at Bonn, see KGW I-4: 44, 64.
[86] Barnes 1986: 17.
[87] Nietzsche published three papers on Laertius. However, the second and third deal with a miscellany of topics and are neither so unified nor so innovative as Nietzsche's first and major contribution. See Gigante 1994: 9–13.
[88] See Bornmann 1989: 472–489. Porter 2000a: 127–166.

has been almost entirely ignored, at least by his biographers (but not by scholars), and for understandable reasons.[89] The topics and modes of argument are arcane and the influence on the philosopher's later work is not immediately evident. Nonetheless, Nietzsche's philological studies represent a dimension of his life that occupied far more time and effort than anything else he accomplished during this period. It is inconceivable that they did not instill in him habits of thought and views of history that he would retain for a considerable time to come.[90] They merit inspection, if only because they represent a road not taken and because they provided a covert way to study philosophy.

There is yet another reason for their neglect. Nietzsche's earliest and most important works center, not on masterpieces of classical literature, which might interest the non-professional, but on collections of texts which few but philologists have ever heard of and which were compiled centuries after the classical eras had passed. Readers today may think of Greek and Latin writers as composing integral books such as the *Aeneid* or the *Satyricon*. This was true in the Golden and Silver Ages, but after the second century both writing and reading skills declined and compendiums became popular. The public came to prize handbooks and schoolbooks in which selections from earlier works were excerpted and sometimes jumbled. These books were scrapbooks, as were the lexicographies which philologists particularly favored.[91] The advantage of such collections lay in their preservation of ancient texts so that today they often serve as scholars' only source for earlier writings. The disadvantages are obvious. In a miscellany it can be difficult to know which texts are genuine, where an extract starts or ends, and to what extent they have been altered.

In several of his early articles and lectures to the Philological Society Nietzsche examined such collections and tried to tease out the stages through which they were composed or changed. In three presentations, for example – those on Theognis, the Suda (which he called the Suidas), and a list of the writings of Aristotle – he began with a given version and worked his way forwards or backwards, trying to determine what had happened to the original to account for the mangled version available now. In all cases, the start or endpoints (the "original" text or the edition currently published), served only as the introductory topic of his

---

[89] Scholars, as opposed to biographers, have been more inquiring, and the pace has picked up in recent years. See, for example, O'Flaherty *et al.* 1979; Barnes 1986; Conway and Rehn 1992; Borsche *et al.* 1994; Porter 2000a and 2000b; Bishop 2004; Benne 2005; Berry 2010; Jensen 2013; and Jensen and Heit 2014.
[90] Emden 2008: 42 ff.   [91] Reynolds and Wilson 1974: 31–33.

researches. Nietzsche's focus was not on the first or last manuscripts but rather the transit between, the literary relay as texts were passed from one scholar to the next and occasionally changed in the process. It was the plurality and shifts of sources, not their first or final fixture that drew his attention. While technically he might be said to deal in *Quellenforschung*, studies in the source of texts, he was by no means a foundationalist.[92] This is the more striking since philologists of his time often occupied themselves either with recension (the attempt to create a reliable edition of a particular work), or emendation (attempts to correct a faulty reading),[93] both of which attempted to establish a more reliable (and possibly final) text. Nietzsche never engaged with the first and hardly with the second. His stress fell firmly on temporal transformation, the slide through time, and not on the inert productions of any specific era.

This preference for multiplicity over unique productions is also implicit in Nietzsche's treatment of Diogenes Laertius, a writer of whom virtually nothing is known except that he flourished in the third century C.E. Nietzsche states that he was first drawn to that author's *Lives and opinions of eminent philosophers* as early as his first semester in Leipzig, that is, before March 1866.[94] One might think that Schopenhauer, who often referenced Diogenes, would have led him to the book.[95] If so, Nietzsche doesn't acknowledge this, stating only that he felt an immediate affinity for the problems that the work proposed.[96] He certainly didn't praise Diogenes as a scholar. This much-admired author had supposedly written a carefully researched history of Greek philosophers in which he personally assessed the relevant evidence and summarized it in a comprehensive survey written in his own words. Nietzsche believed little of it. He claimed that Diogenes was a plagiarist and that his book was mostly an assemblage of earlier documents, Diogenes' contribution consisting mostly of a series of little poems. Such a hypothesis allowed Nietzsche to treat the book rather like the other compendia he had been analyzing, and he made it his task, first, to demonstrate that the *Lives and opinions* was in fact such a compilation, and second, to track down its actual sources.

---

[92] Porter 2000a: 48.
[93] For a brief discussion of recension and emendation, see Reynolds and Wilson 1974: 207–208. See also Kenney 1974. For a more extended treatment, and one that repeatedly references both Ritschl and Bernays, see Timpanaro 2005.
[94] KGW I-4: 526.
[95] Lange also cites Diogenes, but Nietzsche had already begun to study the *Lives and opinions* before March 1866, whereas he did not read *The history of materialism* until that summer.
[96] KGW I-5: 38.

Nietzsche's arguments that Diogenes was a fraud are unimportant in this context.[97] The stress here falls rather on those aspects of Diogenes that Nietzsche did not discuss publicly because they had little to do with his profession. What that author provided was the opportunity to investigate philosophy under the guise of pursuing philology. It also offered him an alternative to his philosophers of choice. Diogenes could never inform his views with the intellectual subtlety of Schopenhauer and Lange, but the *Lives and opinions of eminent philosophers* had an imaginative force which impressed him and offered a view of philosophy different from those he would encounter elsewhere. His German masters gave Nietzsche one set of terms; Diogenes gave him another.

For a start, Diogenes provided a 300-year history of Greek philosophy from Thales to Epicurus, delineating not just individuals, but the interplay and opposition of teachers, students, and peers. Although most philosophers receive dedicated chapters and are emphatically treated as individuals, the book is ordered according to lineages and schools, and accordingly its protagonists also function as transmitters and transformers of a particular approach to reality. Also, in strong contrast to Schopenhauer and Lange, both of whom deliver unequivocal and magisterial surveys of their fields, the book of Diogenes offers a multiplicity of voices, so that the effect is polyphonal, one philosopher, then another, sounding off, though none so dominantly as to provide, as it were, the final word on any subject. Epicurus ends the book, but he is in no way presented as a consummation. He just happens to come last.

Further, as the title indicates, Diogenes offers a series of *biographies* – accounts of each philosopher's life in which philosophical positions and behavior are presented and implicitly entwined. Diogenes revels in anecdotes and apt quotations, and his book is replete with heterogeneous and often pungent tales that combine the appeal of backstairs gossip with suggestions of spiritual enlightenment. Here, for example, are excerpts from his account of Zeno the Stoic:

> It is stated ... that he consulted the oracle to know what he should do to attain the best life, and that the god's response was that he should take on the complexion of the dead. Whereupon, perceiving what this meant, he studied ancient authors.[98]

---

[97] For accounts of the argument in Nietzsche's essay, see Barnes 1986: 16–40; Gigante 1994: 3–16; and Jensen 2013: 27–31.
[98] Diogenes Laertius 1925 II: 111.

Apollonious of Tyre tells us how, when Crates laid hold on [Zeno] by the cloak to drag him from Stilpo, Zeno said, "The right way to seize a philosopher, Crates, is by the ears: persuade me then and drag me off by them; but, if you use violence, my body will be with you, but my mind with Stilpo."[99]

The story goes that Zeno of Citium after enduring many hardships by reason of old age was set free, some say by ceasing to take food; others say that once when he had tripped he beat with his hand upon the earth and cried, "I come of my own accord; why then call me?"[100] Whereupon Zeno "died on the spot through holding his breath."[101]

It should not be thought that Diogenes limits himself to apothegms and anecdotes. He makes a serious attempt to name the books and present the doctrines of each philosopher. Thus, in addition to his wayward account of Zeno's life he includes twenty-one pages on Stoic logic, twenty-two pages on Stoic ethics, and thirteen pages on Stoic physics and metaphysics.[102] He also presents lists of each philosopher's books – data which, however flawed, could prove invaluable to the investigating scholar. For Nietzsche, at least, his book might seem absurd, but it could not be dismissed.

In fact, the impression Nietzsche ultimately conveys is one of involuntary admiration. He clearly thought that Diogenes was an egregious fraud, and he frequently railed at him as stupid, impudent, and careless.[103] Yet his was a lover's quarrel, and for all his baffled vituperation, he could not help but embrace the man's book and refer to it affectionately, particularly when comparing it to the philosophic histories of the nineteenth century.[104] Citations from *Lives and opinions* (almost never acknowledged) appear in several of his later books,[105] although most obviously in *Philosophy in the tragic age of the Greeks*. Diogenes' biographical approach also provided the basis for Nietzsche's contention, both in that work's "Alternate preface" and later in "Schopenhauer as educator" and even in *Beyond good and*

---

[99] Diogenes Laertius 1925 II: 134–137.   [100] Diogenes Laertius 1925 II: 143.
[101] Diogenes Laertius 1925 II: 141.
[102] These can be found in Diogenes Laertius 1925 II as follows: logic: 151–193; ethics: 193–237; physics and metaphysics: 237–263. The number of pages listed for each subject have been halved since this edition is bilingual.
[103] This is not an attitude that other philologists have tended to share. Joseph Scaliger had called Diogenes *homo eruditissimus*, as Nietzsche acknowledged. BAW IV: 217. Barnes 1986 shows that much of Nietzsche's treatment is untenable (24–35). Gigante upholds Laertius as well. Gigante 1994: 5.
[104] See passages cited by Barnes 1986: 21.
[105] For example, in UO III: 8, the reference to honors accorded Zeno come from Diogenes, 117, 121. The claims that Socrates helped Euripides write his plays in *The birth of tragedy* (Section 13) also comes from Diogenes, I, 149.

evil[106] that the most important legacy of philosophers was their lives, the way they embodied their thought and expressed it through their deeds.[107]

Paradoxically, given his contention that the work was a fraud, Nietzsche could import Diogenes' book (and its philosophical subject matter) directly into his professional studies in a way he could never do with Schopenhauer and Lange. The *Lives and opinions of eminent philosophers* would eventually provide the subject matter for two articles, one in two parts, all published in the *Rheinisches Museum*, as well as a third piece published later as part of a *Festschrift*.[108] It further served as the background for his work on Democritus and Menippus. During his Leipzig years Nietzsche probably read him more sustainedly and carefully than the books of any more recent philosopher, quite possibly including Schopenhauer. He may have loved the latter, but Diogenes was part of his job.

Up to now when reviewing Nietzsche's philological researches, discussion has been limited to a few of the texts he "published," whether literally in the *Rheinisches Museum* or figuratively, as addresses before the Philological Society. He also lectured, wrote papers, or repeatedly considered a host of other topics, including Menippus and the Cynics, the possible contemporaneity of Hesiod and Homer, and a history of literary studies by the ancients. The last was never finished, and its loss continues to occasion regret, for this attempt to link artistic productions and subsequent scholarship in a symbiosis that led from Homer to Alexandria and forward to the Romans was a work that only Nietzsche could have completed.[109] In later times Nietzsche would express regrets at having to forego completing tasks that seemed particularly "his." Probably he was thinking of certain Basel insights, but he would also be remembering projects such as this which were devised in Leipzig but which proved abortive. If Nietzsche had any premonitions of these lost opportunities during the late 1860s, they could only have reinforced his pained sense of bafflement. He had hoped that his life would prove significant. Now it appeared that he had taken a wrong turn, and he saw no way to correct this. Earlier, he had lectured Deussen on the need to choose a profession early and to choose philology in particular. Nietzsche never explicitly retracted that advice, but if he remembered it now, the effect must have been mortifying. Intemperate remarks began to pepper his letters and notebooks as he cast about, trying to extricate himself from this misfortune.

---

[106] BGE 6.   [107] See, for example, UO III: 3.   [108] See n. 87.
[109] Gerratana 1994. Compare KSAB II: 248–249.

4

In 1867 Nietzsche was only beginning to be disgruntled professionally, and his disquiet was tempered by his growing rapport with Rohde. As mentioned, their association moved to a new level towards the end of June, when they took horseback riding lessons together. Meanwhile, Nietzsche was not averse to festivities, and he enjoyed himself considerably that spring and summer. He, Rohde, and members of the Philological Society frequented the Schützenhaus, a spacious dining establishment with multiple decks, both indoors and outdoors, where they drank, dined, and listened to concerts.[110] Alone, the two young men took walks in the Rosental, a park north of the university, where they sat on the banks of the river Pleisse and baptized an especially placid spot "Nirvana."[111] They also spent evenings in the theater and later would exchange arch letters regarding notable actresses. Rohde recalled that during the summer the pair spent half and even full days in "real laziness," idle times that in his eyes brought "the richest profit."[112] Profitable or not, all this entertainment, coupled with Nietzsche's preparation for a lecture to the Philological Society on Homer and Hesiod, took its toll.[113] As August 1, the deadline for the Diogenes Laertius paper, approached, Nietzsche found himself seriously behind. Fortunately, he was adept at quick composition, and late into the deadline's eve and "with not another hour to be lost," he wrote down his findings and ran with the manuscript to the home of his friend. Rohde was waiting with glasses and wine.[114]

On the day afterward, with a claim that his new landlords were overcharging him, Nietzsche prematurely vacated his apartment.[115] Since he would not leave Leipzig for another week, he moved into the Italienische Garten, one floor above his friend.[116] This was probably the day he had in mind when he later said that he had finally "surrendered" to friendship with Rohde. Both men were now free to stop working and to look forward to new developments in their lives. Nietzsche had resolved to take no more classes, thus discarding the title of "*Student*," a somewhat technical term in German, which he regarded as unsuited to his level of accomplishment.[117] Further, both men had decided to quit Ritschl and to leave Leipzig, Rohde to relocate to the University of Kiel, Nietzsche to the University of Berlin.

---

[110] KGW I-4: 493, 527, 529.
[111] KSAB II: 234, 235, 247; KGW I-4: 527–528, 530. See Heise 2000: 100. The Pleisse later became so polluted that it was deflected to a pipeline beneath the city.
[112] KGB I-4: 475–476.   [113] KGW I-4: 526.   [114] KGW I-4: 526–527.   [115] KSAB II: 219, 221.
[116] KGW I-4: 529.   [117] KSAB II: 329. See also "Farewell to being a student" KGW I-4: 529.

He considered the philology department at the latter hostile to Ritschl,[118] but Gersdorff, Deussen, Mushacke, and Pinder all lived in that city, as did many former members of the Philological Society,[119] not to mention Wilhelm Corssen, a beloved Schulpforte instructor.[120] A circle of friends would already be in place. The decisive motive, however, was almost certainly one that had concerned Nietzsche since he first arrived in Leipzig. If he did not eventually attend a Prussian school, his employment possibilities in that country would be limited.[121] Accordingly, he informed Rohde, Mushacke, Deussen, his mother, his guardian, and eventually Ritschl himself of his decision,[122] and he hired a "slave" (his term) to pack his books, papers, and other worldly goods.[123]

With such practical matters resolved, he could throw himself into celebrations with abandon. During this period he saw Offenbach's "*La belle Hélène*," delighting in its catchy tunes and probably in its sprightly mockery of the Greeks. (The libretto depicts Paris's abduction of Helen from Menelaus.) So indelibly did this operetta impress him that he would hum its melodies to cheer himself up in the military,[124] and he would cite it twice covertly in his final books.[125] Meanwhile, a round of gatherings hosted by comrades celebrated the departures of the two men. Nietzsche rhapsodized, "Nothing but farewell parties, all rather happy than sad," and he added elegiacally, "Leipzig dies out slowly in our ears."[126]

Leaving the city was a milestone, and since he assumed he was not coming back, it called for another autobiography, one that Nietzsche titled, "Retrospect of my two years at Leipzig."[127] Less self-probing than earlier such works, it began with Nietzsche's retreat from Bonn and described his first days in Leipzig, the discovery of Schopenhauer, Ritschl's acclaim for his Theognis paper, and the latter's request that Nietzsche and others establish the Philological Society. Most of the rest of the piece depicted various friends and instructors Nietzsche found in the

---

[118] KSAB II: 107, 230.   [119] KSAB II: 215.
[120] Corssen had left Schulpforte at Michaelmas, 1866. Rosmiarek *et al.* 2003: 329.
[121] Nietzsche was aware that if he did not take the so-called "state examination," he would not be allowed to teach in a Prussian Gymnasium. Fallon 1980: 39. In a letter to Mushacke, he indicates that he will attend Berlin exclusively to take the state examinations. See KSAB II: 254. Compare 217.
[122] For Nietzsche's proposed transfer to Berlin, see KSAB II: 217, 219, 220–221, 222; KGB I-3: 207, 209; KGW I-4: 530. The *Sittenzeugnis* (a university certificate) that Nietzsche received at the end of the semester indicates that he had left the school for good. Heise 2000: 112–113. It does appear that Nietzsche had a last-minute change of plans, decided before his draft, but this would require extended treatment to explain.
[123] KSAB II: 222.   [124] KSAB II: 235.   [125] CW: "Postscript" and TI: "Skirmishes," 1.
[126] KSAB II: 223.
[127] KGW I-4: 506–530. For more on this autobiography, see Afterword, Section 1.

city; and it closed with the Diogenes Laertius contest and Nietzsche's developing friendship with Rohde. He stressed that their companionship was founded on appreciation for Schopenhauer, and he finished with an invocation of this master by describing "Nirvana," the private and peaceful location by the Pleisse that he and Rohde had "baptized." The two companions, he stressed, enjoyed it "like artists," rapt in "pure contemplation and momentarily released from the stresses of the restless will to life."[128]

On August 8 they were released from stress in a more tangible if less Schopenhaurean manner, departing Leipzig for a two-week tour of mostly rural Bohemia and Bavaria. They were delighted to be free, "like birds in the air" (Rohde's phrase),[129] and when they returned, they did not mourn, for both assumed that they would reunite shortly in Paris. Nietzsche returned from this idyll to Naumburg to resume work. He was just beginning to criticize philology, and he had yet to show any decline in enthusiasm or interest. On the contrary, he had two tasks pending, one of which he attacked with zeal. Before leaving Leipzig, he and Rohde had proposed that they and other students compose a *Festschrift* (tentatively titled *Symbola*)[130] in honor of Ritschl. This project was initiated as early as July 3, and by the first week of August, they had assembled a team of nine (including Nietzsche and Rohde) to complete the book.[131] Nietzsche had chosen to investigate the number and names of writings by Democritus, none of which (except for fragments) were extant, and he set to work on this project with the more industry since he was trying to avoid a less inviting task.[132] Ritschl had requested that he prepare an index for the *Rheinisches Museum*, a series which would encompass twenty-four volumes. One can scarcely imagine an assignment less suited to Nietzsche's strengths, for this would involve much drudgery, little need for imagination, and no opportunity for display of literary flair. A pupil more dedicated to philology might have welcomed poring over hundreds of articles stretching back decades, but the prospect would not have drawn Nietzsche in the best of circumstances, and he was certainly not so disposed now. Besides, a previous experience had already given him a bad taste for such work. In 1866 he had been asked to prepare a lexicon for an edition of Aeschylus. That endeavor had fallen through, ostensibly because Nietzsche

---

[128] KGW I-4: 527–528.   [129] BAW III: 423.   [130] KGB I-4: 657.
[131] These would be Nietzsche, Rohde, Ernst Windisch, Wilhelm Roscher, Ludwig Wilhelm August Theodor Clemm, Reinhold Dressler, Georg Andresen, Otto Kohl, and Sigismund Sussmann Heynemann.
[132] Nietzsche was frank about neglecting one task for the other. See KSAB II: 224, 232.

didn't trust the professor,[133] but at the time a friend had questioned whether this was the right project for him,[134] and Nietzsche himself had found the work boring.[135] Now he had another such task on his hands, and although he rarely complained, the facts speak for themselves. He would eventually complete it – with help from his sister – but he would not do so for nearly a year and a half, and the process would require reminders from his professor.[136]

Meanwhile, he pursued other philological endeavors. He was considering writing a book on the Suda with Diederich Volkmann, his former instructor at Schulpforte,[137] and he looked forward to a professional conference that would take place in nearby Halle at the end of September. There he hoped to observe masters in the profession and to socialize with former classmates, and of course he would now wear the glamour of a newly published prodigy. Nietzsche in fact attended the gathering and his letters indicate that he enjoyed himself immensely – he called it "for the time being, the joyous finale, or let us say the coda, of my philological overture."[138] Nonetheless, the event was overshadowed by two absences – neither Ritschl nor Mushacke appeared – and by some disturbing news. As a male Prussian Nietzsche was subject to the draft. He had long before been informed that he would have to report for duty no later than October 1, 1867, but he seems either to have forgotten this or to assume that his poor vision would lead to an exemption.[139] Now, after years of waiting for that Damoclean sword to descend, he discovered that very weekend that his bad eyesight did not exempt him and that he could expect to report for duty in less than two weeks.[140] In the past he had occasionally sought to enlist on his own terms, and he made one last effort, dashing off to Berlin to try to join the service there. (He spent the night with Paul Deussen.) He was not accepted and would have to perform his service in Naumburg. It is ironic that after he had hoped to discard his status as student and to seek release from academic pressures, he found his wish so unexpectedly granted. More ironic still, this adventure would open horizons and liberate him in an unexpected way.

---

[133] KGW I-4: 521.   [134] KGB I-3: 145.   [135] KSAB II: 167.
[136] Letters from Ritschl questioning progress: KGB I-3: 279–280, 290–291; letters from Nietzsche promising compliance: KSAB II: 313–314 and 317–318.
[137] KSAB II: 242–243.   [138] KSAB II: 231.   [139] KSAB I: 275.
[140] Compare letters from Gersdorff: KGB I-3: 116, 195–196. Förster-Nietzsche 1895: 259; and 1912: 167, states that inspectors examined Nietzsche's spectacles rather than his sight. She does not explain why he should have been wearing – and apparently coping successfully with – unsuitably weak lenses.

CHAPTER 13

"Become what you are"

The human being who doesn't want to belong to the masses just needs to stop going easy on himself: let him follow his conscience, which calls to him: "Be yourself! You are not any of those things which you currently do, think, desire."[1]

I

One might expect Nietzsche to dislike military service, since it was unsuited to his talents and it removed him from his friends. Instead, in the beginning at least, he proved acquiescent and even appreciative. This partly reflected an admiration for the army that had begun in childhood when he enjoyed watching soldiers at their drills.[2] This esteem was reinforced in 1866 when he cheered the Prussian troops during war. In the aftermath of that conflict, he wrote Gersdorff, who was under arms, that to switch to military life after academia seemed a healthy alternative, for it offered "an effective contrast" to school.[3] Gersdorff demurred,[4] but Nietzsche was consistent enough to retain this view when forced to endure it himself. He wrote Mushacke that he compared his unexpected induction to a "zesty meal ... laid on the table of my life." Unable to refuse it, "I tried it and found it not so bad. It tasted especially good after the effeminacy that comes from the way of living and way of studying that derives from being a student. And so I got used to thinking of the year in the military as one of those means we use to compensate one-sided instruction."[5]

It should be noted that Nietzsche's military experiences were comparatively benign. Although the law called for three years of active service, he served only one because he qualified for the *Einjährige-Patent*, a privilege

---

[1] UO III: 1; KSA I: 338. [2] KGW I-1: 302–303. [3] KSAB II: 210. [4] KGB I-3: 202.
[5] KSAB II: 253. Variations of these views occur repeatedly in letters to his friends. See KSAB II: 240, 242, 246, 247.

awarded those who had achieved a certain level of education.[6] Since such persons were expected to pay for their own gear, food, and lodging, he was posted to his own hometown (as opposed to some hinterland), and he lived, not in a barracks, but in his mother's house. Every noon and evening he went home to his family and to his devoted mother's meals.

Despite these privileges Nietzsche found his new life difficult. He had been assigned to a cavalry artillery unit, and although he frequently wrote about horses and even kept a list of equine anatomy in his notebooks,[7] he rarely mentioned munitions in his letters and not at all in his private papers. With his poor eyesight, he was unlikely to be a good shot, and if he had been skilled with powder and shells he would have said so. He did claim to be liked – "Everyone here from the captain to the gunners wishes me well"[8] – and he was told that as a horseman he had the best seat in the unit, a compliment of which he was understandably proud.[9]

Meanwhile, his schedule proved exhausting. He wrote Gersdorff that he was required to work eleven hours per day (with an hour off for lunch), six days a week, not to mention the time spent on officer training instruction and sundry chores such as feeding the horses on Sunday evenings.[10] This regimen was later lightened, but Nietzsche still found his workload hard. After explaining the advantages of military life to Mushacke, he changed the subject, stating that he would rather talk about something other than the army, since he wrote to friends in order to forget it.[11] For all his attempts to recognize the positive aspects of soldiering, Nietzsche knew that he belonged somewhere else. Accordingly, as the months went by he grew restive. "[M]y time as well as the best part of my intellectual power and energy is wasted in this eternal circuit of military drills," he wrote.[12] He referred to his enlisted peers as "moronic recruits,"[13] and he pined for his former life, which he remembered as one "of free self-determination, in the epicurean pleasure of knowledge and the arts, among people with aspirations like one's own, close to a lovable teacher and ... in the constant company of [Rohde]."[14]

---

[6] In theory Nietzsche should subsequently have been subject to maneuvers and afterwards been on call in the reserves. He was spared these requirements, probably because upon assuming his position in Switzerland he gave up his Prussian citizenship.

[7] KGW I-4: 433. At some point in the coming year Nietzsche investigated *Mulomedecinae*, a work on veterinary medicine by Vegetius which apparently dealt, among other matters, with the medical issues of horses. KGW I-5: 65–69.

[8] KSAB II: 247.   [9] KSAB II: 241, 247, 256.   [10] KSAB II: 240–241.   [11] KSAB II: 253.

[12] KSAB II: 254.   [13] KSAB II: 242.

[14] KSAB II: 234. Translation by Christopher Middleton. For the full letter in English, see Middleton 1969: 24–28.

Unburdening himself to the latter, Nietzsche summed up the advantages and drawbacks of his position. "My friend," he wrote, "this life is now truly lonely and friendless. There are no stimulants except those which I give myself, nothing of that harmonious chord of souls [known elsewhere]." On the other hand, "This life is definitely uncomfortable but, consumed as an *entremets*, definitely useful. It is a constant summons to a person's energy and is especially tasty as an antidote against crippling skepticism, the effect of which we have so often observed together. *One learns one's own nature in the process*, how it fosters its revelation among alien, mostly rough people and without the help of scholarship [*Wissenschaft*] and that traditional reputation which determines our worth for our friends and society."[15] (Emphasis added.)

The final sentence is striking. Nietzsche believed that he could best discover his "nature," a project he had ardently pursued throughout his youth, not by dealing with peers, but when largely isolated from sympathetic persons and from institutions that favored his abilities. Other human beings might help to nurture and shape him, but he tended to mistrust them and sought instead some residuum of identity independent of social and interpersonal inflections. To put it metaphorically, he believed that to find himself he must go into the desert.

Nietzsche was scarcely so isolated as he claimed. He lived with his mother and sister and moved among families and environs he had known since early childhood. Yet with the exception of one vague allusion, he never mentions these old acquaintances in his letters, and he seems to have regarded himself as fundamentally stranded.[16] This may say something about his chronic inattention to support structures; Nietzsche always wanted to believe that he was self-sufficient. He neglects to mention, for example, that his mother had coffee waiting every morning when he got up at 5 a.m.[17] Nonetheless, during the day and among soldiers, he was – metaphorically, at least – as solitary as he claimed. This loneliness had its advantages. Military strictures didn't touch his fundamental needs or ambitions. Soldiers neither knew nor cared about his studies, and their indifference created a free zone in which he could commune uninhibitedly with his own ideas. Although he had never before lived under such tyrannical regulations, he was liberated from academic pressures and supervision. For an entire year he could consider the nature of philology unhampered by the scrutiny of instructors and peers.

---

[15] KSAB II: 247.   [16] For the single allusion, see KSAB II: 256.
[17] Franziska Nietzsche 1994: 40.

2

On October 31, 1867, Nietzsche's paper on Diogenes Laertius received the university prize. He noted sardonically that he had won because his was the only entry,[18] but he was pleased by the honor and disappointed that he could not attend the celebratory party in Leipzig. Nietzsche seemed particularly touched by the official encomium that accompanied the award and that lavishly praised the author's skills.[19] (Ritschl filed a separate appreciation.) He also observed that both Ritschl and the committee had cited the paper's Greek epigraph, "*Genoi' hoios essi,*" "Become such as you are," a phrase he would later reconfigure as "Become what you are."[20] Nietzsche took this expression from the second of Pindar's *Pythian odes,* somewhat broadening the original meaning by the omission of a modifying term.[21] The phrase clearly inspired him, for he mentioned it in three letters written at this time[22] and later invoked the German version in five books.[23] When he made it the subtitle of his final autobiography – "How one becomes what one is" – he implicitly declared it a central principle of his personal and philosophic development.

Despite the motto's pedigree and suggestive resonance, it is difficult to grasp what Nietzsche meant by it and why he chose to deploy it as he did. Logically, the expression might appear to be either tautologous or circular. ("[You,] become/be what you [already] are.") For perhaps this reason, James I. Porter has remarked, "[The expression] has no literal meaning, but only a strategic one."[24] Much depends on the initial verb, which translators of Pindar render variously as "Be" and "Become," although it is derived from *gignomai*, "to become."[25] "Be what you are" suggests that the addressee is somewhat alienated from fundamental values and needs to be recalled to

---

[18] KSAB II: 230.
[19] KSAB II: 237–238 and 247–248. It is striking that in the latter letter he would include a bitter remark about Ritschl, calling him a panderer (*Kuppler*) (248).
[20] The phrasing is slightly different in each citation. In HAH I: 263, Nietzsche writes, "so dass [jeder] wirklich ein Talent wird, also wird, was er ist." In GS 270, "Was sagt dein Gewissen?" he replies, "'Du sollst der werden, der du bist.'" (Note the change in relative pronoun.) The subtitle of EH reads, "Wie man wird, was man ist." (Again a change in pronoun.)
[21] Line 72. The original line reads "*Genoi' hoios essi mathon.*" Nietzsche eliminated the final word. Translations of the original (including "mathon") vary, but they mostly circle around the meaning, "Be the sort of man you learned [or were taught] to be." See Hamilton 2004: 59. For a more resonant and wide-ranging survey of translations see Babich 2003: 31–33.
[22] KSAB II: 235, 237, 247.
[23] UO IV: 262; HAH I: 263; GS: 270, 335; Z IV, I: EH subtitle. See also EH, "Clever," 9. The phrase also surfaces in his notebooks, as in KSA VIII: 340, and it is of course implicit in the demand, "Be yourself," which opens the Schopenhauer essay.
[24] Porter 2000a: 197. For discussion of the paradoxes engendered, see Leiter 1998.
[25] I am grateful to Mark Anderson for confirming this.

them. "Become what you are" introduces a temporal dimension, indicating that the command will remain in force for a long time (possibly a lifetime) and involve the gradual transition from a spurious to a more genuine identity.[26] Both assume that a human being has an ideal self which somehow subsists independently of single actions or temporary views.

A hidden aspect of the motto can be observed through the ways Nietzsche deployed it while at Leipzig. It might seem puzzling, for example, that he put it at the head of his essay on Diogenes Laertius. The epigraph, which apparently demands existential authenticity, seems out of place when applied to Diogenes, a man who in Nietzsche's view emphatically did not become "himself" at all but plagiarized wholesale from the books of others.[27] In a separate symbolic gesture, Nietzsche shared the maxim with his "philosophical comrade," Erwin Rohde.[28] When he reported to the latter that he had won the prize, he remembered how the two had erected a memorial at Nirvana, their riverside refuge, and that it bore "the solemn words from me that have proven to be victorious, *Genoi' hoios essi.*"[29] Here, a double-edged aspect to the phrase is more evident. Positively, it invokes a high and noble insight that Nietzsche intends to uphold. The use of the word "victorious," however, suggests a defensive posture and a negative, agonistic dimension: Nietzsche must achieve this personal goal in the teeth of opposition. To that extent, "*Genoi' hoios essi*" serves as a battle cry against forces conceived to be hostile. To become what is, one must avoid becoming what one is not. Hidden within the affirmative summons lies a corresponding repudiation.[30]

Without unequivocal evidence one cannot be certain what obstacles Nietzsche had in mind. However, one might note that the Diogenes Laertius essay was his first publication explicitly to challenge the received opinions of his elders. Diogenes' probity had been acclaimed by no less an authority than Joseph Scaliger, one of the most important philologists of the previous 500 years,[31] and the great man's successors had shown little

---

[26] In his German versions, Nietzsche unequivocally uses the verb "Werde," "become."
[27] In a letter to Gersdorff, Nietzsche mentions that the phrase appeared at the top of the Laertius paper, but he refers to it, not as an epigraph, but as "my motto." KSAB II: 237.
[28] KGW I-4: 420. This salute occurs amid notes for the essay, "On Schopenhauer" and raises the possibility that Nietzsche had intended to dedicate that essay to Rohde.
[29] KSAB II: 235. This translation is based on that of Christopher Middleton 1969: 28. For more on Nietzsche and Rohde's "Nirvana," see Chapter 12, Section 4.
[30] Compare "Schopenhauer as Educator," Section 4: "[Schopenhauer] realizes that others would like to cheat him of himself ... He resists this, pricks up his ears, and decides: 'I want to remain my own!'" Translation by Richard T. Gray, slightly modified. KSA I: 374.
[31] BAW IV: 217.

inclination to dissent from the master's opinion. Since Nietzsche was still only an undergraduate, he may have hesitated to risk his academic career by presenting views that the current experts might view as impertinent. Significantly, when he prepared the final published edition he removed the epigraph and offered to soften some of the polemical remarks, a gesture that Ritschl deemed "appropriate."[32]

Nietzsche was not always so respectful of his masters, nor was the cheek of the Diogenes piece limited to its language. Only two months later and speaking of this very article, Nietzsche would blithely observe, "There was no way to avoid now and then giving a philologist a slap."[33] In early 1867, however, and at a time when he was only just beginning to share misgivings with Rohde, he was less prone to exhibit such *lèse-majesté* directly. One might surmise then that he found the Pinder quote an inspirational motto when taking the first, courageous step of disagreeing with the established authorities, his own way of declaring that this was where he took a stand. Under this interpretation, it was not meant to resonate with the essay's internal contents but rather to issue a challenge to the reader from the start. This understanding of the motto as act of defiance fits both the motto's appearance in the paper and the role that it served in the shrine he built with Rohde.

Under this interpretation one might well ask, what might these insidious temptations be? Before considering this question, one should notice that the assumptions behind Nietzsche's maxim are remarkably similar to those that animate Humboldtian *Bildung*. Both stress aspiration, activity, and self-development. Nietzsche even echoes some of Humboldt's language, as when the latter said of the Greeks that they, as no other people, "had become what they could become."[34] The only immediately obvious difference between the two is that Humboldt is less militant and *Bildung* enjoins no martial overthrow of alien influences. This does not mean that Humboldt was an intellectual pacifist. As an administrator he had vigorously battled alternative theories of education, particularly those that called for religious or practically useful instruction. *Within* the bounds of his theory, however, the sole negative condition that he recognized was that of passivity, the somnolent condition of human beings who had yet to awaken to their powers. To that extent Humboldt's vision was less environmentally sensitive than that of his inheritor, who had been alarmed by anti-Humboldtian considerations as early as his sixteenth year. At that time (1861) Nietzsche had recognized how difficult it was to become oneself

---

[32] KSAB II: 243; KGB I-3: 220.   [33] KSAB II: 255.   [34] Quoted in Sweet 1980 II: 27.

when cultural and social pressures had already informed the putatively free student. It was in order to come to terms with just those limitations that he had prepared his notes on "Fate and history" and "Freedom of will and fate."[35] Now, six years later, and from a vastly more sophisticated point of view, he was ready to return to those issues and to reconsider *Bildung*.

There exists no unequivocal textual evidence to confirm this, but it appears that as Nietzsche matured, he became mistrustful of *Bildung* and even demoted it to secondary importance, transferring its salvageable aspects to his new maxim. Certainly, from this time on he tended to disparage that expression while simultaneously espousing the values most associated with it.[36] What, then, was the difference? As earlier explained,[37] Humboldt conceived *Bildung* and *Wissenschaft* as complementary unities, each growing by extending the other. We must conceive Nietzsche as potentially severing this reciprocity, treating organized scholarship and the burgeoning self as separate domains, with the emphasis planted on the second. Earlier it was asked, what alienating pressures did Nietzsche intend his motto to resist? The answer seems to have been *Wissenschaft* itself. It was the sacrifice of the student's personhood on the altar of knowledge that he deplored and refused to endorse. "It is not primarily our duty to serve *Wissenschaft* and then one's self but completely the opposite," he wrote, adding, "If someone has a surplus of intellectual strength, then after his subjective needs are met he will attend to the needs of humanity. The reverse is cruelty and barbarism." In other words, the needs and ambitions of the student were superior to the demands of knowledge, and Nietzsche drew the pedagogic corollary, "One should tell students this so that they will set up their studies accordingly."[38]

One might argue that Nietzsche had overstated his position. His quarrel was not really with *Wissenschaft* in general but with philology, and not even with philology itself so much as with the field as currently practiced. Further, in putting the stress on the individual, as opposed to intellectual fields, he was actually endorsing the core values of Humboldt himself. However, as shown in the preceding chapter, the methods and the very meaning of *Wissenschaft* had shifted since Humboldt instituted his reform. The rise of the natural sciences and an ever stricter professionalization among professors, exemplified and fed by the research imperative, a comparatively new practice, had led to it becoming more specialized and

---

[35] This process was described in Chapter 6, Sections 4, 6, and 7.   [36] KSAB II: 322.
[37] Chapter 12, Section 2.   [38] KGW I-4: 222.

positivistic and above all less unitary.[39] Nietzsche's quarrel was not just with current philology but with the forms of science and scholarship as currently practiced. He continued to respect many of its aspects, as is evident in his admiration for Ritschl, not to mention his regard for Lange and the natural sciences. Nonetheless, he put his human needs first and, as will be seen, decided to reconfigure *Wissenschaft* on those terms. He did not abandon his studies, although he apparently considered this.[40] Instead, he proposed to pursue them in a different way. During his struggle with the Democritus project he attempted to discover an approach to scholarship that he could ingest as his own.

3

Drained by exercise and isolated from friends, Nietzsche pursued the one thing without which he could scarcely bear to live, substantive work. The projects he had accepted before induction – the *Rheinisches Museum* index and the Democritus article – remained unfinished and therefore available as occasions for activity. Ritschl had arranged for him to have access to the twenty-three completed volumes of the journal (the twenty-fourth was still in progress) as Nietzsche acknowledged toward the end of September.[41] Nonetheless, he seems to have postponed work on this project until late in the following summer. Instead, he concentrated on the Democritus paper and registered in his journals the intensity and the changing nature of his views on that man and his philosophy.

From a philosophical point of view Nietzsche had obvious reasons to study Democritus. Schopenhauer had mentioned him frequently and favorably, and Lange viewed him as the first consistent materialist as well as the first philosopher systematically to exclude teleology from causal accounts. Over the winter Nietzsche came to admire the man's character and to find his atomistic doctrines "poetic."[42] As James I. Porter has noted, his studies of this "laughing philosopher" would influence his philosophy from this time onward.[43] Philosophically, Nietzsche's interest in this figure was, if anything, overdetermined.

From a professional point of view, however, Nietzsche was not a philosopher, but a philologist; and if he chose to investigate Democritus, he would need philological issues as his pretext. He turned the project into

---

[39] For the development of the research imperative, see Turner 1974.
[40] See Rohde's admonition: KGB I-3: 244.   [41] KSAB II: 224. See also 318.
[42] For the association of Democritus' cosmology with poetry, see KGW I-4: 380, 402, 414.
[43] Porter 2000a: *passim*.

an homage to Valentin Rose, a classicist whose work he greatly admired.[44] Nietzsche prized Rose's prickly and rebarbative character, as well as his refusal to accommodate his readers. If the scholar sometimes seemed willfully obscure, Nietzsche construed this as a gesture of independence, and he noted with wonder that "[Rose] was reluctant to make gifts, and he gave with one hand while with the other he sought to protect himself from contact with the public." More colorfully, Nietzsche compared him to a person who digs up gold coins, then buries them again but at least indicates to neighbors where they might be found.[45]

Rose awakened Nietzsche to a vision of larger issues in philology, particularly those relating to "pseudepigrapha," that is, to books falsely ascribed to well-known authors from the past. Thus, if a magician from the third century BCE wanted to issue a book, he was more likely to find a public if he attributed it to Democritus than to himself.[46] Misattribution was also common for more respectable reasons. If a book exemplified the teachings of a known philosopher, it made sense to ascribe the work directly to the head of the school even if it was written by a follower.[47] For these and other reasons, pseudepigrapha – Nietzsche sometimes called them "counterfeits" – were pervasive among the Greeks; and Nietzsche believed that Rose had been the first to award them sustained attention. Past philologists had tended to treat such falsely ascribed works as incidental nuisances, either to be ferreted out and dismissed or to be themselves organized under the heading of a new author, such as the "Pseudo-Dionysus." Rose was different. Nietzsche claimed that the latter's accomplishment had been to abandon such ad hoc treatment and to examine their place and discovery more systematically and comprehensively. "To summarize all those counterfeit tendencies, to seek an inner connection among those innumerable [literary works], in short to include the pseudepigraphic writings in the history of Greek literature, that is Rose's achievement."[48]

Because he was following another author's lead rather than building on his own discoveries, Nietzsche's new project – the attempt to determine the number of works actually written by Democritus – introduced him to

---

[44] For Nietzsche's encounters with Rose, see KGW I-4: 83; KSAB II: 186; and especially KGW I-4: 160–174. For more on Nietzsche and Rose see Porter 2000a: 36–40; BAW IV: 598–600.
[45] KGW I-4: 445.
[46] The reference is to Bolus, a magician whom Nietzsche characterized as operating a "factory" of Democritean forgeries. KGW I-4: 307 ff.
[47] Porter mentions the confusion wrought by doxographical works as well. Porter 2000a: 39.
[48] KGW I-4: 446–447.

philological issues in which he had little experience.[49] It may be recalled that virtually all his earlier explorations had involved issues of transmission – attempts to trace the provenance of later documents and to consider the ways books were preserved or transformed over time. In those cases he had at least possessed a citable text (Diogenes' *Lives*, a Theognis redaction, a listing of Aristotle's writings), which he could use as a reference point. For Democritus no books survived. There remained only fragments, and these seemed so obscure as to be virtually unusable. (Nietzsche scarcely mentioned them except to complain that the most recent edition was flawed.) Instead, he had to compare widely varying testimonials, as augmented by circumstantial evidence. The Alexandrians had listed 300 books by Democritus, whereas Demetrius of Magnesia, a touchstone for Nietzsche, declared that he had written only two.[50] Even this low number might be excessive, for to produce even two in the era before Socrates seems to have been quite rare.[51] How, 2,500 years later and with not a single book surviving, could the actual number be determined?

Nietzsche sifted Democritus' life and times for evidence and clues. He investigated the reasons witnesses might have to lie.[52] He puzzled over ways the Greeks ascribed authorship.[53] He pondered philosophical schools and Democritus' membership in these.[54] He examined incidents in Democritus' biography and whether these had implications for his books. (If he traveled in Egypt he would have known certain things discussed only in that country.)[55] Nietzsche also had to consider the possibility that Democritus had been confused with others of the same name – there was a Democritus of Chios, for example[56] – or that his musical works might have been written by somebody else entirely.[57] In short, Nietzsche had to resolve a multitude of seemingly minor issues before he could begin to render judgment on Democritus' works with confidence.[58]

Meanwhile, the more searchingly he investigated, the more inexorably any conclusive judgments tended to disintegrate in his hands. As he wrote Rohde in the spring, "The entire business has become rather dubious and keeps crumbling before my passably rigorous philological conscience."[59] Eventually, he had to endure the embarrassment of asking for a deadline

---

[49] It is arguable that this sort of problem would not have appealed to Ritschl, who believed that philology should center on texts, not speculations. Benne 2005: 62.
[50] KGW I-4: 173, 198.   [51] KGW I-4: 237–239, 241, 199.   [52] KGW I-4: 326–327.
[53] KGW I-4: 238–242.   [54] KGW I-4: 172–173 and a multitude of others.   [55] KGW I-4: 379.
[56] KGW I-4: 381.   [57] KGW I-4: 329.   [58] KSAB II: 270–271.
[59] KSAB II: 262. Translation (slightly altered) from Porter 2000a: 46.

extension. He would need to submit his paper in November instead of spring.[60] Nietzsche had apparently assumed a project that was impractical in his current situation, but he refused to be defeated. He acknowledged instead that he would first have to resolve the secondary problems mentioned earlier and that this would delay submission. As it turned out, this postponement would be indefinitely extended, for Nietzsche was not the only contributor to have problems with his article. With the exceptions of Rohde and one other colleague,[61] none of the *Festschrift* co-authors followed through on their papers, a failure that resulted in high dudgeon on Nietzsche's part.[62] As a result, the book would not be published, a prospect that Rohde took more in his stride, archly commenting, "From this the world might surmise that Father Ritschl's philological potency is exhausted."[63] No longer pressed to hurry, Nietzsche seized the opportunity to stop working on Democritus altogether, postponing the project for "sometime in the coming years" after he had done a great deal of preliminary work.[64] (In fact he returned to it in the early winter.)[65]

4

Although Nietzsche faced a host of difficulties with the Democritus project, one might note that the problem that he cited when requesting an extension was that "The entire business ... keeps crumbling before my passably rigorous philological conscience." He was beginning to turn his formidable gift for critique against his own efforts and in the process to risk what he must have always dreaded, ceasing to be productive. On the one hand he prized skepticism – Rose's determination to question tradition was one of his traits that Nietzsche most admired. Nonetheless, one must distinguish between (a) methodological skepticism, which questions assertions in the interests of sound reasoning and acceptable proof; and (b) practical skepticism, which scrutinizes motives and effectiveness so scrupulously that one may have difficulty acting at all. While Nietzsche praised the first, it was easy situationally to slide into the second. Disciples of Schopenhauer were particularly susceptible to such paralysis, for they would ultimately consider exercise of the will futile and even "sinful." Nietzsche and Rohde knew a sad case of just this malaise and bewailed the fate of a Leipzig philology student, whom Rohde characterized as "the

---

[60] KSAB II: 249–250. [61] Sigismund Heynemann. KSAB II: 277–278.
[62] KSAB II: 272–274; KGB 1–3: 250–252, 255–256. [63] KGB I-3: 256. [64] KSAB II: 270–271.
[65] KSAB II: 350.

luckless [Heinrich] Romundt, who in unhappy clairvoyance concerning the great secret of purposelessness of action seems to have gone wholly to ruin."[66] The two men sympathized with this friend, but they also seem to have regarded him as an object lesson in what to avoid. They did not find this easy. Nietzsche reported that his own attitude toward philology was so undermined by doubts that he was chronically tempted to abandon it. Thus, when he won the prize for his Diogenes essay he wrote that he was happy with certain lines in Ritschl's encomium, "because they encourage me to forge ahead on a path which I was tempted, *out of skepticism*, to leave."[67] (Emphasis added.) Similarly, and as already quoted, Nietzsche found in the rigors of military life "an antidote against the *crippling skepticism* the effect of which we so often have observed together."[68] (Emphasis added.) Rohde too confessed to such dangerous leanings, and remarked, "I have always carried through in practice the principle not to let myself be beaten down by such thoughts."[69] An *acedia* born of skepticism was a temptation which both friends recognized and battled.

Nietzsche was probably helped by his sanguine temperament, that fundament of hope and ambition which made it difficult for him to stop being creative, regardless of his negative views. Nonetheless, he was not always able to bring his projects to a close, and with the exception of the index, he would not complete a single work he pursued that year in Naumburg.[70] He might enthuse that "The limits of skepticism ... are not yet fixed ... One has not yet exhausted the strengths of this method."[71] Nonetheless, he was experiencing the negative side of such a scorched-earth policy and he began to seek an exit from his impasse, not by abandoning skepticism but by pushing through to what he considered its other side. As he was wont to say, prefiguring an analogy he would make later, "[Skepticism] is no symptom of sickness in our scholarship. Rather one must not forget that in virtue of its particular nature skepticism devours its own children, that it tends to reach a boundary where it turns around and returns on the same path that it had just left."[72]

He was in effect recognizing the positive values implicit in the negativity of doubt. If Nietzsche was a formidable critic, it should not be thought that he found faults out of caprice or as a reflection of his saturnine personality. Rather that personality proceeded from efforts to rein in a fundamentally

---

[66] KGB I-3: 237, 259; KGW I-4: 517; KSAB II: 351.   [67] KSAB II: 237.
[68] KSAB II: 247. The "we" refers to Nietzsche and Rohde.   [69] KGB I-3: 237.
[70] The phrase, "project he planned," is intended to exclude the index to the *Rheinisches Museum*, which was a project *assigned*.
[71] KGW I-4: 394. Compare BGE: 208–210.   [72] KGW I-4: 407.

positive outlook, to keep it from overstepping its bounds and behaving as did his mother, who believed in every passing preacher. If he examined claims sternly, it was in the faith that better solutions might be found and that he should accept nothing less. In other words, his skepticism proceeded from faith in high standards, not negativity. It was thus comparatively obvious for him to reverse the poles and to inspect his current skepticism for its positive side, for the unacknowledged premises that allowed him to recognize that certain views were flawed. Thus in a letter to Gersdorff he remarked, "when my skeptical survey of all the consequences took it all in, I slowly turned the image around in my hands," in accordance with the principle of "the rescue of negation through negation."[73] In this case Nietzsche was referring to his image of Democritus, which he tried to reconceive from an ideal vantage point and then to infer from that what sort of books such a man might have written. In doing so, he piled hypothesis upon hypothesis, until the approach collapsed under its own absurdity. A month and a half later he again found himself baffled,[74] and he sought other ways to resolve the impasse.

Nietzsche was prodigal in devising solutions to these difficulties. His Naumburg notebooks teem with insights made on the fly, notations that are often vividly expressed and that reflect the energy and excitement of a mind expanding its vision and range. Nonetheless, they can be difficult to decipher by a reader who lacks the context in which they were first recorded. Also, Nietzsche frequently outran his own mind, that is, he would no sooner sketch an idea than he would glimpse a larger perspective and abandon the first for the fresher outlook, often repeating the process until he left a trail of vestiges in his wake. It would be gratifying to state that he made a clear and comprehensive breakthrough that either resolved his problems or took them to a higher level. Had he had done so, he would probably have written a paper to record it. His notebooks display rather a host of often brilliantly written passages that push at intellectual boundaries but do not quite transcend them. This is not to deny that a comprehensive reconstruction of an underlying theory could not be gained. To do so, however, would exceed the scope of this biography, which must limit itself to the following sadly inadequate summations.

First, Nietzsche examined philological principles which, despite their pretensions to objectivity, he considered fundamentally aesthetic. To give an example already discussed by James I. Porter, he noted that when the Alexandrians tested passages in the Homeric text for authenticity, they

[73] KSAB II: 255. [74] KSAB II: 262.

were drawn to those sections by their own taste. When they anathematized or approved lines, they couched their judgments in scholarly terms, but ultimately their decisions were based on the perceived poetic vitality of the passage under review.[75]

Second, Nietzsche studied the history of scholarship (*Wissenschaft*) during ancient times, arguing that these activities were parasitic on the works of artistic genius that they proposed to examine. Scholarship was devised to help those not poetically endowed to assimilate and propagate the works of their visionary superiors. He did not construe this view as inherently negative. While the premise might prove humbling for those who overestimated their profession, his primary focus was on the ways scholarship historically developed – the methods through which an audience codified and refined its reception of works that it already found admirable. He proposed then to show how these initial efforts were further modified and elaborated as scholarship endured through the ages, issuing in the work of the classical philologists of his own time.[76]

Finally, Nietzsche began to reconsider certain practices of scholarship, such as the acknowledgement of sources.[77] A personal experience may have served as the catalyst for this move. After the young man's paper on Diogenes Laertius won the university prize, Nietzsche showed the original to Diederich Volkmann, the Suda expert with whom he had been working since at least the previous summer. This was the first time that Volkmann had seen the paper, and he believed that Nietzsche was planning to publish under his own name discoveries that were properly his. In a letter to Ritschl Nietzsche explained that the two had been working independently and had come by separate ways to similar conclusions. "Neither of us has priority on that [discovery]; but it would be embarrassing and troubling for me, given my friendship with the excellent Volkmann, if through earlier publication my work achieved an *apparent* priority."[78] (Emphasis Nietzsche's.) Accordingly, he asked permission for Volkmann to publish an article that would complement his own. Ritschl agreed, but to Nietzsche's annoyance, Volkmann first delayed, then decided not to issue a paper after all, holding up Nietzsche's piece in the process. The young man professed himself surprised that a professor from Schulpforte

---

[75] Porter 2000a: 63.
[76] This is the principal theme of the literary history mentioned in Chapter 12, Section 3.
[77] Egon Flaig has argued that scholars of the time frequently borrowed from one another without attribution. Flaig 2003: 11. He fails to explain why so many writers (Volkmann, for example, and later Bernays) complained of such appropriation.
[78] KSAB II: 244.

could so mismanage his time, but the reins were back in his hands.[79] He dispatched his final work promptly to Ritschl, adding an appendix in the spring.

Nonetheless, the experience possibly prompted him to consider the supposed duty of a scholar to acknowledge sources. In his notebooks Nietzsche argued that while it was plainly dishonest for mediocre researchers not to credit predecessors, "the superior thinker" so transfigures any ideas received that to identify their originators becomes an irrelevance.[80] One can trace at least one source of Nietzsche's later aversion to footnotes here. Curiously for a historian, he seems only concerned with issues of originality, whereas at least since Ranke and arguably since Niebuhr the function of footnotes has been rather to provide evidence for an assertion so that later researchers could follow a trail to its source.[81]

Meanwhile, in these and other deliberations too numerous to discuss, Nietzsche took philology into his own hands in the sense that he tried to determine for himself its origins, functions, methods, and limits. He could do this only by asking himself what aspects of philology seemed true to him and following through on the implications. (One might recall his contention that scholarship was ultimately based on aesthetic grounds.) To an extent, he was invoking the motto, "*Genoi' hoios essi*," not just with regard to his extracurricular behavior, but taking it into the house of *Wissenschaft*. In the spring of 1867 he had made that union literal – by imprinting a personal motto onto a technical paper submitted to the academy. Now, during his year in Naumburg, he worked to bring these two worlds yet closer. Personally, he would observe his own values; academically, he would discover an approach to philology true to his intuitions.[82] Nietzsche knew the established rules, and he could obey them when he wished. Left to his own devices, however, he took the opportunity to see things differently, exploring the bases of scholarship in the light of his own responses.

Unfortunately, he had peers and even superiors to satisfy. As Nietzsche surely knew, the methods and scope of scholarship are not the creation of an individual human being but reflect the protocols of a community that has constructed its norms over millennia. Accordingly, one might consider how dangerous, both academically and perhaps epistemologically, his course of action might be. That the young man was brilliant and insightful

---

[79] KSAB II: 251, 255. For Volkmann's letter see KGB I-3: 228. [80] KGW I-5: 38, but see 367.
[81] Grafton 1997: 15 presents what in Nietzsche's time would have been the standard view: "The text persuades, the notes prove."
[82] For a fundamental critique of philology, see KGW I-5: 96–98.

goes without saying. However, he was also only twenty-three years old, and there were aspects of the academic regimen which he had not yet experienced over time and so could not appreciate. He also might not realize – although in the end perhaps he did not care – how viscerally and unanimously university authorities might respond when he put his new views into action. He would discover this in 1872, when he published his first book.

5

In early March, 1868, five months into his service, Nietzsche suffered a serious accident.[83] He had been housebound throughout winter and when spring arrived, he was anxious to resume horseback riding. One day, while working with what he called "the most fiery and unruly animal in the battery," he tried to leap on its back and missed, his chest striking the front of the saddle. He sensed a quivering tear on his left side but tried to ignore it. After a day and a half of mounting pain he twice fainted; and on the following day he found himself "almost nailed to the bed" with severe pain and high fever.[84] The military doctor discovered that he had torn a couple of muscles and bruised the breastbone. It was soon evident that he also suffered internal bleeding and infection. For ten days Nietzsche endured pain, fever, and eventually enterogastritis. Not only was he bleeding internally, but the pus exuding from the infection was subcutaneous as well and had no way to exit. The doctor had to cut repeatedly through the skin in order to leech it, and eventually a drainage canal was installed so that the liquid could discharge externally. During this time Nietzsche received morphine nightly so that he could sleep,[85] and his letters indicate that he occasionally passed out. Writing Ritschl, he stated that he had to relearn how to walk.[86] Worse, his wounds did not heal, and eventually physicians diagnosed damage to the sternum.

On April 1, a little less than a month after the accident, he received his only military promotion, from private to private first class. Such an advance might be viewed as ironic since, given his pain and weakness, Nietzsche was surely incapable of performing any military duties. Instead,

---

[83] The accident probably took place on March 5 or 6. See Volz 1990: 362, as well as KSAB II: 261, 292. An earlier mention of illness (KSAB II: 259) clearly does not refer to the accident.
[84] KSAB II: 292.
[85] KSAB II: 262. Volz summarizes, somewhat extends Nietzsche's account, and gives the medicines he was administered: Volz 1990: 153–155, 361–365.
[86] KSAB II: 267.

he seized the opportunity to rechannel his sufferings into an extraordinary burst of productivity.[87] Unaware of the accident, Rohde had sent him a study of "The ass," a work at that time attributed to Lucian,[88] and he asked for comments. Despite his medical condition, Nietzsche obliged, writing a half a page of critique, while citing authorities and correcting infelicities in his friend's presentation.[89] During the following month (between April 3 and May 12), he read a dissertation on "Kant's view on freedom of the will," reviewed an edition of Hesiod's *Theogony* for a Leipzig journal, added an addendum to his Diogenes Laertius article, gathered materials for a proposed dissertation, "The concept of the organic since Kant," and reworked his Simonides essay into an article for the *Rheinisches Museum*.[90] He suffered severely while accomplishing all this but continued anyway, reporting to Ritschl on May 26, "The wound on the sternum is still open, and the suppuration has begun to invade the bones, so that recently to my astonishment a piece of my skeleton, an ossicle, has appeared." He added with some pride and undeniable truth, "My patience wears thin but on the whole intense philological and philosophical activity keeps me strong and upright."[91]

This extraordinary productivity may reflect a dam breaking after he was no longer oppressed by military duties. It may also express his relief at having specific tasks to accomplish after his frustration with the chronically unraveling Democritus project. It certainly indicates awareness that his time could be short and that if he didn't produce now the opportunity might be lost forever. As he wrote to Rohde:

> Not only is my illness not over ... but the worst is probably yet to come. The suppuration continues, the breastbone is affected, and today the doctor even proposed an operation in the very near future. At issue is the rejection of a whole chunk of bones; further, they must cut off the weak parts and then "reduce" ... that is, "saw off" the affected bones, namely, the breastbone. When one is under the knife and saw of the surgeons, you know well by what a slight thread hangs the thing that one calls life. There comes a little suppuration fever – out goes the little light. My feelings were strange when the first little bone of my skeleton suddenly swam out of a drainage canal and it slowly became evident that plans for a Paris trip or for *Habilitation* were possibly impossible. The precariousness of existence is never so evident as when one gets to see a little piece of one's skeleton.

---

[87] It should be recalled that throughout this period he was at home and cared for by his mother and sister. Franziska recalls "the twenty-one weeks spent nursing." Franziska Nietzsche 1994: 40.
[88] This is no longer considered to be by Lucian and is cited under the name of Pseudo-Lucian.
[89] KSAB II: 262–264. After writing this, Nietzsche collapsed and had to wait three days before completing the letter.
[90] KSAB II: 265, 266, 267, 274, 279.   [91] KSAB II: 280.

Incidentally, I work eagerly "while it is day" on philological issues ... I have generally devoted my involuntary idleness to a greater focus on and tidying up of my studies. Specific intentions are poured into a more specific form. Half-sensed insights germinate on all sides. No, dear friend, one does not extinguish me quite so quickly.[92]

Nietzsche's aspirations were not limited to philology. In the letter to Ritschl he mentions "philological and *philosophical* activity," (emphasis added), and during this period of physical prostration he decided to get not one, but two degrees, the second in philosophy.[93] This would involve much work and divide his focus – exactly the compromised concentration he had deplored at Bonn.[94] Nonetheless, he acted on this ambition for a while, and to win his degree in philosophy he decided to write a paper on "The concept of the organic since Kant" – he also called it "On teleology" – a work "half-philosophic, half-scientific," very much as Lange's had been.[95] Although Nietzsche did considerable research and wrote Deussen that the preliminary work on his thesis was "fairly complete,"[96] the notes he compiled are sufficiently difficult to interpret that few have made a serious attempt.[97] It appears that he intended to reject teleological approaches of any kind, a stance that reflects his understanding of Lange and Democritus. It accords less well with his enthusiasm for Schopenhauer, whose work, as one might expect in a philosophy based on will, is replete with teleological processes, however non-teleological it might prove in the end. It was probably also during this period that Nietzsche wrote an extended critique of Schopenhauer's metaphysics.[98] While Sandro Barbera has revealed that these notes drew on the arguments of others (notably Rudolf Haym),[99] Nietzsche does not dispute those criticisms, and while Haym's (and by extension, Nietzsche's) analysis is not quite fair, it scarcely mattered. He had already been persuaded by the devastating arguments of Friedrich Lange. Neither of these philosophic sketches, incidentally, was completed. Nietzsche never mentioned the Schopenhauer critique, and he abandoned the Kant dissertation as unsuitable.[100]

---

[92] KSAB II: 289. For the biblical quotation see John 9:4.   [93] KSAB II: 265.
[94] See Chapter 6, Sections 1 and 5.
[95] In letters to friends Nietzsche twice lists the title as "[On] the concept of the organic since Kant."(KSAB II: 269 and 274.) In his papers the heading is given as "On teleology."
[96] KSAB II: 269.   [97] Exceptions: Crawford 1988 and Swift 2005.
[98] KGW I-4: 418–427, 429–430. For a summary of his arguments in English, see Janaway 1998: 18–19; for translations into English, see Janaway 1998:258–265, and Crawford 1988: 226–232, reprinted in Ansell Pearson and Large 2006: 24–29.
[99] Barbera 1995 and 1999.   [100] KSAB II: 274.

As he watched bits of his breastbone emerge and began frequently to compare himself to Sophocles' Philoctetes, Nietzsche turned with surprising intensity to an old friend, the often harangued and patronized Paul Deussen. In fairness to Nietzsche, Deussen had behaved deviously, making promises he had not kept – notably an assurance that he would enroll in philology at Leipzig. He had also silently and repeatedly ignored his friend's entreaties to visit him either at the university or at Naumburg. Nietzsche now began to request, even to implore, a visit. At the beginning of June when his illness was far advanced, he wrote, "When you leave home again [after the holidays] to endure the torture in Berlin, force yourself to travel to Naumburg."[101] Three weeks later (June 22), he described his situation vividly – "One small bone after the other comes out of the drainage canal and shows that the breastbone is badly damaged" – and he appended what, despite its humorous tone, amounted to a plea: "You must ... visit Naumburg on your way back to Berlin. Basically it is practically your duty to visit your sick friend sometime. It would be absolutely too horrible not to do it; even the divine Plato would grant you no absolution for this sin."[102]

Deussen did not come, nor is any letter extant giving his reasons. Instead Nietzsche found himself visited by two of the students who had promised – and failed – to write papers for the abortive *Festschrift*. One of them, Ernst Windisch, was devoted to Nietzsche and would do him several notable favors in the coming year. (It was he who had procured his friend the position as critic for the distinguished Leipzig journal.) Meanwhile, Windisch had recently switched his field of concentration to Sanskrit, and he now studied under Hermann Brockhaus, husband to Ottilie Brockhaus, a sister of Richard Wagner, a connection that would turn out to be important. Other than these two, Nietzsche seems to have received no visits from his many colleagues in Leipzig, a reflection on the short attention span of male undergraduates but also an indication of how few his close friends really were.

Meanwhile, Nietzsche was correct when he warned that an operation impended. On June 25, he visited the surgeon, Dr. Richard Volkmann, in Halle. Volkmann had been discovered by Franziska,[103] and of all Nietzsche's doctors, he was incomparably the most enterprising and had

---

[101] KSAB II: 282. Although Nietzsche does not mention his illness in this letter, he concludes, "Write me in Naumburg. Your letter will reach me so long as there is still life in me. Yet even this flickering thing can sometime go out" (285).
[102] KSAB II: 290. [103] Franziska Nietzsche 1994: 40.

the most distinguished future before him.[104] During the War of 1866 he had treated soldiers in the aftermath of the Battle of Königgrätz, and he become an expert in the treatment of gangrene. Nietzsche caught him near the outset of his career, and this enterprising doctor may have saved the future philosopher's life. Volkmann advised him to postpone surgery and instead spend a month at his own spa in nearby Bad Wittekind.[105] If he did not then improve, he could go under the knife. Nietzsche left no record of how he responded to this interview, but he apparently returned that very afternoon to Naumburg, packed, and left for Leipzig where he visited the Ritschls, as well as friends. He then proceeded to Wittekind on June 30. He must have been under exceptional pressure, and apparently at this time he bonded with Ritschl's wife, Sophie Ritschl, with new appreciation.[106]

Sophie Ritschl had presented young Nietzsche a book on music.[107] Shortly after entering the spa, he followed her example by giving someone else a book in turn. His own selection, however, proved less felicitous, and its reception reveals much about dynamics in the Naumburg household at this time. After his ten-month sojourn at home, the longest he had stayed there since the age of thirteen, Nietzsche's departure must have left a vacuum in the family situation. Elisabeth described the sense of absence in a letter. "Where are the animated dialogues between you and dear Mama? Where then the pleasant call: Liesbeth! that draws me as a neutral party into the fight and where we together decide to what extent the lovely goddess Aesthetics has been insulted? Now all that is over; the rest is silence."[108] If she was already mourning her brother's departure, his gift cannot have cheered her. Elisabeth's birthday had fallen on July 10, and the spa-bound Nietzsche sent her a volume entitled *Order and beauty at the domestic hearth*. Elisabeth, who was neither beautiful nor inordinately devoted to housework, responded ironically to this selection and reminded her brother that she was not without intelligence, as she proved by citing (and correctly applying) a phrase from Schopenhauer's *Parerga and paralipomena*.[109] Perhaps responding to a hidden concern behind her brother's gift, she also advised him that she was quite at ease at the prospect of becoming an "old maid." She made this comment with wry humor, but it was potentially a serious issue for Elisabeth, not so much for romantic as

---

[104] Trieder 2006. 38–41. Volkmann would later pioneer a host of surgical procedures and receive titles of nobility. He also wrote a book of fairy tales so successfully received that it is still available in a Reclam edition.
[105] Wittekind is now part of Halle.   [106] KSAB II: 296.
[107] For an extended study of the book and Nietzsche's response, see Prange 2011.
[108] KGB I-3: 271.   [109] KGB I-3: 274

for economic reasons. If her brother had brought up this possibility obliquely, her mother, who had always been concerned about her marriageability, may be presumed to have spelled out such a fate in graphic detail, perhaps citing the cases of two family members[110] who, never having married or being widowed, sometimes lived in genuine poverty and dependency. Tempers were clearly rising in the Naumburg home, for Elisabeth shortly decamped to go on holiday in eastern Saxony and in a letter she mentions squabbles.[111]

One would think that if Nietzsche was remanded to a spa and trying to heal so as to avoid surgery, he would live quietly, take the waters, drink tea, and have his wounds treated daily with iodine.[112] It appears that his sojourn began that way, but three weeks into his stay his physician congratulated him on a speedy recovery and told him that an operation would not be necessary.[113] Nietzsche was not yet discharged, but he seized the opportunity temporarily to depart Wittekind in order to visit the Ritschls and to attend a music festival at Altenburg.[114] This unorthodox convalescence seems to have done him good. By July 29, he was back in Wittekind and was told by Volkmann that he could depart "in a few days."[115] With the assistance of his bustling mother (and possibly his sister), he was able to bid the spa farewell on August 2.

The brutal ordeal which had lasted five months was now over, its only permanent signs, scars and a dip in the breast where bones had been lost.[116] Nietzsche was still vulnerable to relapse and had to take baths and observe precautions, but fundamentally he was healed.[117] As for the army, he looked forward to being declared unfit for service,[118] although he would not be officially discharged until his birthday, a full year after induction.[119] "My career as warrior has not set the stage on fire," he conceded,[120] and for a time he tried to redeem this misfortune by pursuing (unsuccessfully) earlier attempts to become an officer. It was during this period that at Rohde's request[121] he had a photograph made of himself, apparently in an officer's uniform, for it depicts him with a sword. Aside from the damage to his chest, this picture would be his sole memento from his arduous year in the army. It is regrettable, then, that it turned out to be unflattering, a judgment Nietzsche himself implicitly rendered when he tried to explain to Rohde what had gone wrong. It showed him, he admitted, in a somewhat aggressive pose, accosting his

---

[110] Sidonie Knieling and Lina Nietzsche. [111] KGB I-3: 282. [112] KSAB II: 300.
[113] KSAB II: 308. [114] See Prange 2011: 58 ff. [115] KSAB II: 301, 302. [116] KSAB II: 308.
[117] KSAB II: 311. [118] KSAB II: 308–309. [119] KSAB II: 324–325. [120] KSAB II: 292.
[121] KGB I-3: 247.

friend rudely with drawn saber and with "an irritable and unpleasant" expression on his face. "But why does the miserable photographer annoy us . . . ? Why must we always be ready with our sword? And when we're about to rush precipitously upon [him], what does he do? He ducks under his mantle and shouts, 'Freeze!'"[122]

[122] KSAB II: 307.

CHAPTER 14

The gift horse

My future lies in the dark before me, but that doesn't bother me.[1]

I

During the final months of his convalescence Nietzsche had ample grounds for satisfaction. His military career was drawing to a close. His latest paper on the *Danaelied* had been accepted by the *Rheinisches Museum*. He had just escaped a surgery that could have proved fatal. Having weathered such challenges, he had little to fear from what might be construed as the endgame of his student years. In the German states of the time he would be required to pass a grueling round of examinations, then take two degrees: the *Promotion* (his doctorate) and the *Habilitation* (an advanced degree, which served as a prerequisite for the right to teach).[2] In theory each of the latter would require a separate dissertation, the second quite ambitious; yet none of this inordinately oppressed him. He seems to have believed that he could skip the tests,[3] and he showed little concern for the theses he would be required to write.[4] He had, after all, produced a great deal already.

Beyond school there loomed the dazzling prospect of the trip to Paris. Nietzsche was not sure when he would travel there, but according to Ritschl and in at least one of Nietzsche's own letters, he had set the date for the following Easter, that is, in less than six months.[5] His visions of

---

[1] KGW I-4: 506.
[2] The *Habilitation* did not in itself confer permission to teach but it was a prerequisite. Paulsen 1885: 130–131. For a brief history, see Boockmann 1999: 211–214.
[3] KSAB II: 276. Nietzsche was indeed spared the examinations. However, this exception was unique in the history of the university. Heise 2000: 181.
[4] Nietzsche frequently speculated on dissertation topics such as Hesychius (KGW I-5: 71–73, 310–315) and patronymics (KGW I-5: 315–319, 321–328, 329–330, 331–333). For other examples, see KGW I-4: 437, 32; KGW I-5: 177, 338, 356; KSAB II: 214, 259, 274, 324.
[5] KGB I-4: 548; KSAB II: 309, 311.

this idyll were dreamy and unfocused. He and Rohde were aware of the city's unsavory reputation – Rohde wryly cited a novel called *Ruined in Paris*[6] – and Nietzsche humorously envisioned a life of romantic dissipation "so as to learn the divine power of the cancan and to drink 'yellow poison' [absinthe]."[7] More often he imagined himself and other invited friends[8] as constituting a hub of German scholarship within the city.[9] Above all, he envisioned forming with Rohde "a pair of philosophical *flâneurs* that people would get used to seeing everywhere together."[10] Such fantasies were encouraged by his even more enthusiastic comrade, for this was a shared enterprise, and much of its appeal lay in the prospect of reunion. "But please don't forget our Paris trip," Rohde entreated. "My real reason for going is not philological or ethical but the opportunity to spend time with you before we embark on sterner tasks."[11]

Given such prospects, it is unsurprising that Nietzsche should have reentered Leipzig on a discernible note of triumph.[12] As mentioned earlier, he had decided to discard the odious name, "*Student*."[13] Now he made it clear that he had also outgrown the juvenile activities that went with that demeaning status. (He would abstain from theater and inns.)[14] He further instructed his family to write him as "Herr Doctor Nietzsche," a request which showed that he was getting the jump on a new and more distinguished identity.[15]

Finally, he had resolved "to become more of a society figure."[16] He must have mentioned this ambition to Windisch, for two days after his arrival in Leipzig his friend arranged for him to room in the mansion of Karl Biedermann, a formidable ideologue on the Leipzig political scene.[17] Although Nietzsche made fun of his host, he was also impressed and understandably so.[18] Initially drawn by philology, Biedermann had begun his career as a philosophy professor and in his youth had published a two-volume study of German philosophy from Kant to his own time.[19] He had then turned to politics and throughout the Revolution of 1848 had

---

[6] KGB I-3: 243.   [7] KSAB II: 304.
[8] Mushacke, Gersdorff, Deussen, Romundt, and Kleinpaul were also asked to visit. See KSAB II: 205, 309, 313; KGB I-3: 245–246.
[9] See, for example, KGW I-4: 434–435.   [10] KSAB II: 358.   [11] KGB I-3: 297–298. See also 311.
[12] KSAB II: 310.   [13] Chapter 12, Section 4.   [14] KSAB II: 330, 331.   [15] KSAB II: 326.
[16] KSAB II: 321.
[17] The following is based on Bazillion 1990: 44–48, 50–53, 63–89, 153–184, 219, 246–251, 313.
[18] KSAB II: 331. He had already begun to mock the man as early as August 1866. KSAB II: 150, 159. See also 181.
[19] The philosophers treated were Kant, Fichte, Schelling, Hegel, and Herbart.

held influential offices.[20] The royalist authorities had already threatened him for such leftist activities, and in 1853–1854 they sentenced him to two months in prison and the loss of his post at the university. Nearly ten years in exile followed, during which Biedermann edited several periodicals including the *Deutsche Allgemeine Zeitung*, a review read by liberals throughout Germany. Not until 1863 had he returned to Leipzig. Two years later, he regained his professorship.[21]

It was in this man's house that Nietzsche would spend the next few months; and with the dwelling went Biedermann's social and political environment, including much of Leipzig's political and cultural elite. Nietzsche had heretofore viewed the city's haut-monde from the distance of undergraduate ignominy. Now he dined twice daily with a fashionable set (although today some of the guests sound a little louche), and while he might mock these figures, he was probably pleased to find himself in their midst. Among the table guests with whom he consorted were an actress whom he and Rohde had once admired and the son of the Paris music publisher, Gustave Flaxland.[22] At Biedermann's Nietzsche also encountered Heinrich Laube, the playwright, director, and former friend of Wagner, who had just moved from Vienna to take the reins of the Leipzig *Stadttheater*.[23] Nietzsche clearly enjoyed socializing with these glamorous figures: he sent a photograph of the actress to Rohde and he described Laube at length in a letter.[24] He also invited Gustav Krug to visit his new abode so that his friend could appreciate his change in status since the previous year, "when I was half Schopenhauer, half a junior officer."[25]

Nietzsche was aware that he would eventually have to settle down and complete his graduation requirements, and he expected afterward to spend several years as a *Privatdozent*.[26] The latter were degreed teachers with no salaried position, who were allowed to tutor students and deliver lectures in

---

[20] James Sheehan called him called "the prime mover" of the Revolution of 1848 in Saxony. Sheehan 1989: 670. Among other activities Biedermann was a member of the delegation that presented the pan-German crown to Friedrich Wilhelm IV. (The king notoriously refused.) As Nietzsche noted, his wife was sister to Otto Koch, the mayor of Leipzig. KSAB II: 331.

[21] After unification Biedermann would become a representative to the Reichstag.

[22] Flaxland held the French rights to much of Schumann's music, as well as to four of Wagner's operas *Rienzi, Der fliegende Holländer, Tannhäuser*, and *Lohengrin*. In a letter Nietzsche called his tablemate "the greatest music publisher in Paris," but he seems to have confused the father with the son. KSAB II: 331.

[23] In his youth Laube had been a good friend to Richard Wagner. However, he had just published a negative review of *Die Meistersinger*, which was reprinted in a Leipzig journal, and Wagner never forgave him. Newman 1933–1946 IV: 143–145.

[24] KSAB II: 332, 351.

[25] KSAB II: 343. Nietzsche was of course not a junior office the year before, although he was in training to receive a commission.

[26] KSAB II: 329.

the same halls as the professors themselves.[27] *Privatdozents* often had to linger for decades while waiting for some faculty member to die and free a post; and Nietzsche referred to their lot as one of "distilled hopelessness."[28] Yet he probably looked forward to entering their ranks, for *Privatdozents* occupied a middle ground between professor and student and therefore enjoyed less formal commitment.[29]

In any case, he confessed himself in no hurry to secure academic office. "Do you really want to jump as quickly as possible and with both feet immediately into a school position?" he asked Deussen. "My wish is the opposite: to keep free from such external fetters as long as possible."[30] Nietzsche might be a tireless worker but he never liked to live under constraints ("*external* fetters"), and he intended to postpone professional life as long as he could. Meanwhile, he had other affairs to occupy him. He still had not completed Ritschl's index, and during the first week of November he lectured the Philological Society on Menippus and the Cynics. He also reviewed several books for Friedrich Zarncke's *Literarisches Centralblatt*, the periodical to which he had contributed the previous spring.[31] Conspicuously absent from these activities was any sort of directed work that could issue in a dissertation, although Nietzsche made copious entries on this topic in his notebooks.

His concern with social distinction may have reflected a shift in his legal status. On October 15, 1868, Nietzsche had turned twenty-four years old, and he was apparently now permitted to emancipate himself from the control of his guardian.[32] The latter had been appointed at his father's death and had disbursed funds to Nietzsche from 1849 to the present, often using Franziska as an intermediary. Although Bernhard Daechsel's supervision had never been oppressive, the very existence of such an arrangement would have chafed on his fiercely independent ward. It appears that the legal transfer was complete in mid-November, and Nietzsche could at last control his own finances.[33] It was at this time that he at last informed his mother that he could also attend to his own laundry.[34]

---

[27] See Paulsen 1895: 126; McClelland 1980: 166–168; Fallon 1980: 43–44.   [28] KSAB II: 276.
[29] For Nietzsche's embrace of this status, see KSAB II: 329.   [30] KSAB II: 206.
[31] At the *Centralblatt* he shared critical duties with his former Schulpforte tutor, Max Heinze. Meanwhile, Alfred Fleckeisen, a Latinist and friend of Ritschl, had requested submissions for the *Jahrbücher für classische Philologie*, a request Nietzsche accepted, although he seems never to have written for that venue. KGB I-4: 20–21.
[32] Although Nietzsche celebrated his twenty-fourth birthday on October 15, 1868, the legal proceedings drew on until at least mid-November. Since Nietzsche was in Leipzig the arrangements seem to have been handled mostly by Franziska.
[33] I am unable to discover the sum which Nietzsche inherited from Erdmuthe and now had at his disposal. It was considerable enough for Ritschl to take note. Stroux 1925: 35.
[34] KSAB II: 333.

Nietzsche's recent birthday also figured symbolically. He believed that by the age of twenty-four an individual's frame of mind was fundamentally formed and to that extent fixed. As he would write several months later, "I should consider that a human being who is twenty-four years old already has the most important aspects of his life behind him, even if he only later achieves what makes his life worthwhile. Until about this age the young soul still extracts the typical from all the experiences that form its life and thought, and it will never, ever emerge from the world of these types."[35] While this judgment may have been influenced by the age at which it was delivered, Nietzsche does seem to have believed he was now entering into his majority in a more than legal sense. Liberated from his previous shyness, he embraced Leipzig's social life, consorting extra-academically with his teachers[36] and resuming horseback riding.[37] In addition to his prestigious work for Zarncke, he was hired by Biedermann to serve as a newspaper critic (covering both music and lectures) for the *Deutsche Allgemeine Zeitung*, a position which led to him sitting beside distinguished music critics at concerts.[38] He was also admitted to Laube's salons, where he would have been privy to much behind-the-scenes information and gossip.[39] For the first time in his life, Friedrich Nietzsche cut a glamorous figure, and he seemed to like it.

2

At some point during the year 1868 Nietzsche became smitten with the music of Richard Wagner. It cannot be proved that he disliked the work of this composer before, but the evidence suggests vacillation between tepid enthusiasm[40] and disdainful rejection.[41] As late as his recent stay in Naumburg (and quite possibly the spring of 1868) he could give a list of six musical passages which served him as touchstones, and all were

---

[35] KGW I-5: 45.
[36] In addition to his outings with the Ritschls, Nietzsche socialized with his teacher Georg Curtius and his wife (KSAB II: 336) and with the Brockhaus families. KSAB II: 347.
[37] KSAB II: 347. See also KGB I-4: 534.
[38] KSAB II: 332. No articles by Nietzsche have been identified as appearing in this newspaper. KGB I-4: 525.
[39] Thus, Nietzsche informs his family that Biedermann was the illegitimate brother of Friedrich Ferdinand von Beust, the former Minister of State and Foreign Affairs of Saxony. KSAB II: 334. For admission to Laube's salon, see KSAB II: 373.
[40] See Prange 2011.
[41] See, for example, KSAB II: 174, KGW I-4: 127–128, and KGW I-4: 518, where Nietzsche quarrels with the Wagnerite Hüffer. Prior to 1867 Nietzsche seems occasionally to have liked Wagner's writings, but not his music.

composed by either Schumann or Beethoven.[42] As that year progressed, however, his taste began to change.[43] In a letter to Sophie Ritschl, dated July 2, 1868, Nietzsche alludes to an unspecified faux pas and concedes, "The clubfoot of Wagner and Schopenhauer is difficult to hide."[44] Given the young man's devotion to Schopenhauer, his linkage of that name with Wagner's suggests an extraordinary rise in the latter's stock. Significantly, *Die Meistersinger von Nürnberg*, "my favorite opera" as he would later call it,[45] had premiered in Munich just two weeks earlier, on June 21. That event was closely covered by the *Neue Zeitschrift für Musik*, the distinguished music journal emanating from Leipzig,[46] and Nietzsche was surely aware. He was at last encountering a music drama by the composer that spoke to him personally, and Frederick Love has suggested that he purchased a copy of the piano score at this time.[47] (Shortly thereafter he would be able to play the "Prize song" from that opera for others.) Further, as may be recalled, Nietzsche's month at Wittekind (July 1868) centered on music, and he left at one point to attend a festival of new music at Altenburg.[48] While no works by Wagner were performed there, he would have been, so to speak, in the lion's den – Wagner was one of the four co-founders[49] – and he would have encountered enthusiasts fresh from having heard *Meistersinger* in person.[50]

Whatever may have led to the change, it appeared to have been comparatively lasting, as letters to Deussen and Rohde attest.[51] In early October Nietzsche came across some reviews hostile to the composer written by Otto Jahn, and he declared them deficient in vision.[52] He probably introduced the "Prize song" from *Meistersinger* to Rohde during a visit the latter paid in August, and he certainly played it for Sophie Ritschl in Leipzig. If there was any doubt before, an experience in a concert house seemed to seal his conversion. Under the auspices of the *Deutsche Allgemeine Zeitung*,[53] he attended a concert on October 27, and wrote, "This evening I was ... revitalized with both the Prelude to *Tristan und*

---

[42] KGW I-4: 434. [43] KGW I-4: 430.
[44] KSAB II: 299. Nietzsche may have been taking issue with Ehlert's book, which Sophie Ritschl gave him. See Chapter 13, Section 5. Ehlert was at best diffident concerning Wagner. Prange 2011: 56–57.
[45] KSAB III: 4. See also KSAB II: 364. Compare Love 1963: 63. [46] Love 1963: 52.
[47] Love 1963: 53–54.
[48] He had arrived with the book on music given him by Sophie Ritschl; he immediately ordered music paper; and he left after several weeks to attend a music conference.
[49] According to Martine Prange, the festival was founded by Franz Liszt, Richard Wagner, Hans von Bülow, and Franz Brendel in 1861. Prange 2011: 583.
[50] See KSAB II: 305–306, where Nietzsche mentions "Side note [*Excurs*] on Wagner's *Meistersinger*."
[51] KSAB II: 316, 322. [52] KSAB II: 322.
[53] No reviews by Nietzsche appear to have been published in this newspaper. See n. 38.

Isolde and the Overture to *Meistersinger*. I cannot convince my heart to be critically cool to this music. Every fiber, every nerve quivers in me, and it's been a long time since I have had such an enduring feeling of rapture as with the latter overture."[54]

By the end of October at the latest then, Nietzsche had succumbed to the spell of Wagner's music and to that extent was a passionate Wagnerian. He even dreamed of enjoying some proximity to the great man, for, as mentioned previously, Windisch was pursuing graduate studies in Sanskrit under the supervision of Hermann Brockhaus, and he therefore knew the latter's wife, the former Ottilie Wagner. As Nietzsche had written before leaving Naumburg, "I ... have decided to address myself to a woman of whom wonderful things are told, the wife of Professor Brockhaus and sister of Richard Wagner. Windisch ... has an extraordinary opinion of her abilities."[55]

There is no evidence that Nietzsche followed through on this resolve. However, his wish was unexpectedly granted due to a series of events which had nothing to do with him but had taken place mostly in Switzerland, Bavaria, and Italy. In November 1868 and despite the stunning success of *Die Meistersinger*, Richard Wagner found himself in a state of crisis. Although his first wife was still alive, he had plunged into an affair with Cosima von Bülow, and their four-year liaison had just reached a turning point. Cosima, the daughter of Franz Liszt, was married to Hans von Bülow, a master pianist and one of Wagner's greatest champions.[56] Although von Bülow was not happy about his wife's relationship, he had suffered it, even as Cosima bore two daughters to Wagner in circumstances difficult to overlook. Ludwig II, the king of Bavaria, had also been compromised, for Richard and Cosima persuaded him to sign a public declaration that the king himself could vouch for the purity of their affections.[57]

On October 3, 1868, less than two weeks before Nietzsche left Naumburg for Leipzig, Cosima, pregnant with Wagner's third child, finally requested a divorce. Her beleaguered husband balked at first, but the secret was out. On November 1, Wagner went to Munich in hopes of placating the king, who was now aware that he had been publicly gulled.

---

[54] KSAB II: 332. This was not the first time Nietzsche had heard these pieces. Apart from his experiences with the piano scores of *Tristan* (1862) and *Meistersinger* (1868), he almost certainly attended a concert in November 1865, in which both pieces were played. KGB I-4: 385.

[55] KSAB II: 321. [56] Von Bülow conducted the *Meistersinger* premiere.

[57] This paragraph and the one that follows are based on Gregor-Dellin 1983: 341, 370–371, 376, 378–382, and Newman 1933–1946 IV: 52, 136, 141–142, 153–173.

Ludwig refused to see him, and it occurred to the composer that he might lose his royal pension, an unpleasant prospect, as it constituted his principal source of income. Faced with the possible loss of Cosima, the certain public exposure, and the jeopardy of his relationship with the king, Wagner reflected that it was time to see his family, and he decided to travel across Bavaria and Thuringia to visit Ottilie Brockhaus in Leipzig. (Another sister, Luise, also lived in that city.) On November 2, a month after Cosima had written her fatal letter, he left Munich, and one week later – still with no resolution in sight – he made the acquaintance of Friedrich Nietzsche.

Since Wagner was traveling incognito to avoid publicity (the Brockhaus servants had been sworn to silence) there was no way for Nietzsche to know on his own that the composer was in Leipzig. Intimates of the family circle were aware, however, and these included Ernst Windisch, who on November 6 wrote his friend: "If you want to meet Richard Wagner, come to the theater café at quarter to four."[58] From there the two men rushed to the Brockhaus home, only to find out that the composer had gone out. The family then graciously extended an invitation for November 8, the following Sunday night. Their willingness to entertain the young men reflected the wish of Wagner himself, who, earlier in the week had made the acquaintance of Sophie Ritschl. When the composer played her the "Prize song" from *Meistersinger*, she had responded that she already knew it, having heard it performed by one Friedrich Nietzsche. Wagner then asked to meet this admirable young man, and the encounter had led to Windisch's note and now the Sunday invitation.

When Nietzsche and Windisch arrived on Sunday, they found themselves alone with immediate members of the Brockhaus family and with "the master," as most of his associates called the great composer. Wagner could be extraordinarily entertaining, and he charmed Nietzsche that night, making fun of effete conductors, the Leipzig dialect, and university philosophers, even as he confided that he too was an aficionado of Arthur Schopenhauer. He also played and sang passages from *Meistersinger* both before and after dinner, and at the evening's end he read autobiographical accounts of his student life in Leipzig – stories that so amused Nietzsche that he could not think of them afterward without laughing. Wagner also invited the young man to visit him at his villa on Lake Lucerne, and he asked him to instruct Ottilie Brockhaus and her family in his music. These flatteries were thrilling enough to throw the young student "off the rails"

[58] KSAB II: 337.

(his expression), and he could only exorcise their effect by writing to Rohde.[59] In the aftermath Nietzsche said nothing more of tutoring the Brockhauses, a socially questionable proposition since the husband was not only his academic superior but belonged to a family which ranked among the city's commercial elite. (Brockhaus was younger brother to the famous publishers.)[60] Regardless whether Nietzsche served as preceptor, however, he did at least socialize with the family,[61] and he paid rapt attention when Ottilie provided information on her famous brother.

Nietzsche's infatuation continued well after the composer's departure. Within two weeks of that dazzling evening, he was reading *Opera and drama*, a manifesto by the composer; and at the end of January 1869 he would attend a performance of *Die Meistersinger* in Dresden.[62] He further found in Schopenhauer characterizations of "the genius" which he believed eminently suited to Wagner.[63] He may not at the time have envisioned meeting the great man again, but his imagination had been inflamed. He may also have begun subtly to reconsider his loyalties, for this was a period in which his anger with Ritschl boiled over so badly that for the first time he made his displeasure known even to the professor himself.

3

If during this period Nietzsche cultivated his social connections somewhat to the neglect of his studies, he had reasons which have not yet been considered. On October 20, he received a memorandum from Reinhold Klotz, the current head of the philology department, indicating that he could not take his *Promotion*, much less his *Habilitation*, until he had been enrolled as a university student for at least five years.[64] Since Nietzsche had matriculated in Bonn in October 1864, the implication was that he could not achieve his doctorate for at least another year.[65] He was accordingly inclined to let his academic affairs coast and to content himself with desultory studies and free-ranging inquiries.[66] This is not to say that he neglected academic politics. Nietzsche continued to attend meetings and

---

[59] KSAB II: 337–341.
[60] Hermann was son to Friedrich Arnold, who had founded the publishing house, F.A. Brockhaus. After the father's death Hermann's older brothers, Friedrich and Heinrich, took over the business.
[61] KSAB II: 347.   [62] KSAB II: 346, 361, 378–379.   [63] KSAB II: 352–353.   [64] KGB I-3: 295.
[65] See KSAB II: 337, 368. Ritschl acknowledges the same. Stroux 1925: 32.
[66] Although most of Nietzsche's friends (Rohde, Romundt, Deussen, Hüffer) secured their *Habilitation* at comparatively young ages, this was apparently unusual. McClelland notes that during "the period 1850–69, the average age was as high as 28.5 [years old]." McClelland 1980: 350, n. 10.

to monitor activities of the Philological Society, and at least once he promoted the advancement of a student by reviewing his work in the *Centralblatt*.[67] He also urged a colleague to submit an article to the *Rheinisches Museum*.[68]

One of these interventions cast a long shadow. It may be recalled that in mid-March Rohde had sent Nietzsche a paper on "The ass," a fiction thought to be written by Lucian. This was to have been Rohde's contribution to the *Festschrift* for Ritschl, and when that project foundered, Rohde thought to use it for one of his dissertations. (It had already won a university prize and had plainly impressed the Kiel faculty.) Nietzsche believed it should instead appear in the *Rheinisches Museum*, and he assured his friend that he would see that it was published. Nietzsche forwarded it to Ritschl, and Ritschl seems to have looked favorably on the project.[69] Shortly afterward, however, Ritschl's enthusiasm began to cool, partly because another student had submitted a thesis on the same subject, a work that he found "brilliant."[70] Ritschl then asked Rohde to address this new paper, a request which Rohde construed as a rejection. Hurt and angry, he unburdened his views to his friend,[71] who went to Ritschl and took him to task in terms to which the latter was clearly not accustomed. "I spoke with him quite coolly," wrote Nietzsche, "which shocked him a lot."[72]

In itself this incident was unimportant and in any case it ended happily. Thanks again to Windisch, Nietzsche procured a publisher for Rohde's article.[73] Meanwhile, Ritschl changed his mind and a revised version would appear in the *Rheinisches Museum* after all. Nonetheless, Ritschl's shock during the meeting with Nietzsche shows that he was largely and perhaps wholly unaware of the distance his pupil had traveled over the preceding fifteen months. In his eyes, the young man was still his loyal student. He certainly did not know that the latter had recently referred to him as "a pander for philology,"[74] an insult referring to his habit of wooing students through praise and interesting projects. Nietzsche's process of disenchantment had developed largely in the lonely precincts of Naumburg – far from the reach of his teacher. When, as would shortly occur, Ritschl would warmly endorse this pupil, he would be unaware of the latter's recent disillusionment.

---

[67] KSAB II: 335.   [68] KSAB II: 278.   [69] KSAB II: 280, 286.   [70] KSAB II: 304–305.
[71] KGB I-3: 302–304. Rohde forwarded Ritschl's letter to Nietzsche. It has since disappeared.
[72] KSAB II: 341.
[73] KSAB II: 346, 348, 354. Nietzsche reviewed it for the *Literarisches Centralblatt*. KGB I-4: 535.
[74] KSAB II: 248.

Beyond Ritschl's surprise, the incident probably intensified Nietzsche's animus toward his teacher. During his time at Naumburg he had mocked Ritschl for professional reasons. Now his teacher had slighted his closest friend, and Nietzsche's mistrust assumed a personal coloring.[75] When, eventually, Ritschl accepted Rohde's manuscript, Nietzsche interpreted his change of heart in the most contemptuous way possible. In late February, during the closing phases of the events which will occupy the next section, he wrote his friend, "Father Ritschl has recently spoken out about your [article]. Naturally, he never read [it]."[76] Since Nietzsche made this biting comment at a time when he had reason to be exceptionally grateful to Ritschl, it can be assumed that his mistrust of the man remained unassuaged by later developments.

As for Rohde, when Windisch (but as he thought, Nietzsche) found a publisher for the orphaned paper, he was enraptured and gratefully wrote that would reciprocate if his friend ever needed help.[77] The day would indeed come when Rohde could assist Nietzsche; and while he no doubt wanted to give his friend the support and help he deserved, he surely also remembered the undischarged debt which lay between them. When, eventually, Rohde publicly endorsed his friend's scholarship, it would come at some cost to his own career.[78]

4

One month after the confrontation with his protégé, Ritschl received a letter from Adolf Kiessling, a former student who taught classical philology at the University of Basel. Kiessling had accepted a job at the Johanneum in Hamburg (the same Gymnasium that Rohde had attended), and he asked if Ritschl could suggest a successor at Basel. Kiessling himself brought up the name of Friedrich Nietzsche, whose articles he had seen in the *Rheinisches Museum*, and Ritschl commended his pupil in the strongest terms.[79] Nietzsche might not yet have received his *Promotion*, much less his *Habilitation*, Ritschl wrote, but "I would stake my entire philological and academic reputation that the affair would turn out splendidly."[80]

---

[75] One might note that KSAB II: 344–345, the most venomous letter Nietzsche wrote during his student years on the subject of philologists, was composed a little over a week after his confrontation with Ritschl.
[76] KSAB II: 379.   [77] KGB I-3: 313.
[78] Calder 1983: 240–247; Däuble 1976: 330. (Däuble was Rohde's granddaughter.) According to Calder, Rohde himself recognized the professional damage done by his participation in this quarrel.
[79] For a detailed account of the hiring process and copies of the letters sent, see Stroux 1925: 7–55. A shorter account is given in His 2002: 161.
[80] Stroux 1925: 33.

Apparently on the same day, Ritschl received another letter, this one from Wilhelm Vischer-Bilfinger, a classics professor at Basel who was highly placed administratively and responsible for choosing applicants to fill the same vacancy. Vischer-Bilfinger did not himself ask Ritschl for suggestions but merely inquired his opinion concerning a candidate already under consideration (Gustav Uhlig). In his reply Ritschl confessed himself unable to judge Uhlig, but he enclosed his response to Kiessling in which he had enthusiastically praised Nietzsche's abilities. Despite this unsolicited recommendation, Vischer seems not to have taken Nietzsche as a serious candidate at first – not until December when Hermann Usener, Ritschl's replacement in Basel, also proposed the young man. Even then Vischer included Ritchl's protégé as merely one applicant among others and by no means in first place. In other words and contrary to the standard narrative of these events, Ritschl's recommendation was neither requested by the Basel authorities nor was it given weight until seconded by another professor.[81]

A lengthy correspondence ensued, as these academic eminences debated the fate of the unsuspecting student. At first Ritschl seemed doubtful that his fellow faculty members would allow Nietzsche to graduate early – "that would never happen in Germany," he wrote.[82] Meanwhile, the Basel faculty had doubts of their own, and as late as January 9 were still considering competitors to Nietzsche.[83] (They also inquired of a Leipzig student whether Nietzsche was really so esteemed as his sponsor claimed.) If in the end they did select Nietzsche, it was for a variety of reasons, including Ritschl's recommendation and perhaps the allure of one practical benefit: citing Nietzsche's inexperience they declined to offer him the same title or salary as his more conventionally qualified predecessor.[84]

While these negotiations were wending their way through committees, the two young men – oblivious of the great plans being readied for one of them – eagerly awaited their impending trip. Rohde wrote that, unusually for him, he looked forward to the new year, hoping in its course to encounter "the Fata Morgana, known as happiness ... I have never been introduced to her; perhaps she lives in Paris."[85] Nietzsche answered with a 123-word hymn to that "inconceivably high miracle," a *friend* (his emphasis), although near its end he announced that he had just been called to the inner city of Leipzig. "Now returned, I tremble in every limb and can't even unburden myself by pouring my heart out to you."[86]

[81] Stroux 1925: 51–52. [82] Stroux 1925: 34. [83] Stroux 1925: 45. [84] Stroux 1925: 46, 49.
[85] KGB I-3: 324. [86] KSAB II: 357.

Ritschl had believed himself obliged to inform Nietzsche of his possible appointment, for Basel needed to know whether he was amenable before proceeding.[87] Nietzsche, hearing the news, believed that he had no real choice but to consent.[88] However, his emotional response was from the beginning mixed – he describes himself as both pleased and dismayed – and ultimately negative. He was flattered by the unexpected stroke of good fortune. He was also shocked and eventually angered by this early and to him premature promotion into the grim world of professional responsibility. At the very point when, in his own mind, he had stepped onto a grander stage, outgrowing philology as currently practiced, Ritschl had remanded him to a world he found pinched and dreary. He was further sensitive to the pain the news would cause his friend. Rohde was indeed devastated. Conceding that he was not sanguine by temperament and that he rarely believed that great hopes would come to fruition, he confessed, "Yet now that the long feared horror confronts me bodily . . . I am inwardly unarmed."[89] The young man acknowledged the immense honor and good fortune bestowed on his friend, but he could not bring himself to make the impending trip without Nietzsche. "What should I do alone in Paris?"[90]

Nietzsche, meanwhile, had grim duties to attend to. Instead of going at Paris, he was going to Basel, and he was overwhelmed with tasks involving not just academia and packing, but the procurement of a new residence.[91] Ritschl eased the process at every turn, arranging for him to receive his *Promotion* early,[92] to use two articles published in the *Rheinisches Museum* instead of dissertations, and to spare him the examinations. He also moved that the degree be awarded *in absentia*, a violation of protocol that finally proved too much for one of the faculty members, Georg Curtius, who withheld consent. Although Ritschl argued that Nietzsche's case was special and that the spirit of the law must prevail over the letter,[93] Curtius replied that he would not put personal opinions before regulations. He did not sign the *Promotion* document, although he did allow the majority opinion to prevail.[94]

The opening weeks of the year flew by as Ritschl wooed his fellow professors in Leipzig, while in Basel three administrative bodies[95] pondered

---

[87] Stroux 1925: 34–35.   [88] KSAB II: 359.   [89] KGB I-3: 331.
[90] KGB I-3: 341. Eventually, Rohde made a tour of Italy with Wilhelm Roscher, one of the original founders of the Philological Society.
[91] KGW I-5: 167–168.
[92] I see no indication that Nietzsche received his *Habilitation*, a degree usually regarded as indispensable for a professor.
[93] Heise 2000: 182.
[94] Heise 2000: 189. A copy of the *Promotionsakte* is on view in Heise's book, 184–188.
[95] The *Kuratel*, the *Erziehungskollegium*, and the *Kleiner Rat*.

the appointment. During the interim Nietzsche could not resist confidentially informing Rohde, Gersdorff, and his sister. He also had visiting cards printed that bore his new name and title. By January 21, someone had leaked the news in Leipzig, and most of his fellow students were excitedly aware of his prospects. (The culprit appears to have been the young man that Vischer had consulted as to Nietzsche's reputation among the undergraduates.)[96] This put both Nietzsche and Ritschl in an awkward position, and tensions must have mounted as everyone awaited the outcome. By February 10, the three Basel committees had coordinated and made a decision. Vischer contrived to let Nietzsche know in advance,[97] and although the offer was not made officially until the 13th,[98] Nietzsche could pull out his new cards on the 12th, annotate them appropriately, and mail at least seven to relatives and friends. He was probably happy when he wrote them – the announcements themselves are festive – but his sour mood immediately returned, and he responded to some of the letters of congratulation with startling bitterness. When his mother burst into happy tears and ran out to tell the neighbors, he reproved her: "I'm afraid that people in Naumburg are making fun of your joy, and you will not take it badly if I do that myself."[99] When Deussen did not answer with what he considered proper respect, he answered, "Worthy friend, if your last letter is not due to some accidental mental disturbances, I must request that we regard our relationship as herewith ended."[100]

Franziska's reply is not extant, but Deussen reported that he was aghast. Unaware of what could have provoked Nietzsche's outburst, he tried to assure his friend of his support and made apologies that the latter grudgingly accepted. Nietzsche himself must have been confused. For all his disappointment, he was aware of the honor accorded him.[101] He also recognized one advantage in the transfer to Basel: "Lucerne [Wagner's home] is no longer beyond my reach."[102] Nonetheless, he was angry too, and his smoldering rage was only exacerbated by the riotous joy of family, friends, and associates who assumed that he must be delighted over his luck. "I live here in the ash-grey clouds of loneliness," he wrote, comparing his ostensibly festive situation to a wild carnival before the Ash Wednesday of professional work. He was particularly pained that none of his acquaintances sensed his despair. "They let themselves be blinded by the title Professor and believe I am the happiest man under the sun."[103]

---

[96] Stroux 1925: 37–38. [97] KSAB II: 368. [98] Stroux 1925: 50, 53. [99] KSAB II: 373.
[100] KSAB II: 374. [101] KSAB II: 359. [102] KSAB II: 360. See also 371.
[103] KSAB II: 377, 379.

Meanwhile and beyond his degree, Nietzsche had three practical tasks to complete. After one and a half years, the long-postponed *Rheinisches Museum* index still hung fire, and he worked on it further, with help from his sister.[104] He also needed to procure housing in Basel, and he arranged to secure the lodgings of the departed Kiessling.[105] Finally, Vischer-Bilfinger asked him to give up his Prussian citizenship so that he would not be drafted in the event of war. This was not university policy, and indeed it was a practice frowned upon by the governments of Zurich and Bern, which disapproved of having stateless immigrants on Swiss soil. Nonetheless, Kiessling – also a Prussian and a former militia member – had made this sacrifice, and apparently Basel asked Nietzsche to do the same. (Vischer-Bilfinger's request is no longer extant.) Nietzsche concurred without evident demurral. However, since he would never secure Swiss citizenship (which could in any case be offered only after eight years of residence), he remained a man without a country for the rest of his life.[106]

5

In the midst of so much confusion, Nietzsche found a refuge where he could devise, if not a course through the storm, at least a map of the terrain. The Basel authorities had requested a curriculum vitae, and he seized the occasion to immerse himself in the pleasures of autobiography. Nietzsche would probably have written a history of recent events in any case. Throughout adolescence he had proved an indefatigable chronicler of his life, both of the details and the grander contours. It would have been uncharacteristic if at this juncture, the close of childhood and youth, he had not produced some sort of memorial. Of course, the circumstances of its writing – a brief for his future employer and one that centered on his professional career – did not allow him to be as frank as he might have wished. His account does not mention any family member except his father, nor does it touch on such extracurricular influences as Schopenhauer, Lange, or even Rose. Obviously, he suppresses his chagrin at being forced into a career he had hoped to keep at bay, and above all he cannot acknowledge his doubts concerning philology. Indeed, his final version, the one he forwarded to Basel, was so anodyne as scarcely to repay

---

[104] Förster-Nietzsche 1895 I: 301–303. For extended discussion on the index see Brobjer 2000: 157–161; Benne 2005: 54, n. 87.
[105] KSAB II: 383.   [106] His 2002: 163, 168–173.

reading.[107] Discussion here will concentrate on the earlier drafts which, despite their self-imposed limitations, provide a narrative of considerable sweep and insight.

In a preliminary note, Nietzsche salutes a drive which he views as basic, imperious, and ultimately beneficent in the educational consequences it brings: "a certain philosophic seriousness that [is] never satisfied except in the face of naked truth and [by] a fearlessness, indeed, an embrace of tough and wicked consequences." He observes that it was this ruthless tendency which "saved ... my talents ... from diffuse leakage in every direction."[108] This same earnestness will underwrite a striking feature of this autobiography, its determination not to flatter the author but to view his development impersonally. In another preliminary sketch Nietzsche considers a range of motivations that might induce a student to choose philology as career. These run from the simple need to find a remunerative job to the serene sureness of a master, who could light on insights and discoveries almost by instinct. Rather abashed, Nietzsche acknowledges that he does not fall within this last category but would have to include himself in the ranks below. "It is not easy to admit [this], but it is honest."[109]

This determination to be "honest," to engage in ruthless self-exposure, is particularly evident in the autobiography's opening sections. There, Nietzsche gives no quarter to such fond imaginings as his hope that he might become a musician or his claim that his philological career might reflect inborn necessity. This was to be the final autobiography of his youth, and it makes a sad contrast with Nietzsche's first, written as a thirteen-year-old boy. Then he had marveled at the way his history presented a mirror to the self, the latter envisioned as inviting promise. Now the self is on display in quite another fashion, as an organism pinned to the table for dissection. The tone is sardonic, arguably bitter, as the author peels away layers to reveal a self stripped of pretensions or consolatory self-evasions.

"My upbringing was left up to me in its principal aspects," he begins, in a passage cited earlier. "My father, a Protestant country minister in Thuringia, died all too soon; I lacked the strict and superior guidance of a masculine intellect. When as a boy I came to Schulpforte, I got to know only a surrogate for fatherly upbringing, the uniform discipline of a regulated school. But just this almost military coercion which, because it

---

[107] KSAB II: 366–368; KGW I-5: 55–57. Compare Stroux 1925: 38–39. [108] KGW I-5: 42.
[109] KGW I-5: 44.

is supposed to work on the mass, treats the individual coolly and superficially, led me back to myself again."[110]

As noted, Nietzsche largely eliminates his family from consideration. The effect is to present himself as being raised by schools. Having also introduced the central conflict of his academic career – the ways he would alternately accommodate and resist his training – he turns to his love for learning and the arts, treating these, not as admirable traits, but as rebellious maneuvers, designed to keep discipline at bay. "I saved my private leanings and activities from the monotonous law; I lived a secret cult of specific arts; I strove through an overwrought addiction to universal knowledge and enjoyment to break the rigidity of a compulsorily assigned order and use of time."[111]

Of all his non-academic drives Nietzsche presents only one as autonomous and not fundamentally defensive and reactive. "Certain external contingencies were missing for me; otherwise I would have dared then to become a musician, for from my ninth year I felt the strongest draw toward music." Even this desire came to naught, for as just stated, he lacked the necessary support, and he makes fun of his attempts to prove otherwise. "In that happy situation where one doesn't yet recognize the limits of one's talent and considers everything one loves as attainable, I wrote down numberless compositions and acquired a more than dilettantish knowledge of musical theory. Only towards the close of my life at Pforta and in full self-knowledge did I give up all artistic plans for life; from then on, philology entered the resulting gap."[112]

Nietzsche considers the appeals of his newly chosen major. From a practical viewpoint Schulpforte's stress on Greek and Latin offered a rich environment for the budding classicist. Yet the profession's deeper draw lay in what it could offer ethically, as a corrective to his dispersive drives. "I sought a counterweight to the changeable and restless earlier propensities, a field, which could be promoted with cool sobriety, with logical coldness, with steady work, without the results immediately touching the heart. I then thought to find all of this in philology." Yet the most persuasive incentive hearkened back to the boy's need for masculine guidance. "I found splendid teachers of philology, on whose personalities I based my judgment of their discipline." Inspired by these masters and psychologically buttressed by the sobriety of their practice, he produced his papers on Ermanarich and Theognis, works of which he was manifestly proud.[113]

[110] KGW I-5: 52.   [111] KGW I-5: 52.   [112] KGW I-5: 52–53.   [113] KGW I-5: 53–54.

Having graduated from Schulpforte, Nietzsche went to Bonn, where he encountered problems for which his former school had left him unprepared. He knew a great deal, yet he found himself unable to express this, a mismatch between inside and outside that he would analyze at greater length five years later.[114] He also suggests that his primary focus at Bonn had been a philological approach to New Testament studies, an emphasis which seems questionable, given that he took no religion classes after his first term. Further, Nietzsche plays down his return to classical philology, indicating only that he audited (as opposed to enrolled in) philological lectures. He also makes clear that he there conceived great respect for Friedrich Ritschl. (Otto Jahn goes unmentioned.)[115]

After paying so much attention to his psychological development at Schulpforte and Bonn, Nietzsche largely shelves this topic when he reaches his Leipzig years. The implication is that he had found his home and therewith a resolution to earlier difficulties. "In Leipzig I could breathe again," he begins, and he describes the talents that he developed through interplay with fellow students and the excitement he experienced when Ritschl praised the paper on Theognis. From that point on, he recounts a rather perfunctory recital of events: the Diogenes Laertius essay, induction into the army, the accident, and his subsequent productions, notably work on the *Danaelied* and his contributions to Zarncke's *Literarisches Centralblatt*. He closes with the reasons which had led him to postpone completion of his *Promotion* and *Habilitation*.[116]

The above account amalgamates four drafts, all written with the brisk clarity and grace that distinguish almost all Nietzsche's productions from this period. His depiction of his first nineteen years in particular displays a concise and pitiless incisiveness which suggests that he is rendering final judgment on the hopes and futilities of childhood. His discussion of his time at Bonn and particularly Leipzig is, by comparison, colorless. There he is content to rattle off the principal events, as though he had lost interest and was just complying with his task. He was very busy when writing these sketches (January 1869), and perhaps he lacked time to investigate more searchingly. His uncustomary superficiality, however, may also reflect a concern that he had considered earlier, then dismissed. In the autumn of 1867 Nietzsche had entertained notions that undermined the very possibility of writing reliable autobiography and made even more problematic the prospect of putting one to use. This surmise, which will be treated in the

[114] UO II: 4.   [115] KGW I-5: 54, 47–48.   [116] KGW I-5: 48–50.

Afterword, may well have undercut his enthusiasm for this, the final autobiography of its kind that he would write.

6

In any case during January and early February this young man who so disliked pressures was harried by a host of academic deadlines. The acceptance by Basel (February 13) by no means put an end to them, for it arrived well over a month before he would actually receive his degree (March 25). By that time, however, Nietzsche had already departed for the comforts of Naumburg where he still had work to do (the index), but he could at least bask in the soothing ministrations of his mother and sister. Even this idyll had a time limit. On April 12, a little less than one month after arrival in Naumburg, he took a cart to the train station and boarded the first of a number of connections that would eventually deliver him to Switzerland.

Nietzsche's route from Naumburg to Basel was highly circuitous and involved visits to old haunts and a ride down a particularly picturesque section of the Rhine. It is hard not to view this journey as a farewell tour of sites he had known, a retrospective of the life in the Germany he was about to leave. From Naumburg he traveled to Cologne, then to Bonn, where his happiness in visiting old venues suggests that his memories of his first year were more positive than he usually admitted. He then traveled by steamer to Biebrich, later incorporated into Wiesbaden, and from there by train to Wiesbaden itself, also on the Rhine. In Heidelberg he met friends from Leipzig and worked on "Homer and classical philology," the first public lecture he would deliver in his new home. While at last en route to Switzerland, again by train, he overheard some young people report that *Die Meistersinger* was playing in nearby Karlsruhe. Unable to resist this final excursion, Nietzsche made sure that his railway ticket would still be valid and made a detour to enjoy a performance of "my favorite opera." Only then did he make the final stage of his journey, arriving in Basel on April 19, 1869 at 2 p.m. in the afternoon.[117] Here, as he foresaw, his story would take a radically new turn. It was the end of his youth.

Rather than leave Nietzsche on that long journey, which really belongs to the next stage of his biography, it seems best to let him bow out on April 11, his final night in Naumburg, when he reviewed his past and wrote three letters. He addressed the first to Wilhelmine Oehler, his maternal

[117] KSAB III: 3–4.

grandmother, who since her expulsion from Pobles had lived with various children and was now residing in Merseburg.[118] The letter itself is rich in platitudes and was plainly written out of duty. It is, nonetheless, a duty that he performed. Friedrich Nietzsche sent his grandmother a copy of his diploma.

A letter to Gersdorff is more revealing. "My dear friend," it begins, "the final deadline has arrived, the last evening that I will spend in my home; early tomorrow it's out into the wide wide world ... in a difficult and oppressive atmosphere of duty and work." The writer worries that he will become a "philistine," a dull and blinkered member of the adult world that students liked to mock.[119] Nietzsche believes that his philosophic seriousness will preserve him from so dire a fate, but certain forms of professional deformation will take their toll. He is clearly aware of doors about to close, and the best he can hope is to communicate this sense of "the true and essential problems of life and thought" to his students. "[L]et us try to use this life so that when we are happily redeemed from it, others will bless it as worthwhile."[120]

To Deussen, who had only just earned his *Promotion* (but not his *Habilitation*) and was beginning his first job as an assistant teacher,[121] Nietzsche offers a simpler farewell. He sees them both as facing the same fate and sharing a similar moral outlook. "Let us try, each in his place, each in his way, to breathe and to accustom ourselves to a temporarily oppressive atmosphere." Then, remembering their time at Pforta, he addresses his friend more intimately. "And so, begin your profession, with the faithfulness and care that I know in you from your schooldays, with [your] eye on an ideal, with a longing to realize the same."

Reading these letters one might notice how little Nietzsche looks forward to his new life. What friends clearly saw as an opportunity and occasion for celebration he regards as the performance of a melancholy duty, which may have happy consequences for others, but not for him. True to his Schopenhauerean principles, he shows not a trace of hopeful expectation or enthusiasm for the future. His mood is rather steeped in mourning, and this might lead one to think that, for all his supposed dedication to what was to come, Nietzsche was more bound to the past than he recognized. Of course, he was deeply familiar with Leipzig, whereas any impressions of Basel were imaginary, and becoming a

---

[118] For an account of Wilhelmine Oehler's moves after her husband's death, see Rosmiarek *et al.* 2003: 357.
[119] For a characterization of "philistine" in this sense, see Nietzsche himself in UO I: 2; KSA I: 165–167.
[120] KSAB II: 385, 386.   [121] Feldhoff 2008: 67.

professor does not seem to have been the future he had hoped for. Nonetheless, nostalgia had been a sustained and powerful element in Nietzsche's early psychology. He had repeatedly mourned various departures – from Röcken, from Pobles, and from the past itself through the deaths of various aunts, whose passing he had viewed as a kind of extinction that left him alone. Even his love of anniversaries and the composition of autobiographies tended to recall – and celebrate – the very past they affected to transcend. To that extent the comparatively violent rupture of his Basel transfer may have worked positively. Nietzsche's effort to transcend and outgrow his inveterate sadness would prove one of the vital tasks of his existence. Now that he was snatched definitively from all he had loved, he could begin his life afresh.

Afterword: the autobiographer

It would be odd if what someone most prefers to do and does most skillfully, did not reappear in the overall form of his life.[1]

I

With Nietzsche's departure from Leipzig to assume professional duties, the first phase of his life was over. To that extent the biography at hand is complete, and this Afterword deals with literary matters that seem best addressed separately. Why did Nietzsche abandon his practice of autobiography at this time? Did he later revive it in other forms? If so, how might we distinguish these early attempts conceptually from those he produced later? These are legitimate questions, but it can be problematic to interpret a text by Nietzsche if one is not versed in the contexts within which it arose. Since answering the second and third questions would require a sustained immersion in the later notebooks – and a gestation period at least as long as that taken by this book – any attempts to address events after 1869 must be regarded as tentative.

One can nonetheless say the following. Whatever Nietzsche's reasons for ceasing to write autobiography, he seems not to have abandoned his earlier premises – at least not during the period described in this book. He did, however, question them. As early as the autumn of 1867, little more than a year before his final venture in self-portraiture, he expressed doubts, only to dismiss them. At that time, troubled by comments he had encountered in Goethe and in a book by Julius Bahnsen,[2] he began to wonder if he had been wrong from the beginning. Those initial questions surface in notes he compiled around the time he wrote his "Retrospect of my two years at Leipzig," that is, in the late summer or early autumn of 1867:

[1] UO IV: 2; KSA I: 435.   [2] BAW IV: 635.

Afterword: the autobiographer

<u>Self-observation</u>

It deceives.

Know yourself.

Through actions, not by watching.

Those who measure themselves by an ideal, learn to know themselves only in their weaknesses. But even the extent of these is unknown to them.

—

Observation inhibits energy: it separates and breaks apart.

—

Instinct is best.

—

Self-observation, a weapon against outside influences.

—

Self-observation as a developmental illness.

—

Our acts must occur unconsciously.[3]

At first glance these notes may appear unfocused and even somewhat contradictory. Repeated readings reveal that, despite the title, Nietzsche is less engaged with self-observation than with the secondary heading, "Know yourself."[4] He is absorbed in particular with the degree to which self-observation assists self-knowledge and the extent to which the use of such assistance is harmful. Self-observation has its uses, notably as a weapon against outside influences. Nonetheless, he stresses its inadequacies and places his faith in unreflective responses. "[Self-observation] deceives." "We must know ourselves through actions, not by watching [*Betrachten*]." "Our acts must occur unconsciously." "Instinct is best."[5]

It bears saying that the German title of this text ("*Selbstbeobachtung*") is often translated "introspection," and the reader might take Nietzsche to be reiterating the viewpoint he had held since 1858. Already with "From my life" he had assumed that the self is better understood through interpreting its actions in an objective way than by exploring one's interior introspectively. He did not believe that one should look in one's heart and write. That is why he concentrated on composing autobiographies in the first place instead of producing such introspective works as "On moods." Thus, as we might expect, he seems to contrast self-observation with actions, as when he writes, "Know yourself: through actions, not through observing." Yet this cannot be the position enunciated here. If such were Nietzsche's point, he would oppose self-observation (introspection) to his own use of

---

[3] KGW I-4: 489.
[4] The spacing here corresponds to Nietzsche's manuscript. The KGW version misrepresents the spacing of the two headers. For a photocopy of the original see BAW IV: 228–229.
[5] Compare formulations in KGB I-3: 236; KSAB II: 265.

autobiography, the latter a preferable way to examine actions. In fact the contrasting term here is *instinct*, construed as an alternative to consciousness. In other words he is questioning *any* conscious attempt to understand and direct the self, presumably including his earlier experiments with autobiography. In effect he regards all deliberate attempts to guide the self as disruptive, and he implicitly advises himself to forego them.

If this were Nietzsche's last word on the subject, we would need no further reason to determine why he quit autobiography. Construing it as a product of conscious examination – and any interpretations it made would certainly be conscious – he would consider it intrusive and likely to impede the more efficient operations of the unconscious self. The self would take care of the self far better without the interference of some executive ego.

As it happened, the doubts registered in "Self-observation" were only entertained, not affirmed, at the time. We know this because Nietzsche addressed and quite explicitly rejected them in "Retrospect of my two years at Leipzig," his autobiography written around the same time in 1867.[6] That memoir began as follows:

> My future lies in the dark before me, but that doesn't bother me. I have the same attitude toward my past. On the whole I forget it very quickly and only changes and confirmations of character show me from time to time that I have lived though it. In this way of living one will be surprised by one's own developmental process [*Bildungsgang*], without understanding it; and I do not fail to recognize that this has advantages, that the continual observation and evaluation of the naïve expressions of character tend to disturb and seem easily to hinder its growth.[7]

This is very similar to the point of view presented in "Self-observation." Attempts to understand and guide the self just get in the way and probably should be avoided. In fact, if the passage had ended here, one might ask why Nietzsche did not immediately lay down his pen. He would have no reason save nostalgia and an antiquarian interest to write a word further. As the succeeding passage makes clear, however, Nietzsche did not believe what he had just written. He was introducing a point of view that he proposed only to reject. He immediately continued:

> Nonetheless, it occurs to me that such conscious conduct of life is disturbing only in appearance and only for a time. Think of the foot soldier, who is at first afraid he'll forget how to walk altogether, because he is directed to lift his foot consciously and thereby to keep his mistakes in view. What counts is to instill a second nature in him; he then walks just as freely as before. It is very easy to find the moral of this fable, and the following pages should show

[6] See Chapter 12, Section 4. [7] KGW I-4: 506.

that I have found it. I want to observe (*betrachten*) myself and, in order not to begin with an unmediated "today," I will commence with the course of the last two years.[8]

With the almost defiant declaration of that final sentence, he launches a richly detailed narrative of his initial Leipzig years, one which constitutes arguably the most elegant and comprehensive autobiography that he produced during his youth.

In the autumn of 1867, then, Nietzsche was affirming old practices, but not without reservations. I suspect that those concerns ran deeper than the text discloses and that they were indeed a factor in his abandonment of the kind of autobiography written up to that time. He could keep his doubts at bay by limiting them to the issue of self-guidance, commands to the self which inevitably were conscious and potentially intrusive. There is another use of consciousness which he doesn't address, however. Autobiographies are, so to speak, mute. Mere accounts of action have to be interpreted before they can be put to use, and such interpretation is itself a conscious act which may superimpose itself upon the presumably intrinsic (but as yet unknown) meaning of an action. Only consciously can one determine what an act expresses. Nietzsche doesn't actually say this, so that any attempt to impute this can only be speculative. What is certain is that with his departure for Basel Nietzsche did cease to practice what we might call personal autobiography,[9] and he left his reasons ultimately undivulged. His silence should cause no surprise. He was writing for himself alone and had no occasion to record explanations which he already knew.

Of course, Nietzsche could have a plethora of external, non-philosophical reasons for abandoning this practice. He may also have ceased to write autobiographies because he had no leisure in Basel. Perhaps his association with Richard Wagner opened paths that convinced him to leave older ways behind. It may be that, having reached the age of twenty-four, he believed that his character was established and that further examination of his past was fruitless.

Another ground is possible but unlikely. At the time when Nietzsche first bonded with Rohde he adopted the saying, "Become what you are," as a personal motto.[10] One might argue that he found in this future-oriented injunction a complement to and even a replacement for the past-centered approach proper to autobiography. He accordingly discarded the one for the other. This is quite possibly true in the long run. A passage in UO III: 1 suggests that Nietzsche adopted just this policy at Basel.[11] If so however, the

---

[8] KGW I-4: 506–507.   [9] I owe this term to Lee Quinby.   [10] See Chapter 13, Section 2.
[11] See the paragraph beginning, "But how are we to find ourselves again." KSA I: 340–341.

transition is unlikely to have occurred during the period under consideration. If "Become what you are" was so important to him in Leipzig, one would expect to see it invoked repeatedly in his notebooks and letters and to surface imposingly when he ceased to write autobiography. In fact, he seems to have foregrounded this expression during only one period, the spring of 1867 when he was writing his paper on Diogenes Laertius. He did mention it three times afterwards,[12] but those invocations were nostalgic, not assertive, and the phrase then vanished from his written communications, not to reemerge until late 1874 and even then only in paraphrase.[13] No grounds exist for believing that it replaced or even threatened Nietzsche's regard for autobiography up to 1869.

Ultimately, then, we simply do not know why Nietzsche ceased to engage in self-portraiture of this kind. We can only observe that it is true. This is not to deny that he did not later engage in other forms of autobiographical self-presentation, but these had different audiences, purposes, and forms.

2

As already stated, it seems imprudent to make judgments concerning Nietzsche's later use of autobiography without close examination of all the texts. One might assume, for example, that published works are by definition written for other people and to that extent incapable of meeting the private uses served by earlier such works. Surely that would offer one reason to consider Nietzsche's later autobiographies essentially different from those written in his youth. Unfortunately, such a view would not take into account background notes made prior to publication. We have just seen, for example, how just such a public document, in this case the curriculum vitae for Basel, was preceded by texts of a very different (and much more vital) sort. It may be that some of Nietzsche's later autobiographies also originate in less well-known but similarly immediate sketches.

Given the nature of Nietzsche's later self-portraits, however, this seems unlikely. Those later depictions tend to represent his past as a process which is largely over and done with and now being viewed from a distance. Thus, he depicts himself as having once been a subterranean creature mining below the ken of other human beings,[14] or as a person

---
[12] KSAB II: 235, 237, 247.
[13] Although the expression is not invoked explicitly, it underwrites the appeal made in UO III: 1.
[14] D: Preface, 2.

demoralized by his own doubts who underwent a lengthy convalescence.[15] Unlike earlier self-portraits, these are scarcely up-to-the-moment bulletins on his psychological conditions. Nietzsche is at pains to stress the contrary in the preface to *Human, all too human* II. There, he states, "My writings speak *only* of my overcomings ... [This process] has always first required the time, the convalescence, the remoteness, the distance, until the desire moved within me ... 'to represent' (or whatever one wants to call it) retrospectively for knowledge something that had been experienced and survived, any sort of act or fate. To that extent, all my writings, with one single, yet essential, exception, should be *backdated* – they always speak of something 'behind-me.'"[16] (Emphases Nietzsche's.) This retrospective stance seems intrinsic to Nietzsche's published autobiographies, both those implicit in the *Unfashionable observations* and the prefaces to his books and his final review, *Ecce homo*. He always treats his past as something survived or transcended, as in any case done with. The autobiographies of his youth, by contrast, read like glimpses into a life in progress, a life the very meaning of which is at stake and must be resolved at all costs. They tell a story by no means ended, and everything depends on the author to bring it to a successful close. The anxiety implicit in these narratives seems far removed from the serenity of Nietzsche's later self-reflections.

Nietzsche's later autobiographies were probably different for another reason. His early efforts had depended on a particular psychology, which he came increasingly to modify and abandon.[17] His notion of self was already in flux during adolescence, as seen in his attempts both to accommodate and parry the threat of environmental determinism. He extended his views further when he proposed that one could create an environment for oneself (one's own *physis*) by engaging in fields which would foster certain drives and capacities at the expense of others. He undoubtedly explored his belief in an unconscious more searchingly after reading Schopenhauer. In later years, his modifications were more drastic, as when he came to reject the Cartesian belief in the ego, leaving the self a shifting system informed by competing drives. Readers have already noted ways in which *Ecce homo* attempted to recognize and mediate this quite different psychology.[18] We could surmise, then, that as Nietzsche's views of the self evolved, so would the kinds of self-portraiture he would produce.

---

[15] HAH I: Preface, 2–7.   [16] HAH II: Preface, 1. Translation: Gary Handwerk.
[17] See, for example, Liebscher 2010; Acampora 2013: ch. 5; Jensen 2013: 192–201.
[18] See, for example, Wright 2006.

For these reasons I believe I am correct in claiming that after 1869 Nietzsche ceased to write personal autobiographies of the kind composed during his youth. However satisfying these might have been as accounts of his past, these earlier reminiscences were written to meet more visceral ends – as a means to self-knowledge and to self-guidance in the immediate present. When he ceased to apply them to those purposes – and we do not know why; we just know that it is true – he ceased as well to write autobiography of the corresponding type. He did not lose the habit of keeping memoranda, and he occasionally recorded distant memories. He even eventually wrote other autobiographies, although these took a different form. The self-transformations of the kind he pursued in his youth and the literary mirrors which inspired them, had, however, come to an end. He was ready to try something new.

Bibliography

Acampora, Christa Davis 2013. *Contesting Nietzsche*. University of Chicago Press
Agthe, Kai, Rittig, Roland, and Ziemann, Rüdiger eds. 2006. *Ich dichte fort, bis dieses Leben schwindet: Beiträge zu Leben und Werk Ernst Ortlepps für Hermann Josef Schmidt*. Schriften der Ernst-Ortlepp-Gesellschaft zu Zeitz. No. 3. Halle: Mitteldeutscher Verlag
Andler, Charles 1958. *Nietzsche: sa vie et sa pensée*. Vol. I. Paris: Gallimard
Anrich, Ernst 1960. *Die Idee der deutschen Universität und die Reform der deutschen Universitäten*. Darmstadt: Wissenschaftliche Buchgesellschaft
Ansell Pearson, Keith and Large, Duncan eds. 2006. *The Nietzsche reader*. Oxford: Blackwell Publishing
Babich, Babette E. 2003. "Nietzsche's imperative as a friend's encomium: on becoming the one you are, ethics, and blessing." *Nietzsche-Studien* 32: 29–58
Baird, William 1992. *History of New Testament research*. 2 vols. Minneapolis, MN: Fortress Press
Barbera, Sandro 1995. "Eine Quelle der frühen Schopenhauer-Kritik Nietzsches: Rudolf Hayms Aufsatz 'Arthur Schopenhauer.'" *Nietzsche-Studien* 24: 124–136
  1999. "Eine Quelle der frühen Schopenhauer-Kritik Nietzsches. Rudolf Hayms Aufsatz 'Arthur Schopenhauer'" in *Entdecken und Verraten: Zu Leben und Werk Friedrich Nietzsches*. Andreas Schirmer and Rüdiger Schmidt eds. Weimar: Verlag Hermann Böhlaus Nachfolger: 59–66
Barclay, David E. 1995. *Frederick William IV and the Prussian monarchy: 1840–1861*. Oxford: Clarendon Press
Barnes, Jonathan 1986. "Nietzsche and Diogenes Laertius." *Nietzsche-Studien* 15: 16–40.
Bazillion, Richard J. 1990. *Modernizing Germany: Karl Biedermann's career in the Kingdom of Saxony: 1835–1901*. New York/Bonn/Frankfurt-am-Main/Paris: Peter Lang
Beiser, Frederick C. 2014. *After Hegel: German philosophy 1840–1900*. Princeton University Press
Benders, Raymond J. and Öttermann, Stephen; with Reich, Hauke and Spiegel, Sibylle (Stiftung Weimarer Klassik) 2000. *Friedrich Nietzsche: Chronik in Bildern und Texten*. Munich/Vienna: Carl Hanser Verlag (hardbound), Stiftung Weimarer Klassik bei Deutscher Taschenbuch Verlag (paperback)

Benne, Christian 2005. *Nietzsche und die historisch-kritische Philologie.* Berlin/New York: Walter de Gruyter
Bergmann, Peter 1987. *Nietzsche, "the last antipolitical German."* Bloomington, IN: Indiana University Press
Berry, Jessica 2010. *Nietzsche and the skeptical tradition.* Oxford University Press
Bezold, Friedrich von 1920. *Geschichte der Rheinischen Friedrich-Wilhelms-Universität: von der Gründung bis zum Jahr 1870.* Bonn: A. Marcus & E. Webers Verlag
Biller, Thomas and Häffner, Hans-Heinrich 2001. "Die Stadtbefestigung von Naumburg – Geschichte und Erhaltung" in *Naumburg an der Saale: Beiträge zur Baugeschichte und Stadtsanierung.* City of Naumburg ed. Petersberg: Michael Imhof Verlag: 239–260
Bishop, Paul ed. 2004. *Nietzsche and antiquity: his reaction and response to the classical tradition.* Rochester: Camden House
Blackbourn, David and Evans, Richard J. 1991. *The German bourgeoisie: essays on the social history of the German middle class from the late eighteenth to the early twentieth century.* London/New York: Routledge
Blue, Daniel 2007. "What was Nietzsche's nationality?" *Journal of Nietzsche Studies* 33: 73–82
  2012. "Biography and scholarship: a reply to Professor Young." *Journal of Nietzsche Studies:* 43(2) 368–372
Blunck, Richard 1953. *Friedrich Nietzsche: Kindheit und Jugend.* Munich/Basel: Ernst Reinhardt Verlag
Bödeker, Hans Erich 1989. "Die 'gebildeten Stände' im späten 18. und frühen 19. Jahrhundert: Zugehörigkeit und Abgrenzungen, Mentalitäten und Handlungspotentiale" in *Bildungsbürgertum im 19. Jahrhundert.* Vol. IV. Jürgen Kocka ed. Stuttgart: Klett-Cotta: 21–52
Bohley, Reiner 1976. "Über die Landesschule zur Pforte: Materialen aus der Schulzeit Nietzsches." *Nietzsche-Studien* 5: 298–320
  1980. "Nietzsches Taufe. 'Was meinst du, will aus diesem Kindlein werden?'" *Nietzsche-Studien* 9: 383–405
  1987. "Nietzsches christliche Erziehung." *Nietzsche-Studien* 16: 164–196
  1989. "Nietzsches christliche Erziehung." *Nietzsche-Studien* 18: 377–395
  2007. *Die Christlichkeit einer Schule: Schulpforte zur Schulzeit Nietzsches.* Kai Agthe ed. Jena/Quedlinburg: Verlag. Dr. Bussert & Stadeler
Bollack, Jean 1998. *Jacob Bernays: un homme entre deux mondes.* Villeneuf d'Ascq (Nord): Presses Universitaires de Septentrion
Boockmann, Hartmut 1999. *Wissen und Widerstand: Geschichte der deutschen Universität.* Berlin: Siedler Verlag
Borkowsky, Ernst 1897. *Geschichte der Stadt Naumburg an der Saale.* Stuttgart: Hobbing & Büchle
Bornmann, F. 1989. "Nietzsches metrische Studien." *Nietzsche-Studien* 18: 472–489
Borsche, Tilman, Gerratana, Federico and Venturelli, Aldo eds. 1994. *'Centauren-Geburten: Wissenschaft, Kunst und Philosophie beim jungen Nietzsche.* Berlin/New York: Walter de Gruyter

Bowra, C. M. 1960. *Early Greek elegists*. Cambridge: W. Heffer & Sons Ltd
Breazeale, Daniel 1989. "Lange, Nietzsche, and Stack, the question of 'influence.'" *International Studies in Philosophy* 20(2): 91–101
Briggs, Ward W. and Calder, William M. III eds. 1990. *Classical scholarship: a biographical encyclopedia*. New York/London: Garland Publishing Inc.
Brobjer, Thomas H. 1998. "An undiscovered short published autobiographical presentation by Nietzsche from 1872." *Nietzsche-Studien* 27: 446–447
  1999. "Nietzsche's education at the Naumburg Domgymnasium 1855–1858." *Nietzsche-Studien* 28: 302–322
  2000. "Nietzsche's forgotten book: the index to the *Rheinisches Museum für Philologie*." *New Nietzsche Studies* 4(1, 2): 157–161
  2001a. "A discussion and source of Hölderlin's influence on Nietzsche. Nietzsche's use of William Neumann's *Hölderlin*." *Nietzsche-Studien* 30: 397–412
  2001b. "Why did Nietzsche receive a scholarship to study at Schulpforta?" *Nietzsche-Studien* 30: 322–328
  2008. *Nietzsche's philosophical context: an intellectual biography*. University of Chicago Press
Brose, Eric Dorn 2013. *German history 1789–1871: From the Holy Roman Empire to the Bismarckian Reich*. Revised. Providence, RI/Oxford: Berhahn Books
Bruford, W. H. 1975. *The German tradition of self-cultivation: 'Bildung' from Humboldt to Thomas Mann*. Cambridge University Press
Burrow, J. W. 1969. "Editor's introduction" in Wilhelm von Humboldt, *The limits of state action*. J. W. Burrow ed. Cambridge University Press. vii–xliii
Butler, Nicholas Murray 1895. "Introduction: the relation of the German universities to the problems of higher education in the United States" in Friedrich Paulsen, *The German universities: their character and historical development*. Edward Delavan Perry tr. New York/London: Macmillan and Co: ix–xxxi
Calder, William Musgrave III 1983. "The Wilamowitz-Nietzsche struggle: new documents and a reappraisal." *Nietzsche-Studien* 12: 214–254
  1991. "What did Ulrich von Wilamowitz-Moellendorff learn from Otto Jahn?" in *Otto Jahn (1813–1868)*. William M. Calder III, Hubert Cancik and Bernhard Kytzler eds. Stuttgart: Franz Steiner Verlag: 195–203
Calder, William M. III, Cancik, Hubert and Kytzler, Bernhard eds. 1991. *Otto Jahn (1813–1868)*. Stuttgart: Franz Steiner Verlag
Campioni, Giuliano, D'Iorio, Paolo, Fornari, Maria Cristina, Fronterotta, Francesco, Orsucci, Andrea and Müller-Buck, Renate eds. 2003. *Nietzsches persönliche Bibliothek*. Berlin/New York: Walter de Gruyter
Cancik, Hubert 1985. "Erwin Rohde – ein Philologe der Bismarckzeit" in *Semper Apertus: Sechshundert Jahre Ruprecht-Karls-Universität Heidelberg 1386–1986*. Berlin/Heidelberg/New York/Tokyo: Springer-Verlag: 436–505
Carr, William 1987. *A history of Germany: 1815–1985*. 3rd edn. London/New York/Melbourne/Auckland: Edward Arnold (A division of Hodder & Stoughton)

1991. *The origins of the wars of German unification.* London/New York: Longman
Cate, Curtis 2002. *Friedrich Nietzsche.* London: Hutchinson
Clark, Christopher 1993. "The politics of revival: Pietists, aristocrats, and the state church in early nineteenth-century Prussia" in *Between reform, reaction, and resistance: studies in the history of German conservatism from 1789 to 1945.* Larry Eugene Jones and James Retallack eds. Providence, RI: Berg Publishers: 31–60
 2004. "Religion" in *Germany 1800–1870.* Jonathan Sperber ed. Oxford University Press: 162–184
 2006. *Iron kingdom: the rise and downfall of Prussia, 1600–1947.* Cambridge, MA: Belknap Press
Cocks, Geoffrey and Jarausch, Konrad H. eds. 1990. *German professions, 1800–1950.* Oxford University Press
Colson, Bruno 2013. *Leipzig: La bataille des nations: 16–19 octobre 1813.* Paris: Perrin
Conway, Daniel W. and Rehn, Rudolph eds. 1992. *Nietzsche und die antike Philosophie.* Trier: Wissenschaftlicher Verlag
Cousin, Victor 1833. "Rapport sur l'état de l'instruction dans quelques pays d'Allemagne, et particulièrement en Prusse." Tr. unknown. *Edinburgh Review*: 116: 505–542
Crawford, Claudia 1988. *The beginnings of Nietzsche's theory of language.* Berlin/New York: Walter de Gruyter
Däuble, Hedwig 1976. "Friedrich Nietzsche und Erwin Rohde: mit bisher ungedruckten Briefen." *Nietzsche-Studien* 5: 321–354
Daum, Andreas W. 2004. "Wissenschaft and knowledge" in *Germany 1800–1870.* Jonathan Sperber ed. Oxford University Press: 137–161
Deussen, Paul 1901. *Erinnerungen an Friedrich Nietzsche: mit einem Porträt und drei Briefen in Faksimile.* Leipzig: F.A. Brockhaus
 1922. *Mein Leben.* Dr.Erika Rosenthal-Deussen ed. Leipzig: F. A. Brockhaus
Diehl, Carl 1978. *Americans and German scholarship 1770–1870.* New Haven, CT: Yale University Press
Diethe, Carol 2003. *Nietzsche's sister and the will to power: a biography of Elisabeth Förster-Nietzsche.* Champaign, IL: University of Illinois Press
Diogenes Laertius 1925. *Lives of eminent philosophers.* 2 vols. R.D. Hicks tr. (Loeb Classical Library, Harvard University Press.) London: William Heinemann Ltd
Dorgeloh, Annette 2003. *Das Künstlerehepaar Lipsius: Zur Berliner Porträtmalerei um 1900.* Berlin: Akademie Verlag GmbH
Ebers, Georg 1969. *Richard Lepsius: Ein Lebensbild.* Osnabrück: O. Zeller
Edmunds, J.M. ed. and tr. 1931. *Elegy and iambus, being the remains of all the Greek elegiac and iambic poets from Callinus to Crates excepting the choliambic writers, with the Anacreonta.* Vol. I. Cambridge, MA: Harvard University Press
Elias, Norbert 1996. *The Germans: power struggles and the development of habitus in the nineteenth and twentieth centuries.* Michael Schröter ed. Eric Dunning and Stephen Mennell tr. Columbia University Press

Emden, Christian J. 2008. *Friedrich Nietzsche and the politics of history*. Cambridge University Press
Emerson, Ralph Waldo 1983. *Essays and lectures*. Joel Porte ed. New York: The Library of America
Engelhardt, Ulrich 1986. *"Bildungsbürgertum": Begriffs- und Dogmengeschichte eines Etiketts*. Industrielle Welt 43, Stuttgart: Klett-Cotta
Erdman, Bart 2005. *Misquoting Jesus: the story behind who changed the Bible and why*. HarperSanFrancisco
Esdaile, Charles J. 1995. *The wars of Napoleon*. London: Longman
Fallon, Daniel 1980. *The German university: a heroic ideal in conflict with the modern world*. Boulder, CO: Colorado Associated University Press
Feldhoff, Heiner 2008. *Nietzsches Freund: Die Lebensgeschichte des Paul Deussen*. Cologne/Weimar/Vienna: Böhlau Verlag GmbH & Cie
Feuerbach, Ludwig 1956. *Das Wesen des Christentums*. 2 vols. Berlin: Akademie-Verlag
  1957. *The essence of Christianity*. George Eliot tr. New York: Harper
Figes, Orlando 2010. *The Crimean War: a history*. New York: Metropolitan Books
Figl, Johann 1984. *Dialektik der Gewalt: Nietzsches hermeneutische Religionsphilosophie mit Berücksichtigung unveröffentlichter Manuskripte*. Düsseldorf: Patmos Verlag
  1995a. "Die Abteilung I im Kontext der Kritischen Gesamtausgabe der Werke Nietzsches." *Nietzsche-Studien* 24: 315–323
  1995b. "Geburtstag und Totenkult: zur Religiosität des Kindes Nietzsche." *Nietzscheforschung* 2: 21–34
  1999. "Das religiös-pädogogische Kindheitsmilieu Nietzsches. Eine biographisch-philosophische Interpretation früherer Aufzeichnungen" in *Entdecken und Verraten: Zu Leben und Werk Friedrich Nietzsches*. Andreas Schirmer and Rüdiger Schmidt eds. Weimar: Verlag Hermann Böhlaus Nachfolger: 24–36
  2007. *Nietzsche und die Religionen: Transkulturelle Perspektiven seines Bildungs- und Denkweges*. Berlin/New York: Walter de Gruyter
Figueira, Thomas J. and Nagy, Gregory eds. 1985. *Theognis of Megara: poetry and the polis*. Baltimore, MD: Johns Hopkins University Press
Flaig, Egon 2003. "Jacob Burckhardt, Greek culture and modernity" in *Out of Arcadia: classics and politics in Germany in the age of Burckhardt, Nietzsche and Wilamowitz*. Ingo Gildenhard and Martin Rühl eds. London: Institute of Classical Studies, School of Advanced Study, University of London: 7–39
Förster-Nietzsche, Elisabeth 1895. *Das Leben Friedrich Nietzsche's*. Vol. 1. Leipzig: C. G. Naumann
  1912. *The young Nietzsche*. Anthony M. Ludovici tr. London: William Heinemann
Fortlage, Carl 1852. *Genetische Geschichte der Philosophie seit Kant*. Leipzig: F. A. Brockhaus
Frei, Hans W. 1974. *The eclipse of Biblical narrative: a study in eighteenth and nineteenth century hermeneutics*. New Haven, CT: Yale University Press

Gagliardo, John G. 1980. *Reich and nation: the Holy Roman Empire as idea and reality, 1763–1806*. Bloomington, IN: Indiana University Press

Gerber, Douglas E. 1999. *Greek elegiac poetry: from the seventh to the fifth centuries B.C.* Cambridge, MA: Harvard University Press: 326–350

Gerratana, Federico 1994. "'Jetzt zieht mich das Allgemein-Menschliche an': ein Streifzug durch Nietzsches Aufzeichnungen zu einer 'Geschichte der literarischen Studien'" in *Centauren-Geburten: Wissenschaft, Kunst und Philosophie beim jungen Nietzsche*. Tilman Borsche, Federico Gerratana, and Aldo Venturelli eds. Berlin/New York: Walter de Gruyter: 326–350.

Gigante, Marcello 1994. "Friedrich Nietzsche und Diogenes Laertius" in *Centauren-Geburten: Wissenschaft, Kunst und Philosophie beim jungen Nietzsche*. Tilman Borsche, Federico Gerratana, and Aldo Venturelli eds. Berlin/New York: Walter de Gruyter: 3–16

1999. "Nietzsche und die klassische Philologie" in *"Jedes Wort ist ein Vorurteil": Philologie und Philosophie in Nietzsches Denken*. Manfried Riedel ed. Cologne/Weimar/Vienna: Böhlau Verlag

Gildenhard, Ingo and Rühl, Martin 2003. *Out of Arcadia: classics and politics in Germany in the age of Burckhardt, Nietzsche and Wilamowitz*. London: Institute of Classical Studies, School of Advanced Study, University of London

Gildersleeve, Basil L. 1884. "Friedrich Ritschl." *American Journal of Philology* 5(3): 339–355

Gilman, Sander L. 1979. "Pforta zur Zeit Nietzsches." *Nietzsche-Studien* 8: 398–426

Gilman, Sander L. ed. 1987. *Conversations with Nietzsche: a life in the words of his contemporaries*. David J. Parent tr. Oxford University Press

Gilman, Sander L. and Reichenbach, Ingeborg eds. 1981. *Begegnungen mit Nietzsche*. Bonn: Bouvier Verlag Herbert Grundmann

Gladen, Paulgerhard with Becker, Ulrich 1986. *Gaudeamus igitur: die studentischen Verbindingun einst und jetzt*. Munich: Callwey

Glucker, John and Laks, André with Véronique Barre eds. 1996. *Jacob Bernays: Un philologue juif*. Villeneuf d'Ascq (Nord): Presses Universitaires de Septentrion

Goch, Klaus 1994. *Franziska Nietzsche: ein biographisches Porträt*. Frankfurt am Main: Insel Verlag

1995a. "Franziska Nietzsche in Röcken. Ein Blick auf die deutsch-protestantische Pfarrhauskultur." *Nietzscheforschung* 2: 107–140

1995b. "Lyrischer Familienkosmos: Bemerkungen zu Nietzsches poetischer Kindheitserfahrung." *Nietzscheforschung* 3: 103–125

2000. *Nietzsches Vater oder Die Katastrophe des deutschen Protestantismus: Eine Biographie*. Berlin: Akademie Verlag

Goldfrank, David M. 1994. *The origins of the Crimean War*. London: Longman

Grafton, Anthony 1997. *The footnote: a curious history*. Cambridge, MA: Harvard University Press

Green, Abigail 2001. *Fatherlands: state-building and nationhood in nineteenth-century Germany*. Cambridge University Press

2004. "Political and diplomatic movements, 1850–1870: national movement, liberal movement, great power struggles, and the creation of the German empire" in Jonathan Sperber ed., *Germany 1800–1870*. Oxford University Press: 69–90

Gregor-Dellin, Martin 1983. *Richard Wagner: his life, his work, his century.* J. Maxwell Brownjohn tr. San Diego, CA: Harcourt Brace Jovanovich, Publishers

Gregory, Frederick 1977. *Scientific materialism in nineteenth century Germany.* Dordrecht/Boston, MA: D. Reidel Publishing Company

Hahn, Scott W. and Wiker, Benjamin 2013. *Politicizing the Bible: the roots of historical criticism and the secularization of scripture, 1300–1700.* New York: Crossroad Publishing Company

Hamilton, John 2004. "Ecce philologus: Nietzsche and Pindar's second Pythian ode" in *Nietzsche and antiquity: his reaction and response to the classical tradition.* Paul Bishop ed. Rochester: Camden House: 54–69

Harris, Horton 1973. *David Friedrich Strauss and his theology.* Cambridge University Press

1975. *The Tübingen School.* Oxford: Clarendon Press

Hart, James Morgan 1874. *German universities: a narrative of personal experience, together with recent statistical information, practical suggestions, and a comparison of the German, English and American systems of higher education.* New York: G. P. Putnam's Sons

Hayman, Ronald 1980. *Nietzsche: a critical life.* Oxford University Press

Hege, Fritz 1958. *Naumburg: Stadt und Dom. Mit Bildern von Fritz Hege und einem Vorwort von Rosemarie Schuder.* Weimar: Volksverlag Weimar

Heise, Ulf 2000. *"Ei da ist ja auch Herr Nietzsche": Leipziger Werdejahre eines Philosophen.* Beucha: Saxe-Verlag

Henrich, Dieter 2003. *Between Kant and Hegel: lectures on German idealism.* David S. Pacini ed. Cambridge, MA: Harvard University Press

Herter, Hans 1975. "Aus der Geschichte der Klassischen Philologie in Bonn" in *Kleine Schriften.* Ernst Vogt ed. Munich: Wilhelm Fink Verlag: 648–664

Heumann, Hans, Bohner, Claus, Ilgen, Christoph, Maser, Peter, and Weihe, Justus 1994. *Schulpforta: Tradition und Wandel einer Eliteschule.* Erfurt: Verlagshaus Thüringen

His, Eduard 2002. *Friedrich Nietzsches Heimatlosigkeit.* Basler Zeitschrift für Geschichte und Altertumskunde. Vol. 40. Basel: Verlag der historischen und antiquarischen Gesellschaft, Universitätsbibliothek Basel, 1941; reprinted Basel: Schwabe & Co. AG

Hödl, Hans Gerald 1994a. "Dichtung oder Wahrheit? Einige vorbereitende Anmerkungen zu Nietzsches erster Autobiographie und ihrer Analyse von H. J. Schmidt." *Nietzsche-Studien* 23: 285–306

1994b. "Nietzsches Gervinuslektüre 1862 im Kontext seiner geschichtsphilosophischen Reflexionen in 'Fatum und Geschichte.'" *Nietzscheforschung* 1: 365–382

1998. "Der Alte Ortlepp war es übrigens nicht ... Philologie für Spurenleser." *Nietzsche-Studien* 27: 440–445

2009. *Der letzte Jünger des Philosophen Dionysos: Studien zur systematischen Bedeutung von Nietzsches Selbstthematisierungen im Kontext seiner Religionskritik*. Berlin/New York: Walter de Gruyter
Hollingdale, R. J. 1973. *Nietzsche*. London/Boston, MA: Routledge & Kegan Paul
  1999. *Nietzsche: the man and his philosophy*. Cambridge University Press
Howitt, William 1969. *Life in Germany; or scenes, impressions, and every-day life of the Germans, including the popular songs, sports, and habits of the students of the universities*. New York: AMS Press, reprinted from the London edition of 1849
Hübinger, Paul Egon 1964. "Heinrich v. Sybel und der Bonner Philologenkrieg." *Historisches Jahrbuch* 83: 162–216
Humboldt, Wilhelm von 1960–. *Werke in fünf Bänden*. Andreas Flitner and Klaus Giel eds. Stuttgart: J. G. Cotta'sche Buchhandling
  1969. *The limits of state action*. J. W. Burrow ed. with introduction and notes. Cambridge University Press
Janaway, Christopher 1998. "Schopenhauer as Nietzsche's educator" in *Willing and nothingness: Schopenhauer as Nietzsche's educator*. Christopher Janaway ed. Oxford: Clarendon Press: 13–36
  2010. "The real essence of human beings: Schopenhauer and the unconscious will" in *Thinking the unconscious: nineteenth-century German thought*. Angus Nicholls and Martin Liebscher eds. Cambridge University Press: 140–155
Janaway, Christopher ed. 1998. *Willing and nothingness: Schopenhauer as Nietzsche's educator*. Oxford: Clarendon Press
Janz, Curt Paul 1972. *Die Briefe Friedrich Nietzsches: Textprobleme und ihre Bedeutung für Biographie und Doxographie*. Zürich: Editio academica
  1978. *Friedrich Nietzsche: Biographie*. 3 vols. Munich: Carl Hanser Verlag
Janz, Curt Paul ed. 1976. *Friedrich Nietzsche: der musikalische Nachlass*. Basel: Bärenreiter-Verlag
Jarausch, Konrad H. 1974. "The sources of student unrest, 1815–1848" in *The university in society: Europe, Scotland, and the United States from the 16th to the 20th century*. Vol. II. Lawrence Stone ed. Princeton University Press: 533–569
  1982. *Students, society, and politics in imperial Germany: the rise of academic illiberalism*. Princeton University Press
  1984. *Deutsche Studenten: 1800–1970*. Frankfurt am Main: Surhkamp Verlag
  1990. "The German professions in history and theory" in *German professions, 1800–1950*. Geoffrey Cocks and Konrad H. Jarausch eds. Oxford University Press: 9–24
Jeismann, Karl-Ernst 1990. "'... der gelehrte Unterricht in den Händen des Staates': zum Bildungsbegriff in den preussischen Gymnasialprogrammen des Vormärz" in *Bildungsbürgertum im 19. Jahrhundert*. Vol. II. Reinhart Koselleck ed. Stuttgart: Klett Cotta: 317–345
Jensen, Anthony K. 2013. *Nietzsche's philosophy of history*. Cambridge University Press
Jensen, Anthony K. and Heit, Helmut eds. 2014. *Nietzsche as a scholar of antiquity*. London: Bloomsbury

Kamenka, Eugene 1969. *The philosophy of Ludwig Feuerbach*. New York: Praeger Publishers
Kenney, E. J. 1974. *The classical text: aspects of editing in the age of the printed book*. Berkeley/Los Angeles: University of California Press
Kjaer, Jørgen 1990. *Nietzsche: die Zerstörung der Humanität durch "Mutterliebe."* Opladen: Westdeutscher Verlag
Klencke, Hermann 1851. *Alexander von Humboldt: ein biographisches Denkmal*. Leipzig: Verlag von Otto Spamer
Kocka, Jürgen 1989. "Bildungsbürgertum – Gesellschaftliche Formation oder Historikerkonstrukt?" in *Bildungsbürgertum im 19. Jahrhundert*. Vol. IV. Jürgen Kocka ed. Stuttgart: Ernst Klett Verlag für Wissen und Bildung GmbH u. Col, KG
Kocka, Jürgen ed. 1989. *Bildungsbürgertum im 19. Jahrhundert*. Vol. IV. Stuttgart: Ernst Klett Verlag für Wissen und Bildung GmbH u. Col, KG
Kocka, Jürgen and Mitchell, Allan 1993. *Bourgeois society in nineteenth-century Europe*. Providence, RI/Oxford: Berg Publishers Ltd: 9–20
Köhler, Joachim 2002. *Zarathustra's secret: the interior life of Friedrich Nietzsche*. Ronald Taylor tr. New Haven, CT: Yale University Press
Köhnke, Klaus Christian 1986. *Entstehung und Aufstieg des Neukantianismus: die deutsche Universitätsphilosophie zwischen Idealismus und Positivsmus*. Frankfurt am Main: Suhrkamp Verlag
Koselleck, Reinhart 1990. "Einleitung – Zur anthropologischen und semantischen Struktur der Bildung" in *Bildungsbürgertum im 19. Jahrhundert*. Vol. II. Reinhart Koselleck ed. Stuttgart: Klett Cotta: 11–46
Krentz, Edgar 1975. *The historical-critical method*. Philadelphia, PA: Fortress Press
La Vopa, Anthony J. 1980. *Prussian schoolteachers: profession and office, 1763–1848*. Chapel Hill, NC: University of North Carolina Press
  1990. "Specialists against specialization: Hellenism as professional ideology in German classical studies" in *German professions, 1800–1950*. Geoffrey Cocks and Konrad H. Jarausch eds. Oxford University Press: 27–45
Lange, Friedrich Albert 1866. *Geschichte des Materialismus und Kritik seiner Bedeutung in der Gegenwart*. Iserlohn: Verlag von J. Bädeker
  1892. *The history of materialism and criticism of its present importance*. 3rd edn of English version. Ernest Chester Thomas tr. New York: The Humanities Press
Large, D. 1995. "Nietzsche and the figure of Columbus." *Nietzsche-Studien* 24: 162–183
Law, David R. 2012. *The historical-critical method: a guide for the perplexed*. London: Continuum
Legrelle, Arsène 1866. *A travers la Saxe, Souvenirs et études*. Whitefish, MT: Kessinger Legacy Reprints
Leiter, Brian 1998. "The paradox of fatalism and self-creation in Nietzsche" in *Willing and nothingness: Schopenhauer as Nietzsche's educator*. Christopher Janaway ed. Oxford: Clarendon Press: 217–257

Lepsius, M. Reiner 1992. "Das Bildungsbürgertum als ständische Vergesellschaftung" in *Bildungsbürgertum im 19. Jahrhundert*. Vol. III: M. Rainer Lepsius ed: 8–18

Levinger, Matthew 2000. *Enlightened nationalism: the transformation of Prussian political culture, 1806–1848*. Oxford University Press

Liébert, Georges 2004. *Nietzsche and music*. David Pellauer and Graham Parkes tr. University of Chicago Press

Liebscher, Martin 2010. "Friedrich Nietzsche's perspectives on the unconscious" in *Thinking the unconscious: nineteenth-century German thought*. Angus Nicholls and Martin Liebscher eds. Cambridge University Press: 241–260

Love, Frederick R. 1963. *Young Nietzsche and the Wagnerian experience*. Chapel Hill, NC: University of North Carolina Press

Maier, Gerhard 1977. *The end of the historical-critical method*. Edwin W. Leverenz and Rudolpf F. Norden tr. St. Louis, MO: Concordia Publishing House

Mandelkow, Karl Robert 1990. "Die bürgerliche Bildung in der Rezeptionsgeschichte der deutschen Klassik" in *Bildungsbürgertum im 19. Jahrhundert*. Vol. II. Reinhart Koselleck ed. Stuttgart: Klett Cotta: 181–196

Marchand, Suzanne L. 1996. *Down from Olympus: archaeology and philhellenism in Germany, 1750–1970*. Princeton University Press

Mathien, Thomas and Wright, D.G. eds. 2006. *Autobiography as philosophy: the philosophical uses of self-presentation*. Abingdon: Routledge

McClelland, Charles E. 1980. *State, society and university in Germany: 1700–1914*. Cambridge University Press

Middleton, Christopher ed. and tr. 1969. *Selected letters of Friedrich Nietzsche*. Indianapolis, IN: Hacket Publishing Company, Inc.

Migotti, Mark 1991. *The early Nietzsche and the question of redemption*. Doctoral thesis for Yale University

Müller, Carl Werner 1990. "Otto Jahn" in *Classical scholarship: a biographical encyclopedia*. Ward W. Briggs and William M. Calder III eds. New York/London: Garland Publishing Inc.: 227–238

  1991. *Otto Jahn: mit einem Verzeichnis seiner Schriften*. Stuttgart/Leipzig: B. G. Teubner

Müller, Detlef K. and Zymek, Bernd with Hermann, Ulrich 1987. *Datenhandbuch zur deutschen Bildungsgeschichte, Bd II: Höhere und mittlere Schulen: 1. Teil: Sozialgeschichte und Statistik des Schulsystems in den Staaten des Deutschen Reiches, 1800–1945*. Göttingen: Vandenhoeck & Ruprecht

Müller, H. von 2002. "Nietzsches Vorfahren." Evelyn S. Krummel and Richard F. Krummel eds. *Nietzsche-Studien* 31: 253–275

Müller, Renate G. 1994. "'De regus gestis Mithridatis.' Ein lateinischer Schulaufsatz Nietzsches im Spannungsfeld zwischen Quellenstudium und Selbstdarstellung." *Nietzscheforschung* 1: 351–363

Müller-Buck, Renate 1998. "'Naumburger Tugend' oder 'Tugend der Redlichkeit': Elisabeth Förster-Nietzsche und das Nietzsche-Archiv." *Nietzscheforschung* 4: 319–335

Bibliography

Nehamas, Alexander 1985. *Nietzsche: life as literature*. Cambridge, MA: Harvard University Press
Neill, Stephen 1964. *The interpretation of the New Testament, 1861–1961*. The Firth Lectures, 1962. Oxford University Press
Newman, Ernest 1933–1946. *The life of Richard Wagner*. 4 vols. New York: Alfred A. Knopf
Nicholls, Angus and Liebscher, Martin eds. 2010. *Thinking the unconscious: nineteenth-century German thought*. Cambridge University Press
Niemeyer, Christian 1998. *Nietzsches andere Vernunft: Psychologische Aspekte in Biographie und Werk*. Darmstadt: Wissenschaftliche Buchgesellschaft
  2014. "Elisabeth Förster-Nietzsche im Kontext. Eine Antwort auf Robert C. Holub." *Nietzsche-Studien* 43: 152–171
Nietzsche, Franziska 1994. *Der entmündigte Philosoph: Briefe von Franziska Nietzsche an Adalbert Oehler aus den Jahren 1889–1897*. Gernot U. Gabel and Carl Helmuth Jagenberg eds. Hürth: Gabel Verlag
Nipperdey, Thomas 1996. *Germany from Napoleon to Bismarck: 1800–1866*. Daniel Nolan tr. Princeton University Press
Oehler, Adalbert 1940. *Nietzsches Mutter*. Munich: C. H. Beck
Oehler, Ralf 2002. "Ein Beitrag zu Nietzsches Großvater David Ernst Oehler (1787–1859)." *Nietzsche-Studien* 31: 276–277
O'Flaherty, James C., Sellner, Timothy F., and Helm, Robert M. eds. 1979. *Studies in Nietzsche and the classical tradition*. 2nd edn. Chapel Hill, NC: University of North Carolina Press
Pahncke, Robert 1956. *Schulpforte: Geschichte des Zisterzienserklosters Pforte*. Leipzig: Köhler & Amelang
Parkes, Graham 1994. *Composing the soul: reaches of Nietzsche's psychology*. University of Chicago Press
Paulsen, Friedrich 1885. *Geschichte des gelehrten Unterrichts: Auf den deutschen Schulen und Universitäten vom Ausgang des Mittelalters bis zur Gegenwart, mit besonderer Rücksicht auf den klassischen Unterricht*. Leipzig: Verlag von Veit & Comp.
  1895. *The German universities: their character and historical development*. Edward Delavan Perry tr. New York/London: Macmillan and Co.
Pernet, Martin 1989. *Das Christentum im Leben des jungen Friedrich Nietzsche*. Opladen: Westdeutscher Verlag. Studien zur Sozialwissenschaft, Bd. 79
  1990. "Friedrich Nietzsche über Gustav Krug, seinen 'Ältesten Frund und Bruder in Arte Musica': Aus dem Nachlass der Familie Krug." *Nietzsche-Studien*, 19: 488–518
Peters, John C. and McClellan, Ely 1875. "A history of the travels of Asiatic cholera: in Asia and Europe" in *The Cholera epidemic of 1873 in the United States*. John M. Woodworth, United States Surgeon General's Office. Washington, DC: Government Printing Office: 514–705
Pfeiffer, Dr. Ludwig 1867. "Beschreibung der hauptsächlichtsten Ortsepidemien mit den Lokal-Verhältnissen: Naumburg" in *Die Cholera-Verhältnisse Thüringens*. Munich: R. Oldenbourg: 32–42

Pfeiffer, Rudolf 1968, 1976. *History of classical scholarship*. 2 vols. Oxford: Clarendon Press
Pletsch, Carl 1991. *Young Nietzsche: becoming a genius*. New York: The Free Press
Podach, Eric F. 1930. *Nietzsches Zusammenbruch: Beiträge zu einer Biographie auf Grund unveröffentlicher Dokumente*. Heidelberg: Niels Kampmann Verlag
  1932. *Gestalten um Nietzsche: Mit unveröffentlichten Dokumenten zur Geschichte seines Lebens und seines Werks*. Weimar: Erich Lichtenstein Verlag
Porter, James I. 2000a. *Nietzsche and the philology of the future*. Stanford University Press
  2000b. *The invention of Dionysus: an essay on* The birth of tragedy. Stanford University Press
Prange, Martine 2011. "Was Nietzsche ever a true Wagnerian? Nietzsche's late turn to and early doubt about Richard Wagner." *Nietzsche-Studien* 40: 43–71
Reich, Hauke 2004. *Nietzsche-Zeitgenossenlexikon: Verwandte und Vorfahren, Freunde und Feinde, Verehrer und Kritiker von Friedrich Nietzsche*. Basel: Schwage, AG
Reynolds, L. D. and Wilson, N. G. 1974. *Scribes and scholars: a guide to the transmission of Greek and Latin literature*. 2nd edn. Oxford: Clarendon Press
Ribbeck, Otto 1969. *Friedrich Wilhelm Ritschl: ein Beitrag zur Geschichte der Philologie*. 2 vols. Neudruck der Ausgabe 1879–1881. Osnabrück: Otto Zeller
Rich, Norman 1985. *Why the Crimean War? A cautionary tale*. Hanover, NH: University Press of New England
Ringer, Fritz K. 1969. *The decline of the German mandarins: the German academic community, 1890–1933*. Cambridge, MA: Harvard University Press
Rosenberg, Hans 1958. *Bureaucracy, aristocracy and autocracy: the Prussian experience 1660–1815*. Cambridge, MA: Harvard University Press
Rosmiarek, Ralf, Heimer, Falko, and Buchta, Alexander 2001. "Fundstücke – 'Mein lieber Herzensfritz'; Unveröffentliche Briefe: Elisabeth Förster-Nietzsche an Franziska und Friedrich Nietzsche: Aus den Jahren 1891 und 1892." *Nietzsche-Studien* 30: 364–380
  2003. "Wie man mit Herrn Hammer datiert –: Neudatierungen und Bemerkungen zu Briefen von und an Nietzsche aus dem Jahr 1858 innerhalb der Kritischen Gesamtausgabe von Nietzsche's Briefwechsel (KGB)." *Nietzsche-Studien* 32: 313–364
Ross, Werner 1980. *Der ängstliche Adler: Friedrich Nietzsches Leben*. Munich: Deutscher Taschenbuch Verlag
Safranski, Rüdiger 1989. *Schopenhauer and the wild years of philosophy*. Ewald Osers tr. Cambridge, MA: Harvard University Press
  2002. *Nietzsche: a philosophical biography*. Shelley Frisch tr. New York: W. W. Norton & Co.
Salaquarda, Jörg 1978. "Lange und Nietzsche." *Nietzsche-Studien* 7: 236–253
Schirmer, Andreas and Schmidt, Rüdiger eds. 1999. *Entdecken und Verraten: Zu Leben und Werk Friedrich Nietzsches*. Weimar: Verlag Hermann Böhlaus Nachfolger

Schlechta, Karl 1954–1956. "Philologischer Nachbericht" in *Friedrich Nietzsche: Werke in drei Bänden*. Munich: Carl Hanser Verlag. Vol. III: 1383–1432
Schmidt, Hermann Josef 1991–1994. *Nietzsche absconditus oder Spurenlesen bei Nietzsche*. 4 vols. Berlin/Aschaffenburg: IBDK Verlag
  2001. *Der alte Ortlepp war's wohl doch, oder, Für mehr Mut, Kompetenz und Redlichkeit in der Nietzscheinterpretation*. Aschaffenburg: A Libri Verlag. [Copyright by author, 2000]
Schnädelbach, Herbert 1984. *Philosophy in Germany: 1831–1933*. Eric Matthews tr. Cambridge University Press
Schopenhauer, Arthur 1969. *The world as will and representation*. 2 vols. E.F.J. Payne tr. New York: Dover Publications
Schröter, Axel 2011. *August von Kotzebue: Erfolgsautor zwischen Aufklärung, Klassik und Frühromantik*. Weimarer Verlagsgesellschaft
Schubert, Ernst 1989. *Naumburg: Dom und Altstadt*. Photography by Fritz Hege. 2nd edn. Leipzig: Köhler & Ameling
Schulze, Hagen 1991. *The course of German nationalism: from Frederick the Great to Bismarck, 1763–1867*. Sarah Hansbury-Tenison tr. Cambridge University Press
  1998. *Germany: a new history*. Deborah Lucas Schneider tr. Cambridge, MA: Harvard University Press
Schweitzer, Albert 1960. *The quest of the historical Jesus: a critical study of its progress from Reimarus to Wrede*. W. Montgomery, tr. New York: Macmillan Company
Sheehan, James J. 1989. *German history 1770–1866*. Oxford: Clarendon Press
Simms, Brendan 1998. *The struggle for mastery in Germany, 1779–1850*. New York: St. Martin's Press
Sommer, Andreas Urs 2000. "Vom Nützen und Nachteil kritischer Quellenforschung." *Nietzsche-Studien* 29: 302–316
  2013. *Kommentar zu Nietzsches Der Antichrist, Ecce homo, Dionysos-Dithyramben, Nietzsche contra Wagner*. Berlin: Walter de Gruyter GmbH
Sorkin, David 1983. "Wilhelm von Humboldt: the theory and practice of self-formation (*Bildung*), 1791–1810." *Journal of the History of Ideas*. 44(1): 55–73
  1987. *The transformation of German Jewry, 1780–1840*. Oxford University Press
Sperber, Jonathan ed. 2004. *Germany 1800–1870*. Oxford University Press
Spranger, Eduard 1928. *Wilhelm von Humboldt und die Humanitätsidee*. 2nd edn. Berlin: Verlag von Reuther & Reichard
Stack, George J. 1983. *Nietzsche and Lange*. Berlin: Walter de Gruyter
  1992. *Nietzsche and Emerson: an elective affinity*. Athens, OH: Ohio University Press
Stern, Fritz 1961. *The politics of cultural despair: a study in the rise of the Germanic ideology*. Oakland, CA: University of California Press
Stone, Lawrence 1974. *The university in society: Europe, Scotland, and the United States from the 16th to the 20th century*. 2 vols. Princeton University Press

Strauss, David Friedrich 1970. *The life of Jesus, critically examined.* Marian Evans tr. 2 vols. New York: Calvin Blanchard. 1860 Repub. St. Clair Shores, MI: Scholarly Press
  2005. *Das Leben Jesu für das deutsche Volk bearbeitet.* Orig. Leipzig: F.A. Brockhaus. 1864 Repub. Elibron Classics Replica Edition, Adament Media Corporation
Stroux, Johannes 1925. *Nietzsches Professur in Basel.* Jena: Frommannsche Buchhandlung (Walter Biedermann)
Sweet, Paul Robinson 1978 and 1980. *Wilhelm von Humboldt: a biography.* 2 vols. Columbus, OH: Ohio State University Press
Swift, Paul A. 2005. *Becoming Nietzsche: early reflections on Democritus, Schopenhauer and Kant.* Lanham, MD/Boulder, CO/New York/Toronto/Oxford: Lexington Books
Taylor, A.J.P. 1945. *The course of German history: a survey of the development of Germany since 1815.* London: Hamish Hamilton
Teuteberg, René 1986. *Basler Geschichte.* 2nd edn. Basel: Christoph Merian Verlag
Thatcher, David S. 1974. "Nietzsche and Byron." *Nietzsche-Studien* 3: 130–151
Timpanaro, Sebastiano 2005. *The genesis of Lachmann's method.* Glenn W. Most ed. and tr. University of Chicago Press
Trieder, Simone 2006. *Richard von Volkmann-Leander. Chirug und Literat. literarisches Porträt.* Halle: Mitteldeutscher Verlag GmbH
Turner, R. Steven 1974. "University reformers and professorial scholarship in Germany 1760–1806" in *The university in society: Europe, Scotland, and the United States from the 16th to the 20th century.* Vol. II. Lawrence Stone ed. Princeton University Press: 495–531
  1980a. "The *Bildungsbürgertum* and the learned professions in Prussia, 1770–1830: The origins of a class." *Histoire sociale – Social History* 12(25) 105–135
  1980b. "The Prussian universities and the concept of research." *Internationales Archiv für Sozialgeschichte der deutschen Literatur* 5: 69–93
Van Rey, Manfred 2001. *Bonner Stadtgeschichte kurzgefasst: von der Vorgeschichte bis zur Gegenwart.* Bonn: Bouvier Verlag
Verrecchia, Anacleto 1986. *Zarahustras Ende: die Katastrophe Nietzsches in Turin.* Peter Pawlowsky tr. Vienna/Cologne/Graz: Hermann Böhlaus Nachf.
Vierhaus, Rudolf 1972. "Bildung" in *Geschichtliche Grundbegriffe: Historisches Lexicon zur politisch-sozialen Sprache in Deutschland.* Vol. I. Otto Brunner, Werner Conze, and Reinhart Koselleck eds. Stuttgart: Ernst Klett Verlag: 508–551
Vogt, Ernst 1990. "Friedrich Ritschl" in *Classical scholarship: a biographical encyclopedia.* Ward W. Briggs and William M. Calder III eds. New York/London: Garland Publishing Inc.: 389–394
Volz, Pia Daniela 1990. *Nietzsche im Labyrinth seiner Krankheit: Eine medizinisch-biographische Untersuchung.* Würzburg: Königshausen & Neumann
Wagner, Siegfried 2001. *Stadtmuseum Naumburg: Führer durch die Dauerstellung im Haus zur Hohen Lilie. 1. Das bürgerliche Naumburg von den Anfängen der Stadtgeschichte bis zum Ende des 19. Jahrhunderts.* Naumburg: Druckservice A. Schirmer

Wawro, Geoffrey 1996. *The Austro-Prussian War: Austria's war with Prussia and Italy in 1866.* Cambridge University Press
Weber, R.G.S. 1986. *The German student corps in the Third Reich.* Houndsmills/Basingstoke: MacMillan Press Ltd
Wehler, Hans-Ulrich 1989. "Deutsches Bildungsbürgertum in vergleichender Perspektive – Elemente eines 'Sonderwegs'" in *Bildungsbürgertum im 19. Jahrhundert.* Vol. IV. Jürgen Kocka ed. Stuttgart: Klett-Cotta: 215–237
Weil, Hans 1967. *Die Entstehung des deutschen Bildungsprinzips.* 2nd edn. Bonn: H. Bouvier & Co. Verlag
Wilamowitz-Moellendorff, Ulrich von 1928. *Erinnerungen: 1848–1914.* 2nd edn. Leipzig: Verlag von K.F. Köhler
Willey, Thomas E. 1978. *Back to Kant: the revival of Kantianism in German social and historical thought, 1860–1914.* Detroit, IL: Wayne State University Press
Williamson, David D. 2005. *Germany since 1815: a nation forged and renewed.* Houndmills/Basingstoke: Palgrave Macmillan
Winkler, Heinrich 2006. *Germany: the long road west,* Vol. 1, *1789–1933.* Alexander J. Sager tr. Oxford University Press
Wollek, Christian 2010. *Die lateinischen Texte des Schülers Nietzsche: Übersetzung und Kommentar.* Marburg: Tectum Verlag
Wright, D.G. 2006. "The subject of Nietzsche's *Ecce homo*" in *Autobiography as philosophy: the philosophical uses of self-presentation.* Thomas Mathien and D.G. Wright eds. Abingdon: Routledge: 211–229
Young, Julian 2010. *Friedrich Nietzsche: a philosophical biography.* Cambridge University Press
Zammito, John H. 2002. *Kant, Herder, and the birth of anthropology.* University of Chicago Press
Zimmermann, Heinrich 1967. *Neutestamentliche Methodenlehre: Darstellung der historisch-kritischen Methode.* 3rd edn. Stuttgart: Verlag Kath. Bibelwerk

Index

Acampora, Christa Davis, 12, 319n
Aeschylus, 188, 227, 244, 269
Agthe, Kai, 143n, 144n
Almrich, 96, 144
Altenburg, 20, 21, 28
Anderson, Mark, 12, 274n
Andreas-Salomé, Lou, 7
Ansell Pearson, Keith, 132n, 133n, 134n, 135n, 137n, 166n, 171n, 288n
Austro-Prussian War, 231–232
Awakening movement, 20, 46, 47, 60, 61

Babich, Babette E., 274n
Baird, William, 121n, 122n
Barbera, Sandro, 288, 288n
Barclay, David E., 16n, 27n, 98n
Barnes, Jonathan, 261n, 262n, 264n, 265n
Basel, 261n, 303, 304, 305, 306, 307, 311, 317
  Unversity of, 303
Baur, Ferdinand Christian, 192, 192n
Bazillion, Richard J., 48n, 212n, 232n
Beecher, Henry Ward, 196
Beethoven, Ludwig van, 147, 298
Beiser, Frederick C., 192n
Benders, Raymond J., 58n, 94n, 110n, 157n, 158n
Benne, Christian, 174n, 181n, 262n, 280n, 307n
Bergmann, Peter, 7n, 11, 11n, 34n, 48n, 100n
Berlin, 198, 202, 206, 211
  Unversity of, 105n, 180, 267
Bernays, Jacob, 181, 263n, 284n
Berry, Jessica, 262n
Beseler, Wilhelm, 198, 198n, 199
Bezold, Friedrich von, 182n, 184n, 197n, 198n, 200n
Biedermann, Karl, 48n, 294, 295, 297, 297n
Bildung, 4, 5n, 10, 43, 91, 104, 125, 126, 136, 205
  and philology, 103–105
  and *Wissenschaft*, 170, 258–259, 277
  contrasted with *Erziehung*, 101–102

cultivation, 45
education, 101–102
social class, 43–44
increasing irrelevance, 44–45, 242–243, 256–257
Nietzsche's rejection, 277
self-development, 102
Biller, Thomas, 34n
Bishop, Paul, 262n
Bismarck, Otto von, 48, 232, 233, 234, 235, 236, 256
Blue, Daniel, 15n, 213n
Blunck, Richard, 6n, 7n, 11, 11n, 30n, 32n, 98n, 100n, 251n, 255n
Bödeker, Hans Erich, 44n, 45n, 258n
Bohley, Reiner, 17n, 18n, 20n, 22n, 23n, 27n, 28n, 30n, 32n, 37n, 45n, 47n, 49n, 51n, 54n, 58n, 60n, 63n, 75n, 78n, 79, 79n, 95n, 100n, 107n, 125n, 144, 144n, 150n, 151n, 152n, 165n, 174n
Bollack, Jean, 181n
Bonn, 11, 150, 174, 188, 189, 191, 194, 197, 198, 201, 202, 204, 205, 206, 207
  history, 179–180
  University of, 150, 173, 174, 178, 181, 197
Boockmann, Hartmut, 293n
Bornmann, F., 261n
Borsche, Tilman, 262n
Brahms, Johannes, 148
Braune, Richard, 108, 117n
Breazale, Daniel, 152n
Brobjer, Thomas H., 11, 11n, 57n, 59n, 60n, 63n, 78n, 79n, 94n, 98n, 109n, 110n, 146, 146n, 151, 151n, 152n, 205, 205n, 307n
Brockhaus, Hermann, 289, 299, 301, 301n
Brockhaus, Luise Wagner, 300
Brockhaus, Ottilie Wagner, 289, 299, 300
Brose, Eric Dorn, 15n, 232n
Büchner, Ludwig, 237
Buddensieg, Robert, 78, 107, 148, 149, 150, 151, 155, 159, 161

Index

Buddensieg, Rudolf, 155
Bülow, Cosima von, 299, 300
Bülow, Hans von, 298n, 299, 299n
Burgher school, 37, 38
Burrow, J. W., 104n
Burschenschaften
  drinking and dueling protocols, 185–186
  history, 184–185
Butler, Nicholas Murray, 103n, 182n, 183n
Byron, George Gordon, Lord, 144, 145, 152, 153, 161
  "Manfred", 153–154, 160, 189

Calder, William M. III, 199n, 303n
Campioni, Giuliano, 11, 11n, 145n, 148n, 196n, 249n
Cancik, Hubert, 249n, 251n
Carr, William, 15n
Cate, Curtis, 7n, 11, 11n
Cathedral *Gymnasium*, 39n, 59n, 63n, 77n, 78n, 63, 76, 77, 78, 87, 91, 93, 226
Catullus, 249, 249n
cholera epidemic of 1866, 244
Clark, Christopher, 15n, 16n, 46n
Cologne, 187, 198
Colson, Bruno, 14n
Conway, Daniel W., 262n
Corssen, Wilhelm, 168, 231, 268
Cousin, Victor, 38n,
Crawford, Claudia, 288n
Curtius, Ernst, 257
Curtius, Georg, 297n, 305

Daechsel, Bernhard, 40, 75, 233, 244, 268, 296
  Nietzsche's guardian, 40, 296
Daechsel, Friederike Nietzsche, 31, 75, 215, 244, 245, 246
Dathe, Gustav, 22, 32
Däuble, Hedwig, 7n, 303n
Daum, Andreas W., 37n, 258n
Democritus, 238, 266, 269, 279, 280, 283, 288
Deussen, Paul, 42n, 52, 53n, 94n, 95n, 115, 116n, 117n, 119, 119n, 120, 121, 121n, 122, 123, 127, 143, 143n, 152n, 155, 155n, 156, 156n, 157, 159n, 164, 169, 169n, 173, 175, 175n, 179, 180, 181, 182n, 183, 184, 186, 186n, 187n, 188, 202, 203, 206, 215, 216, 216n, 226, 233, 233n, 241, 242, 248, 250, 252, 258, 259, 260, 266, 268, 288, 289, 294n, 296, 298, 301n, 306, 312
  arrival at Schulpforte, 115–116
  Confirmation, 119–120
  friendship with Nietzsche, 116–117, 164
  tensions with Nietzsche, 117, 155–157, 202, 206–207

Deutsche Allgemeine Zeitung, 295, 297, 298
Devrient, Karl August, 201
Diehl, Carl, 105n
Diethe, Carol, 7, 7n, 55n
Diogenes Laertius, 227, 248, 263, 269
Dorgeloh, Annette, 45n
Dresden, 112

Ebers, Georg, 55n, 78n
Edmunds, J. M., 170n
Ehlert, Louis, 298n
Eilenburg, 14, 15, 19, 20, 23
Elberfeld, 198
Emden, Christian J., 182n, 262n
Emerson, Ralph Waldo, 5, 130, 133, 135, 136, 139, 146n, 153, 163, 165n, 168, 191, 196, 197, 197n, 223
  works
    The Conduct of Life, 130
    "Beauty", 163, 165
    "Considerations by the way", 130n
    Essays, 130
    "Fate", 130–132
    "Intellect", 196–197
    "Wealth", 130
    "Worship", 130
Engelhardt, Ulrich, 43n
Engels, Friedrich, 140, 234
Epicurus, 238
Erdman, Bart, 121n
Ermanarich, 128, 129, 145, 145n, 168, 249, 309
Ernesti, Johann August, 121
Esdaile, Charles J., 15n

Fallon, Daniel, 103n, 105n, 198n, 259n, 268n, 296n
Feldhoff, Heiner, 95n, 116n, 142n, 143n, 168n, 182n, 202n, 312n
Feuerbach, Ludwig, 140n, 211, 223
  teachings, 140–141
Fichte, Johann Gottlieb, 102
Fielding, Henry, 144
Figl, Johann, 11, 11n, 32n, 37n, 69n, 216n
Figueira, Thomas J., 169n, 170n
Fischer, Kuno, 222
Flaig, Egon, 284n
Flaxland, Gustave, 295, 295n
Förster-Nietzsche, Elisabeth, 6, 7, 7n, 8n, 13, 15n, 17n, 23, 23n, 24, 24n, 26, 26n, 28, 28n, 33, 34n, 35, 35n, 36, 38, 39, 40, 41, 46, 51, 53, 54, 56, 57, 58, 61, 63, 64, 73, 73n, 75, 75n, 85, 85n, 94n, 95, 107n, 112, 117, 117n, 154, 160, 160n, 161, 164, 164n, 169n, 175n, 188, 194, 195, 195n, 196, 210, 233, 244, 245n, 270n, 290, 291, 306, 307n, 311

Förster-Nietzsche, Elisabeth (cont.)
  biographies criticized by mother and family, 8, 27, 39
  birth, 28
  concerned over brother's apostasy, 196
  disturbed when brother leaves for Schulpforte, 85
  education, 55n
  examples of questionable stories, 27–28, 34, 38–39, 79–80
  helps brother with *Rheinisches Museum* index, 307
  resigned to remaining unmarried, 290–291
  snubbed by Naumburg society, 194–195
  taught to read by mother, 37
  unreliability as witness and scholar, 6–7
Fortlage, Carl, 205, 205n, 216, 223, 237n
Franconia, 183, 186, 187, 188, 202, 211, 214
Frei, Hans W., 121n
Friedrich Wilhelm IV, king of Prussia, 21, 27, 29, 46, 98, 112, 118

Gagliardo, John G., 232n
Gassendi, Pierre, 238
Gerlach, Ernst Ludwig von, 46
Germania, 118, 123, 127, 132, 135, 146, 147, 153, 154, 164, 185, 227
Gerratana, Federico, 266n
Gersdorff, Carl von, 94n, 117n, 151, 151n, 155, 202, 214, 224, 226, 233, 236, 237, 241, 243, 246, 247, 248, 250, 252, 254n, 268, 270n, 271, 272, 275n, 283, 294n, 306, 312
Gersdorff, Ernst von, 246, 247
Gibbon, Edward, 128n
Gigante, Marcello, 261n, 264n, 265n
Gildersleeve, Basil L., 181n, 197n
Gilman, Sander L., 42n, 53n, 95n, 97n, 100n, 116n, 120n, 121n, 150n, 151n, 154n, 156n, 168n, 169n, 182n, 225n, 254n
Glucker, John, 181n
Goch, Klaus, 8n, 11, 11n, 13, 13n, 14n, 15n, 16n, 17n, 18n, 19, 19n, 20n, 21n, 22n, 23n, 24n, 25n, 26, 26n, 27n, 28n, 29n, 30n, 31n, 32n, 33n, 35n, 36n, 37n, 40n, 44n, 46n, 47n, 49n, 50n, 51n, 52, 52n, 53n, 54n, 58n, 66n, 67n, 73n, 74n, 77n, 78n, 100n, 195n
Goethe, Johann Wolfgang von, 17n, 43, 61n, 102, 143, 144n, 151, 213
Gorenzen, 117, 211
Grafton, Anthony, 285n
Granier, Raimund, 117n, 155
Gray, Richard T., 64n, 137n, 224n, 275n
Green, Abigail, 16n, 48n, 212n, 234n
Gregor-Dellin, Martin, 299n
Gregory, Frederick, 237n, 238n

Gymnasium, 37, 59
  contrasted with university, 103

Häffner, Hans-Heinrich, 34n
Hahn, Scott W., 121n
Halle, 18, 20, 77
Hamburg, 251
Hamilton, John, 274n
Händel, Georg Friedrich, 76, 187
Handwerk, Gary, 319n
Harris, Horton, 192n, 193n
Hart, James Morgan, 184n, 185n, 186n, 201n
Hase, Karl, 141n, 161
Haydn, Joseph, 77, 147
Haym, Rudolf, 222, 288
Hayman, Ronald, 7n, 11, 11n, 30n
Hege, Fritz, 42n
Hegel, Georg Wilhelm Friedrich, 147, 255, 257
Heinze, Max, 149, 150, 157, 159
Heise, Ulf, 11, 11n, 212n, 213, 213n, 225n, 267n, 268n, 293n, 305n
Heit, Helmut, 262n
Helmholtz, Hermann von, 258n
Henrich, Dieter, 217n
Herder, Johann Gottfried von, 102, 102n, 256n
Hermann, Gottfried, 225
Herter, Hans, 181n, 197n
Hesiod, 266, 287
Heumann, Hans, 94n, 95n, 97n, 142n, 143n, 169n, 176n
His, Eduard, 303n, 307n
Hobbes, Thomas, 238
Hödl, Hans Gerald, 3n, 4n, 27n, 37n, 58n, 59n, 61n, 63n, 64n, 66n, 68n, 78n, 79n, 110n, 117n, 144n, 155n, 158n, 160n
Holbach, Baron d', 238
Hölderlin, Friedrich, 144, 145, 146, 146n, 147, 148, 151, 152, 157
Hollingdale, R.J., 11, 11n, 166n
Homer, 266
Horace, 249, 249n
Hübinger, Paul Egon, 197n, 199n
Hüffer, Franz, 297n, 301n
Humboldt, Alexander von, 102, 109
Humboldt, Wilhelm von, 102, 104n, 136, 255, 256, 258, 259, 276, 277
  contrasted with Emerson, 136–137
  coordination of *Bildung* and *Wissenschaft*, 258
  educational innovations, 102–103
  espousal of Latin and Greek, 103–104
  views on Bildung, 102
Hume, David, 238

Ilgen, David, 45n
Institute. *See* Weber Institute

Jahn, Otto, 151, 180, 180n, 197, 199, 200, 205, 224, 298, 310
   early years, 180–181
   hired by Ritschl, 181
   Philologenstreit, 197–199
   regrets and death, 199–200
Janaway, Christopher, 288n
Janz, Curt Paul, 6n, 7, 7n, 10n, 11, 11n, 30n, 32n, 77n, 145n, 146n, 251n, 255n
Jarausch, Konrad H., 104n, 184n, 185n, 205n, 258n
Jean Paul (Johann Paul Friedrich Richter), 144, 144n
Jeismann, Karl-Ernst, 101n, 104n, 105n, 256n, 257n, 259n
Jena, Battle of, 17n
Jensen, Anthony J., 199n, 255n, 262n, 264n
Johann, king of Saxony, 225
Joseph, duke of Saxe-Altenburg, 21, 29
Juvenal, 165, 180n, 202, 249

Kamenka, Eugene, 141n
Kant, Immanuel, 101, 137, 205, 216, 217, 222, 238, 240, 241, 287, 288, 294n
Kaufmann, Walter, 157n
Keil, Karl, 143n, 168
Kenney, E. J., 263n
Kiessling, Adolf, 303, 307
Kjaer, Jørgen, 11, 11n, 52n, 62n, 63n, 65n, 66n
Kleinpaul, Rudolf, 248, 250, 294n
Kletschke, Hermann, 159, 165, 174, 180, 205n
Klotz, Reinhold, 301
Koberstein, Karl August, 45n, 150, 150n, 151, 152n, 168
Kocka, Jürgen, 43n, 258n
Köhler, Joachim, 49n, 58n
Königgrätz, Battle of, 236, 290
Koselleck, Reinhart, 45n, 130n, 256n
Kotzebue, August von, 17n, 184
Krafft, Wilhelm Ludwig, 180n, 191, 192
Krämer, Oskar, 107, 117n, 245
Krause, Johann Friedrich, 47n
Krentz, Edgar, 121n
Kretschmer, Julius, 142n
Krug, Gustav, 37n, 38, 59, 60, 76, 87, 88, 117, 132, 139, 147, 150, 154, 157, 162, 164, 174, 295
Krug, Gustav Adolph, 60, 187
Krüger, Carl Christoph Heinrich, 17n

Lampert, Laurence, 12
Lange, Friedrich Albert, 288, 222, 237, 238, 239, 240, 245, 257n, 261, 264, 266, 278, 288, 307
   History of materialism
      implications, 241–243
      Nietzsche discovers, 237
   themes, 238–240
   treatment of metaphysics, 241
Langensalza, Battle of, 233
Large, Duncan, 68n, 132n, 133n, 134n, 135n, 137n, 166n, 171n, 288n
Lassalle, Ferdinand, 212
Laube, Heinrich, 295, 295n, 297, 297n
La Vopa, Anthony J., 101n, 257n, 257
Law, David R., 121n, 193n, 245n
Legrelle, Arsène, 212n
Leipzig, 14, 21, 31, 143, 203, 212, 226
   Battle of, 14
   history, 212
   Nietzsch's Leipzig, 212
   University of, 149, 174, 180, 203
Leiter, Brian, 223n, 274n
Lepsius, Carl Peter, 55
Lepsius, Friederike Gläser, 45
Lepsius, Johann August, 55
Lepsius, Julie Gläser, 45
Lepsius, Karl Richard, 45, 78
Lepsius, M. Reiner, 44n
Leucippus, 238
Liébert, Georges, 10n
Liebig, Justus von, 237
Liebscher, Martin, 319n
Liszt, Franz, 172, 298n, 299
Literaria, 45, 152
Literarisches Centralblatt, 296, 296n, 302, 302n, 310
Loeb, Paul S., 6n, 12, 12n
Lotze, Rudolf, 245
Love, Frederick R., 10n, 298, 298n
Lucian, 287
Lucretius, 238
Ludwig II, king of Bavaria, 299
Lützen, 28, 28n, 31

Machiavelli, Niccolò, 235
Maier, Gerhard, 121n
Mandelkow, Karl Robert, 61n, 144n
Marchand, Suzanne L., 257n
Marx, Karl, 140
McClellan, Ely, M.D., 244n
McClelland, Charles E., 17n, 105n, 180n, 198n, 258, 258n, 296n, 301n
Mendelssohn, Felix, 60, 60n
Menippus, 266, 296
Mette, Hans Joachim, 125n
Metternich, Klemens von, 29
Mettrie, Julien Offray de la, 238
Meyer, Guido, 79, 117n, 155, 155n, 156, 157, 159, 160, 164, 165
Middleton, Christopher, 196n, 241n, 247n, 272n, 275n

Mozart, Wolfgang Amadeus, 181, 187
Müller, Carl Werner, 180n, 181n, 197n
Müller, Detlef K., 38n
Müller, Hans von, 6n
Müller-Buck, Renate, 6, 6n, 7, 7n, 8n, 128n
Mushacke, Eduard, 211, 212
Mushacke, Hermann, 201n, 202, 204, 206, 208, 209, 211, 212, 213, 214, 215, 226, 233, 237, 241, 246, 248, 254, 268, 268n, 270, 271, 272, 294n

Nagy, Gregory, 169n, 170n
Napoleon I, 14, 14n, 15, 28n, 29, 42, 103
Napoleon III, 62, 235
Naumburg, 11, 31, 34, 35, 36, 37, 42, 48, 49, 53, 55, 58, 61, 73, 80, 86, 88, 93, 96, 107, 111, 118, 144, 149, 151, 179, 195, 203, 205, 208
  description, 34–35
  history, 42–43
  Nietzsche's attitudes, 34–35, 61, 211, 231
  religious tensions, 45–47
  social tensions, 48–49
Neill, Stephen, 121n, 193n
Neue Zeitschrift für Musik, 298
Neumann, William (Arthur Friedrich Bussenius), 152
Newman, Ernest, 299n
Nibelungenlied, 129, 165
Nicholls, Angus, 258n
Niemeyer, Christian, 6n, 11, 11n
Niese, Carl Eduard, 45n, 116, 150
Niethammer, Friedrich Immanuel, 258n
Nietzsche, Auguste, 23, 24, 26, 31, 32, 35, 49
  character, 23, 26
  illness, 24
  death, 73–74
Nietzsche, Carl Ludwig, 8, 11, 13, 14, 14n, 16, 18, 19, 19n, 20, 21, 22, 33, 36, 41, 49, 50, 51, 53, 55, 58, 75, 86, 114, 175, 194, 307, 308
  birth, 14
  childhood, 16
  pact with mother, 18–19
  early illness, 19
  early success, 19–20
  separates somewhat from mother, 20
  at Altenburg, 20–21
  secures pastorate, 21
  anxieties, 21–23
  assembles family, 23–24
  proposes marriage, 24
  dislikes in-laws, 27
  child-rearing practices, 28
  upset over revolution, 29
  collapse, 29–30
  death, 31

Nietzsche, Erdmuthe Krause, 8, 15, 17, 17n, 18, 19, 19n, 20, 23, 25, 26, 32, 35, 36, 38, 39, 45, 46, 47, 53, 55, 67, 73, 77, 78, 114, 121, 184, 296n
  first marriage, 17
  second marriage, 15
  rigor with son, 19
  relocates to Röcken, 23
  return to Naumburg, 32, 47
  hymnbook controversy, 47–48
  Naumburg contacts, 55
  finances, 17n, 296n
  death, 74
Nietzsche, Franziska Oehler, 24n, 273n, 7, 8, 8n, 11, 23n, 24, 25, 26, 27, 28n, 30n, 31, 32n, 33, 33n, 35, 36, 37, 37n, 39, 39n, 40, 40n, 41, 46n, 49, 49n, 55, 66, 66n, 67, 67n, 73, 74, 75, 76n, 77n, 85, 96, 150, 154, 157, 161, 162, 165, 187, 194, 195, 200, 210, 225, 244, 246, 250, 268, 287n, 289n, 291, 296, 296n, 306, 311
  childhood, 25
  engagement and wedding, 25
  difficulties assimilating to Nietzsche family, 25–27
  gives birth to three children, 27, 28
  husband's funeral, 31
  death of son, Joseph, 32, 49
  teaches children to read, 37
  hardships in Naumburg, 49
  keeps journal, 49–50
  religious views, 50–51
  as disciplinarian, 51–52
  temperament, 52–53
  enrolls son in burgher school, 39–40
  visits parents, 53
  teaches children to rhyme, 66
  blocks attempt to send son to Halle, 77–78
  teaches son music, 76
  sends son to Schulpforte, 78, 79
  reproaches son at Pforta, 158
  rapprochement with son at Pforta, 161, 162
  writes son in Bonn, 194–195
  response to son's apostasy, 195–196
  reproaches son for expenditures, 201
  emotional involvement with son, 210
  financial situation, 74n
  response to son's graduation, 306
Nietzsche, Friedrich
  birth, 27
  early childhood, 28
  response to father's death, 30, 31–32
  guardianship established, 40
  arrives in Naumburg, 34–35
  attends burgher school, 40
  enters Weber Institute, 59

Index

friendship with Wilhelm Pinder and Gustav Krug, 59–60
games during Crimean War, 62–63
religious views during childhood, 58, 91–92
transfers to Cathedral *Gymnasium*, 63
begins to write poetry, 66–69
explores music, 76–77
awaits scholarship, 84–85
writes "From my life", 86
arrives at Pforta, 93–95
dedicates himself to scholarship, 108–109
worries over lack of focus, 110, 175–176, 188, 308, 309
made Primus, 109, 110n
befriends Deussen, 116–117
Confirmation, 119–120, 122
possible influence of Ernst Ortlepp, 144–145
writes anthropological essays and "The course of my life", 123–127
fascination with Ermanarich, 128–129
chooses Max Heinze as tutor, 149–150
friendship with Guido Meyer, 155
begins reading Emerson, 129–130
delivert "Fate and history" to Germania, 132–133
increasing skepticism concerning Christianity, 123–124, 127, 132–133, 137, 139–142
troubles with authorities, 157–158, 159–160
chooses Hermann Kletschke as tutor, 159
reconsider Pforta friendships, 163–165
worries over future profession, 162–163
rejects career in arts, 167–168, 309
commits to philology, 168, 309
writes valedictory autobiography at Schulptorte, 175
travels to Bonn, 311
attitudes toward Franconia, 185, 186, 201–202, 204, 214
friendship with Gersdorff, 202–203
publicly rejects Christianity, 195
friendship with Mushacke, 202, 204
difficulty weaning self from mother, 210
meets Eduard Mushacke, 211–212
initial unhappiness in Leipzig, 213–214, 215
reads Schopenhauer, 216
reads Diogenes Laertius, 264–266
co-founds Philological Society, 225–226
socializes with Philological Society, 226–227
Ritschl as mentor, 227, 229
observes Austro-Prussian War, 232–236
reads Friedrich Albert Lange, 236–243
aroids cholera epidemic, 244
responds to Rosalie Nietzsche's death, 246
develops friendship with Rohde, 249, 250, 251–252
envisions trip to Paris, 250, 294

Leipzig amusements, 267
uses Pindar motto, 274–276
reevaluates philology, 253–254
decides to attend University of Berlin, 267–268
departs Leipzig, 268
writes Leipzig retrospect, 268
serves as enlisted man in army, 271–273
works on Democritus project, 278, 279–281
admires Valentin Rose, 278–279
confronts skepticism, 281–282,
"Survives riding accident and aftermath", 286, 289–290, 291
returns to Leipzig, 294
resents unexpected promotion, 305, 306
prepares curriculum vitae for Bases, 307
endures riding accident and convalescence, 286, 289–290, 291
lodges at Biedermann's, 294
emancipates from guardianship, 296
meets Richard Wagner, 300–301
quarrels with Ritschl, 302
writes farewell letters, 311–312
travels to Basel, 311
schools
  burgher school, 37–38
  Weker Institute, 58–59
  Cathedral *Gymnasium*, 63
  Schulpforte, 94–95, 99–100
  University of Bonn, 180
  University of Leipzig, 213
photographs
  Confirmation, 119
  Byronic, 154
  Franconia group portrait, 187
  in military uniform, 292
autobiographies, 2–5
  "From my life", 85–92
  "The course of my life", 125–127
  "My life", 166–167
  "Farewell", 175–176
  possible Bonn autobiography, 209
  "Retrospect of my two years at Leipzig", 268–269, 316–317
  "Sketches for curriculum vitae", 307–311
essays and lectures
  "Hunters and fishers", 123
  "The childhood of peoples", 123–124
  "Letter to my friend, in which I recommend that he read my favorite poet", 151
  "Ermanarich, Ostgothenkönig", 129
  "Concerning the dramatic works of Byron", 153
  "Fate and history", 132–135
  "Freedom of the will and fate", 135–136

Nietzsche, Friedrich (cont.)
  "The poetical achievements of
    W. Pinder", 164
  "Character study of Cassius from 'Julius
    Caesar'", 164–165
  "Napoleon III als Präsident, 235
  "On moods", 171–173
  musical compositions
    early music, 77
    Christmas oratorio, 127
    "Pain is the keynote of nature", 127
    "Slavic" works, 145
  philological and philosophical works
    "De Theognide Megarensi", 169–170
    "Zur Geschichte der Theognideischen
      Spruchsammlung", 226
    "De Laertii Diogenis fontibus", 267
    Die Gestaltung der Sage von Ostgothen
      Nänig, 170–171, 309
    Ermanarich bis in das 1200 "Jahrhundert",
      170–171, 309
    "Die PINAKES der aristotelischen
      Schriften.", 262
    Democritus projects, 279–281
    "Der Danae Klage", 287
    "On Schopenhauer", 288
    "On the concept of the organic since
      Kant", 288
    Index to *Rheinisches Museum*, 269, 278
    "Self-observation", 315
    "Über die litterarhistorischen Quellen des
      Suidas", 262
    Philosophy in the tragic age of the Greeks, 265
  poems, fiction, and plays
    "The gods on Olympus", 63–64,
    birthday presentation to mother, 67
    "The youthful years of Cyrus", 69n
    "The transience of happiness", 70
    "Andromeda", 71
    "Alfonso", 71
    "Rinaldo", 71
    "Skipper's song", 80–82
    "*Wohin*", 84
    "Two larks", 82–84
    "Colombo", 82
    "Six Serbian folksongs", 145
    "Cantabo musae", 156
    "Ermanarichs Tod", 129n
  published works
    The birth of tragedy, 265n
    "David Strauss, the confessor and the
      writer", 312n
    "On the utility and hability", 13
    "Schopenhauer as educator", 115, 265, 271,
      275n, 318n
  "Richard Wagner in Bayreuth", 231, 314n
  Unfashionable observations, 319
  Human, all too human I, 208n, 223n, 274n,
    319n
  Human, all too human II, 319n
  Dawn, 318n
  The gay science, 229n, 274n
  Thus spoke Zarathustra, 274n
  Beyond good and evil, 93, 229n, 265–266
  On the genealogy of morals, 169
  Twilight of the idols, 229n
  Ecce homo, 57, 274n, 319
Nietzsche, Friedrich August Ludwig, 14, 15, 16,
  17, 46, 121
Nietzsche, Lina, 16n, 75, 244, 291n
Nietzsche, Ludwig Joseph, 28, 32, 49, 88
Nietzsche, Rosalie, 23, 24, 26, 32, 35, 54, 66, 73,
  74, 76, 109, 153, 154, 161, 189, 191, 194, 195,
  215, 244, 246, 247, 249
  moves to Röcken, 23
  advises Franziska, 26
  quarrels with Franziska, 26
  mother's death, 74
  moves after mother's death, 74–75
  death, 246
  Nietzsche's esteem, 246
Nipperdey, Thomas, 15n, 231n
Nirvana, 275n, 267, 269, 275

O'Flaherty, James C., 262n
Oehler, Adalbert, 22n, 23n, 24n, 25n, 26n, 28,
  28n, 30n, 33n, 35n, 37n, 39n, 50n, 51n,
  54n, 55n, 58n, 67n, 74n, 76n, 231n
Oehler, David Ernst, 8, 24, 24n, 36, 37n, 46n, 53,
  54, 78, 112, 114
Oehler, Edmund, 52, 117, 195, 196, 211
Oehler, Max, 11
Oehler, Oscar, 8n, 96
Oehler, Ralf, 24n, 54n
Oehler, Richard, 51n, 52n
Oehler, Wilhelmine Hahn, 25, 26, 54, 311
Offenbach, Jacques, 268
Olhausen, Justus, 198, 199
Opitz, Juliane (Julie) Nietzsche, 245
Ortlepp, Ernst, 141n, 143, 143n, 145, 145n,
  152, 168
Osswald, Gustav Adolf, 79
Overbeck, Franz, 7
Ovid, 249

Pahncke, Robert, 99n
Parkes, Graham, 7n, 11, 11n, 171n
Patti, Adelina, 201
Paulsen, Friedrich, 103n, 104n, 183n, 198n, 205,
  206, 206n, 256, 256n, 257n, 293n, 296n

Index

Payne, E. F. J., 218n
Pernet, Martin, 6n, 11, 11n, 17n, 18n, 20n, 21n, 22n, 24n, 25n, 26n, 27n, 29n, 34n, 37n, 38n, 43n, 45n, 46n, 47n, 50n, 51n, 53n, 54n, 59n, 60n, 75n, 76n, 77n, 78n, 99n, 100n, 119n, 121n, 142n, 150n, 161n, 174n, 179n, 180n, 186n, 187n, 188n, 195n
Persius, 165, 180n
Pestalozzi, Johann Heinrich, 101
Peter, Karl, 142, 151, 168
Peters, John C. M.D., 244n
Petőfi, Sándor, 146, 146n
Pfeiffer, Rudolf, 197n
Pforta. *See* Schulpforte
Philological Society, 227, 229, 249, 262, 266, 267, 268, 296, 302, 305n
Pinder, Caroline, 55, 59
Pinder, Eduard, 60, 61
Pinder, Gottlieb Ernst, 47, 55
Pinder, Wilhelm, 37n, 38, 59, 60, 61, 63, 87, 88, 97, 111, 117, 118, 132, 139, 144, 146, 150, 154, 163, 164, 174, 235, 236, 248, 268
  champions Hölderlin, 146
  general character, 60
Plato, 182, 205, 223
Plauen, 23, 25, 245
Plautus, 180n, 249
Pleisse, 267, 269
Pletsch, Carl, 11, 11n, 12n, 30n
Pobles, 24, 53, 55, 113, 245
Podach, Erich F., 6n, 11n
Porter, James I., 209n, 261n, 263n, 274, 274n, 278, 278n, 279n, 280n, 283, 284n
Prange, Martine, 290n, 291n, 297n, 298n
Pre-Socratics, 205

Quinby, Lee, 12, 317n

Rehn, Rudolf, 262n
Reich, Hauke, 22n
Reynolds, L. D., 262n
Rheinisches Museum, 226, 266, 278, 287, 293, 302, 303, 305, 307
Ribbeck, Otto, 181n, 197n, 199n, 213n, 224n, 225n, 228n, 249n, 254, 254n, 255, 255n, 256n
Ringer, Fritz K., 44n, 258n
Ritschl, Friedrich, 281, 8, 180, 180n, 197, 199, 200, 203, 224, 225, 226, 227, 228, 229, 237, 245, 249, 263n, 268, 269, 270, 270n, 274, 274n, 276, 278, 280n, 282, 284, 285, 286, 287, 288, 290, 293, 296, 301, 301n, 302, 302n, 303, 304, 305, 310
  personality and character, 228–229

Philologenstreit, 197–199
  poor health, 224–225
  inaugural address, 225
  proposes Philological Society, 225–226
  praises Theognis paper, 226
  traits shared with Nietzsche, 227–228
  arranges Nietzsche's early promotion, 305
  misunderstanding over Rohde, 302
Ritschl, Ida, 226
Ritschl, Sophie, 225, 229, 290, 298, 298n, 300, 301n
Rochau, Ludwig August von, 48
Röcken, 11, 21, 24, 25, 26, 29, 33, 34, 35, 36, 37, 54, 55, 86, 88, 95, 96, 111, 113, 114, 245
Rohde, Erwin, 237, 254, 254n, 260, 267, 268, 269, 269n, 272, 275, 275n, 276, 278n, 280, 281, 282, 287, 291, 294, 295, 298, 301n, 302, 302n, 303, 303n, 304, 305, 306
Rohn (first name unknown), 213, 237
Romundt, Heinrich, 237, 248, 282, 294n, 301n
Roscher, Wilhelm, 269n, 305n
Rose, Valentin, 281, 307
  pseudepigrapha, 279
Rosenberg, Hans, 44n
Rosental, 267
Rosmiarek, Ralf, 17n, 28n, 38n, 40n, 46n, 55n, 60n, 96n, 108n, 268n, 312n
Ross, Werner, 7n, 11, 11n, 98n, 144n, 156n, 185n, 187n, 213n, 228, 228n
Rossleben, 18
Rousseau, Jean-Jacques, 101, 206

Safranski, Rüdiger, 17n
Salaquarda, Jörg, 237n
Scaliger, Joseph, 275
Schaarschmidt, Karl, 181, 182, 182n, 200, 205, 216, 223
Schelling, Friedrich Wilhelm Joseph, 147
Schenkel, Rudolf, 174, 174n, 214
Schiller, Friedrich, 43, 61n, 102, 144n, 151
Schlechta, Karl, 6n, 7, 63n
Schlottmann, Konstantin, 180n, 192
Schmid, Hedwig Nietzsche, 245
Schmidt, Hermann Josef, 3n, 10, 10n, 11, 11n, 18n, 28n, 32n, 55n, 58n, 64n, 67n, 70n, 71, 71n, 72, 75n, 76n, 79n, 80n, 82n, 83n, 95n, 97n, 109n, 124n, 144n, 150n
Schnädelbach, Herbert, 257n, 258n, 259n
Schopenhauer, Arthur, 205, 205n, 216, 217, 221, 222, 223, 229, 235, 237, 240, 241, 247, 255, 263, 264, 268, 278, 288, 290, 298, 300, 301, 307, 319
  metaphysical vision, 216–221
Schubert, Ernst, 34n

Schulpforte, 11, 190, 191
    conflicts with government, 100n, 150n
    landscape, 94
    mission, 97–98, 99–100
    regulations, 95–96
    reputation, 78
    variety of names, 99n
    weaknesses, 142–143
Schulze, Gottlob Ernst, 217
Schulze, Hagen, 15n, 48n, 231n
Schumann, Clara, 60, 60n, 201
Schumann, Robert, 60, 143, 147, 148, 161, 185, 298
    "Manfred overture (from "Manfred: Dramatic poem with music in three parts")", 188, 189
Schweitzer, Albert, 193n
Semler, Johann Salomo, 122
Shakespeare, William, 144, 145, 153
Sheehan, James J., 15n, 48n, 231n, 295n
Simms, Brendan, 15n, 232n
Simonides, 200n, 261n, 287
Simrock, Karl Joseph, 200
Sommer, Andreas Urs, 2n, 152n
Sorkin, David, 101n, 137n
Springer, Anton, 150, 180, 182, 188, 199n, 200
Stack, George J., 132n, 133n, 134n, 135n, 137n, 139n, 237n
Steiner, Rudolf, 11
Steinhart, Carl, 45n, 120, 143, 150n, 168, 174n, 182n, 205
Stern, Fritz, 48n
Sterne, Laurence, 144, 144n
Stirner, Max, 211
Stöckert, Georg, 117n, 155, 155n, 184
Strauss, David Friedrich, 124n, 192, 193, 193n, 195n, 208, 211, 223, 245n
    Life of Jesus summarized, 192–193
    Life of Jesus for the German people summarized, 193
Stroux, Johannes, 301n, 303n, 304n, 305n, 306n, 308n
Suda, 170n, 270, 284
Sweet, Paul Robinson, 101n, 102n, 103n, 258n, 276n
Swift, Paul A., 288n
Sybel, Heinrich von, 180, 180n, 182, 199n
Symbola, 269

Thatcher, David S., 145n, 154n
Theognis, 170n, 249, 309
    character and poems, 169
Timpanaro, Sebastiano, 121n, 263n
Tinsley, David F., 12, 212n
Trieder, Simone, 290n
Turner, R. Steven, 17n, 257n, 258n, 278n

Universities, 183n, 103
    freedom offered students, 182–183, 205–206
Usener, Hermann, 304

van Rey, 179n
Verrecchia, Anacleto, 11, 11n
Vierhaus, Rudolf, 91n, 101n, 102n, 257n
Vischer-Bilfinger, Wilhelm, 304, 307
Vogt, Ernst, 181n
Volkmann, Diederich, 152, 152n, 169n, 175n, 231, 270, 284, 284n, 285n
Volkmann, Richard, 289, 291
Volz, Pia Daniela, 30n, 32n, 112n, 203n, 286n

Wachsmuth, Curt, 45
Wagner, Richard, 140, 147, 295, 297, 298, 298n, 299, 300, 301, 306, 317
    Die Meistersinger von Nürnberg, 295n, 298, 298n, 299, 299n, 300, 301, 311
Wagner, Siegfried, 42n
Wawro, Geoffrey, 232n
Weber Institute, 59n, 93n, 59, 63, 76, 77, 85, 87
Weber, Carl Moritz, 59, 93
Wehler, Hans-Ulrich, 44n
Weil, Hans, 101n, 102n
Weimar, 198
Weisse, Christian, 245
Welcker, Friedrich Gottlieb, 181
Wenkel, Friedrich August, 161n
Wiker, Benjamin, 121n
Wilamowitz-Moellendorff, Ulrich von, 94n, 95n, 97n, 100, 100n, 103n, 111, 111n, 142n, 151n, 179n, 183n, 200n
Wilhelm I, king of Prussia, 98, 118
Willey, Thomas E., 245n
Williamson, David D., 232n
Wilson, N. G., 262n
Windisch, Ernst, 269n, 289, 294, 299, 300, 301n, 302, 303
Winkler, Heinrich August, 232n, 234n
Wissenschaft, 10, 103
Wolf, Friedrich August, 104
Wolleck, Christian, 156n, 169n, 170n
Wright, D.G., 319n

Young, Julian, 7n, 11, 11n, 47n

Zammito, John H., 44n
Zarncke, Friedrich, 296, 297
Zeno the Stoic, 264
Zimmermann, Heinrich, 121n
Zymek, Bernd, 38n